CLOUDLESS MIND

Volume 1

CLOUDLESS MIND

Conversations on Buddhahood

with

Daniel P. Brown, PhD

SENTIENT PUBLICATIONS

First Sentient Publications edition 2025

Transcribed and edited by: Susan Pottish and Scott V. Anderson MD

A paperback original
Book design and cover design by Laura Waltje

Library of Congress Control Number: 2024952907
Publisher's Cataloging-in-Publication Data

Names: Brown, Daniel P., 1948-2022, author.

Title: Cloudless mind : conversations on Buddhahood , volume 1 / with Daniel P. Brown, PhD.

Description: Includes bibliographical references. | Boulder, CO: Sentient Publications, LLC, 2025.

Identifiers: LCCN: 2024952907 | ISBN: 9781591813545 (vol. 1) | 9781591813569 (vol. 2) | 9781591813583 (vol. 3)
Subjects: LCSH Buddha (The concept) | Buddhahood. | Buddhism. | Meditation--Buddhism. | Spiritual life--Buddhism. | BISAC RELIGION / Buddhism / Tibetan | BODY, MIND & SPIRIT / Mindfulness & Meditation | PSYCHOLOGY / Psychotherapy / Spiritually Integrated
Classification: LCC BQ7612 .B76 2025 v. 1 | DDC 294.3/923--dc23

Printed in the United States of America
10 9 8 7 6 5 4 3 2 1

SENTIENT PUBLICATIONS
A Limited Liability Company
PO Box 1851
Boulder, CO 80306
www.sentientpublications.com

Contents

May the knowledge, guidance, and wisdom shared by Dan Brown in this collection be helpful to all in understanding their path to wellbeing and freedom in this life.

Editor's Foreword

Daniel P. Brown, PhD was known professionally as Doctor Brown, but in his interactions with students and colleagues, as in the question-and-answer sessions making up this book, he was always addressed simply as Dan. He spent forty-six years as a clinical psychologist, and researcher; he was also an expert witness on trauma and the veracity of children's memories and testified in courts across the U.S. as well as at War Crimes Tribunals in eastern Europe. This deep expertise gave him a unique perspective on and a depth of knowledge of human potential—both positive and negative. His forty-five years as an authorized teacher of Buddhist practices to Westerners gave him an opportunity to integrate his psychological knowledge with the wisdom of the Buddhist path to spiritual awakening. The ultimate principle guiding him, in all areas in which he worked, was to enhance the wellbeing of others.[1]

In 2008 Dan began inviting students, friends, and associates to join him at a meeting room in a small two-story building in Newton Center, Massachusetts, to explore spiritual and psychological understandings of healing, positive growth potential, and flourishing for human beings, including the path to spiritual awakening and enlightenment as presented in Tibetan Buddhism and as Dan had been teaching for decades by then. The recordings of these sessions by students began in 2012.

---

1 For a fuller picture of Dan's work over the years, please see his biography and C.V. at the end of the book.

There were no guidelines given for questions. People were invited to ask questions about "whatever." Thus, neither Dan nor anyone else knew what the topics would be on any given night, and yet Dan often gave his answers to the myriad subjects raised in rather astonishing detail.

The pointing-out style of teaching that Dan developed was not something he did on his own. First, at the direction of H. H. the Dalai Lama, Dan hiked to a remote area of Tibet and sat with a yogi practitioner who demonstrated "rainbow body" (physically dissolving into light and then reappearing) to Dan, while describing in words what he was doing at each stage of the way. The yogi also told him specifically never to practice or teach what he saw. The question in Dan's mind remained, "Why did His Holiness send me there? What was I supposed to learn?" After nearly two years, he understood that the benefit of that encounter was to have the experience of learning from a teacher who was teaching him by "pointing out" each stage of a practice. After that, and after fifteen years of teaching meditation in the traditional manner with Denma Locho Rinpoche, a high lama in the Gelugpa lineage (assigned to teach with Dan by H. H. the Dalai Lama), Dan proposed an innovative method using "pointing out" instructions when they taught together to increase efficacy in learning by students. The increased efficacy was demonstrated so well to Denma Locho Rinpoche that he gave Dan permission to continue teaching in that pointing out way on his own. (Dan published *Pointing Out the Great Way: The Stages of Meditation in the Mahāmudrā Tradition* in 2006 as an homage to his teachers.)

In 2009 Dan partnered with his longtime spiritual friend, Rahob Tulku Rinpoche, and they agreed that Dan would prepare students for the higher transmissions to be given by Rinpoche. Rahob Tulku was viewed by H.H. the Dalai Lama as an emanation of Guru Padmasambhava for our time. Although living quietly at a small center in Petersburg, New York, Rinpoche became well-known and beloved by many of Dan's students as he met them individually to give them guidance in their practice either in retreats with Dan or at his small center in upstate New York. When Dan mentions "Rinpoche" in the Wednesday Night talks, it is Rahob Tulku Rinpoche to whom he is referring.

Also, Dan made it clear that he would never teach alone, meaning he was always overseen and held accountable by a lineage master. While he often had to be the sole teacher at his retreats, he preferred to have a co-teacher whenever possible. There were multiple reasons for this, including the understanding that teaching by oneself could easily lead to a sense of "self-importance," which, in

Dan's view, was a disastrous failing.[2] Thus he taught his wife, Gretchen Nelson (a physical therapist and yoga teacher), to teach his pointing-out way, and they taught together internationally for nearly thirteen years.

His commitment to being accountable and overseen expanded later when Dan discovered and began studying and practicing teachings from the Bon tradition that preceded Buddhism in Tibet. At that time, Dan became a heart-student of H.H. the 33rd Menri Trizin, whom Dan recognized as his Root Lama in 2014 and who encouraged Dan both to teach and to translate texts never translated before into English. This he did in collaboration with Geshe Sonam Gurang, a Bon Geshe also accountable to H.H. Menri Trizin.

Because Wednesday Night sessions rarely focused on a single topic, the titles given to each chapter in this collection consist simply of the date each took place and a subheading of "themes," attempting to capture something of the range of that evening's questions and answers. Also, as the talks often included conversation, the conversational style has been preserved throughout, with no attempt to edit Dan or questioners into something like "written" material. On occasion, if it seemed like Dan left out a word accidentally or because a word was inaudible on the tape, the most likely missing word has been put in brackets [like this] or indicating a group response like [Laughter]. Also, because the names of people asking questions were mostly inaudible or unknown, the people who asked questions are identified simply as Student 1, Student 2, etc.

When Dan does mention someone's name, it has been changed to honor their privacy.

On another slightly technical note, Dan often used Tibetan words in his responses to people, particularly when explicating the Tibetan Buddhist interpretation of a given topic. Instead of using a formal glossary that gives Wylie transliterations (which does not convey pronunciation), the approach chosen here was to give the best phonetic rendering of the words Dan spoke as heard on the recordings, just as he said them.

---

2 He cited the declaration by one of the early Christian Desert Fathers that self-importance, or pride, was "the eighth deadly sin." Nevertheless, several of Dan's students, both in the U.S. and abroad, have chosen to teach on their own. Dan would not have approved of this, giving his wife, Gretchen Nelson, sole authority to train and approve new teachers. For information on approved teachers, please contact admin@pointingoutthegreatway.com.

Another aspect of Dan's later work included pioneering neuroscientific research using EEG measures in relation to levels of mind. His goal was not to show that the brain was the cause or the source of mind nor of its awakening, but rather to show that as awakening progresses there are also detectable changes in the brain's activity. Some thirty of his students were assessed by Dan and an assistant teacher for their capacity to shift into and out of a number of what he called the "basis of operation," or well-established and continuous states of mind, including "awakened awareness," and then, in a laboratory environment, participants underwent brainwave evaluation while making those shifts.

This research was sponsored by the Fetzer Foundation and performed in the neuroscience lab of Judson Brewer, MD PhD in Boston at UMass Medical School. (See the Wednesday night talk #65 of July 19, 2017 for a basic description of the study.) The results reported by Dan were "stellar" because they showed uniquely high levels of activation of specific centers in the brain when the subject shifted through levels of mind they had learned from Dan, and most especially when shifting to the level of awakened awareness.

To our knowledge, this kind of research had never been done before. In a meeting to review the results of the study, a representative of the Fetzer Foundation and a representative of the National Academy of Sciences found the outcomes to be highly valuable and worthy of further research funding. Unfortunately, that additional research didn't happen because the lab was closed during the Covid pandemic, and Dan passed away in April of 2022.

It has recently come to our attention that there are several new initiatives in contemplative neuroscience (CN) to investigate deeper levels of practice than have been the focus (of CN) previously. Among these initiatives are the Harvard Meditation Research Project,[3] and the initiatives reported in a recent article in *Scientific American*—"Advanced Meditation Alters Consciousness and our Basic Sense of Self"[4]—that provides a link to Dan's innovative study.

In the Wednesday night conversations, Dan describes steps, stages, levels, and ranges of spiritual development. He describes the spiritual path according

---

3 Mass General Meditation Research. "Research." Massachusetts General Hospital. https://meditation.mgh.harvard.edu/research/.

4 Zanes, Anna. "Advanced Meditation Alters Consciousness and Our Basic Sense of Self." Scientific American, Joe 24, 2024. https://www.scientificamerican.com/article/advanced-meditation-alters-consciousness-and-our-basic-sense-of-self/.

to three progressive maps, with explicit instructions along the way, and also warning practitioners against trying to jump ahead. He made it clear that just because the map is there, if a particular location is not where you are, it's better that you don't focus on that location. Why? Because if you're not there yet, you will be thinking about it, using ideas, images, or concepts; and such thinking about it, he says, actually hardens the mind and makes it more difficult to experience awakening. So, even though Dan discusses the full range of experiences, it is not to encourage people to imagine them, but rather to know that there is a path that leads to their natural and spontaneous appearance.

Finally, at the start of each Wednesday night meeting, Dan would routinely ask for people attending for the first time to identify themselves and speak a bit about how and why they came to the meeting. Sometimes those conversations went on for quite a while. Then, at the end of the introductions, Dan would clarify for everyone the purpose and structure of the meeting, which was, first, to create a completely open forum for questions that anyone might have about literally anything; and second, once the question and answer period was over, there would be a bathroom break and people would reassemble for a guided meditation—what Dan called "meditation improv"—in which he created on the spot a novel guided meditation to give people some direct experience of what had been spoken about earlier in the evening. (Those meditations were not transcribed and thus are not part of this collection.)

Because the opening conversations were often personal, and also repetitive, rather than repeat the introductory descriptions by Dan for each Wednesday Night meeting, one very simple version has been included at the beginning of each talk, namely, "Welcome everybody. You have a question?"

The reason there is no introduction for the first talk presented in this text is that on that particular occasion Dan did something unusual, introducing the topic for the night without asking for questions, and then offering a summary of the Buddhist path to enlightenment. While not planned by anyone, of course, it does seem to be a wonderful introduction in this publication to the scope and depth that Dan presents throughout the Wednesday Night talks, and thus also seems a perfect opening. We hope you will delight in the experientially derived scope and depth of Dan's unique integration of Eastern Wisdom traditions and Western psychology.

Susan Pottish & Scott V. Anderson, M.D.

April 25, 2012

Themes: The Three Maps to Buddhahood

Dan

I think I'll do something a little different tonight, having just returned from a retreat. I think what I'll try and do with the time, since we have a big group, and we have a group in hyperspace [the internet], is to try and be somewhat explicit about the nature of this path from beginning to end. Maybe that will help you to understand the remarkable, elegant, orderliness of this path to buddhahood.

There are essentially three maps. First, there's the roadmap that in Indo-Tibetan Buddhism and the Essence traditions takes you from the very beginning of these practices up through getting a taste of the true nature of the mind, "a taste of awakening" as we call it. There's a second map that is designed to give methods that stabilize that awakening up to the point that you have it all the time, 24/7. And there's a third map which starts when you have awakening all the time, or most of the time, and brings you to full buddhahood. Having been working on that map, the way that this unfolds is now much more clear to me. So, I thought it might be useful to spell it all out, so that at least intellectually you'll have some sense of where this thing starts from and where it takes you to.

In the vehicle of the Mahāyāna, or the "lofty vehicle" as it's called, the Great Vehicle, starting with the first map, which those of you who take the retreats have some familiarity with, but even before that, these practices traditionally start with preliminaries. There's a whole world in that. We could spend ten years just talking about preliminary practices. And in the Tibetan traditions some of those have become quite routinized and stereotyped. You can think about 100,000 prostrations, but that's not a useful way of thinking about it.

There are four main areas that we cover in preliminary practices, four things that need to get done. The first thing that needs to get done is something like—we would call them in the West—motivational practices. When you're caught up in the busy-ness of everyday life, what is it that leads you to set as a priority any kind of spiritual practice, so that you actually set aside not only time to do that, but make it the central focus of your life and living in the world, rather than something that you dabble at or think is a good idea? In Western psychological terms, we call that a "stage of change problem."

In Western psychological terms, people are pre-contemplative or contemplative. They're in the action stage or in the maintenance stage, within four stages of change. Most people go into psychotherapy when they're contemplative. They've contemplated, first, the fact that there's something wrong with their life, and number two, they've contemplated that there is some course of action that they can take. We know from Western research that there are a lot of people out there who are pre-contemplative. They either don't know they have problems, and everybody else may see that they do, or they know they have problems, but they haven't quite got around to how they're going to go about doing anything about that in any kind of systematic way. In either case, they're not ready for therapy.

Likewise in the East, there's a literature in Tibetan Buddhism similar to the stage of change literature in the West. The idea is that spiritual practice is hard. It takes a lot of work and there are many people who are not motivated to do it. So, the motivational practices in Tibetan Buddhism are called *lözhi*, the four attitudes. They're done in sequence. And the first thing you do is you look at what's called precious opportunity, or *daljor*. It's a visualization you do in the context of everyday life. You think about other lives that you might've been born into other than what you have now.

You think about being born into a life where you lose your mental faculties, let's say, dementia. Lots of people have that these days. You imagine it as if that were your life; do a quick visualization on that, drop it and come back to right now, to what you have now, how you actually enjoy the full mental capacities and intelligence to do a practice like this. Then, you imagine all the people who go through life-threatening medical illnesses, and you imagine that that's your lot in life. Then, you drop that, and you come back to what you have now, which is that most of you enjoy reasonable health to support doing this practice. Then, you imagine the context of the culture we live in. You imagine all the people who live in war torn cultures, what it's like, as if that's what you were growing up in, where everything is in chaos. And then, you imagine that you live in a culture where things are reasonably safe even after 9/11. Then, you imagine all the people throughout history who lived in times where they didn't have exposure to spiritual practices, and you imagine, in contrast, how fortunate you are.

And each one of these scenes hammers home the point of the preciousness of what you have. You have reasonable health, you have the intelligence, you have the stability of a culture; you have exposure to all the teachings, complete bodies of teachings. You have a community of practitioners that you can do this with, so you don't have to do it alone, and favorable conditions to practice under. That's a lot. And after you go through the visualization enough times, you get the point that this is a rare and precious opportunity.

Then, the next thing you do is you imagine impermanence. Nothing lasts. Think of all the material things in your life that wear out. I just came back from India with my brand-new luggage bag. The bag handle lasted basically two flights. [Laughter] Now it's time for another one. Impermanence. Everything changes. Think of all the relationships in your life that you've been through. Nothing lasts. And ultimately, when you go through all the things in life materially, interpersonally, all the things that don't last, then you come and look at yourself. You look at the aging process, and you actually visualize your own aging, and it culminates with visualizing your own death. You rehearse it.

That makes the motivation a little bit more urgent, moves you along a bit, and maybe spiritual practice is something that would be useful because if you do these practices, there is no death. It's not possible. It's just the body going. As Rinpoche says, "Body like a hotel; you guest." [Laughter] Better to have a five-star hotel, [Laughter] but, still you're the guest. It doesn't last, right? The stars progressively go as you get older. [Laughter] Is there anything good about aging?

Student 1

Yes!

Dan

Maybe the wisdom that comes with it. Yes. Okay.

So, the third one is called causes and effects of karma, like a cost benefit analysis. You imagine different wholesome and unwholesome actions that you engage in, behaviors, and then you sort of predict how that's going to impact you and others over time. Sort of string it out. Predict the future. And then after you see what you can imagine to be the destructive effects of certain courses of actions, it just makes it harder to go there, including all the time that you waste with things that go nowhere. When you finish that, it not only hammers home the point even more clearly that there's a certain urgency here, but it begins to affect not just your attitude but your behavior. You begin to think more about your behavior and start to reprioritize things.

And the last is the suffering of the six realms of *samsāra*. You go through all of the suffering of the hell realms, and all the suffering of the hungry ghost realms, and all the sufferings of the animal realms, and the god realms, and the demigod realms and the human realms. We were talking about the demigod realms—that's where the movie stars live. Those are our demigods, in their own kind of hell—rich and famous and miserable. So, after you go through these four *lözhi* or attitudes, the outcome, if you do them enough, is that you change your attitude and therefore, slowly in the context of your everyday life, also your behavior.

So, you begin to increase the motivation to think about the value of spiritual practice and to actually start organizing your life around doing it. You accomplish what in Western terms we call stage of change. You become contemplative. I don't mean that in the meditation sense. It means in the sense that you're thinking that there's a course of action here that's more useful than others, and the rest of the stuff doesn't matter so much. Then, the rest of the preliminaries, what you might work on—well, there are three big areas.

If you watch your mind and all of the spontaneous states that come up during the day, in our ordinary experience, they're predominantly negative states. So, the next area to cover is how in your everyday life to shift the balance so that there's more positive states coming up than negative states, because if you don't do those kinds of practices then you play out all the problems on the meditation pillow. If you go right into meditation and you have more negative states than positive states, meditation doesn't feel very good. Too much negative stuff comes up, and the likelihood is that you'll get sick of the meditation, or, in Western terms, you'll develop a phobia of meditating. But, if you follow the natural sequence of this, what happens instead is you shift the balance slowly over time through these practices so that more positive states come up than negative states. That's when you're ready to meditate.

Then, lastly, the last big thing to cover as part of preliminary practices is instilling the view of where these practices will take you: the view of the ultimate state of awakening, your true nature, and the full manifestation of that awakening, enlightenment. Usually, guru yoga is how you instill that. You put forth an image of some embodiment of that ultimate state, like Padmasambhava or whomever, and you visualize it in such a way that it activates your own buddha nature, your own awakened nature. And then you finish the visualization with the idea that your mind in its original buddha nature state and the ultimate state of Padmasambhava's mind are inseparable. They're one and the same. You all have that same buddha nature. It's just clouded over.

The presumption here is that everybody is awake all the time. Awakening isn't some state you ultimately find. It's always here. Every moment, it's here. There are too many clouds, so you don't see it. The sun always shines, but we don't see it when it rains. So, when the clouds clear up, we say the sun comes out, but the sun doesn't come out. The sun is always shining. Awakening doesn't come out. The brilliant nature of an awakened mind is always shining. You just don't see it because your mind is full of clouds. So, when you do the guru yoga, it sort of activates that nature. It gets it started again here. You want to clean it up.

Okay. Those are the essential ingredients of preliminary practices. The next series of meditations is to train the mind. Concentrate. The purpose of concentration is to stabilize the mind and free it from its distractibility. You keep bringing the mind back over and over again to some object, and directing the mind back, intensifying on that object, so the mind stays more and more closely engaged with just the intended concentration object and doesn't go anywhere else. The opposite of concentration is distraction. The extreme opposite of that is what we call in the West Attention Deficit Disorder.

When you're training concentration, you're training *newa*, which means to stay. The mind stays more and more. First you train what's called continuous staying. Maybe the mind stays on the concentration object. You might use the rising and falling of the breath as the object. It might stay for a few milliseconds, but if you keep bringing the mind back many, many times there's a cumulative learning effect of that. We tie the rope of mindfulness onto the object time and time again and the mind learns to stay. Ultimately, it will stay continuously, five, ten minutes at a time; ultimately, as long as you want.

Then, you'll notice that there's background noise. You're only partially staying on the object because what you're really doing is apportioning maybe twenty percent of your attention to the concentration object while at the same time, you're still engaging all that background noise of thought. Tibetans call that *necha*, partial staying. So, there are methods to help you to develop what's called complete staying. And when you develop both continuous and complete staying, the mind pretty much stays on the concentration object fully.

If you continue to train your concentration, you can stay on that object so closely that all the dynamic energy that makes up the breath, the body as the meditation object, will change. It's not a solid object anymore. The body loses its solidity, the breath loses its solidity. If you really concentrate intensely, you start to see the concentration object is just energy. You're shifting from what we call the coarse level of mind that has content to the subtle level of mind, of mind moments, a hundred thousand bursts of energy and movement in the blink of an eyelash. You open up that whole level of mind.

Then, you have to learn to concentrate all over again. It's sort of like shifting from a stable target to a moving target. It's a whole different set of rules. Sometimes we call that the difference between concentration with support and concentration without support. You learn to stabilize the mind at the subtle level. It doesn't really mean concentration without support. It means concentration as less of a support, because the object's sort of always moving and changing, so it's not as easy to latch onto it. So, it's less of a support. But when you get into that range and you perfect the concentration, you'll find that you can continue concentration with continuous and complete staying. And it gets more and more natural, and ultimately automatic, so that you can stay on the concentration object with absolutely no effort and no need to apply any remedies anymore. Ultimately, when you perfect concentration, whatever you intend to put the mind on, it stays on it for as long as you want it to stay on it without going anywhere else. There's not an instant of distraction.

When you get deeply concentrated, all that background noise of thought stops. There's no thought elaboration. The Tibetan word for concentration is *shine* [pronounced she-nay], a compound term. *Newa* means staying, and *shiwa* means calm. It means, from the mind perspective, the mind stays continuously over time, as long as you want, and completely at any given point of time on the meditation object without going anywhere else. And, it means from the events of the mind, there's no thought content, absent of any thought. *Shine* literally means staying-hyphen-calming meditation. We say the mind becomes serviceable. At that level you're operating out of intention, not attention. Whatever you put your mind on, whatever you intend to put it on, the mind stays on that fully.

You can think of the ordinary mind as being like a wild elephant. When you train it with concentration, you have the full strength and intelligence of that elephant mind to work for you. Whatever you put it on, it stays on that. It doesn't go anywhere else. There's no extraneous thought anymore. That's useful.

Why do we train concentration? It does two things. It supports the insight practices. First, because one of the outcomes of concentration is what we call mental pliancy, *shinshong*. Mental pliancy means that the mind operates with the speed of intention, very quick, much quicker than thought, much quicker than attention. The more you have mental pliancy, the greater the speed of the mind. You can focus on things with the quickness of the speed of light. And you're going to need that quickness for some of the higher realizations, because the ability to follow the path when you're given pointing out instructions, at a certain point, you're not thinking about those instructions anymore. You're just following what's being pointed out. The mind will follow it with its intention. You get out of the way, and don't have to think about it. The mind will just follow it. We can carry you directly into awakening with the instructions. They have worked for thousands of years. If you have enough mental pliancy, because the mind will simply follow what's being described without thought.

But, the second thing is that concentration supplies stability of mind, because when you get to the higher realizations, it's always about *dawa*, view. The view is the meditation. But without concentration, the view isn't stable. You think that when you look into the nature of the mind, it's like putting a light on things in the mind and seeing how the mind constructs experience. And looking even deeper into the real nature of the mind, the looking is like putting a candle flame to something so you can see it. But stability through concentration, where the concentration provides the stability of that candle flame. If you don't train concentration, it's like trying to look with a candle that's always flickering in the wind. So, what you see gets distorted because the candle flame is always flickering. But if you train solid concentration, your view is unshakeable, like a mountain. Then, it's easy to open up these practices. That's concentration.

Then, comes insight. There are two levels of insight, ordinary and extraordinary. In ordinary insight, we look into how the mind constructs experience, how it constructs sense of self, how it constructs external reality, and how it constructs time and space. Those are the big three ordinary insights. Emptiness means ... actually, it's an unfortunate term. It doesn't mean things go away or that they have no substance. A good synonym for emptiness is "mere construction." The mind is constructivist. It's always making representations. That's how it works. And when you look at things as empty through emptiness meditations, it's not that they don't exist. What you're seeing is the way they really are. They're just constructions. The problem is that we reify those constructions, *nozhin*. We make them too real or too solid.

For example, emptiness of self. Kids aren't born with a sense of self. They develop a sense of self around eighteen months, right smack in the middle of when kids develop representational thinking. A sense of self is a construction. It's a representation, useful in everyday life. It's useful to have Dan. My whole life is organized around Dan-ness. Right? It's a central organizing principle, but ultimately, I forget that it's just a construction. And if I forget that things are a construction, there are two consequences: *zinpa*, the self has grab. All my experiences filter through the self, and my experience then has grab. I develop likes and dislikes and preferences, and all that grab creates more and more suffering. And second, *mümpa*: the self becomes like a massive cloud, and all the stories and constructions around the self are like more and more clouds building up. They become too solid because we think the self is too real and too serious. We forget it's just a construction. With that comes *mümpa*, the capacity to obscure. It clouds over our true nature.

I'm not trying to get rid of the self. When I do emptiness practice, I'm trying to get rid of its capacity to obscure. External reality becomes a solid structure of mind. I think there's a world out there. Time becomes a construction of mind. It gets reified. Relatively speaking, time is useful. It's a central organizing principle. We all operate by it, but we forget it's merely a construction. The construction of time as an internal structure of mind isn't really complete until about eight years of age, late in childhood. It's useful. I organize a lot of my day around time, relatively speaking, but ultimately, I forget that time is an empty construction. I actually think there's an external time, a cosmic time clock somewhere, in Greenwich. [Laughter] With the reification of that time clock, it creates grab. Now I race around like crazy trying to get deadlines done. A lot of suffering comes from that, and it creates *mümpa*, the capacity to obscure. I forget the timeless, boundless nature of awareness, part of my true nature.

Each one of these emptiness practices helps you to see things just the way they are, as merely constructions in such a way that they no longer obscure. You don't have to get rid of them. I don't have to get rid of Dan, I don't have to get rid of time. I just have to get rid of their capacity to obscure. That's what the Heart Sutra is all about. Many of you know this. Some of you are new tonight, so I'll say it. Each one of these practices in the Heart Sutra cleans up a cloud so that the result of doing emptiness practice is what we call "shifting your basis of operation," shifting it to some level of awareness. It's all about awareness that you wouldn't have seen before.

Gate gate pāragate pārasamgate bodhi svāhā. In Sanskrit, it means "gone (*gate*), gone (*gate*), gone beyond (*pāragate*), gone way beyond (*pārasamgate*), Oooh, what a realization (*bodhi svāhā*)!"

First "gone." You think in your everyday life. You confuse awareness and thought. You think they're the same thing. If you concentrate enough, most thought elaboration will stop so you'll have long periods of stillness. What comes out of that is in your direct experience, not conceptually, the direct experience of operating out of awareness rather than operating out of thought mode. It's sort of nice. Awareness gone beyond thought, the first *gate*.

Then, if you practice emptiness of self, you search for the self. It's unfindable as a construction of mind. It keeps receding from your awareness. What's left after you do the emptiness of self-meditation is a level of awareness that's cleaned up of personal identity. I shift my basis of operation. So now I'm operating out of awareness itself, which is cleaned up of Dan. I go back to the meditation. Dan isn't doing the meditation anymore. Awareness itself is. That's the second *gate*, awareness itself gone beyond personal identity.

Pāragate—still that awareness will fluctuate and the experiences in the field of awareness will fluctuate in time. So, I do Nagarjuna's emptiness of time meditation, or what is called the "beyond three times" meditation in Mahāmudrā. There are various ways of doing this. And I'll open up a level of awareness that's timeless and boundless because time and space are together. That's a huge shift. That's the beginning of the gateway of the Mahāyāna. That's what all the Nagarjuna dialectical practices are about. Now I open up a level of awareness that's huge and timeless and boundless, ever-present, changeless awareness—*pārasamgate*—timeless, boundless awareness gone way beyond the conception of time.

Now I'm in the realm of the Essence traditions. Now I'm operating at of a level of experience that's vast. Within the field of that experience, at the subtle level of mind, everything is interconnected. That's where Mahāmudrā practices like Ocean and Waves are useful. Now I can let everything arise within the field of that awareness, but I'm looking at where I'm looking at it from. That's more interesting. I'm looking at all that stuff that arises from the field of boundless, changeless awareness, like an ocean of boundless, changeless awareness looking at its own waves. Everything will come up as another momentary construction, empty. And whatever arises in that field dissipates within that field. And there's your first taste of spacious freedom within the vastness of that space. The awareness remains absolutely still, without any grab. There's your beginning taste of freedom.

I can deepen that realization to nonduality. Now, I can come to see that the field of awareness and what gets expressed within it are the same thing, just as the ocean and the waves are inseparable. There are a lot of popular teachings these days on nonduality. Nonduality is not to be confused with awakening, but it's a good precursor.

Now, if I press further with my inquiry, what I'm noticing is that things come up in this ocean of awareness. And at some point, when I watch these waves arise, like waves on an ocean, I realize that they're empty constructions. But, if I press further with that intention, the quickness of the mentally pliant mind, I can start nailing the realization much more quickly. As soon as something begins to arise, I already know it and its true nature as empty. Moment by moment by moment, I nail it that quickly, not after the fact, right at the moment. Everything will come up spontaneously and quickly, already expressed as empty. But there will still be a lot of assumptions that I'm making in the background of my awareness. I like to think of them sort of like windows that are minimized on your computer that influence your operating system.

You have to step back with your best intelligence and absolute honesty and look at all the assumptions that are operating about your practice that you're not seeing as empty. And all that's got to come into it, too; all the assumptions that you're necessarily going to have problems or have had or will have certain problems. Those are empty ideas. All assumptions that you can't do this, empty ideas. All assumptions that there's a certain outcome that you're looking for that you will get, or you won't get, all empty ideas. All assumptions about certain states being more or less desirable—empty ideas. The whole thing goes into the hopper.

Come to know what it means to practice. See everything as empty, the emphasis being on everything. Then, you extend your range of application of emptiness to everything that possibly could come up in your field of experience. When you have immediacy and range, you'll have an extraordinary *samādhi* called "automatic emptiness." Everything comes up very quickly, spontaneously, every moment already expressed as empty. And at that point, you don't have to do anything anymore because any attempt to do anything in the meditation is empty upon arising. But more importantly, that is the foundational state for all the advanced practices. Why? Because it clears conceptualization. Because as soon as you notice the tendency to conceptualize about state or outcome, immediately it's expressed as empty, and it clears itself. As Tilopa says, "Then the mind becomes like a crystal-clear pool of water when all the mud of conceptualization settles." There's something about the lucidity of that awareness that will become more transparent to you.

Mind what I'm saying: [with] the higher teachings, if you try and think your way through it conceptually, you harden the mind and you actually damage yourself. You'll harden the mind so that it's harder to awaken. Don't jump ahead and try and take the advanced teachings until you establish a good foundation of automatic emptiness because it's the only thing that corrects for the conceptualization in a way that increases the likelihood that you'll get a taste of awakening.

With that as your foundational state, then you can open up to a taste of an awakened mind. But here's the last big cloud: your information processing system.

Right here, every moment is an ocean of boundless awareness-love, which is your true nature. It's always right here, but you don't see it, because your information processing system, by definition, operates to partialize. And as long as it partializes, it obscures the totality of what's always right here.

So, let's think of your information processing system in terms of speed, from slowest to highest. It takes about a half a second to two or three seconds to think something out. Quicker than that is attention. To direct your mind to something, to pay attention, takes about two hundred milliseconds. To be aware of something is much quicker than that. In Western terms, we can measure awareness, as far as our electronic board will take us, in about five milliseconds. That's because the machine is limited. Awareness works at the speed of light—much, much quicker than attention. And the quickest process of your information processing system is called—actually, we don't even have a word for it in the West. I like to translate it as "particularizing." And I like to translate particularizing, *illa machepa,* as the tendency of the mind towards something that makes it something particular, like an action potential. In every moment that's the quickest operation of our information processing system. But, you see, here's the issue. If what is right here all the time is a boundless ocean of awareness-love, you're never going to directly experience that through conceptualization. As the great Dzogchen scholar says, "The function of conceptualization is to delineate." When I develop a concept, I'm saying this as opposed to that, and delineation means we're partializing, we're segmenting and breaking up the totality of reality that's always right here.

At a higher speed, every time I pay attention to something, I'm partializing. At the highest speed, every time I make the tendency of the mind towards anything, I'm partializing it. See, everything that your information processing system does, in every moment, and at any level or speed of processing, obscures the true nature that's always right here.

So, what are called "crossing over instructions" help you to not get rid of your information processing system, but to get rid of its capacity to obscure. If you're given those instructions and you're in the right state of automatic emptiness, conceptualization won't get in the way. Attention won't get in the way. And with setting up the right view with what are called in Mahāmudrā "non-meditation instructions," or in Dzogchen "*trekchö*"—thoroughly cutting through instructions, which refer to cutting through individual consciousness or cutting through your information processing operations that obscure—you will open up awakened awareness.

You'll find that you will shift your basis of operation so you're operating out of awakened awareness rather than ordinary awareness. *Pārasamgate*—awareness gone way, way beyond the operations of your information processing system. Ooh, what a realization, *bodhi svāhā.*

What is that like? Well, from the self-emptiness side, or the negation side of the equation, you find that you've shifted out of the constraints of your individual consciousness so that you are now operating out of this boundless ocean of awareness-love that has no location, no reference points. Other than that, there's nothing you can say about it. Or as Mipham says, "Even to say, 'this is it' is to miss the mark."

Then, from the other-emptiness or the positive affirming side of that equation, the only thing you can say is that there's something self-evident about the nature of awakened awareness that's different from ordinary awareness. It has *dangpa*, brightness. It has *gnar*, it has intensity. It has *hrige*, it has awakeness. And there's something about that lucidity that's so different from ordinary awareness. Not that it's just boundless; not that it's nondual. But the brilliance of its knowing is what characterizes it as different. Like the sun that shines brilliantly when the clouds clear up; it's self-evident.

But mind you, all you do is *chak*—set up the conditions. The self doesn't awaken. Dan doesn't get awakened. If you clear away the structures of the mind like the self and set up the conditions, then the awakening happens to itself by itself. Why? Because it's part of the hard wiring. Buddha nature knows its own intelligence, it knows its own path. Just get out of the way. Then you get a taste of what Tashi Namgyal calls "little flames." That's the first map.

Now, the second map is how you make those little flames a forest fire. You have to develop that. The Tibetan word is *chungwa*, to nurture something. You've got to give it some care. You have to nurture it and bring out this awakening through a process of *gompa*, familiarization, until it's so familiar to you that you have it all the time. Some of you know what I'm talking about and you're working on that with Rinpoche or with the advanced courses.

So, how do you get it from one little flame to have awakening 24/7? There are three things you do. The first is you set up exactly the same kind of conditions that established the awakening before. You use the same kind of non-meditation instructions in Mahāmudrā, or *trekchö*, thoroughly cutting through instructions, in Dzogchen. And set up the conditions just right. And if you get them just right, it will keep opening up. And what you're looking for here is frequency and duration. You're looking at establishing the condition so that on the pillow and then eventually off the pillow you open up awakening more frequently, and for longer and longer periods of time, longer durations. And then it will cloud over again.

This idea that "you awaken and that's it" is not usually the course here. Or as Dzogchen Ponlop says, "Most people who awaken put the snooze alarm back on a lot." It clouds over naturally because of all the habits of mind. But you have to keep working on this. You have to nurture it.

So, the second set of practices is to look at what clouds it over. Or as one of our students coined it, "You look at your favorite clouds." Each of you with your best intelligence will find that for you there are certain patterns of what clouds it over. The cloud of self—all the stories that go with the self; that's a big cloud. It's likely to keep coming back. That was what the Sufi master Hafiz said, to look at "the tiresome project of self."

Then, external reality. The great Dzogchen master Longchenpa, says, "As soon as they get off the pillow, out-there-ness comes back." There's the solidity of time, getting lost in thought, getting lost in emotional states, getting lost as yogis, getting lost in special states—bliss, luminosity, stillness. These are the usual clouds. You have to look at what your favorite clouds are and practice emptiness.

What do you practice? It depends on what your basis of operation is.

With your best intelligence, if you're operating out of your ordinary mind and you have thoughts that get in the way or emotions that get in the way, you practice emptiness of thought and emptiness of emotion. If at that time you're operating out of awakened awareness, you view the thought and emotion as the liveliness of an awakened mind. Because awakened awareness has what we call *tsal*, liveliness. It's always expressing itself to itself. And then you view the thoughts as no more than the expression of that awakened awareness so it can be none other than that. So how can it possibly cloud it over? And you either do emptiness practice or liveliness practice depending on what your basis of operation is—ordinary mind versus awakened mind. Either way, you have to clean up the clouds.

And the third set of practices is metacognitive practices. As you go about your life, on and off the pillow, ask yourself the question, "What's my basis of operation right now? Am I lost in thought mode? Am I operating out of self? Am I in timeless boundless mode? Am I in nondual mode? Or am I in awakened mode?" If you keep looking, you're going to train that metacognitive awareness. And the result of that is going to be, over time, just by looking into it, immediately it starts shifting in the direction of awakening.

Or you can do the relational view of that metacognitive training. You can develop a special heart connection with a teacher. Many of you have done that with Rinpoche. And as soon as you think of Rinpoche, you shift into awakening. Or you do it through guru yoga. Many of you do Padmasambhava guru yoga. And as soon as you have the idea of Padmasambhava, you shift into awakening.

And all these three practices—setting up the view, looking at your clouds, practicing metacognitive abilities—all of these things are designed to increase the frequency and duration of operating out of awakened awareness, the infinite ocean of awareness-love. In my view, it's easier to do that on the pillow and then take it off the pillow. Most people start getting little flames of awakening towards the end of a retreat. They come back; they get it in more retreats, and they start finding that in the retreats they get it earlier in the week rather than just at the tail end of it. If you do it a lot, you find you get it almost always while you're sitting. And you find in your daily practice that you have it pretty much on the pillow all the time. Then you can start taking it off the pillow.

A good practice at that point is to set your view up, shift into awakening mode on the pillow, and as soon as you shift into awakening mode, play it out a bit, nurture it a bit on the pillow, and then get it right off the pillow, and take it off. Then there's a set of practices that we call "mixing practices." Your task is to mix awakened awareness with everyday activity. Mix it into movement. Take it off the pillow and mix your awakening into exercise. Mix it into walking. Mix it into sitting. Mix it into all daily activities. Mix it into speech. When I was with Menri,[1] he had me sit out in front of his door. And his schedule's sort of like the Dalai Lama's because he's the Dalai Lama's meditation teacher. So, as a senior person he gets one person after another coming to see him. So, one of the things he made me do is sit outside and say "Hi" to everybody and talk with them while they were waiting to see him. And the task was that I had to mix the awakening into all those conversations.

Then you have to mix it into thought and the practices of mind—I'd mix it into while I was sitting at the computer composing something. That was interesting. Then after a while, all the activities of body, speech, and mind are mixed into awakening. And after a while, you start mixing it into everything else, including the task of the exercises that then carry that awakening into deep sleep and to dreaming sleep. So, you basically have it all the time, 24/7. That completes the second map. And when you have it 24/7, pretty much all the time, that's the next major accomplishment.

And the third map is the map that takes you to full buddhahood. There are four areas of buddha training.

The first begins with what's called automatic *dharmakāya* release. There are three levels of automaticity: *samādhi* or deep concentration going all by itself during the concentration series; automatic emptiness during the emptiness meditations; and now we get the third and last automaticity and the most important one. It's called *rangdröl*, which means "self-liberation." But a more accurate translation would be "automatic *dharmakāya* release."

---

1 H.H. the 33rd Menri Trizen, Dan's first lineage Master who was in the Bon tradition.

Here's what happens. You set up your view like an infinite vast expanse. But you add something to that view. You view that infinite vast expanse as the groundless ground of being from which everything arises in an unconditioned way, as reflected by the brilliant flashes of awakened awareness every moment by moment. We call that the inseparable, nondual pair of groundless ground and awakened awareness.

So, when everything arises, every moment comes up in an unconditioned way, and it immediately dissipates. You don't engage in anything. And one thing that changes is it's no longer about emptiness practice. Everything that comes up is like drawing on water; it leaves no trace. And the key is that things come up in an unconditioned way from groundless ground and disappear into groundless ground without any mental engagement. The technical terms for that in Dzogchen are *panglam*, don't accept anything, don't reject anything; leave it alone, *tsomar*.

Whatever comes up is just there as part of the groundless ground. If it events, it goes back. There's no ordinary mind engaging it anymore. It's just reflected by *rigpa*, awakened awareness. Like things coming up in a mirror are not affected by the mirror. The mirror isn't affected by the things that come up because it's all the same. And here's what happens if you hold it like that as your view: at this stage, the view is the meditation. The view is the meditation. If you hold it like that, everything that comes up every moment leaves no karmic trace. That's the beginning of buddha training. It means there are no further karmic impressions because what makes memory traces, karmic traces, is mental engagement.

Since you're not doing any of that anymore—because there's nobody home in there to engage anything, it's all groundless ground—what's going to happen? All the previous karmic traces come up at an accelerated rate and release themselves. And that process of automatic release every moment leads along a path of what's called "*dharmadhātu* exhaustion."

At first, what will come up will be lots of very quick, very fleeting impressions from your life. Memories of your life just come up and they're gone at an accelerated rate. Awakened awareness watches all the personal memories from life just come up and release themselves. All the stuff of all the relationships that you have that have lots of grab in them, they all just come up and they go. All the stuff about strong emotional states in your life just come up and they go.

And after a while, all that stuff starts to wind down and the same stuff comes up from previous lives. And it all comes and goes. And the endpoint of that, through this accelerated process, is that there are no negative states left in the continuum of your experience across lifetimes. You're extinguishing all negative states.

And what will flourish or shine forth is *kadak*, the original purity of all the positive states of mind. It's not like they suddenly come up and you transform anything. That positivity is always there, but it's obscured by all the negative stuff. And when it clears, it's clean. We call that *drima* [pronounced dree-may]—stainless mind. It's so clean and pure and wondrous. And the awakened awareness at that point is just stably brilliant and wondrous. And there are no negative states left anymore. That's *dharmadhātu* exhaustion or "the clearing of the impure visions" as it's called.

The first part of buddha training is the exhaustion of all negative states and the flourishing of all positive states. There are eighty positive qualities of a buddha mind. When I was in retreat going over this stuff, at the end of the retreat, Menri was teasing me about it. And he said, "You Western psychologists—*nyermang, nyermang*!" And I said, "Yes, we get pre-occupied with negative emotional states." And then I said, "Yes, I'm a professional about negative emotional states. I specialize in them with people." [Laughter] And he says, "What's the matter with that?" And I said, "*mümpa*." He says, "Yes! *mümpa*, they all obscure." He says, "Look at your mind now and look at the difference." And I said, "Well, it's vast. It's absolutely crystaline clear. It's clean. It's stainless as if there aren't any impurities whatsoever, and it's rather remarkably wondrous."

He says, "Well, why waste all this time on all these negative states? [Laughter] Why waste all your time on the clouds when you can dwell in the sun?" He made his point. See?

So, the first domain of the third map of buddha training is the transformation of affect. It doesn't transform, it just gets rid of the clouds. It seems to transform though. Nothing left is negative. The ultimate of that? *Kuntuzangpo*—everything good.

Now, the second domain is the seeming transformation of perception because we see stuff and we have the habit and ordinary mind of things in an out-here world. But we don't see anything out here. What we're seeing is the mind's capacity to make representations. Awareness expresses itself. It's constructive; it makes representations. There's no outside world that we're seeing. What we're seeing is what the mind has represented. We're seeing the mind's awareness because we can't see anything other than that. This is what we see.

But what's going to happen is that somewhere along this process of buddha training, you'll start to look more carefully at the issue of perception. And you're going to look really at the issue of how awareness creates all of this show. All of this is the display, the dance, the *rolpa*, the play of awareness. And you start looking at how, you don't look; *rigpa* looks into itself; awakened awareness looks at itself making its own display. And that's quite remarkable.

What will naturally unfold is how the display is constructed by the spontaneous play of awakened awareness. In the slower path, it's called the five wisdom energies. The outcome is that you're going to see everything in terms of energy and light. There's nothing solid left anymore. The quick path, the hyperspace path along that same way, is the Lamps practice, the secret energy channels. And in the secret energy channel practices, you open up the pathway to look at how the world is constructed. Out of the eyes, there's a film upon which all of existence is projected. And that begins what are called the *tögal* visions. What you start to see is the lively dance of awakened awareness every moment, and that awakened dance will start to be more and more fluid, and nothing is solid. You see the world through the fluid movement of awakened awareness as it expresses itself.

And then awakened awareness will express itself not so much in fluidness, but it will create all of these tigles, like very quick moving energy, little bubbles of energy, sort of like watching water boil. You get many, many bubbles very quickly. And then it all slows down and you get perfect spheres appearing in empty space. And the spheres get more and more organized. It's sort of like looking at cells under a microscope, it's very organic. And of course there's no duality. And then what you start to see is that all the tigles and the cells and the energy, they start to produce bursts of energy, brilliant rainbows, colors. And that pretty much finishes the first level of visions.

Then in the second level, all of those visions, all that fluid dance of energy patterns itself, and you start getting patterns. And you watch the organization—and there you're going to learn something that goes beyond liveliness. What you're going to learn is that *rigpa* not only expresses itself to its own liveliness, it organizes itself to itself. That's a really important point.

And in the third level, you're going to watch *rigpa*, awakened awareness, start organizing worlds. This is just one bubble. You're going to watch the myriads of worlds being organized, and there's your key to all at-once-ness. All those worlds begin to get organized, and you just watch the whole dance of the worlds organizing itself, and the awareness pervades all those multiple myriads of worlds at once.

What's left if you follow that path? There's no solidity left in the world whatsoever. The only thing that's left is the body becomes light. Sound becomes pure sound, and pure sound isn't hearing that piece of paper or the bell. Awakened awareness has a sound. You can hear it. Always here. It's soft and alive and you can hear it.

And if there's no duality left and you watch this whole show, here's an interesting thing that happens. You see, earlier you probably had a lot of difficulty with thought, and you tried to catch thought with your awareness. What is thought? It's a movement through the mind. It has a certain directionality to it. What happens when you hold your awakened awareness all the time? You notice that awakened awareness has a directionality to it. Right? And when you have absolutely no duality in the mind, here's what happens. The directionality of thought and the directionality of awakened awareness are not different anymore. They're the same thing. We call that "discriminating wisdom," the absolute pinpointed precision of that intention. And ultimately that turns to light, so all that's left are rays of light.

You're not going to get rid of that directionality. But if you clean it up, it's no longer the directionality of thought movement. It's no longer the directionality of awakened awareness. It's like the rays of light that are crystal clear every moment. Everything is reduced to light, sound, and light rays. That's the world that you live in—not very solid, and rather magical. Sometimes in the Dzogchen texts that's described as *hedawa*, the condition of chronic wonder.

So, now the body's really interesting because if you follow the secret channels in the body, not the central channel practices—see, the trouble with central channel practice is that you have to represent it, do all this work to visualize the side channels and clearing them of all their impurities, and then visualizing the central channel. And you can squeeze the pot, vase breathing, and you can squeeze all the *tigles*, the energy, into the central channel and let it rise and heat it up and all. It's a lot of work. But if you're operating out of *dharmakāya* release, all you have to do is take the view of an awakened mind, like an infinite vast expanse. And with the simple intention of looking at the body, it spontaneously arises in groundless ground like an empty glass bottle filled with light, hanging in empty space. And all you have to do is put the intention to look at the channel and it will spontaneously arise perfectly clear in that body, King of Samādhi, pinpointed focus against the backdrop of infinite vast expanse.

You don't have to do anything anymore, no representation. The channels spontaneously reveal themselves to themselves. And you watch the energy flow through those channels. There's no you watching it. It's reflected by awakened awareness spontaneously, and the flames surge every moment. And what happens is the body gets more and more transparent, and more and more light until there's absolutely nothing left but clear light body.

The imprint of the body stays as long as you're alive. But as Rinpoche says, "Body like hotel, you guest." Now, the hotel's pretty bright, cleaned up, crystal clean. It doesn't even take long to do. It just opens up itself to itself. Then you get a taste of clear light body. And if you follow those practices right down to the elements in the body, which will naturally open up with the rainbow lights, the outcome of that is rainbow body. The body is reduced to nothing more than rainbow light because all of those elements that seem solid are just light and color. Then you've mastered fully the process of living and dying. There is no death. So, the third part of the map or the third domain is the transformation or seeming transformation of the body, the clear light body, and ultimately to rainbow body.

Now the fourth and last part of the domain is if you follow the dance of how awakened awareness organizes itself to itself, and you follow the path of how it keeps organizing and displaying with the worlds, that's the key to what will open up into the limitless buddha realms and all the mind-to-mind transmissions, what seem to be like downloads of teachings. The path has its own intelligence at that point. But those teachings aren't out there. They're all within the field of awakened mind, so you know everything you need to know along the way.

And, ultimately, the mind's awareness will pervade all of those realms. The infinite thousands, myriads of realms, are like one great sphere, Tigle Chenpo. And they all get unified in one ultimate reality that's at once completely empty and completely full. It contains the content of all realms and times. And your mind pervades all of that and you manifest the bodies of enlightenment. At once, the infinite vast expanse of ocean-love: the *dharmakāya*. At once the brilliant intensity and radiance of awakening: the *sambhogakāya*. And at once the myriad of displays that appear in various realms for various reasons: the *nirmānakāyas*.

And all that's left at that point is enlightened conduct, enlightened activity, which is the operation of perfect conduct for the sake of helping beings in that ocean. It's game over at that point; the end of the path. No negative states, the flourishing of all positive states in a mind that has "cracked the eggshell," as it's called, and that pervades many realms and times simultaneously for the sake of helping beings across all of those. The scope of that mind is limitless. Enlightened activity is inexhaustible. The best measure of realization is *choepa*, conduct. And when it's the conduct of a buddha, we call that "enlightened activity."

So, my friends, that's a description of the whole path. Now you've got to do it.

May 5, 2012

Themes: Internal and External Refuge; Trust; Aspiration; Conduct

Dan

Welcome everyone.

So, the format is that we open this up for whatever—either questions specifically about meditation practice, which nobody ever does, or questions about spiritual practice in everyday life. We see where that takes us, and we translate that into meditation of some sort or another for the second half of the class. It's wide open.

Student 1

I've been reciting the four refuges day by day as often as I can remember. And they've been a good way to offset …

Dan

The four refuge objects, you mean?

Student 1

Yeah, in the teachers, Buddha, *dharma*, and *sangha* …

Dan

Okay.

Student 1

Just chanting that over and over. And they've been a good offset to becoming aware of where I'm grasping at wanting more of something or less of something in my life. As that settled down, though, lately I've been becoming aware of how I still, though, really am so invested in refuge in the basics in my life, like home, family, some stable finances, health, and that I'm still seeking refuge there more of the time than I am in the Buddha, *dharma*, and *sangha*.

Dan

How's that working out of this Asian culture? [Dan chuckles.]

Student 1

So, I just wondered if you could comment on that about the way to truly take the refuges completely. I guess I'm realizing more and more how profound a shift it is.

Dan

Yes, it is. Let's start with the idea of taking refuge. It may not be clear to people. So, let's review that. When you take refuge, there are two forms of it. The conventional form, or what's called "external refuge," is you take refuge in the Buddha, the *dharma*, the *sangha*; and those are called "the three jewels." Externally, when you take refuge in the Buddha, you're taking refuge in a person who is the epitome of what it means to realize what's possible. The word buddha means realized. So, to take refuge in the Buddha means that you have faith in the fact that throughout history there was a Buddha Shakyamuni, and since [then] many, many more buddhas who were able to fully realize their mind—I suppose what we would call complete actualization in Western terms. So, the Buddha provides a kind of exemplar, or a model for what's possible. This is the final result.

I remember towards the end of my nine years of living with my Root Lama, summers between college and graduate school, just before he died in 1979. And one of the last things he said to me was, "When you came here, you expected me to teach you how to meditate. And you probably feel disappointed that I didn't do that the way you wanted because I didn't show you very specific meditation methods." He said, "Those are easy to learn and there are many places that you'll learn them, but that's not what you got."

He said, "I started studying when I was four years old, and I finished when I was fifty-five." He was eighty-nine at the time. And he said, "What you got in your nine years being here is what it's like to be around somebody who's fully realized the mind. This is what it's like. And if you see that and you've understood through the time of being with me the value of that, with your own intelligence and resourcefulness, you'll go out and figure out how to do the same thing until your mind and my mind are inseparable. And if you don't see the value of that, you won't do anything with it. That's what you get." And what he was really saying was the gift of being there was a chance to actually spend a lot of time with somebody who's fully realized and lives it as a way of being.

And that lesson, as a refuge object, as we would say in the *dharma*, is far more important than any specific methods that I learned. Because what he offered was a living example of what's possible for each and every person. And the gift was to be around somebody like that for that long. So, when you take refuge in the Buddha externally, you're having a faith, an act of faith that this development of your own mind and its refinement to full buddhahood is quite possible for you. And secondly, there's some taking refuge in the *dharma*. And the taking refuge in the *dharma* means that you take refuge in a body of teachings that work.

These practices have been around a long time. The practices from Shakyamuni Buddha stem back twenty-five hundred years, from Tonpa Shenrab five thousand years. The Elephant Path of concentration goes back fifteen hundred years. There isn't anybody in the Tibetan tradition that doesn't learn the concentration, the nine stages of concentration, the Semnegu. That means thousands and thousands of people have used it. And the reason why it stays around is because it works. In Western medicine, we use language like "empirically supported" treatments.

Taking refuge in the *dharma* is taking refuge into something that's empirically supported or proven, not in the Western bullshit sense of advertising when we say some medicine is clinically proven as a way of giving it an official stamp, which is completely garbage. But the fact that many people use these practices, and they use them over and over the generations because they tend to work for each generation. And unlike new products in the West that are advertised, there's no "new improvements."

They're conservative; they don't change much because they work. And they're usually taught the same way each generation because they work for each generation. So why change what works?

So, when you take refuge in the *dharma*, what you're really saying to yourself is, "I'm having an act of faith here that these practices have worked for so many people, not just to teach them to meditate, but to awaken their mind, to bring it to full buddhahood. And then I can do that too."

And then thirdly, you take refuge in the *sangha*. The *sangha* is the community of people who support your practice. Now, that's a little bit more complex because, you see, in the West people tend to be very competitive with each other. And I suppose that's true even of Tibetans to be fiercely competitive. But within the domain of the *dharma*, there's no place for competition. There's no place for jealousy. There's no place for wishing that you would advance better than others.

One of the Four Immeasurables is joy for others' gain, the positive opposite of competition and jealousy, [such that] you take a genuine joy in seeing other people get there even before you do. But, if you have a precious *sangha* that lives that, then you have people who are there supporting you in your best development. It's nontoxic. That's a rare thing in this culture. So, if you find that, it's like a shelter. Many of you people know that because you have that here. Special. There's no place for competition; there's no place for jealousy. It's about support.

The Tibetan translation of the word *sangha* is really interesting: *Gendun*. *Gewa* is virtue. *Dunpa* is a best friend. To take refuge in the *sangha* from the Tibetan point of view is to have a community of people who are going to be your best friends to support your best development. Literally, it means "friends of virtue" or "virtuous friends." Now, when you find that, that's special. We don't do that in the West. We're competitive with each other. We undermine each other. We want to do better than anybody else. I'm reminded of this line from South Park, which is clearly a *dharma* teaching [Laughter], and the devil throws a coming out party for himself. People are kind to him, so he has a fit of remorse. So, he starts listing all the awful things he did throughout history and the punch line is, "And I did all these awful things but never as bad as what junior high school girls do to each other." [Laughter] And you notice a certain cutting-through honesty about that. That's really painful to hear. I mean, we're hearing all about that with the bullying stuff now. It's painful. But that's the culture our kids start with. It's flawed. And as adults we just grow on that culture, make more of it. So, to find the refuge—and it is refuge from the nightmare of all that, of people who are genuinely kind and helpful and supportive and want the best for you—that's what it means to have a genuine *sangha*. But at the beginning you don't know those people, so it's an act of faith again. That's external refuge.

Internal refuge is a little different. It's what one would do in the Essence tradition like Dzogchen, the Great Completion practice, or in Mahāmudrā, the Great Seal practice. There, you don't take refuge in the Buddha because there's no buddhas. It's just an empty construction of mind. Ultimately, what you take refuge in is your own mind's capacity, buddha nature. Everybody is already fully awake. The view in the Essence traditions is that everybody is awake all the time, they just don't realize it. And the analogy is like the sun that's covered by clouds. When the clouds clear, we say, "Well, the sun just came out." The sun didn't just come out. The sun's always shining. But when the clouds clear, it appears to you that it just happened. The sun came out. Your awakened nature is always shining. You just don't see it because of the clouds. So, you take refuge in your own buddha nature. You have to activate it, clear away the clouds through emptiness practice. So, what's shining forth, the real precious jewel is the jewel of your own mind, fully realized. And that mind manifests all the qualities of a full buddha. There are no negative states in a buddha mind through a process of what's called *dharmadhātu* exhaustion. You eradicate all negative states from this lifetime and all previous lifetimes. And what comes forth is a flourishing of eighty positive qualities of a buddha mind. And a mind that has a scope, a range that covers the entire possibility of everything that could be on all levels at all times at once, what we call all-at-once-ness. That's the scope of a buddha mind. That's the omniscient component of awakening. Very different from the older Theravādin Buddhism, where awakening meant liberation, the absence of suffering. The absence of a negative isn't the development of a positive. In the Mahāyāna, in addition to liberation from negative states, complete liberation from negative states, you cause a flourishing of all the eighty positive qualities of a buddha mind. And the mind pervades you with its awakened awareness to such vast scope, it encompasses everything in one great sphere. All realms and times, all seeming individual consciousnesses are contained within that mind, an enlightened mind. And within that sphere, a buddha tirelessly acts to help beings. We call that enlightened activity.

So, you take refuge in the fact that your mind is already programmed as part of the hard-wiring for that to occur. That's refuge in buddha nature, not in external Buddha. Secondly, you take refuge in not the *dharma* as an external body of teachings, but your own inner resourcefulness—all the positive qualities, the seven factors of awakening, the six perfections, the quality of absolute trust in yourself. You take refuge in your own intelligence; you take refuge in your own resourcefulness. That's deep confidence, or better, assurance that you have everything you need within your own capacity to bring about that realization. And if you have that, you see, buddha nature has its own intelligence. And you know that the further you get along the path. The further you get along the path, you activate your own innate buddha nature intelligence. So, the path shows itself to itself more and more. Just get out of the way. At some point the path just goes by itself—easy.

Everything shows itself to itself. Bob doesn't awaken. Awakening happens to itself by itself when Bob gets out of the way. The refinement of that awakening, so you have it at all times, happens to itself by itself. And when that gets fully automatic, the rest of the path will reveal itself to itself. There's no teachers anymore. You get what seem to be complete bodies of teachings. They'll seem like downloads from buddhas—it's called mind-to-mind transmission, but there are no buddhas out there. It's all contained within your own mind. How stunning.

I was talking with His Holiness Menri Trizin about that on my last retreat with him, and I said, "It just sort of reveals itself to itself." He said, "Yeah, I sort of like that. Come back to me when you're further along. Let me know what you've realized." No further instructions. [Dan laughs.] I knew exactly what he was saying. He knew exactly what I was saying.

So thirdly, rather than taking refuge in external *sangha*, you take refuge in all of relative reality. The whole display is here for only two purposes. Every moment of the awakened mind is a gesture of compassion. As we say in Dzogchen, a great liberation practice, the Great Completion practice, "the intention of an awakened mind every moment is necessarily the intention of compassion, *gonpa*," the intention of compassion. That's the compassion side of the equation. The other thing we can say in Mahāmudrā is the intention of every moment of the awakened mind is to show itself to itself so the realization can realize itself. That's why it's called Mahāmudrā, which literally means the great gesture. Every moment of relative reality is another gesture to you until you get it. Infinitely inexhaustible gestures to you until you get it. We're all sort of slow learners here. The mind has many displays and all of that is for the benefit of realization. That's the wisdom side of the equation. And they're both the same—wisdom and compassion, two sides, the same thing. The great gesture, an invitation.

If you see it just the way it is, every moment is an invitation that deepens awakened realization.

So, you see, all of relative reality—not just our precious community of kind beings that are supportive—everything, all of the stuff of reality, is useful. You put yourself in the midst of all the stuff just to let the realization shine forth in the midst of all the stuff. Nothing needs to be changed. How wonderful is that?

I travel all the time for these courses now—this is the fourth trip in a row where the airlines have lost my bags, and this is the second trip in two retreats where they lost all my meditation stuff, and this time I don't think I'm going to get it back. I think it's completely gone. So, I have to get on a plane Monday with absolutely nothing left to teach with except my mind. And there's something that's wonderfully freeing about this whole mess. [Laughter] It's fine. So maybe I don't have the music for the course, but what do I need this stuff for? I've got to show you without the stuff. So maybe it will come back, maybe it won't come back. But does it really make any difference? And there's the freedom. We want stuff. We all want stuff.

So, those are internal and external refuge objects. There's a little bit different twist in the Tibetan from the Indian system with this because in the original Mahāyāna, which came from India, there were the Three Jewels. But the Tibetans did something else. They added a fourth and that's the lama. And the lama is the embodiment of all the other three jewels. The lama is the embodiment of the fully realized state. The lama is the embodiment of the perfect teacher because buddhas know how to teach people at different capacities with different methods. There are 84,000 methods in Buddhism, all for different capacities. And since the buddha mind works on all those levels at once, the buddha gets it, how to teach each person at the right level, even simultaneously. And the lama represents all the positive qualities of the mind that offer the best support for the development of your practice.

So, in that sense, you see, the lama becomes the embodiment of all the Three Jewels. So that's where the fourth object comes in. Now, that's not uncomplicated because you see, in the older tradition, the lama was a reserve title for somebody who's done lots of practice. In the original tradition, you didn't get to call yourself a lama. People called you lama over a lifetime of your being and living that, and how you were with people. That's a real lama. Because the ultimate test and the authenticity of any realization is always conduct. That's a lama, how they live.

But then it got watered down a lot. The traditional view was you get called a lama if you've done your twelve years of studying all the texts, which is a rigorous training. It's better than our four years of PhD or whatever it takes here, sometimes less, sometimes more, but it's not twelve years, unless you went to the University of Chicago like me where everybody took ten or twelve years because it was only a graduate school, primarily. And in those days, that's what people did. But, generally speaking, it's not as rigorous as lama training and the philosophical training. And then after twelve years of learning all the texts, it's three years of meditation retreat. And in the oldest days, that model is watered down from a lama, you see. It's not about conduct.

And there used to be competencies that were demonstrated. But you see, it's deteriorated a lot in the traditions. Now you can clock your hours. I mean, it's no different from how Western academics deteriorate. It used to be much more rigorous. I remember once teaching in the medical school in summers in Portugal and I went to a doctoral dissertation and my god, it's like stepping into the Middle Ages. They still dress up in the robes. It's a three-day event, a public affair, not just with your dissertation advisors, but the entire community comes to test you. They still do it the old way. Amazing. You've got to know your stuff because they tested competency.

But now in the West, that's broken down. Now everybody gets an A. Or you can get pass/fail; you don't even get grades anymore. All you have to do is clock your time. And there are similar versions of that in the monastic tradition. What's broken down a lot is that a lot of people call themselves lamas just by virtue of taking a three-year retreat. And that happened more because when the last Kalu came around, he told Westerners if they took the three-year retreat, they could call themselves lamas. So now we have all these Western lamas. But some people take the retreat and never got any instructions, certainly didn't have to demonstrate competencies. So, you see, now the word means nothing anymore.

I remember when I was in Burma in 1980 doing the *Visuddhimagga*, and you had to go through all the stages of the practice, and the final exam was you had to go before three of the masters and they called out the states randomly and you had to produce them on the spot. And they judged the authenticity based on the speed by which you could produce that state and the quality of how you describe it, because if you have that kind of mental pliancy, you can shift to any level of mind. In other words, they were doing a final exam of competency. It wasn't enough just to clock the time on the pillow or what some people call "the odometer principle" in the West. If you clock mileage, that means you get somewhere. Well, most people clock a lot of miles, you don't get anywhere. So, you see, the "take refuge in the Lama" in the old tradition meant something. That wasn't a title you could pin on the donkey. It was a title that you earned through a lifestyle of being a certain way. And it didn't represent self or self-importance. And they said it represented a way of being that was authentic. And there's no self-involvement in any of that. It couldn't possibly be. So, it's a little more complicated in the West now. Everybody's a teacher.

So that's what I would say about the structure of taking refuge. Now, the change in the experience of taking refuge is a whole other dimension of this. And the first is taking refuge that aspires towards those goals. So, let's say with external refuge. So, it means that you develop the aspiration that you could develop the practice to become a buddha. But then again, you've got to take yourself seriously and you're going to bump across all those limiting beliefs. "Me, a buddha? *Moi*?" [Laughter] Why not? You have buddha nature.

What are we doing this for? It's about awakening. It's not about sitting quietly; it's not about stress reduction. It's about awakening. So, let's be honest about it. Why waste your time doing anything else? So, you have to at least entertain the possibility, and that requires kind of an act of faith.

But beyond that, it means developing that faith enough that you start aspiring towards that. And it starts to become, when you have the faith that aspires, what you're really developing is a central organizing principle. You start to organize your practice around wanting that. And then what's going to happen to all the wasted time of everyday life? All that stuff just gets less important.

Many of you know this story, but when I used to teach with Denma Locho Rinpoche, who's now the head of the Gelugpa, one day we were teaching in the West and the student asked a question, "What do I do with laziness?" And he said, "No. Laziness is for monks in the monastery. You Westerners, your disease is busyness. That's your laziness." Two sides of the same thing. Good comment, busyness. And you see, what happens is that all that busyness, for extraneous reasons, it's not going to get us anywhere in life, you begin to get less interested in all that kind of stuff. It changes over time.

That's the first step: faith, which aspires, or trust, which aspires. I like the word trust better than faith.

The second is faith or trust that believes. What does that mean? It means that now you've organized a spiritual practice and you've done it a lot and you've made a place for it in your life, like you have done. And what begins to happen after a while? You begin to see what you're capable of doing. We call that in Western psychology, self-efficacy. You actually begin more and more progressively to draw the conclusion that you can actually do this practice and it gets you somewhere. And after a while, you develop confidence. But more than that, after a while, you start to develop a positive and firm belief, a conviction that this is really quite possible for you.

Remember, Western cognitive psychologists say that unlike negative self-talk, which is sort of a moment-by-moment evaluation of our state—not a very good one—negative or irrational beliefs develop very slowly over time; it takes years to develop a negative belief. But the one thing that's unique about negative belief, according to Western cognitive therapists, is that once you develop a negative belief, it's relatively intractable, impervious to change. Which means if you encounter new experiences that run contrary to belief, the natural human tendency is to throw out the new experience and keep the fixed belief, however irrational it may be.

So, it takes a lot to sort of whack those beliefs because they're stable structures of mind. But that also applies to positive beliefs. They develop slowly over time, too. And like any belief, like a negative belief, beliefs operate in the background of our awareness and they have a lot of influence, like minimized windows in the computer that cause the computer to crash. The positive beliefs also operate in the background of the awareness and have a lot of influence. That's what it means to have trust or faith that believes.

There's a certain point in time where it's not just aspiring towards something, but in your own direct experience you've seen over and over again the positive effects of doing the practice. It proves itself to itself. Then at some point, you just know where it's going to take you. That's a belief, and it doesn't change much after that. And it's going to have a lot of positive influence in the background of your awareness and what you do because all the other things don't matter so much. And you become more single-minded about where you're going with that. That's the second stage, faith which believes.

The third step is when that transforms into behavior, conduct. Now that belief becomes a central organizing principle, first probably more in terms of how you organize your practice. What is it going to mean? You've all been through that, I'm just articulating it. It probably means that you're probably going to make a central place for a daily practice. It probably means that at some point it's going to dawn on you that you're going to have to take it off the pillow. And that how you bring emptiness practice or your view of whatever level of practicing you want, whether it be practicing liveliness from an awakened state, or whatever the view is, you're going to have to take that off the pillow. And that means that you can't separate out the everyday life from the twenty minutes you're doing your meditation. And you're probably going to enlist more and more of your behavior in the service of the development. And after a while, you're probably going to enlist all the stuff, all the negative stuff of everyday life in the service of spiritual development. So, there isn't anything other than relative reality after a while. That becomes the vehicle of your spiritual development. All the stuff is useful. Every moment counts.

In other words, the activity of the mind becomes the stuff and the medium of practice every moment on and off the pillow. But after a while, it's not even about activity. It's not about what you do; it's just a way of living. It's a way of being. That's the ultimate of the development of that kind of faith. So, you see, in that sense, in terms of progressive experience, you become the refuge object in the way you're living your life. Same mind, but different. My teacher used to tell me, my Root Lama: "Same mind, but different." It took a long time to figure that out. He meant develop your own mind until the awakened mind of the teacher, or any refuge object like Padmasambhava, in your mind, your own awakened buddha nature, are inseparable. You've manifested the same, then there's no difference anymore.

Now, there's another meaning of refuge that's important. And that is, if you think of the Western connotation of the word refuge, it means going for protection. And it means that when you call forth refuge objects, buddhas, you have to understand here that buddhas are not ordinary beings. They're non-ordinary beings. Buddhas only manifest in this appearing reality, in what we call their *nirmāṇakāya* aspect, only manifest for the sake of helping beings. It's the Buddhist version of *Field of Dreams*. If you build it, they will come. In other words, if you call forth non-ordinary beings, then you ought to take seriously that you're not just visualizing them in your head.

The intention of calling forth realized beings that comes from your own heart causes a linking from heart-to-heart. Remember, in Buddhism, when we go "body, speech, mind." Look where mind is: it's heart-mind. The mind is in the heart. So, when you put the intention into calling forth a refuge object, which is a non-ordinary being, you are making a heart-to-heart connection. And when you call them forth, it's not a visual representation, although the act of making the mental representation visually actually requires greater karmic strength. So, it strengthens the connection, but it's not about the visual image. You're calling forth beings who never die, who are, in one sense, always right here. Of course, they're not even out there, from a certain perspective, because you lose duality after a while.

But when you call forth beings, they come. Rinpoche told a story about this that some of you've heard in maybe in an advanced retreat. See, one of the great masters, of course, was Guru Rinpoche, Padmasambhava, [who] was a great, probably the greatest master in this tradition, in the Tibetan tradition, who lived in the [eighth] century. And he was a remarkable being. There are not many beings of that ilk. He took up in a local kingdom and did his practice. The king didn't really like him very much and didn't know what these crazy yogis were doing. And the kingdoms in those days were about five hundred people and not very big.

So, the king was threatened by him and killed him, except he reconstituted himself. And the king killed him in a different way and he reconstituted himself. And then it got worse because the king's daughter got fascinated with Padmasambhava and took up with Padmasambhava in the practice. And then the king got really enraged and killed him in more violent ways and he reconstituted himself. And then finally, the king killed him and his daughter, his own daughter, and they both reconstituted themselves. And after twelve rounds of this, the king got the point that this wasn't working out very well, and then decided to sort of learn from them instead. And the king became enlightened and the entire community became enlightened.

Then Padmasambhava went to Nalanda University, a great Buddhist university. He mastered all of the textual tradition of which there are 84,000 volumes. He learned all the psychic powers, and he had other unusual things. He was then invited to bring teachings to Tibet from India. He [had meditated in] a place called Rewalsar in northern India. And he accepted the invitation, and on the way, he used his psychic abilities to tame all the gods and demons and make them protectors of the *dharma*.

And then he went into a retreat for twelve years. And because he had the capacity to see across all realms and times, he wrote the terma text. He realized that for different times in history there would be different teachings necessary.

And he wrote them for the future to be discovered by certain people at certain times when they were needed. There were twenty-four bundles of terma text. Half of them have been discovered. One of them is very famous because it contains amongst many other texts, all the texts on the teachings of *The Tibetan Book of the Dead* because he realized he could see in the future at some point, people's attitude towards death would really deteriorate. So, they would need special teachings to sort of get back on track.

So, all these teachings would've put people on track by writing them for the future, by seeing it in the future and then leaving them behind for the future, which is sort of like science fiction-like. But that's how he worked. And according to tradition, he never died. He moved to the West and he lives in the Copper Mountain. And if you call him forth, he comes.

Now, our Rinpoche who we teach with is the emanation of Guru Rinpoche, who lives in the West, and for years lived in the Copper Mountain of Arizona. He is Guru Rinpoche for this generation of bringing the teachings to the West. But Rinpoche told us a story about Guru Pema[2] where, at the height of Nalanda, they were debating the Hindus who represented Patanjali's Yoga Sutras. And in the Hindu debate it was much superior to the Buddhists. So, they went to the Abbott and said, "We're going to lose this debate." And the Abbott said, "Well, why don't you get Guru Pema to do it?"

And of course, he had previously disappeared or died, but he never dies, three hundred years earlier. So, the Abbott said, "No, if you call him, he'll come. Non-ordinary beings come if you call him." So, they called him and he came flying through the air, and he debated the Indians and won. The Indians thought there was something funny because the perimeters of the debate place were all sealed. And there was a count, the headcount of fifty people on each side, and the Indians couldn't figure out how all of a sudden there were fifty-one of the Buddhists because nobody could get in and out of this place.

So, there was always this protest about whether the Buddhists cheated because they had an extra person, but they couldn't explain how they got an extra person. But the moral of the story that he was saying is, "If you call them, you take the attitude that they come forth as real beings." Why is that useful to think of? Because non-ordinary beings who have a realized mind, they can give

---

2 Another way of referring to Padmasambhava: Guru Pema

you what's called *chingilap*. *Chinwa* means to give, and *lapa* means a wave, like a wave on the ocean.

And what they give you is the gift of influence. In other words, from the side of awakened *dharmakāya* space, if you call forth a non-ordinary being, or if you take refuge in a non-ordinary being, calling them forth means making a heart connection directly to their enlightened mindstream. And, out of kindness, what they can do by you putting in the intention to calling them forth, is they will respond in kind by offering you the gift of influence. You can strengthen that by making a request. You ask them to intervene and to clear your mind of obscurations. And they'll offer *wang*, influence. Now, that's deteriorated in the West. We call that empowerments and Western students go around to a lama and they collect empowerments. The word *wang* doesn't mean empowerment. It means influence.

There's not stuff you're collecting. What you're asking for is a direct intervention from the side of awakened *dharmakāya* space to clean away the clouds. But here's the deal, you don't just get it for free. You've got to match it with effort. If you go to an empowerment, or you don't go to an empowerment ceremony, if you call forth a non-ordinary being in guru yoga and then you don't do the practice, whatever influence will wane very quickly. If you match it with the effort, you double the effect. It's like a matching grant. Then it works.

And they'll help clear away the clouds until there's no clouds left because non-ordinary beings have the capacity to directly intervene in your own mindstream. It's the Buddhist equivalent of grace. So, that's the extraordinary version of taking refuge.

So, there's the protection piece. I remember Geshe Wangyal, my Root Lama, saying [something] to me once—it was an unusual time. And I was just a student; I was like twenty years old, but he could foresee things. And I remember one day—he liked to water his plants at night; he had a big garden; he liked to water his flowers and watch the bees—he was watering the flowers and I was sitting outside translating and he just dropped the hose suddenly and he came over and got right in my face. He looked at me and he said, "Pay attention." And he said, "If you take refuge in the *dharma*, you will always be protected. Do you understand?" And he was urgent about it. "Do you understand? You will always be protected. Please understand what I'm saying." And it sent chills down my spine because it came suddenly and out of nowhere, and I felt he was telling me about the future.

And my own life has proven that to be true to me because as many of you know, I work in the trauma and the abuse field, and that's involved dangerousness. When I did my testimony before the War Crimes Tribunal, I'd take the plane over to Schipol[3], the night train, the plane, which was difficult. Before anybody else got off the plane, the UN security forces would escort me off. Then every day I went, I had a different car and a different bomb watcher. And I would testify in a plexiglass bubble because the war was still going on. And the whole idea was to disrupt the testimony.

And I worked on the Bobby Kennedy assassination. I made it on the Patriot Act. With all my traveling, I think I will forever be harassed at airports. But I don't feel unsafe. It is not possible. So, yesterday I was sitting all day doing a forensic examination on a person who is completely violent. People were terrified of her. We sat and we chatted for the whole day; it went just fine. No risk; not possible. So, you see, if you take refuge and you bring it to the level that you now are understanding, it's really profound. There are no risks. There are no fears. But it's not grandiose, it's deeply humbling.

Even in Western terms, there was John Bowlby, the grandfather of attachment that said, "The fundamental function of the attachment system is the protection of the species." First thing, secure parents are fiercely protective, but not overprotective of their kids. And you take refuge in the *dharma* protectors, they're fiercely protective. You can count on that.

And you can count on the gift of influence. It has an effect. Many of you in the retreats now have had a taste of awakening. Many of you have developed that, so it's strong. Do you really think that it has anything to do with me? I'm just a minor player in this. But the influence is strong because you took refuge, and the non-ordinary beings who transmit that. I'm just a translator.

---

3 The Schipohl Amsterdam Airport that serves the Hague, Netherlands, site of the International Criminal Tribunal for the former Yugoslavia where Dan served as an expert witness.

May 30, 2012

Themes: Unfolding Levels of Motivation; Awakening; Conduct

Dan

Welcome everyone. You have a question?

Student 1

This is something that I've been thinking about. It initially stemmed from what I do for a living and then has expanded, as things always tend to, into the practice. And it's like I've been watching the way my patients are with us and the way staff members and families are with those patients with whom I work, and what I was curious about is: what it is that motivates family members to become involved in care, the patient's care. Or staff members? What brings them to the kind of work that we do? And I think that those motivations and motives aren't always clear. So, I'm thinking too about the evolution of my practice, which has to do with what motivated me to come originally, and how that has changed along the way. And so one of the things that I've been thinking about and noticing is that there is an interaction between motivation and realization in that I think that realization doesn't really flourish without a certain level of motivation. So, I wondered if you could talk a bit about motivation and interaction and so on.

Dan

Wow, okay. I suppose we need to talk about initial motivation and resultant motivation or resultant motivations, plural.

Student 2

Can you just repeat the question?

Dan

The question was that she was wondering about how, in her own coming to this practice and seeing in her work, which is basically work with the elderly, how that led her to wonder about the motivations that bring people to do things, like for example the motivation to get started in a spiritual practice. And she was saying that for herself, she's noticed how that motivation has changed through the practice and she wants to know about the—I'm going to reword it here—the interaction effect between realization and motivation, how each affects the other. Is that fair to say?

Student 1

Yes. Yes, thank you.

Dan

Okay. And there are two types of motivations that cause people to come to spiritual practice, at least in the Indo-Tibetan Buddhist tradition. And the standard answer, the common answer, is that people come to meditation practice because they're unhappy. People come to spiritual practice because they're unhappy. We become acutely aware of the suffering in life, either our own or others or both. We're unhappy, and people seek spiritual practice as a way out. And that would be the main reason for practice. I suppose we could refine that and say that in the course of a life, people vary in the degree to which they are unhappy in themselves. So, they're not always predisposed to spiritual practice then. They're predisposed to spiritual practice at times when they're acutely aware of that unhappiness, or, which is often the situation, they have some sort of crisis in their life; it makes them more amenable to reevaluate their life and then come to spiritual practice. So, that would be the main motivation.

The other less common answer in Buddhism is encounter with a non-ordinary spiritual being. And one of the most interesting Tibetan texts that I translated many years ago, and I put a big chunk of that in the *Pointing out the Great Way* book because it just fascinated because I had not seen anything like it. But, when I first started reading mostly Mahāmudrā texts from Tibetan for my doctoral dissertation, I remember not knowing how to get a hold of the texts. And everybody said that the person who was collecting and preserving the Tibetan library was Gene Smith, who died this last November. So, I found his phone number in Delhi and called him up and said, "How do I get such and such Tibetan texts?" And he said to me, "Well, they're in your library at the University of Chicago. I shipped them all there, amongst other places, and I happen to be coming to Chicago in several weeks in the future. I will meet you."

So, Gene and I went to this back room at Regenstein Library at the University of Chicago, and with our hammers and crowbars opened these big crates where there were many, many hundreds of books, block print books, Tibetan books. And he went through it like a kid in a candy shop, "You have to read this and you have to read that." And he gave me this one book. He said, "This is very unusual, you won't find anything like it." And he was a lover of the Tibetan literature, the only Westerner who really knows this stuff cold. And when he said that, he meant it. And it was a two-volume set, which is probably over a thousand folios in Tibetan, and by Kunga Tenzin. And the whole analysis was how an encounter with a non-ordinary spiritual being transforms your life.

And, of course, I read it with great fascination because it was a travelogue of my experiences with my Root Lama, all laid out as a path. And it said in that book that the usual motivation to spiritual practice is, you know, unhappiness and suffering, malcontent in life. But the other pathway is encounter with a non-ordinary spiritual being. And in that encounter, there is something unusual about them. And he analyzed it in terms of different stages that you go through. The first is *dunpa*, interest, that in your encounters with this being, who is clearly, they are motivated towards your welfare, that's their main concern is your spiritual welfare, so you keep coming back for more because on some level of mind you sense that this person is unusually kind, unusually concerned about your welfare and the greater picture of life. And even though you may not be able to articulate that, you keep showing curiosity about how they're being with you, and that interest deepens. That's the first step.

And the second is that in being with them long enough, you begin to sense perceptually, you begin to perceive more and more of their good qualities, their positive qualities and how unusual those positive qualities are. Now, I suppose that could deteriorate into idealization, but in the positive sense, it's *merpa*, which is admiration. At some point it dawns on you that this is not a usual being, and they have special qualities. And you keep getting more and more curious about those qualities and who this being is, and you keep getting the direct effect of how they are in your life, which is deeply positive. And you become appreciative of that.

And then if they have, over time, a very deeply positive impact on your life, the third step is *gerpa*, which we translate as respect. But in the commentary to Kunga Tenzin's book, what's explained as *gerpa* means something behavioral. I suppose in the West it's like imitative behavior. If somebody has a deeply positive influence in your life, you want to be like them, and you act like them, and you become more and more like them. And the reason why the word is translated as *gerpa* is if somebody has been deeply positive to you in some way, and only interested in your well-being, then the best respect you could give back for their kindness is to act like them in general towards others.

And then the last step is *mendowa*, admiration-hyphen-respect, where you integrate all that into your own being. And the outcome of that is the desire to lead a life like that, a life of virtue which is only deeply positive. And that's what initiates you to give up the extraneous things in your life that are useless, and to more single-mindedly pursue a spiritual path.

Now, I mean, it's not hard to understand that analysis in Western common-sense terms. Think about somebody in your life who may be a teacher, may be a mentor, somebody who's had deep positive impact on you. For a lot of people that was a teacher, it might've been elementary school or high school. It might've been a mentor or a teacher in college. It might've been a clinical mentor for some of you in the mental health field or the medical field. But we can all think of people, and it's a particular kind of person. It's a person who extended to you an unusual interest in your well-being, your growth and development and learning, and acted out of kindness, with a kind of selfless kindness, towards what was best for you. And we all gravitate towards that. We can all think of people who are like that in our lives. So, there's nothing mystical here about this. And if we think about mentors that did us a good turn, we become more like them.

Roy Schafer, a psychoanalyst in the 1950s who trained at the Menninger Foundation, looked at that process in psychoanalysis. He called it selective identification. In those years, in the 1940s and 1950s, analyses were a long-term thing—they were ten or twenty years. So, this analyst knew everything about your life. They were there all the time, four or five times a week, for you to talk through anything that was the matter. And I suppose if they did you a good turn and you got better and your life got on the right track and you were deeply appreciative of all their selfless devotion to your growth and well-being, then what Roy Schafer was saying is, "The best outcome is not only do you get better, but you identify with positive qualities and you become like them in certain ways."

Plato had that clear a long time ago in his comments about education where he said that real education is necessarily education of character. We don't [just] learn stuff, we become who we are through our relationships with our mentors. It's the qualities of who they are that matter. So, there's a Western literature that touches on this issue, you see. So that's the alternate pathway if you have ... I mean, you see that in schools all the time. Kids get touched by teachers, and it makes all the difference in the world. I mean, for me, I was a somewhat below average student in the first three years in school until fourth grade, until I had Mrs. Merchant. [Laughter] You all have a Mrs. Merchant in your life. And she saw things in me that I couldn't see in myself, and I loved her. And, absolutely overnight, I blossomed in the relationship with her. Not only becoming the smartest kid in the class but the most artistic kid in the class. And on every level of mind, everything just blossomed, and it was all about the relationship. She was not an ordinary being to me. And that started the whole path in my life. Coming from an economically depressed area, that was my pathway out. And I'm deeply grateful for that because everybody I grew up with, my best friends, are either all dead or in jail. Because that whole area now is all, just all crack houses, which is what's happened to most Massachusetts mill towns. That likely would've been the path that anybody else took in that neighborhood. But that encounter made all the difference in the world, you see.

You all know what I'm talking about. That's why I'm here now. My duty is to give that back. And there have been many Mrs. Merchants in my life. Some of them have been teachers, some of them have been mentors, some of them have been spiritual masters, clinical mentors. I have been of good fortune with having many figures that I can think of like that. But it's the alternate pathway. And it's not a bad pathway, you see? So sometimes we're just miserable enough that we're forced to do things differently, and sometimes we're going along and we think everything's just fine until somebody shakes up our whole world. Those are the main pathways.

Western literature offers one slightly different version of the first pathway and that is crisis, turning points. The Greek word for that is *kairos*. And there's a fair amount of literature that shows one of the things that finally leverages change in peoples' lives is when they have some sort of major crisis that disrupts their life. Like the old Taoist phrase, "Crisis means opportunity."[4] So, it's not that we just generally get unhappy about our lives. It's very specific points that there are crises, and that's when people tend to turn more to spiritual practice. And I think that's an accurate depiction of it for many people. So, general dissatisfaction in life, specific crisis points, or encounters with non-ordinary beings—those are the typical answers for causal motivation. As would be said in Tibetan terms: what initiates you to start spiritual practice.

Now, most motivation is self-oriented. Most people who are motivated for spiritual practice don't do it with *bodhisattva* motivation. They're really wanting their own way out of this mess. They want to be happy; they want to have peace of mind; they want to have absence of suffering. It's not usual in this culture that people enter spiritual practice and all the work of that for the sake of other beings. We're not that kind of a culture. It's not built into this culture. And where it seems to be built into the culture, it's mostly representations. So, we do spiritual practice because we think we're benefiting other people, but what we're really doing is creating a representation about ourselves that we like by creating the image of being compassionate. You understand what I mean? And a lot of Western motivated spiritual practice, it has that end in it. It's really to make the self feel good. It's not really about others. It's serving others to make the self feel good. So, there's a kind of a false self-motivation in there. But I don't worry about that too much.

---

4 Robert F. Kennedy was quoted as saying, "The Chinese use two brush strokes to write the word 'crisis'. One brush stroke stands for danger; the other for opportunity. In a crisis, be aware of the danger-but recognize the opportunity" ("In China, a Crisis Is Also an Opportunity." *China Admissions*, April 16, 2020. https://www.china-admissions.com/blog/in-china-a-crisis-is-also-an-opportunity/). While this view of the term is widely held, there are also those who do not agree with the interpretation.

You see, the path has its own intelligence. And it's said that along this path, if you think about the three maps, there's the map that gets you from the beginning to having a taste of awakened nature, true nature. There's the second path that develops that awakening, that nurtures it so you have it all the time, up to having it all the time. And then there's the third path, which is when you have that awakening all the time up to full buddhahood. And it's said that that third path of buddha training does not open unless your motivation is founded in *bodhicitta*, authentic *bodhicitta*. You can't open that gate unless your practice is no longer motivated for your own wish for realizations for the self. It only opens if your motivation has a strong foundation in the wish for the end of suffering and the cause of everything good for all beings. You can't do it. The gate doesn't open.

But see here's the issue which is sort of interesting. The path has its own intelligence, which basically means if you get little flames of awakening, those little flames of awakening are usually accompanied by spontaneous compassion [a student's cell phone goes off with loud music], and sometimes by downloads [Laughter], and spontaneous compassion and spontaneous gratitude, and sometimes an appreciation for devotion.

So, you see the realization results in the authentic increase in the spontaneous expression of compassion. And if you were to take that second map, the more you cultivate the continuity of that awakening so you have it more frequently, you have it for longer duration until you have it all the time. The more you nurture that, the more you are developing that compassion as the natural, and authentic expression of that realization. So, you see, you don't have to worry about getting to that third map and being closed out because you don't have strong ultimate *bodhicitta*, ultimate compassion, because it develops as a consequence of the realization. You don't have to do a visualization at that point. You don't have to do a little compassion training visualization every day. It's the spontaneous expression of the true nature of the state of awakening. So, it's built in, you see. The motivation will naturally change, as you say, as a consequence of the degree to which your realization of awakening deepens.

So, in that sense, the realization results in authentic compassion, and that fuels the compassion. And the more that you develop that compassion, that deepens the realization and it actually determines and shapes the nature of the realizations that you have accessible to you. So, in that sense, you see, realization and compassion are yoked together, and each reinforces the other. The realization develops the compassion, the compassion develops the nature of, and even determines the nature of the realization, you see. So, by the time you get to that third map, the scope of the mind is such that it holds all beings within infinite *dharmakāya* space. It's not hard to open up all-at-once-ness, and open up a mind that operates on all levels of reality simultaneously, and works tirelessly with enlightened activity towards all beings and all levels of reality. It's the natural outgrowth of that yoking of compassion and realization.

So, it's not something you have to think about or decide conceptually. What you're describing is the nature of the compassion changes, the nature of the motivation changes, as a function of the depth of your realization. And at some point, the issue of developing these realizations for the purpose of self will seem perfectly ridiculous. It won't even come up as a question anymore because there isn't so much [of the] remnants of self or self-importance that ever comes up as an issue. The scope of the mind, the intention of the realization, is always for the benefit of the compassion.

So that's what matters. But, I mean, there's another dimension of this. We talked about that in our class this afternoon, and that is that it's only at the very latter stages of this practice, during that third map of buddha training, that realizations and conduct become yoked together and integrated. That's one of the very last changes on the path to buddhahood, when spontaneously emerging activity necessarily arises from *dharmakāya* for the sake of beings. It's always the best fit for whatever the context is at the moment. That's the most difficult thing to develop and it shows the most mature realizations. Then all conduct is a manifestation of awakened activity.

But, prior to that point, it's not out of the question and not uncommon to get some disconnect between realization and conduct. That's why conduct is always the best measure of realization.

Years ago, Jack Engler and I gave Rorschachs to various people at various stages of practice. With Rorschachs, people look at things in the normal waking state, and they see, they project content onto the ink. So, this ink blot looks like a bat. This one looks like a butterfly. This looks like two people dancing. This looks like two animals. These are common responses, popular responses. Well, we found that when people were deep into *samādhi*, before they went into meditation they saw bats, butterflies, people, animals. But after they went into *samādhi* they saw ink, and they didn't make it into anything. They spent just as much time describing the shape, the color, the shading. They just left it the way it was, which is consistent with the idea that when you're deeply concentrated, there is no thought elaboration.

But when we gave Rorschachs to people who were at the very subtle level of mind, storehouse mind, it was exhausting. We had to cut the Rorschachs at ten hours each because there was infinite turning over of mental content—highly unusual, because they could just dip into anything. It was always changing. If we gave them the next day, which we made a mistake of doing with some of the subjects, it was completely different content. That's not usual. There's your storehouse of creativity. But when we gave Rorschachs to people, this was in the Theravadan tradition, and in that tradition there are four gradations of path, four gradations of awakening in stages. And the ones that were from the first path, people who had achieved the first path, they looked like normal Rorschachs, with the full range of conflict that we see in the Rorschachs of ordinary people. But when we scored the Rorschachs with a scoring system for defense effectiveness and defense demand, they had no defensiveness. All their conflicts were right out there, easily and readily disclosed with no conflict. Now, that would be consistent with what the text or the authoritative tradition says, that the initial taste of awakening handles the problem of reactivity. In Western terms, [there's] no psychological defensiveness. But it doesn't change anything other than that.

And what was disturbing is the number of people who had genuine tastes of awakening, first path experiences, who in those Rorschachs, if we looked at them in Western terms, we would say met the criteria for a personality disorder. And that led Jack and I to the conclusion that emotional development and spiritual development are complimentary but separate tracks, and that one could have genuine realization and not be very emotionally evolved; and in fact, could be pretty screwed up and personality disordered, and that somehow the evolution spiritually didn't change any of that stuff. And it helped us understand the guru game, that gurus could come over here having genuine spiritual realization and be rather screwed up. And the only thing that changed is that they don't have that internal reactivity anymore. So, they may not suffer, but in their conduct, they may make lots of other people suffer. And the naive assumption was that somehow spiritual practice necessarily changed one's psychological makeup. And at that level of realization, which was genuine, it did squat. So, that meant that there were people who could purport genuine spiritual realization and have significant psychological problems that would negatively affect other people. That urged us to have some caution here about gurus.

And then we found, however, that a smaller sample size of people who had reached the third or fourth penultimate and ultimate path in that tradition, the arhats, if you will, and there the Rorschachs were not like anything we saw before, ever. They were completely absent of aggression, specifically, and they were generally absent of all negative states. We just didn't see anything like that ever before, which means if you get to the highest stages of realization, there are no negative states left and only positive states, which is what the textual tradition says. And that's what these people did. And I think what was most memorable to me in giving those Rorschachs was who they were in giving them, the imprint they had on me as the evaluator. Because all of those people—there weren't a lot—were non-ordinary people at that point. They were the most deeply loving people I had ever met. And that ocean of love made a lasting impact on me, just being in their presence. It was not ordinary.

So, you see, up to a point, spiritual realizations don't necessarily result in psychological transformation. Along this model that we're using of these three maps, what we would expect in this tradition, in the Essence tradition, is that the fundamental transformation of our psychological makeup, and therefore our conduct, doesn't really change until that third map, and pretty far along the way of that third map. When you achieve the automatic release of all previous karmic states, if you have what I call automatic *dharmakāya* release, where everything arises spontaneously from groundless ground in an unconditioned way and immediately settles back into groundless ground when leaving no trace, no trace goes beyond the practice of emptiness where things lose grab. It means that whatever arises spontaneously doesn't form any new karmic impressions, unless you mentally engage what comes up and then it forms a new karmic impression.

But if you leave everything alone in that continuously awake state, then the only possibility left is for all karmic traces in your storehouse mind to ripen themselves at an accelerated rate, to release themselves until there's nothing left. That's called *dharmadhātu* exhaustion. And the end point of that is no negative states, only positive states, the flourishing of all positive states. That's the point that you'll begin to get a sense of, that's the beginning of really transformation of conduct. That's pretty far along.

If you have awakening all the time, I mean, what does Garab Dorje and the Nyingma tradition say about that, the Dzogchen tradition? If you have awakening all the time and you have initiated that process of *dharmadhātu* release, and you do that all the time, the average time for that to settle out is about six years, if you do it all the time. Not a lifetime. Now, if you accelerate that process with *tögal* practices, the supercharged hyperspace practices, then the average time is about two years. Not a long time. But what you should expect to see is the outcome of that change is fundamental differences, not just in motivation anymore, but conduct.

So, that's why, since it's one of the last things to change is spontaneously emerging conduct from *dharmakāya* space, conduct is the best measure of realization or authenticity of realization. And the epitome of that [is] when the mind opens up to all-at-onceness, and the awakened mind now operates on many planes of reality in different times and spaces, and all that conduct is inexhaustibly oriented towards the compassion towards beings, the welfare of beings. Then we call that conduct, we give it a new name. We call it enlightened activity.

So, if you read the text of the twenty-one Taras, each one of those Taras is a metaphor for a particular type of enlightened activity. It's not about beings with different qualities. It's a metaphor for there being twenty-one types of enlightened conduct of a full buddha. And that's what manifests, that's the epitome of this. Conduct necessarily is the outcome and the best measure of authenticity. And if your conduct doesn't match, it doesn't mean you don't have spiritual realization. It simply means that the spiritual realizations have not evolved enough yet. And it may be, at times, the deterioration of authentic realizations into something more conceptual, and you're back to self. And you engage in certain behaviors to represent self. So again, whether your realization is authentic or whether it's either false, conceptual, on the one hand, or genuine and deteriorated, again, the best marker of that is conduct.

It goes back to when William James wrote his classic *The Varieties of Religious Experience* over a hundred years ago and he was asked the question, "How do you measure the authenticity of spiritual realization?" And his answer was, "By their fruits ye shall know them."[5] Conduct.

Genuine spiritual masters leave behind a legacy of positive change in the world. That's the best measure of realization. It's not about what people say on the internet about their self-discovered realizations, which we have a lot of these days, mostly by people who don't represent lineage traditions. Because you wouldn't say that. When Debbie Solomon from the New York Times interviewed Bob Thurman about his new book on the Dalai Lama, she asked him

---

5 The question was posed to William James (not sure by whom). The reply is a direct quote from the Bible, Matthew 7:16-20.

whether he was enlightened. Bob's answer [or what I was told was his answer] was, "Anybody who said yes to that categorically was not." Good answer. That's why His Holiness the Dalai Lama says, "I'm just a simple monk." Good answer.

Okay, that's a good question. Yes?

Student 2

How has spiritual practice affected your intimate relationships, especially whether family or romantic? I'm very curious about that.

Dan

How has my spiritual practice affected my intimate relationships, family relationship?

Student 2

… attachment and, you know, craving and feeling craved? I don't just mean romantic. I mean, my family is like that. Super, you know, there is just a lot of wanting expressed on both sides and wanting to …

Dan

Yeah, but that's the stuff for practice.

Student 2

Yeah.

Dan

You know, in one of the spontaneous songs of Milarepa, the line goes, "When I get a lot of stuff coming up, even better still." And relationships give us lots of occasions for stuff. So, they're wonderful training grounds for our realization. The closer the relationships we have and all the complications of that, is the medium of the best practice. Attachment, anger, confusion, any good relationship has it all, right? [Enthusiastic group laughter]

Student 2

Yeah. But the reason I'm asking that question is when you're changing the rules on your family members …

Dan

Like how?

Student 2

I mean if, my limited understanding of the way I've changed rules in the last few years is to practice non-attachment to the degree of, all right, I'm not going to flip out on my mom, you know. But …

Dan

I don't agree with that. I think if you're practicing non-attachment, that's not genuine practice. That's a representation of what you think you should be doing. It's an idea and it comes from self. Okay? So, it creates a certain image of the self. Practice would be to see the attachment, to see the anger, to see all of that stuff just the way it is, as constructions of mind, and cut through that with emptiness practice so it loses grab. But if you're trying to, you see, in Mahāyāna terms, if you're trying to make something go away, like to make attachment go away by practicing non-attachment, that is not middle path practice. It's nihilism. And it shades off into trying to represent things conceptually. And that's the practice that one might do in the older Buddhism. But there are improvements that came up in the Mahāyāna. You don't do that. You put yourself into the thick of all that kind of stuff and you see it just the way it is. And when we do emptiness practice, if you do it correctly, you're not going to get rid of that stuff. You're not going to get rid of your attachments. You're not going to get rid of your anger. You're going to get rid of the grab, *dzin-pa* that's associated with those states.

Student 2

I wasn't asking about how you changed internally or the attachment inside. How did your conduct change?

Dan

If you're practicing the stuff of emptiness, things lose grab. You don't leave the attachments, you don't leave the anger, but all that stuff loses grab. And what that likely can mean is you're going to be more honest, more real with your partner, with your family, and you're likely to be softer and kinder with everything. But it's not a representation of certain ways you're going to act. But there are certain negative behaviors that, after a while, when you practice emptiness strongly, you just don't go there because they don't come up. And ultimately it changes to something far more positive. That matters.

Look, I have a partner that I teach with, so that's both good and bad because we face the strain of traveling together all the time and all the stuff of the students. It's difficult. And then we have the stuff that any couple would have. But that's our practice, is to put it all out there. You know? And it's real and it's honest, and neither one of us shirks away from that. And the outcome of that is we try and be kind to each other and support each other. It's much easier doing this together. And if that kind of support lays a foundation so we're easy to be present and more kind to others, that's useful. And the stuff just comes up all the time. And that's not a bad thing. Mostly when it comes up, we deal with it honestly and then usually laugh about it because it doesn't have the same grab anymore. And for me, I consider that good fortune, personally, to have that.

So, look, there's nothing wrong with attachment. It's the grab of attachment, because you're not going to do away with attachments. You're not going to do away with anger until you get to that third map and you have *dharmadhātu* exhaustion. Then you won't have any of that. Up until that point, which is pretty far along the path, you would do better to believe or take the view that all of that stuff is going to come up a lot, and put yourself right in the thick of it. Personally, that's my practice.

And maybe I'm idealistic in some ways, but this is the time that Buddhism will come to the West. And I'm clear that what that means is that if Buddhism is going to survive in the West, it's going to survive in the thick of *samsāra*. To see that people can evolve themselves to buddhahood in the context of *samsāra*, Western *samsāra*, with all of our stuff, that's the lesson that this practice is coming to the West. If they can't work in what we've got here, they're not useful for anything. The mission here is to see that these practices can work in the thick of everyday life here in the West, for all of our stuff. So, we're not trying to change that. We're not trying to represent this as trying to evolve towards non-attachment or being patient and not angry or whatever. All that relative activity is the vehicle to deepen realization. It's the stuff that we use for realization, the full catastrophe of that.

That's the best practice, I think, because it's real. And it's consistent with a relational based way of teaching this. My first mentor in Buddhism was when I was nineteen years old and it was a very unusual person. Her name was Teresina Havens. And the first Buddhism to develop in the West was in 1887 when Carolyn Rhys Davis and her husband formed the Pali Text Society, and they translated the first books of Buddhism in the West into English, in London. That was the first time that Buddhism ever came to the West. And Caroline's main student was Teresina. She was an unusual lady. She got offered an endowed chair, as a woman, to teach Buddhism at Yale in the 1930s.

First of all, women didn't get professorships in the 1930s, particularly in places like that. But what was more unusual was she rejected it because she felt in her heart that you couldn't teach Buddhism academically. You had to live it. And she and her husband lived it through their relationship. They wrote the first things on using relationships and intimacy as the path of buddhahood. That was my first teacher. She had a big impact on me. So, this is not a new thing, you see. Since she was not an ordinary being and was my first encounter with any of this stuff, the legacy that she left me was that you do this in the thick of relationships.

That's Western Buddhism. She had that vision back in the 1930s, and here we are. Their first little pamphlet they wrote was on the spiritual evolution through relationships, intimate relationships. Remarkable. Here we are.

So, I don't practice non-attachment. I practice steeping myself in that stuff, and getting nice and messy with it. [Laughter] And it's all okay. That's the lesson. It's all okay just the way it is. But then the view changes, and none of that stuff gets in the way. That's an important realization. And all that stuff after a while enhances the realization, not obscures it. It's best to use all the stuff of relationships as the vehicle of transformation. So, you welcome all that conflict as a friend.

July 18, 2012

Themes: Usefulness of Concentration and Awareness Training

Dan

Welcome everyone.

Well, since a lot of the new people have insight background, maybe we should say something about the differences. Maybe that would be useful to start with.

There are two broad categories of meditation and they do different things.

When you intend to focus on something in your everyday experience, as soon as you focus on something, your mind won't stay on it. It will go somewhere else. The great American psychologist William James once said that the average time that the mind stays on whatever you intend to focus it on is about three seconds. Unfortunately, modern neuroimaging studies have shown his estimates to be quite true. So, ordinarily we are highly distractible and the mind doesn't stay on whatever we put it on, and immediately it jumps to something else. Where does it go? It either jumps to sense experience or thought or emotion.

Now, potentially, it should be the case that whatever you put your mind on, it stays only on that and on nothing else for as long as you intend to put it on. But that's not the case in our ordinary experience. We have a kind of bad habit of mind, where we are remarkably distractible.

So, concentration meditations are designed to teach you to stay for increasingly longer duration on whatever you intend to focus on. If you think of the mind as [being] like a wild elephant where elephants are smart and strong creatures, they're also very easily spooked. So, on the game preserves, if you frighten the wild elephant, a stampede causes a lot of damage. And your ordinary mind is likened to be like a wild elephant that runs out of control all the time. It's always chasing after either the next thought or the next sense experience, and rarely does it stay on whatever you intend it to stay on.

So, in concentration meditation, it's said that you tie the rope of mindfulness onto whatever the concentration object is. Using our elephant metaphor, it's like tying a chain around the elephant's neck. So, whenever the elephant wanders off, it feels the pull of the chain, and when it wanders off again, it feels the pull of the chain again. And if after a while the elephant figures out that it's not going to go anywhere because it's tied up to the chain, it stops wandering. And likewise, if you tie the mind up to a concentration object, whatever that object may be, it will keep trying to pull away and chase after the next thought or sense experience. But if you keep tying the rope of mindfulness onto the concentration object, and every time it wanders off you pull it back, the cumulative effect of those many times that you pull it back to the concentration object is that the mind stays for longer and longer duration on that concentration object. You train it to stay, and if you train it thoroughly, it should stay on that concentration object for however long you want it. Hours, even.

In one of the classes that everybody's doing today, we were reading a text that said, "If you can stay on, concentrate on the meditation object for four hours that seems pretty good concentration." Imagine focusing on one thing for four hours with no distracting thought, completely absorbed in whatever that concentration object is for four hours. We can't even conceive of that. But that would be a pretty good standard for concentration. When you're concentrating, you're either staying on the concentration object or you're distracted, there's no other possibility. Anything else that the mind is doing at that moment is a distraction. So, the purpose of concentration training is to stay continuously on the object of concentration.

Now, that's one type of meditation. The other broad category of meditation is awareness meditation. In awareness meditation, there's no concentration object. When you practice awareness meditation, the goal is to approximate continuous awareness because in our ordinary, everyday dysfunctional experience, awareness is discontinuous. We have lapses in our awareness. We are forgetful, we're mindless. We have big chunks of our awareness missing where we said, "Well, where was I? I don't even know where this was. Where did I put this?" So, our ordinary awareness is discontinuous. It's broken up. And the purpose of awareness meditation training is to train towards the approximation of continuous uninterrupted awareness.

Examples of awareness meditations in the ideal sense would be something like Krishnamurti's choiceless awareness, being aware of everything moment by moment by moment by moment, without any lapses in that awareness—continuous awareness; or *shikantaza's* "just sitting" style of Zen, where you're aware of everything every moment. That type of meditation was popularized in one of Aldous Huxley's novels where there's a mynah bird who's trained to say, "Here and now, here and now, here and now." [Laughter] In every moment you remind yourself to stay, here and now.

So, there are two ways to train the elephant. In concentration, you put a stake in the ground and tie a chain to the elephant's neck, and every time it wanders off, it gets pulled back by the chain. That's the metaphor for concentration meditation. You tie the mind to one concentration object and you keep pulling it back to that object until it stays continuously.

But the other way of training the elephant is to let it roam free and track it. And no matter where the elephant roams, you never take your eyes off that elephant for one second. And everywhere the elephant goes, you track it continuously. And the elephant will settle down afterwards. And that's a metaphor for awareness meditation, a continuous tracking with continuous awareness.

But you need to understand that training continuous awareness and training the mind to stay on one thing are completely different skills, and therefore completely different types of meditation. They're not the same. It's said however, that if you train one type of meditation to its extreme, the other comes naturally. If you train concentration so thoroughly that you stay every moment on the object, then even without training it, you'll get greater continuity of awareness over time. If you train continuous awareness and approximate continuous awareness every moment, the mind will get naturally concentrated. So, at the beginning, awareness meditations and concentration meditations are distinctly separate and unique skills, but at the upper level of skill development, one becomes the other, and they're not so separable anymore. To stay is to have continuous awareness.

Now, those are the two broad categories of meditation. I understand that for many of you, Burmese mindfulness has been very popular in this country. But you need to understand that Burmese mindfulness is a hybrid. It's a mixture of these two broad categories of meditation, neither one nor the other. Burmese mindfulness was developed about a hundred years ago by a single individual, Mahāsī Sayādaw. In that sense, we can call it a revitalization movement. One individual revitalized the tradition within Burma, which spread to India and Sri Lanka and Thailand, and it became the main form of Buddhism in the last hundred years in South Asia. It represents the older Theravāda Buddhists. But as a revitalization movement, it doesn't represent the lineage that goes back thousands of years.

And Mahāsī Sayādaw made certain compromises in order to make this work for people. One thing he did is he assumed that asking people to do pure mindfulness or pure awareness practice isn't easy to do. If I said to you, "Every moment, just be aware of everything," that doesn't work out so well. So, one of the compromises he made in his hybrid system was to have people do a modest amount of concentration training first. So, you learn to develop some degree of concentration using the rising and falling of the breath as a concentration object. And once the mind gets at least modestly concentrated, the background noise of thought will settle down a bit, and then it's a little bit easier to train mindfulness. Having developed concentration, you then open up the field of mindfulness and you train for continuity of awareness. So mixing concentration into what would otherwise be pure awareness training was one of the big changes in the Burmese system that Mahāsī Sayādaw introduced.

The second huge change that he made was to use labels. He thought that it was very difficult to say to somebody, "Okay, just be aware of everything every moment." So, to assist you with that, he allowed people to use labels. So, what you do is you concentrate until the mind becomes reasonably quiet, just focusing on the rising and falling of the breath. And when you get reasonably concentrated, you open up the field of awareness. You still focus on the rising and falling of the breath as the primary meditation object. And if a thought happens to arise, rather than turning away and focusing back on the concentration object as you would do in pure concentration meditation, what you do instead is you label the fact that at that given moment in time thinking is happening. You don't think about the content of the thought; [it's] just that at that given moment thinking has happened. So, you use the label "thinking, thinking."

If a sound came into your field of awareness at that given moment, you label "hearing, hearing." You don't think about the type or the source of the sound; just that at that given moment hearing is happening. If you looked at something at that moment, seeing—not what you saw, just the fact that at that given moment, seeing is happening. If a body sensation comes in, sensation; If an emotion comes in, feeling—not the content of the emotion or the type of the emotion, just that at that given moment feeling is happening. You notice a shift in your state of consciousness state, and you use the labels moment by moment by moment in order to approximate a greater continuity of awareness, so that as you train the skill of mindfulness, you are approximating continuous awareness and you're correcting for the dysfunction of the ordinary mind, which is discontinuous or interrupted awareness.

And the more you train for continuous awareness, that awareness will allow you to be more present to whatever comes in, in a non-reactive way, because you're not doing anything to anything, you're just being aware of it. In the ordinary mind, the habit of the ordinary mind is that if something comes into our awareness that we like, the mind moves more towards it to make more of it. If something comes into our awareness that we don't like, the mind moves away from it to make less of it. It's a kind of inherent reactivity every moment. But here you're training a kind of continuous nonreactive awareness.

Awareness and concentration are different meditations; they're less at the very advanced stages where they tend to blend in. But if you train awareness, that doesn't mean you're training concentration, and vice versa. In most traditions, you start with concentration as the foundation. Then you train for continuous awareness. Even Mahāsī Sayādaw tried to do that. But concentration training is not that strongly developed, at least in the way that Mahāsī Sayādaw taught it.

Now, in all fairness, within the Burmese tradition, when Mahāsī Sayādaw died, his successor, U Pandita, was very interested in concentration. He took a lot of the Western teachers of mindfulness and brought them back to the Burmese [tradition] and re-schooled them to develop more intense concentration.

The tools of concentration are not well developed within that tradition. If you want great concentration traditions, the two great traditions are the Asanga tradition of concentration in the Indian Mahāyāna Buddhist tradition, or the Patanjali Yoga Sutras, the Indian Hindu system. Those are the traditions that have very well-developed procedures for concentration.

So, the Burmese system that caught on here is a bit of a compromise that has some concentration but not in depth, and some mindfulness using a kind of hybrid system using labels. So, it's a good beginning concentration, it's a good beginning meditation, but it trains neither deep concentration well, nor continuous awareness well. It's a bit of both. So as an introduction, it's a nice way of seeing something about what you can do with training your mind. At some point, some purer systems lead to greater skill in training the mind, in my opinion.

Not all meditations are the same. We tend in the Tibetan tradition to emphasize concentration much more than mindfulness. But concentration trainings, for one reason or another, never caught on in this country, so most people aren't familiar with them. The Asanga tradition is virtually unknown, and the only people that teach it so far that I know are myself and Alan Wallace, in Santa Barbara. And then Patanjali's Yoga Sutras is the great system of meditation. There are eight *aṅgas* or eight limbs to meditation. Unfortunately, the stuff that came over here was the first limb, the first *aṅga*, which is the body postures.

Yoga is very popular in this country. Somehow yoga got mostly dissociated from the mind. It's just a series of postures that people do. That wasn't how it was set up in Patanjali's original system. The postures were just a foundation for training the mind. Most people go to yoga class and then they get five minutes of meditation at the end, hopelessly underdeveloped, not the way it was originally taught by Patanjali. I'm sure Patanjali wouldn't be happy with the way it's been taught in this country. Training the body is a prerequisite to training the mind, but training the body isn't an end in itself. It only helps to train the mind.

So, what do you really want to develop? Well, there are a number of things you want to do. Since we live in the culture of attention deficit disorder, it means as a culture we are very poor in training concentration. We don't have the cultural systems that allow us to train concentration very well. Most older children and adults are very poorly concentrated. So, training yourself to stay on whatever you focus on is a useful, basic skill of everyday living. The opposite of concentration is distractibility. The extreme opposite of concentration is ADHD, attention deficit.

From a neuroimaging point of view, we know a lot about concentration. The anterior cingulate cortex is the attention distribution center of the brain. When you have a competing attention demand, it allows you to decide where to put your attention most. The ACC, or the anterior cingulate cortex, is underactive in people who have ADHD; it's offline. Ritalin selectively activates the ACC and puts it back online, which is why it works for ADHD. When you do concentration meditation, you're activating the ACC. When you hypnotize somebody and put them into a trance state, you're activating the ACC.

The brain is sort of an equal opportunity employer. It doesn't care whether you use drugs or mind-body techniques like concentration or hypnosis. They all do exactly the same thing. They put the concentration center back online. And in this culture, the ACC is underdeveloped in many children and many adults. We call it attention deficit disorder. Why? Well, a lot of that has to do with early attachments, between infants and caregivers.[6]

We know from developmental studies that the frontal areas of the brain, including the ACC, develop more in the context of secure attachment systems. And with disorganized attachments, they remain underdeveloped, which is why kids end up with ADHD. I know the pharmaceutical industry would like you to think that ADHD is biological, even genetic, and therefore they can sell lots of drugs. But the one comparative study we have on genetic factors versus developmental factors shows that the genetic factors account for only a very small amount of the variants of ADHD, unlike what the drug companies would like you to believe. And the largest part of the variance is caused by attachment failure.

Simply put, the kids who develop the frontal areas of the brain, which included the attentional areas of the brain, develop best in the context of secure attachment wherein the kids are very carefully attended to by mothers who are interested in everything about that kid's internal state of mind all the time, and everything about that child's development, who follow and track all the developmental changes. It's in the disorganized attachment [where] mothers are present but not present. They're there, but they're not really there all the time. Those are the kids that are more likely to develop ADHD.

And worse, when the kids are trying to attend to something, it's the mothers who, for their own needs they're constantly distracting the child. Twenty years later those mothers who are highly distracting to their kids are likely to raise kids with attention deficit disorder. Given a culture where we plant kids in front of the TV set and they grow up watching Disney movies rather than being attended to, or go to daycare, it's not surprising that we have a culture

---

6 Attachment has become a focus in clinical psychology, informed by a text written by Dan Brown and David S. Elliott along with others, *Attachment Disturbances in Adults, Treatment for Comprehensive Repair*, W.W. Norton, 2016

where ADHD is the metaphor for the culture. And the frontal areas of the brain remain underdeveloped.

And when kids are carefully attended to, those kids are going to grow up with remarkable attentional capacity. It's not necessarily so much a genetic issue. It's a nurture issue, not a nature issue. And given in addition to the attachment failure, we don't live in a culture where we emphasize paying attention. We don't teach kids how to pay attention in the school system. The kids never learn to pay attention. So, it's not surprising that attention is weak in this country.

Nor do we teach kids general awareness, continuous awareness. We're left with the dysfunction of the ordinary mind. So that means that as adults, you've got to train the mind. There's one study that shows if you train concentration, concentration meditators who meditated for ten years showed an increase in volume and an increase in white matter in the ACC. The brain is not a stable structure of mind. If you use areas of the brain, they develop and grow, they increase in volume, they increase in structure; you lay down new tracks. If you stop using the areas of the brain, those areas of the brain shrink like muscles and atrophy, and you lose structure.

In lots of studies on age-related cognitive decline, the studies are very clear. We're not talking about dementia. We're talking about normal age-related cognitive decline. The studies are very clear. Elderly people who keep active and use their minds don't show age-related cognitive decline in the way we expect otherwise. Those that sit around and do nothing show remarkable age-related cognitive decline. If you stop using your mind, you'll lose it. If you're always using it at an advanced age, the brain changes structure according to usage.

Okay. So, concentration training is like a basic. You learn to focus on one thing and you can stay focused on that as long as you want. Then you go on to look at how the mind constructs experiences, what we call insight meditations in Mahāyāna Buddhism. How mind constructs sense of self; how it constructs external reality; how it constructs time.

But you can't look at how the mind constructs experience if the mind is very unstable. We say it's like a candle flame. If you have a candle flame and a strong wind, what happens to the flame? It's constantly flickering. If you try and look carefully at something where the candle flame is constantly flickering, it's hard to see it, even though it's right there. Trying to get insight into how the mind works with an unstable mind without concentration training, it's like trying to look at the mind with a flickering candle flame. It's hard to see what's there.

But if you train concentration and you make the mind stable so that whatever you put the mind on it stays on that for as long as you want, even hours, then when you look into the nature of the mind and how it constructs experience, you're looking with the candle flame that's steady and never flickers. It's much easier at that point to see into the nature of the mind. So, in that sense, we say concentration training is a prerequisite for insight into how the mind constructs its own experience. That's useful.

Now, awareness training is useful to become less reactive, so you have more presence with what you're doing, and you have a kind of pure non-reactive awareness for whatever comes up in the moment. Awareness training has to do with two things, as I said earlier. It has to do with approximating continuous awareness. And second, awareness is very much associated with the issue of reactivity. The best awareness meditations I ever did came from another Burmese master, not Mahāsī Sayādaw, from a master called Taungpulo Sayadaw, who lived in the forests of Burma, the jungles of Burma. Sometimes he was called the forest dwelling master. And he had a very simple meditation.

If you look into your experience every single moment, there are only four possibilities. If at that given moment the mind likes something, you'll notice a movement of the mind towards that area of focus to make more of it. That's one possibility. If at that given moment the mind doesn't like what's going on, the mind averts from it, moves away from it to make less of it. Those two components, moving towards and moving away, we'll call reactivity. There's an inherent bias in information processing, if you will.

The ordinary mind is constantly reactive to what's happening at that moment. That was Buddha's first sermon on the Four Noble Truths. The first noble truth is *dukkha*, which has often been translated as "the truth of suffering." But that's not a very good translation of the Pali term *dukkha*. *Dukkha* means reactivity.

And it's that movement towards or away—reactivity—that is the root cause of suffering in the older Theravādin Buddhism. So, the first noble truth is reactivity, the built-in reactivity. And you can actually, if you look carefully with a certain quickness of your awareness, you can perceive that reactivity.

Now, you can see the moment that the mind moves towards something to make more of it and moves away from it to make less of it. It's inherent in ordinary information processing.

What's the third possibility? Something comes into our experience and because of our discontinuous awareness, as we mentioned earlier, you miss it.

Boom, went right by, and then after the fact, retroactively we say, "Well, what just happened here? I just missed something." You may not even know what that something is, but you're aware of missing it.

And what's the fourth possibility? You notice some sense you experience, and you're purely aware of it without any reactivity—pure awareness.

Mind moving towards, mind moving away, mind being non-aware, mind being aware without reactivity. Those are the only four possibilities that accompany every aspect of your experience moment by moment, every aspect of your information processing system.

So, Taungpulo Sayadaw's meditations were rather simple. What you do is you use those four categories, and you label every moment of your experience all day long. Mind moving towards, mind moving away, mind being oblivious to what's just happened, pure awareness with non-reactivity. And what do you think you find? You find that in your ordinary experience, those first three moments predominate. You get a lot of moments of mind moving towards, a lot of movements of mind moving away, and a lot of moments where you just were out of it and missed it. And those three moments of experience in Buddhism are called the three poisons, which we often translate as attachments, aversion or hatred, and the third is confusion. But that's not a good translation of the three poisons.

The three poisons are a description of ordinary information processing. And the more accurate translation would be: First poison is mind moving towards to make more of it. Second poison is mind moving away to make less of it. Third poison is out of it, mind dismisses it, the moment of non-awareness. And a fourth desirable possibility is pure non-reactive awareness of whatever came in at that time. So, if you use these labels or ways of categorizing moment by moment experience, and that's all you do, you're going to see that your awareness is predominated by the three poisons, and every now and then a moment of pure awareness. And what do you think is going to happen over time?

If you keep practicing this 24/7, the balance is going to shift in the direction of predominantly pure non-reactive awareness. And ultimately, that's all you're left with is pure non-reactive awareness. A very good meditation. In fact, I'll show it to you; we'll do it after the break. You can see for yourself. A little different from the mindfulness that you're used to.

So, you see, if you start looking into this issue of discontinuous awareness, what you begin to see are two things. Everything changes all of the time. So, the issue of impermanence comes up. Everything goes. But the other thing is that you start to see that when you look into awareness that's inextricably bound up with this issue of reactivity, and this reactivity that's built into moment-by-moment high speed information processing, and that's what keeps generating our suffering. What if whatever came into our awareness, you just left alone with a continuous awareness, without any reactivity whatsoever? Then, good or bad, whatever came into the experience would be equally of interest. And you'd never be distracted for a moment from whatever came into your experience.

In fact, in the older Theravādin Buddhism, there are four gradations of awakening, and with the first gradation of awakening, that reactivity drops off completely. There is continuous awareness of whatever comes into your experience and there's no reactivity, therefore no suffering. You break the link between awareness and reactivity. You train continuous awareness without any reactivity. That's useful. And ultimately you get what's called a liberation component of awakening. You fundamentally rewire your information processing system. There's no reactivity, and you have continuous presence. And then you live a more full life, free from that reactivity, and therefore free from suffering.

But it's not necessary that you train the depth of concentration to get that realization. The danger in systems that just train awareness is you don't really get insight into the nature of how the mind constructs experience. In the Mahāsī Sayādaw system there's very, very little emphasis on training to look at the nature of self. So, you can have relatively continuous awareness and be filled with self-importance. And spiritual pride, of course, is a big problem with whatever you get with your meditation. And there's very little in that system that will clean up that issue. And there's lots of people teaching mindfulness these days in the West, and a great deal of self-importance about their teaching. You all know what I'm talking about.

There's nothing within that mindfulness system that corrects for self-importance. [There are] no teachings on emptiness of self. And even the old Theravādin work on the aggregates and no self in the aggregates isn't emphasized in the Mahāsī Sayādaw system. It doesn't correct for ego. Interesting that that's the system of meditation that caught on so strongly in the West, whose rugged individualism is so strong, and there's nothing about that system that would threaten you or cause you to change that rugged individualism. It's a good match if you don't really want to change yourself at all. But the risk of that is spiritual pride. In my view, if you learned anything from the meditation traditions of any nature, the fundamental lesson is that self-importance isn't terribly important. There are some limitations to this. But, in terms of framing continuous awareness, and in terms of working with the issue of reactivity, there's nothing else like it. It's good for that. [There are] no teachings on emptiness of self. And even the old Theravādin work on the aggregates and no self in the aggregates isn't emphasized in the Mahāsī Sayādaw system. It doesn't correct for that. Interesting that that's the system of meditation that caught on so strongly in the West, whose rugged individualism is so strong, and there's nothing about that system that would threaten you or cause you to change that rugged individualism. It's a good match if you don't really want to change yourself at all. So maybe after the break we'll do basic concentration meditation for the first half and then we'll do awareness meditation for the second half so you can see the difference between the two.

Questions about what I'm talking about so far before we take a break? Yes?

Student 1

[Question is inaudible.]

Dan

Well, mindfulness practice just makes you less reactive, and therefore what we call the coarse level of suffering that you're experiencing in everyday life greatly diminishes as a result of it. But, that's all it does. In the Mahāyāna system, the developments of Buddhism that came later, the realizations were very different, particularly in what are called the Essence traditions like Mahāmudrā, Dzogchen and Great Liberation practice and the *tantras*. And, the Essence traditions all share a common view that all of us have buddha nature. The enlightened mind is always right here. It never goes away, but we have an accumulation of so many bad habits of mind that we can't directly realize it.

It's sort of like the metaphor to use is the clouds and the sun. If it's rainy like it has been earlier today and then all of a sudden the rain stops and the sun comes out, what do we normally say? We say the sun just came out. Is that true? No. The sun was always out. What really happened is the sun was shining all the time, but the clouds would shield it so you didn't see the sun that was always shining out there. And once the clouds cleared up enough, the full radiance of that sun becomes obvious. So, you see, in the Essence tradition, the basic idea here is that the radiance of a fully awakened mind, like the shining of the sun, is always happening, always right here. But you don't see it because of the clouds. Each one of these practices clears away the clouds, so at some point there are no clouds left. Then it becomes obvious.

Now, in the Essence traditions, there's also a different emphasis. And, in your original buddha nature, there are many deeply positive qualities. There are eighty positive qualities associated with a fully enlightened buddha mind. And those are part of the original purity of the mind. Those eighty positive qualities are obscured by all the clouds of the bad habits. So, you see what's fundamentally different in the nature of the realizations in Mahāyāna Buddhism and the old Hinayana Buddhism is that in the old Hinayana Buddhism what you get is the liberation from suffering with no emphasis at all on positive states.

Whereas, in the Mahāyāna, what you get is the liberation from suffering in a way that then no longer obscures the flourishing of all positive states. And what happens is, in the Mahāyāna, a process [begins] where you automatically release all the negative karmic impressions from lifetimes—this process, with certain meditations, is called *dharmadhātu* exhaustion. And the consequence of that is there are no negative states left. At some point in your practice, it dawns upon you that there are no negative states left in your experience, your field of experience, whatsoever. It's all pure states, positive states. It's rather nice.

What causes karmic impressions? When things arise in your field of experience, if you left everything completely alone, there would be no karmic traces. But whatever arises in this vast ocean of awareness-love, which is your awakened true nature, we develop a habit in our information processing system of having the mind pick out particulars. As soon as the mind tends towards anything particular, it's missing the whole, the vast infinite awareness-love that is right here, the vastness of it. As soon as the mind then tries to make more of this or less of that, it fixes that karmic impression. Then if you attend to it, you give it greater strength.

So, at some point in the experience of your meditations, with awakening, you find yourself operating out of an infinite vast expanse of awareness-love, without focusing on anything particular. We say the mind remains completely content and everything occurs in its own right, and the mind has no preferences. Everything is experienced within that infinite field of the groundless ground of awareness.

And therefore, if you have that as a stable experience, every moment that things arise, they leave no trace. They say it's like writing things on water. As soon as they arise, they disappear. So, if you set up the view like that and that's your experience, then no new experiences will lay down any new karmic traces.

And the only thing that's possible is for the previous storehouse of all karmic impressions—first from this lifetime and then from all previous lifetimes—to automatically release themselves. They call it automatic *dharmakāya* release. The end result is there are no negative states left. And there'll be a flourishing of all the positive qualities.

Now, here's the problem. If you're operating out of awakened mind, then that's fine because nothing will leave any trace. But if you're operating out of the constraints of your ordinary information processing system, then you're constantly laying down new karmic impressions. And if you're in an experience and if it's negative, you're going to lay down the strength of negative impression.

But it's not just true with your example of being in some difficult experience. It's also true for spiritual practice. Tilopa, one of the great Mahāmudrā masters, says, look, the problem with ordinary practices of spirituality is that when you are chanting mantras, when you are doing concentration meditation, when you are reading the sutras, when you're doing your sadhana practice, when you're practicing ethical restraints, in the whole range of spiritual practices, still the ordinary mind is moving towards things that it likes and moving away from things that it dislikes. And as long as that is still happening, these practices just create more karmic impressions—maybe positive ones, rather than negative ones. You're never free from that.

So, the only practices that can free you are not specific spiritual practice. The only practices that can free you are the instructions that lead you to awaken, so the mind is no longer moving towards or away from anything. And that's when all these spiritual practices become elaborate illusions to create more karmic impressions. Do you understand what I'm saying?

So, in that sense, when you sleep, when you have the awakened mind that automatically releases everything from groundless ground, every moment, you are beyond karmic impression. Does that mean you can do whatever you want? No. Why? It's a fundamental misunderstanding. Because if you are operating out of a stable awakened mind, every moment or whatever arises spontaneously from groundless ground releases itself in the groundless ground; and operating out of that awakened mind means you're operating out of a boundless, changeless ocean of awareness-love, and the fundamental intention of the awakened mind is compassion.

This whole display is for the benefit of compassion. It's built in. The stronger your awakening, the stronger it will spontaneously express itself as compassion, gratitude, devotion. It doesn't mean you can do anything you want. No, it means your conduct spontaneously more and more comes into accordance with what's necessary for the greater social good.

It's built into the system as the best measure of practice and realization always is. It's the only true test of the realization. How you live your life and live in the world. That's the only measure of spiritual realization. So, you see, it's built in. Awakening is always expressed as the compassion and benefit for others. So, in that sense, you see, the problem that you see in that question isn't a problem at all from a certain perspective. How you act in that situation is the best fit for what's needed because the action spontaneously arises or awakens from awakened *dharmakāya* space. So, then when we worry about actions—because [worry] operates out of an ordinary mind that goes towards things and away from other things—it creates the same problem all over again. You never get off the wheel that way. Does that make it any clearer to you?

Good question.

August 8, 2012

Themes: Everyone Matters, Deserves Respect; Styles of Attachment

Dan

Welcome everyone. You have a question?

Student 1

I studied a lot of transpersonal psychology and I studied Native American shamanism; specifically I went up to the Navajo Reservation, observed different healing ceremonies.

Dan

Well, this is a big topic, but in Indo-Tibetan Buddhism, there are two types of compassion practices. The more common compassion practices that are known in the West have to do with compassion with respect to the suffering of others in the world. So, if you visualize Avalokiteshvara or Chenrezig in Tibetan, Avalokiteshvara or Chenrezig is the Buddha of compassion, unlimited ultimate compassion towards all beings. Sometimes in the paintings, Avalokiteshvara is depicted as having a thousand arms, one to reach out towards every being. So, in the vehicle of the Mahāyāna, nothing is left behind, no one's left behind.

So, one needs the great scope in the inexhaustible compassion of Avalokiteshvara to handle all the suffering in the world. And you visualize yourself as Avalokiteshvara as if your mind and the mind of Avalokiteshvara are inseparable; and through a process of what's called "successive approximation," in your heart, you become more like Avalokiteshvara. His Holiness the Dalai Lama is the embodiment of Avalokiteshvara for this generation. He is Avalokiteshvara.

Then another compassion practice, which is fairly popular in the West, is Talang, which literally means giving—taking in and giving out. So, you imagine taking in the suffering of the world and giving out loving-kindness. Those are fairly well-known practices.

The less known practices are, or the second category of compassion practices have to do with what's called practices related to common humanity. And the basic idea in common humanity practices is that all of us share the same existential concerns all around the world, despite huge differences in people. We all want the same things. Even our enemies want the same things that we want. We all want happiness. We all want to be secure in the world. We all want financial security. We all want health. We all want the best for our families. There isn't anybody in the world that doesn't share a common set of concerns.

So, in common humanity practice, therefore, every human being deserves dignity and respect just by virtue of the fact that we all share the same common humanity. There's no differences. And when you do common humanity practices, you take that view that everyone deserves the same loving-kindness and respect and dignity just by virtue of being human.

Now, what makes that difficult, of course, is we don't like everybody the same way. There's a great deal of research and social psychology in the West that suggests that we make our decisions about who we like and who we dislike almost immediately. Even before we have any interaction with a person, we've already decided. And we don't change that much after that. So, there's a kind of, if you will, bias in social information processing, how we process our perceptions of people in such a way that some people we like, not always for the same rational reasons. That's certainly the case of being in love. And some people we don't like, not always for rational reasons, and a lot of people, we just don't even have on the radar screen. We ignore them.

I once asked my Root Lama just before he died in 1979, I said, "Of all the practices you've done in your life, what did you find the most difficult?" And he said, "Treating everybody exactly the same." The tendency to have preferences is very difficult to overcome. So, the way you overcome those preferences, positive and negative, is with the practice in traditional Tibetan called *Manam*, which basically means all beings as mothers. And in Tibetan culture, the quintessence of human love is the selfless love that a mother gives to her child. She sacrifices her sleep, she sacrifices her body, she sacrifices her time, she sacrifices everything for the growth of this child. So, it's that enormous loving-kindness as exemplified in a mother's love towards a young growing child that in the Tibetan culture is the epitome of all love.

So, what you do is you, in a traditional *manam* visualization, you imagine yourself receiving that kind of completely selfless love, and everything is about your welfare, from your mother, until you can really generate the feeling quality of that. And then you imagine yourself being that kind of loving mother towards an infant. And then with that same state of being, that selfless love that a mother shows, you imagine bringing that same state of mind of selfless love into relationships with people that you know, and you imagine how it influences the relationship. You imagine bringing it into relationships with people you have difficulty with. And it's interesting to see what happens to how you experience the difficulties with that person when you see yourself as their loving mother. And thirdly, you bring it to people that you are neutral about, all the forgotten people in your social field during the day that you're oblivious to.

Now, in Tibetan culture, that's very powerful. You expand the scope of that out until you see yourself as the mother of all beings, and everybody you come in contact with you see from that point of view. And there's a kind of deep concern for who they are just by virtue of their common humanity. Only that concern is the concern of a mother wanting the best for her young child. Everybody now becomes your young child. And in the culmination of that, there are no preferences. All the children are treated equally, and no one is ignored.

The best example of that is, oh, I remember sometime a while back, maybe twenty years ago, His Holiness the Dalai Lama likes science, so he's had through Mind and Life a series of three-day, sometimes seven-day dialogues with scientists around the topic. And there was a three-day dialogue here in Boston about the brain. So, he met with some of the top neurobiologists so he could learn all about the scientific studies and neuroimaging of the brain.

The conference was at Harvard, and he was staying at the Charles Hotel, and he got up to go to his talk and he opened his door and outside there was a woman with a cart, a cleaning woman. And he stopped and said, "Where are you from?" And she spoke in broken English and said something about her country, and he said, "Oh, that's interesting. I've never been there. What's it like growing up there?" And he asked her about her family and why she came here and what her experience was here. And he spent a good deal of time getting to know this person who was in his interpersonal field. Then he went off to his talk, somewhat late.

And the next morning he got up for the second day of the talk and he opened his door and there were about twenty cleaning carts lined up with all of the cleaning ladies for the entire hotel. And he stopped and he talked with all of them because they were in his interpersonal field, and each of them deserves the dignity and respect of being acknowledged. This is a very special and powerful quality, but it's rare, and it needs to be cultivated because what it means is acknowledging all the forgotten people in the world.

I'll add another story here because in my other hat, in my professional life as a Western psychologist, I do a lot of I do a lot of high-profile work in the courts as a trauma expert.

As some of you know, in the last couple of years, one of the cases that we reopened was the Bobby Kennedy assassination [which took place in the kitchen of a hotel]. Bobby had a gift. He had a gift for acknowledging all of the forgotten people. So, I'll tell you the story of Juan. When Bobby was shot, the next day on the front cover of Life magazine there was a picture of a fifteen-year-old busboy who worked in the kitchen, and it's a Pulitzer Prize photo of this boy with a big tear in his eye, with a set of rosary beads saying, "Please, Mr. Kennedy, don't die." I interviewed a lot of the witnesses in the kitchen at the time of the assassination, and I interviewed Juan, the busboy, forty-two years later.

Juan grew up in Mexico and his mother had been remarried. His stepfather was very physically abusive to him, and he was a broken boy with little confidence, a forgotten boy. His family immigrated to Los Angeles and his stepfather worked in the kitchen of the hotel. Juan didn't work in the hotel; he was only fifteen. So, a couple of weeks before the assassination, Bobby gave a talk with Cesar Chavez, who's the champion for the rights of all the underpaid immigrant workers from Mexico. And in the talk, he publicly said that he respected the Mexican immigrant workers because he thought they were honest, hard-working people and they should be acknowledged for all that they contribute to the growth of this country. Juan heard that talk and he felt like he mattered. Bobby immediately became his hero.

So, the assassination was on a Tuesday, primary day, but the weekend before the assassination, they were very crowded at the Ambassador Hotel. So, his stepfather brought him in to help out as a busboy. He wasn't officially hired, but he just needed extra help. So, he was working in the kitchen with his stepfather and a phone call comes down from the presidential suite. It's from Bobby Kennedy asking for room service. So, Juan says to the chief waiter, "This really means a lot to me. I'll wait your tables for two weeks if you let me take this order." He wants to meet his hero. So, he wheels the cart upstairs. Bobby's in the room talking on the telephone—this was before cell phones, of course. He smiles and waves Juan in, they're just the two of them and they're by themselves. It's a big presidential suite. And Juan's never seen anything like this before.

And Bobby tells him to wait, and finishes his phone call, and he hangs up the phone and he goes over to Juan, takes both of his hands like this and says, "Now, who are you? Tell me about yourself." And he does. And Bobby spends about forty-five minutes with him, alone. And Juan walks out elated, and he feels important. For the first time in his life, he feels like he matters. And he thinks to himself, "The next President of the United States knows who I am." And finally, his life matters.

Then doubt sets in and he begins to think, "Nah, he's just a political candidate. This is all just a show." He's obsessed with the doubt. And then he thinks, "Well, there wasn't anybody to show it to. I was just with him by myself. So maybe it was genuine." But he can't let it go, and it really bothers him. So, the day of the primary, he hears this rumor that Bobby's going to come through the kitchen after his talk because, of course, the route got changed at the last minute and the assassination occurred in the kitchen. So, he's going to find out whether Bobby remembers him.

So, the kitchen is very crowded, but he's a kid, so he sort of wiggles his way through the crowd and waits. Bobby comes through the kitchen with him moving the whole crowd this way and sees Juan, and Juan sticks out his hand like that. And Bobby goes, "Hi Juan, nice to see you again." And he just holds his hand and holds his hand, and he won't let it go. This is his hero. And while he's holding his hand, the shots ring out and Bobby falls, and Juan's world is shattered along with the hope of an entire generation. And for the next forty-two years, he carried the guilt of thinking if he didn't hold the hand long enough, maybe the angle of the gun would've been different, and faults himself with this history.

Bobby had a gift, like His Holiness has a gift, being able to acknowledge forgotten people. It's a very rare quality. As my Root Lama said, it's the hardest thing to do. So, when you practice common humanity practice, you have the presence of mind that everybody in your interpersonal field matters. And even in the smallest ways of acknowledging people, it makes a huge difference. More, if you make them feel like they matter and they're important, then you're contributing something to the greater good here. Now, the way you develop that view, in this case the view is through *manam* practice: all beings [including you] as mothers.

But here's the problem. It doesn't work in this culture because Tibetan culture, before the culture was dismantled, was a very child-focused culture, but we're not. So, in my clinical hat, I do a lot of work with attachment and the infant's attachment to the primary caregiver, usually the mother, but it can be the mother or the father or both. In those first two years life, all of human development is organized around that attachment. And we can study when that goes right and when it goes wrong. We can divide infants into secure attachment and what we call insecure attachment. In secure attachment, the infant's relationship to the caregiver serves like a secure base and everything feels right around that.

And as the grandfather of modern attachment studies, John Bowlby in the UK says, security of attachment is the foundation for all development. And when kids get the attachment to the caregiver right, or better when the parents provide that kind of secure attachment, then the natural outgrowth of that is healthy exploratory behavior. Kids are free to explore and discover and the self evolves out of that as a strong and independent self. But if that secure base isn't provided, then something goes wrong with exploratory behavior and development gets off track. So, kids who we call dismissing, they explore but they don't connect. They disconnect. They have a fundamental problem in their life with just connecting in relationships. Kids that we call anxious and preoccupied are fearful. They have inhibitory exploratory behavior. They cling to try and get the attachment system right, but they can't explore. So, they never really developed the self. They're always queuing themselves for what they think others want. And kids that we call disorganized do a bit of both. They alternate back and forth between being clingy and dismissing. They don't do relationships well.

Now, from what data we have in Asian cultures, secure attachment rates are, in traditional Asian cultures, about 80 percent. Secure attachment rates in Europe and North America are just about 63 percent. So, we don't do attachment so well here. Why? Because when you do attachment well, the parents are completely engaged in everything about their children's development. They're present.

The worst thing you can do with kids is be present but not present, or worse, out of it, dissociated. And what most kids get in this culture is what in the attachment field is called "instrumental love." You do all the right things, you feed them, send them off to school, put on the Disney videotapes so you don't have to really attend to them—let them watch TV. And you're done with your tasks, and you have no idea who these little beings are because you're never present to watch all the wondrous stuff that happens in development. And more and more our culture becomes like that. So, the base rates of secure attachment go down.

I remember once years ago I was asked—this must've been almost thirty years ago—and I gave a talk on attachment. Not on attachment, on Tibetan compassion practices to an audience of Western psychoanalysts. And I raised the idea of visualizing all beings as mothers. I mean, they were just horrified at this prospect [Laughter] because in that world the ambivalence towards mothers is so strong, and they're not that kind of figures in this culture.

So, what we've done is sort of modified the protocols a bit here. Because in my clinical reality, rather than the meditation field, I've spent the last twenty years trying to develop protocols that treat attachment pathology in children and adults. And the visualizations help with that. Here's why: Attachment, the intense bond between an infant and caregiver, starts about the second or third month of life. That's pretty clear. But when we study attachment between infants and caregivers, we study them between twelve and twenty months in a standard laboratory situation called "the strange situation paradigm." You put the child and the mother in a strange playroom they've never seen before; you don't give them any instructions. There's a couple of chairs around, there's toys on the floor, and there's a big plastic box filled with toys, but the mother and the child have to negotiate how to get the stuff out of the box.

And you let the mother and child be alone in the room for three minutes and watch how they deal with this situation. Then a stranger comes in, who's really a confederate to the research, and you watch the child's differential response between the mother and the stranger. Then after three minutes, the mother is asked to leave, and you watch what it's like for the child to be with the stranger alone. Then the mother comes back, and you see the child's response to the mother coming back. Then the stranger leaves and then the mother leaves and you see what it's like for the child to be alone. You look at all the combinations.

And secure kids basically show increased organization of their play behavior and increased organization of their state of mind in the presence of the mother.

The internal and external behavioral signs get more and more organized. That's healthy exploratory behavior. Dismissing kids, they don't do the relationship with the mother, they just go right for the toys. They don't show a preferential response to the mother. They make little contact with the mother. They don't care when the stranger comes in. They don't protest when the mother leaves, or they don't seem to make a difference about whether anybody is there, or they play alone. But they easily get frustrated, and they throw the toys a lot. Anxious, preoccupied kids are terribly timid and they show inhibited exploratory behavior, and they need a lot of coaxing to do anything. And when the mother leaves and comes back, they get disorganized when the mother leaves, and then they get really upset and they're inconsolable when the mother comes back. They're very clingy. And disorganized kids do a bit of both. They show lots of clinginess and lots of dismissing stuff, and the behavior gets progressively disorganized.

Now, those four types of attachment configurations are fairly stable throughout childhood into adulthood. It does determine how we act in relationships a lot. But what's really interesting about that is that it's no accident that the stable types of attachment status are observable between twelve and twenty months. Why? Because that's when representational thinking develops in kids. Attachment behavior, the intense bond starts at three, four months, as I said. But the real change in development is not the attachment behavior; it's when the child can represent that behavior in their head. They have an internal map for what relational behavior is going to be like, and all of the other major lines of development—the sense of self, the capacity for internal means to regulate emotions—all that arises from this. So, if you get the internal map wrong, if it's disorganized, for example, then that's going to show a profound effect on self-development. It's not going to happen the way we want, and it's going to have a profound effect on the internal capacity to regulate emotional states. In other words, kids grow up either feeling too much or too little in confusing ways; and they won't have a clear sense of themselves. So, it's not attachment behavior, it's the capacity to represent them and to develop those internal maps or internal working models for relationships, as Bowlby called them. That's what makes the critical difference. So, what does that tell us?

The key to treating attachment problems in the West, people who have that, is not so different from what the Tibetans figured out. The key is visualization practice. Keep visualizing it and visualizing it, and you'll develop a new map. What we developed in the protocols here in the West was using ideal parent figures. Ask people to visualize not what they got in their family of origin, which is always a mixed bag, but in the ideal sense, if they grew up in a family with parents ideally matched to them and their nature, what does secure attachment look like? How would you imagine it?

See, imagination creates possibilities, and you can shape it and reshape it until you get it just right. And we found in the process of doing that, that there are five main functions of healthy attachment. So, I'll go through what they are and then maybe after the break we'll do a visualization on this, and I'll show you how it works with the common humanity practices.

The first is safety and protection. The primary function of attachment is protection of the species. That's why the baby antelope hangs out with the mommy antelope for the first couple of years, so they don't get taken by predators. Humans aren't any different. We have a long attachment span. So, the duty of any parent as an attachment figure is protection, safety. Healthy parents are fiercely protective of their kids, but not overprotective. It's different. Fiercely protective. Treating abuse survivors for over thirty years and helping people work through the experiences and memories of childhood, physical and/or sexual abuse, many, many times, what I began to see was that the much more difficult ground to work through is not the memories of the abusive acts of a parent sexually or physically, but the memories of the failed protector, what the other parent didn't do. That's more difficult to work out because, you see, the fundamental duty of the species is protection, safety. So that's more damaging. It's the parent who lets it happen and thinks that nothing's going on. That's a failure of the first duty of any healthy attachment, which is protection. So healthy attachment means fierce protection.

The second is attunement. Healthy parents are really present, and they're carefully attuned to everything about the child's behavior, everything about the growth and changes in development, but even more so, they're attuned to the child's internal state. They're interested in the child's internal state. And if the parent is constantly present and interested with everything about the child's state, behavior, and development and growth, that's how the child feels held. There's your secure base, because you feel seen. And in the course of development, by the most important attachment figures in our life, in a very deep way, children need to be seen, really seen, in their being. Not for what they do; in their being. That's different.

The third is emotion regulation. When children are upset, secure parents are there and they provide soothing, and comfort, and reassurance. And time and time again, when the parents are providing that behavior of being soothing and comforting during the critical period when children develop representational capacity, they can now represent in their mind the soothing response. And after a while that becomes part of the structure of their own mind. They don't need the mother to be there to soothe them anymore. They can self-soothe because they've taken it in as part of the structure of their own mind.

The fourth, this one, I like to call the joy or delight in the child's being, or better, expressed delight. And this is the root of healthy self-esteem. What is healthy self-esteem? What is self-esteem? I tend to favor a developmental explanation. In the Hempstead Clinic, years ago, Joe Sandler defined it as the following. He said, "Self-esteem is the developmental linkage of positive emotional states with the sense of self." It's one thing to have a sense of self, and during our everyday life we can conjure up our sense of self. We call it evocative memory. I can evoke Dan; I can look at Dan. Now, if I have healthy esteem during the day, if I evoke Dan-ness, I evoke it against the backdrop of good feeling. That's what it means experientially to have healthy esteem. But there's a lot of people out there for whom they never did that. They never fostered that linkage between positive emotion and the sense of self. We call them narcissistically vulnerable.

So, what does it mean? When you evoke the sense of self if you're narcissistic-vulnerable, you evoke the sense of self against the backdrop of no feeling, at which point you're probably high functioning, and you have this fundamental sense that there's something missing in life and you can't quite figure it out. Many people compensate for that with self-agency. So, they do a lot and they're very accomplished. And no matter how much they do, they never feel good about themselves. It's the disease of the entire Western culture, right? Or, you evoke the sense of self against the backdrop of negative feelings, in which case we say you're depression-vulnerable. But what these individuals who are narcissistically vulnerable can't do is evoke the sense of self against the backdrop of positive feeling because they never link those two things together developmentally. Where does that link come from? It comes from expressed delight.

See, the healthiest parents enjoy their kids. They're not just giving instrumental love. They're highly expressive about everything. They delight in everything about this child's being. The Yiddish word, *kvelling*, best captures this, right? They *kvell* about everything that this child is doing, everything about what this child accomplishes, but more, the child's being. They're delighted. This little critter is the whole meaning of their life. And the young children to healthy parents evoke a tremendous sense of love and joy. Not just love, but joy.

You know what I'm talking about as parents, if you have this with your kids. When you're changing your kids, you even love their poop. When they spit up on you, you love being spit up on. It's the most bizarre thing, but it is like that. But the smiles of recognition mean you know what I'm talking about.

Anyway, some parents are always expressing their joy and their delight. They just value everything about this moment-to-moment experience with this wondrous little being. And that expressed effusive positive emotion is internalized by the child, and there's your roots of healthy esteem. But in a culture where parents would best provide instrumental love, plant the kids in front of TV sets, give them video games to play with, where's that going to happen? Where's the source of joy in who you are? So, what are you going to raise, a culture of competent robots with a profound indifference towards life? We are moving in that direction. So that's the fourth necessary function of secure attachment.

And the fifth is that the best parents are champions of their children's self-development. The opposite of that are parents who have agendas, we call them. They want their kids to grow up to be certain things for the parents' needs. It's the hardest thing. The hardest thing to give your kids is their own individuality. The most mature parents are able to say, "I'm curious of who this little being is going to turn out to be." They don't impose anything on the child. They're there as a kind of collaborator with the child, mutually discovering together who this child is going to turn out to be and supporting and encouraging the child to explore because exploratory behavior, playful exploratory behavior is the medium of self-development. And the best parents set that up so that children can explore and discover, and they're there as supports, without imposing agendas, and let that individual of the child flourish. How can you be with a child to bring out the child's best self? That's the critical question here.

So those are the five primary functions of healthy attachment. And of course, rarely do people get them all right, certainly in this culture.

So, what we've done is modify the traditional Tibetan practice and say, "Okay, let's learn from what we know about how to do this in the West." Start the visualization not with parents where it goes flat, where it immediately evokes negative states like ambivalence, anger. That's not going to go anywhere positive. But if you step out of all that stuff and say, "Let's remap it," let's come up with the ideal of getting all of that right and use your imagination to shape it carefully, and let's see where that goes. It's very moving.

And then once you can imagine yourself getting all that as a child with all that you know and don't know, then you imagine yourself as that kind of parent who can give all that. There's the source of your *manam* practice. See yourself as the kind of parent who can give all that. A parent who exemplifies all those five great functions I call "the cherishing parent." Then see yourself bringing that cherishing state of mind as if you were the cherishing parent, bring that same state of mind into relationships with people you know, are close to, to people you have difficulties with, and then to people that you just don't know that you're passing in your interpersonal field.

And then eventually expand the scope of that so you see yourself as that cherishing parent towards all beings. If anybody that you come in contact with, you look through that lens, that view, that'll change how you are with people. It's the hardest practice. Very deep. So that's the gist of it. I don't know about the biological substrate of that too much, but psychologically and emotionally, it feels right. One clinician called it "the righting effect." When you start doing this with patients who have significant attachment problems, first they'll protest doing it, but when they start settling into it, they feel like they're on the right track. And they say, "There's something about this that feels right." And the reason why it feels right is it's part of the hard-wiring.

We're programmed to have this attachment thing work out right. And when it doesn't work out right, everything feels off. So, people feel like they're getting back on the right track. And if you get back on the right track, then you can give it. There's something corrective about it, and you can keep expanding the scope of how you give it, so it works better.

August 15, 2012

Themes: The Profound Influence of Mentors; Fiduciary Relationships

Dan

Welcome everyone.

There's the Western approach to well-being, and there's the Buddhist approach. In the Western approach, just to give a little historical background, starting in mostly the 1990s, there was a development in psychology research on what's now called the positive psychology movement. It was an attempt to do formal psychological research on various positives states. And that research was fledgling, but it was put on the map by Marty Seligman when he became president of the American Psychological Association in the year 2000. And as his campaign platform he pushed for developing research initiatives in positive psychology, and trying to get various kinds of granting agencies to funnel money into research on things such as the development of virtues in character, research into wisdom, research into everyday happiness, research into what's called subjective well-being.

One of the areas of research that developed more recently was research into gratitude. And now there's a fair amount of good research in the West on gratitude and its positive effects on subjective well-being, showing that people who practice gratitude are genuinely happier, and they have greater well-being about their lives. Some of the research is better than others, but Bob Emmons—his first book was called *The Psychology of Ultimate Concerns*—found was that people who had an overarching belief system, either spiritual or humanitarian, where they had a clear vision of what ultimately mattered in life, had less internal contradictions in how they saw themselves. They had greater subjective well-being, and that vision, that spiritual vision of life, served as a kind of central organizing principle in life. They were happier, and in the face of life's difficulties they tended to be more resilient because they had a belief system that helped them get through those difficulties.

Having put out a book on that, his next area of research was on gratitude, and the positive effects of gratitude in terms of well-being and happiness. So now there's a whole bunch of research coming out on why gratitude is a good thing. In the Western research, the basic idea is you reflect on what you appreciate about people and what they've done in your life. There are different approaches to what's emphasized in gratitude. One approach that's very powerful is to reflect on people who had some substantial and positive impact on the course of your life, and to do a visualization around thanking them, expressing appreciation for the effect that they've had on your life. It doesn't make any difference whether that person is alive or not alive; you go back and revisit that, as if you could show them that. Those are important. So, you can revisit them in your mind, and it helps you feel more complete to express those things. So, you allow yourself to go back and reflect upon who is most important and express to them, show them, the changes you have gone through in your life.

I'll give you a personal example of that. Mrs. Merchant. She was my fourth-grade teacher. Before that, I was an average student, not very excited student, had average capacities, no special talents, and grew up in a working-class neighborhood in one of the many Massachusetts mill towns that were failing. The whole culture was failing. Pretty much everybody I grew up with is either in jail or dead. That whole area now is all drugs. [Dan gestures to one of the students present.] You know, you lived there. She and I grew up in the same neighborhood.

Then, in fourth grade, I had this teacher who took a special interest in me. And she fundamentally changed my life. I loved this teacher. I became the teacher's pet, and she was like a good mother figure. I got re-parented. She saw talent in me, and I went from an average to low-average student to absolutely blossoming in every single area, and I also blossomed as an artist. So, the impact is that what I learned from being with her was to look at my own resources that I didn't even know I had, and to have somebody who had faith in me. And I fundamentally transformed. I never turned back after that.

Although I never got help from my parents in terms of going to college because they couldn't afford it, I worked my way through college on three jobs and got a Danforth Scholarship that paid for graduate school at a very good school, the University of Chicago. I'm one of the few kids in my area from that generation that actually went to any college, and the only person from that area and culture that teaches at Harvard Medical School. That's an anomaly for the people I grew up with. And I attribute all of that to Mrs. Merchant.

One time, after I got settled with my first job as a chief psychologist at one of the Harvard hospitals, I decided that I needed to pay some tribute to her, so I went back and looked her up. She was very old. I tried to show her what I had become because of what she had done by having faith in me. It was a big impact for both of us. It made a big difference. And I think, probably, she died shortly thereafter with the knowledge that she had an impact. So that's just one example. I can't say exactly what happened when she did it, but whatever it was, it worked. And I never forgot my roots.

I remember when I first started doing clinical teaching—and I taught for twenty-five years at the social work school at Simmons [University in Boston]. I taught the basic psychopathology course; it was a live interview course, which was lots of fun. And the person who hired me was Sophie Freud, Sigmund's granddaughter, who was the, you know, she was the sequence chair and I remember her saying, "Look, we can't pay hardly anything. You're not going to get any gratification out of what money you're going to make from this job. You have to look at it this way: you're going to have all the young social workers in this region, and this is their core course. Anything they come about thinking, whatever they arrive at clinically, is going to come from your course. So, you're going to affect an entire generation of people, and that's the only way you can look at it in terms of what you're going to get out of this." She was right. And I found that very gratifying, to feel like I could have some kind of effect on shaping a whole generation of clinicians in terms of how they treated people.

So, how many teachers are there in this country that have changed kids' lives like that, that never get any recognition for what they've done? This is one small example. So, I've always appreciated that, and what I've gotten from different teachers, mentors. Then, in addition to those people that have a big impact on your life, there's the everyday expression of gratitude, that's the style of communicating.

When I used to do more couples therapy, you know, the people who came to couples therapy are sort of in the final stages of their relationship, and one is generally dragging the other person in, the one who doesn't want to be there, and they're usually fairly toxic in how they've learned to communicate with each other. So, when doing couples therapy, it's been amazing to me how people who start off loving each other can trash each other so thoroughly on a regular basis. It is just truly amazing what we as human beings do. And one of the homework assignments that I used to give people is that when they got together at the end of the day, each member of the couple-ship had to, no matter how small or large they were, they had to think of three things that they appreciated about their partner that day. And on a regular basis, develop a style of expressing those things. Those little things make a difference. But we don't just have to do that with our spouses. You can do that with anyone you come into contact with. It changes your whole interpersonal field. All the little appreciations for what people do during the day. It changes their attitude towards their work.

For example, the little things that people do to go out of their way to be helpful, it's worth acknowledging those things. If we know anything about behavior reinforcement, we know if people engage in positive, adaptive behaviors, and you reinforce it, you tend to get more of it; and if you don't, you tend to get less of it. So as a culture, as a species, if we develop a style of appreciating what people do, they're likely to do it more for us and others, too. Then you have some positive influence and shape more positive behaviors in our interpersonal world. These things matter. Especially because I think in this culture, it's not our style to appreciate. So that's the Western approach to gratitude.

Then, in Buddhism, it's a little different. With lamaism, Tibetan Buddhism, there certainly are teachers; and, like a good mentor in the West, they change the course of our life, but in a different way. Because, you see, what's being taught there is not a skill that you're learning from a mentor, like in a profession. It's not like learning clinical skills or law skills, or whatever else. What you learn is a direct transmission about the nature of ultimate reality. It's about awakening, and ultimately, enlightenment. It's about your true nature.

Anybody that we've ever worked with in this pointing out style of meditation, at the point that they've gotten some direct taste of awakening to the true nature of the mind, however unstable it might have been, if it's only what Tashi Namgyal calls "little flames of awakening," it changes everything. And every single person who's ever gotten a taste of awakening, however stable or unstable it may be, said this is something they've always known, but didn't know. Because it is your true nature, and it's familiar to you. All that the teachings do is show you the way home. But, once you find your way home, you recognize it, it's familiar to you. The metaphor that is very popular in Dzogchen Great Completion practice is the metaphor of a child's capacity to recognize his or her mother.

So, let's say there's a child in a crowd, and the child loses sight of its mother for some short period of time, and then sees the mother. The child's face will immediately light up with the pleasure and familiarity of finding the mother again. The child has the capacity to recognize what's familiar and run up to the mother and jump into the mother's lap, because it's built in, it's hard-wired, it's part of the imprinting. You can recognize immediately your mother. Children orient towards the mother, and the orienting response happens in the first two or three days of life. And likewise, the capacity [is built in] for the infant of individual consciousness to recognize the mother consciousness, the great ocean of awareness-love—*dharmakāya*—awakened mind. The infant of individual consciousness, it's built in to recognize the mother consciousness. It's familiar, just like child who sees the mother and lights up. You just know it.

So, if you are given the blessing of a set of teachings that will show you true nature, then the natural response is number one, familiarity, *gompa* [in Tibetan]; and number two, gratitude. So, we say that gratitude, it's not like an emotion, it's not like sadness or anger or happiness. Gratitude is the structure of reality. It's built into the way things are. So, the natural and spontaneous expression of an awakened mind is gratitude—the deeper the awakening, the stronger the gratitude. How do you know the awakening is authentic? Well, it's hard to say because we tend, in the West, to confuse it with conceptualizing about awakening. But you're probably on the right track if your awakening is accompanied by strong, spontaneous compassion, strong gratitude, and respect and devotion for what you've been given. And the deeper, the more stable the awakening, the greater the compassion, the greater the gratitude, the greater the respect and devotion.

The teachings are very deep, and they command an ocean of respect and gratitude because it's built into the way things are. So, in that sense, it's both similar and different to the Western stuff. It's not an emotional state. It's part of the structure of being. In that sense it's different, but what's similar about it is that, just like in the West, if a teacher or a mentor does something that changes your life, or a psychotherapist changes your life, you express gratitude for the positive impact on who you've become. Here, it's similar in the sense that, to the teacher or the body of teachings, you express gratitude for the impact on who you've become. But what you are expressing is the spontaneous nature of ultimate reality itself—gratitude. That's the different part. So, it's both similar and different, you see.

But, it's about who you become. Let me give you a Western analogy again. In the 1950s, which was probably the height of the psychoanalytic movement in the West, and by then, you know, Freud, when he did psychoanalysis, they were rather short things. They were three months, six months. He pushed people along and moved them through treatment. But by the 1930s, and particularly the 1940s and into the '50s, psychoanalysis had become ten, twenty-year things, four or five times a week on the couch. It's the old Woody Allen joke: "I've given it ten years. I think I'll give it another ten years and see for myself whether it's gonna work." It had become like that.

But, in the positive sense, if you had an analyst who you'd gotten used to talking to for an hour a day, four or five times a week for ten years, and they were genuinely concerned for your welfare, they knew everything about your life, and you'd gotten used to being able to talk about everything with somebody who accepted you. You didn't have to be defended with them, you could be honest with them, and you could explore and learn to discover. Good therapy, like good attachment, leads to healthy exploratory behavior, except it's internal exploration in this case. It's not exploration of the world. So, if that person has been involved in everything about your life for a decade or longer, and you got better, whatever that means, and you were more content with your life, you had worked out your neurosis, and you were happier, not only did you change, in terms of whatever the problems were that you came to analysis with, but something else happened.

Roy Schafer, an analyst at the Menninger Foundation in the '50s, talked about it in terms of selective identification. What he meant is that you, in appreciation for all the change that you went through in your life based on this person, who has such a central role in your life, you began more and more to identify with certain positive qualities of who they were. And you became like them. So, it wasn't about resolving your neuroses and getting your life to work better. In addition to that, you became like them in certain ways. You identified, hopefully, with the positive qualities. But that became the idea in the West that wasn't just about psychoanalysis, specifically, or psychotherapy, in general. It became a model to understand any kind of mentorship, like Mrs. Merchant, a good teacher. Or like a good clinical mentor, or a mentor in the legal field, or whatever your profession is. We identify with our mentors, and we become more like them. The other day I went to my oldest son's white coat ceremony, which is adorable, as he's starting medical school. When he was in high school, he shadowed a surgeon who worked in the pain clinic. And we were talking about medicine the other day and he said, "Well, I think I might work in the pain field." Well, where do you think that came from? It came from identification with his mentor, of course. He had not made that connection clear, but it seemed perfectly obvious to me, because this guy was good to him. He was a good mentor, and that's what made him go into medicine. We become like that.

Think about people in your life who are mentors, and what qualities you picked up from them. You'll see what it means to selectively identify and become more like your mentors. Plato was very clear on this when he wrote about the education of the state. What he said was that good education necessarily is about character development. It's not about learning content. It's about who we become. It's not about lesson plans. I mean, that's clear to you and the kids that you teach. It's not about their lesson plans. It's who your kids are going to turn out to be, and you're rather single-minded about that. A lot of us, if we had good teachers, we wouldn't have to go into psychotherapy later. [Laughter] Remember that book, *All I Really Need to Know I Learned in Kindergarten*? Remember that? There's a certain truth to that. Good education, good identification figures as teachers correct a lot of things that don't occur in the stage of early attachment. In the attachment field, we call that earned security. Kids learn it outside of the original attachment system if they don't get it fully.

Think about people in your life who've had an impact on you and how you've become like them in certain ways. It's not hard for me to think about that. My clinical mentor was Erika Fromm for thirty-five years. I have her single-minded ethics. It's her voice, not mine. My other clinical mentor was Karl Menninger. When I'm excited and wonder about everything, and am always looking into things new, that's not me, that's Karl. When I tie everything together with this massive encyclopedic integration, that's not me, that's Mircea Eliade, my history of religions professor. Every one of them changed me in certain ways.

My Tibetan nickname is one that my teacher teases me with is Rigpa Kyungde, "the one who's single-minded about awakening." That's not me. That's His Holiness Menri Trizin. He's single-minded about developing that in me, and I picked up the same trait. I am those qualities of all my mentors. And you are, too. Identification changes your character, changes who you are. The essence, the heart of true education, it's always about character. It's who you become. So, if you change in positive ways, through that kind of identification, the spontaneous expression of that change is character, but the true expression of the maturity of that is always conduct. How you act in the world. It goes beyond emotional states like gratitude.

The true measure of spiritual realization is always and necessarily about conduct. How you are. And that's the ultimate expression of spiritual realization, but it's also the ultimate expression of gratitude. It's not that I could go back and meet Mrs. Merchant again and express how grateful I am for the fundamental transformation of this kid. The true expression is how I honor my teachers and who I am. That is a duty. If you have gratitude, it's not negotiable in terms of who you are. So, if you see it that clearly, there's no place for screwing up. It's not part of the system. It doesn't compute. You show it in who you are. That matters.

Just before my Root Lama, Geshe Wangyal, died in 1979, some of you have heard this story before, but it bears repeating. I had lived with him summers over a nine-year span, college and graduate school, and I went there to learn Tibetan language and to learn to meditate. And towards the end of his life he said, "Dan, when you came here you had the expectation that you were going to learn various meditation techniques, and you're probably disappointed. I didn't take you by the hand, and I didn't show you how to do this meditation, that meditation. You didn't learn anything like that from me." He said, "I started studying when I was five years old, and I finished when I was fifty-five." He was eighty-nine, I think, at the time. He said, "What you got is an opportunity to see what it's like for someone who completes the path and brings it through fruition." Implied there, of course, although he didn't use the word, is buddhahood. He was a buddha. And he said, "If in what you see about the time you've been with me, if that state is convincing to you, you have your own intelligence, and you'll figure out how to do the same thing. And if it's not, you won't do anything with it. That's all you get." It was sufficient. But, being in my young twenties, at the time, and not really utilizing it or appreciating it as much as I could when I had that precious time to be with him every day, I didn't press it for everything I could get because I was terrified of him. It's hard living with somebody that reads your mind, at least at that age. Now, it's sort of a relief.

There were times over the years where things would go bad in my life, and I always remember I had this [play]; one of my favorite plays was *Camelot*. There's this scene with King Arthur, where the Round Table has gotten really screwed up. The vision has gone bad and it's getting terribly complicated. And Arthur wanders out to the forest because he needs to find Merlin again. Only, when he gets to the forest, Merlin's no longer there. There were so many times in my life, at crossroads, where things weren't going well, that I wished that Merlin was there again. It felt like wandering in the forest, looking for something that was greatly lost and missing. My Root Lama wasn't there anymore. And I used to have these thoughts about what it would be like, what I could've learned from him if I were older and wiser, whatever that means. It's a nice construction of mind, but at least had something compelling about the construction, so I would think about it. I would think about what it would have been like to have that kind of guidance over the years. I don't do that anymore because I understood what he was saying.

You see, the whole message is here: You have to become that. He used to say, "Same mind, but different." Or in guru yoga we say, "the mind of the Master," like Guru Padme [pronounced Paymay], or whomever, or the Root Lama, held in your mind as inseparable. Think about what that means, and draw it to its ultimate conclusion. The mind of the master and your mind are inseparable. And when you have become that, what's missing? Nothing's missing. The best way of honoring what the deep blessing of being shown the teachings that will bring that out is to become that. What greater way to honor what you've been given, or to express gratitude? Become it, live it, convey it to others in a way that transforms their lives in the same way that it did for you. It's a spiritual Ponzi scheme. Pass it on. [Laughter] It's all empty. It's all illusion, except it works. And it doesn't exploit anybody; it does whatever the positive opposite of exploitation is. It brings out the best so that everything good flourishes. *Kuntuzangpo. Samantabhadra. Kuntuzangpo* means "everything good." So, becoming that means going beyond temporary states, which are more emotion-like states of gratitude. It's the fruition of gratitude.

Any more discussion of that? Anybody else want to chime in on this topic? It's a good topic.

Yes?

Student 1

I'd like to ask you about the challenging side of when you feel angry or when the people that have been your mentors betray you, and therefore you do not become like those people.

Dan

Or worse, they betray you and you become like them. [Laughter] That happens, too.

Student 1

So, I really empathize and can relate to those moments of genuine gratitude, but I'm struggling with some of the opposite.

Dan

That's a great question. What if your mentors betray you?

Well, there are serious karmic consequences. See, in Western terms, we call this a fiduciary duty. And what a fiduciary duty means is that the senior party has a duty owed to the junior party to put aside their own needs, single-mindedly, towards the welfare and growth development of the junior party. So, a parent-child relationship by definition is a fiduciary relationship. A teacher-student relationship is a fiduciary relationship. A doctor-patient or a therapist-patient relationship is a fiduciary relationship. A relationship between a priest or a minister and the clientele is a fiduciary relationship. And it used to be that the banking industry was a fiduciary relationship, [Laughter] but that seems to have gotten forgotten somewhere along the way. But all of those are fiduciary relationships. And that comes with a very clear ethical duty of the senior party to put aside their own needs for the welfare of the junior party. And we know that, in terms of fiduciary violations, the psychological damage from fiduciary violations is very strong.

For example, I don't like what we did with our current version of our Psychiatric Diagnostic Manual in terms of the definition of trauma because they watered it down. They defined a traumatic event in terms of causing threat to one's physical integrity or threat to life. But, there's a huge amount of research that shows that interpersonal trauma is much more damaging. Sexual abuse is usually more damaging than physical abuse. And all kinds of interpersonal trauma are more damaging than non-interpersonal trauma. Of all the interpersonal traumas, fiduciary damage is the worst. None of that is captured in our models for this anymore. But fiduciary violation is a big thing. That's why the sense of betrayal and the damage is so strong around priest abuse and why it's such a big deal. But it's not just the abusing priest. It's the institution, and the cover ups.

Interesting how the whole culture reacts to this. You look not only towards the perpetrator, but look at the outrage of an entire culture around the Sandusky thing.[7] Not about Sandusky, but about the cover up at Penn State. And then bringing down Joe Paterno's statue was sort of like the falling of the statue of Stalin when the Soviet Union fell. It's no different. It's that same kind of rage to get rid of the icon because the icon failed, because the cover up and the advantage for the institution became more important than the individuals involved. And in this culture, we have so many fiduciary violations that the amount of outrage is just stunning, to see this. Because at every level, I mean as a culture, we've all watched our life savings go down the tubes based on the securities and banking industry.

We've all heard many, many examples of abuse of children that are overwhelming everywhere. Nobody is paying their duty as senior parties anymore because we have no leaders that are responsible, or who see their ethical duties. And that's why we're a culture in trouble. And we've all seen many examples of spiritual leaders failing in their fiduciary duties, either most commonly through sexual misconduct or exploitation by power and money, and it's a big deal. The people who are in the senior position who exploit those in the junior position have a huge, from an Eastern point of view, they have huge karmic debt. That's a serious thing. They'll probably come back as cockroaches next lifetime. But I can't say that, because the cockroaches' rights people will get on me [Laughter] for singling out cockroaches. But you know what I mean. It's a serious debt. But on the other hand, as a trauma clinician, I can't be oblivious to the profound effect that fiduciary violations have, particularly in the spiritual field.

And I try to handle that sensitively. We've had a number of people come to our retreats who were damaged by flawed spiritual teachers. And all that I can do is to try and offer them an emotionally corrective experience by not exploiting them and trying to show them the nature of ultimate reality in a way that they can directly appreciate. And in the course of that, do some healing, and maybe get them back on the track, because you see, my duty there is when people are damaged spiritually, they don't just get disillusioned with the flawed teacher. They get disillusioned with the spiritual path. And one of the areas of

---

7 Joe Sandusky, convicted of child sexual abuse in 2012.

significant damage is, they won't practice anymore. So, as a spiritual teacher, my duty is to see if I can provide them with an emotionally corrective experience so they can find their way back into a path that they can trust, and get back on track, and ultimately to awaken to their true nature. And then, in that sense, they're healed. We have a number of students who we've gone through that with. I tend to extend myself more to reaching out to them and trying to do what I can to help them with this issue.

I used to have a woman that I worked closely with, one of the grand old masters in this clinical field and years ago she, this was years ago, she was in the inner circle with Maharishi, and she saw much too much stuff that disillusioned her badly. She was very damaged by that. So, when I met her, she wouldn't practice anything. And I was much younger then. That was when my Root Lama was alive, so I explained the situation to him and brought her to see him a number of times. And that was very good for her. She began to trust the practice again, and he was flawless.

So, what's emotionally corrective for somebody who's been damaged like that is a teacher who has to be flawless. Not as an idea, but in terms of how they are. It is healing. So, it can be repaired, but what I've been trying to say is that the best medicine is prevention. And in this culture, we all participate in the disease of idealization. And because a teacher comes from the East and they have a funny name and they look different, then we tend to think they're a spiritual teacher. That's bullshit. What happened to critical judgment? You know? My Root Lama, my original Root Lama was a Mongolian horse trader. He said, "Finding teacher like buying horse. You have to check out the hooves, you have to check out the teeth. You don't just buy any horse. Do the same with your teacher. Take some time and check them out before you buy." It's a good lesson. We just buy the horse that comes along, lock, stock, and barrel. You can't do that. It's stupid.

There are some guidelines that I push, and get trashed for it. But while I think that it's not always the case, you're likely to be on safer ground in lineage traditions, because there are checks and balances. You know, it's passed down the same way. You just don't go out and do whatever you want. It's a great fortune that at my age I'm still having a senior teacher who's eighty-eight years old. And he busts me all the time, but it keeps me honest over and against my own tendencies, because you have to watch for spiritual pride. But what I've seen where it becomes a mess, there are two things. One is teachers who come over from the East to sort of exploit the West—they have a funny name, and they do funny things and people go, ooh, and that's bad. And some of those are just frauds, they're just charlatans. And the second are teachers that are self-proclaimed. They might have some genuine realization, but they sort of figured it out on their own. It doesn't come as part of a lineage tradition. And with those, you know, it's largely conceptual. And those are the ones who ultimately are flawed. You have to be very careful with them. We have a lot of that kind of self-proclaimed stuff in the West. So that kind of self-importance is just remarkable to me. And there's no place for it. That's where you get in trouble. So, check out the qualities of who the person is, but more, check the context of where they're teaching from. And you're likely to be on safer ground when it represents a lineage tradition, but not always.

Even the lamas who come over, and not just the lamas, but teachers from the East who represent lineage traditions, they come to the West and some bite the dust, particularly if they come from a monastic tradition, because they're not capable of dealing with it. I was always appreciative of my Root Lama, who came over as a representative of the monastic tradition. But, when he came here, he said, "Well, I have to do things differently in the West." So, he had a stable girlfriend for twenty years. He was in his eighties when I knew them together as a couple and she was in her late seventies, and they were an adorable couple. Yeah, it was a terrific model for the West. And he didn't get into all this bullshit that people in the monastic tradition do, where they end up going from one extreme to the other, from celibacy to sexual misconduct. He steeped himself in all the Western relationship stuff just so he could teach in the West because he needed to know about it, and I respected that. That was a good model.

There's been a lot of damage, but I'm hoping what that means is that somewhere along the way people can either retain or develop their metacognitive intelligence and develop better judgment in terms of what teachings and teachers they associate with. Do not suspend your judgment outside the door.

But in that sense, choosing a spiritual teacher is unfortunately about as efficient as falling in love, right? Which means what? You know right away who you're getting involved with, and you want it to be something else, so you suspend all your thoughts about the person's flaws and discover that ten or fifteen years later and say, "Why didn't I do something differently at the beginning?" We do the same thing with spiritual teachers. We park our intelligence outside the door because we want it so bad. And that's stupid. It's better to use your metacognitive intelligence. See what you're getting and what you're not getting.

August 22, 2012

Themes: Interconnectedness; Beyond Time; Positive States

Dan

Welcome everyone. You have a question?

Student 1

I appreciate the opportunity to talk about something I have been thinking a lot about over the last six weeks. Six of my patients have died. I was thinking about the interactions between the patients and the staff, the patients and the families, and thinking about their impact on me and my influence on them. One patient stood out in particular, an unusual gentleman who was with us for two and a half years in a sub-acute facility. He was somebody that people got to know a great deal. He often sat in the reception area talking with people. He sat outside as some of the folks gardened. He fed the birds. So, he had an impact on a lot of people over the course of time. One of the women who works at the nursing home put out candy on his behalf after he passed away on all of the nursing units. In the gift baskets she wrote something that I'll read. It said a great deal about what I have been thinking about. This gentleman, I am going to call Mr. John Smith.

"As you know Mr. John Smith left us on Thursday, July 19th. He came to our facility two and a half years ago and went from being someone who would never come out of his room to someone who barely stayed in it. He came to a rehabilitation center but left a home. He went from being a resident to being a friend. When he was in the hospital, he mentioned not returning to our home because he did not want to be a burden to any of you. Then he realized that this was exactly where he wanted to be, surrounded by his family. And he told them to send him home. Over the past two years, he touched so many lives in so many ways, and he is missed terribly. But as he always said, 'It's alright to be down and out, just not for too long. You have to pick yourself up and go on. Life is too short to be unhappy.' So, take a minute to grieve, but not much longer; it's what he would want."

This woman goes on to say, "A few days before he left, I asked him what we were supposed to do without him. He replied, 'I'll still be around, you just have to listen harder.' So, enjoy the chocolate. It's a final gift from him to you. And the next time you're out in the garden, be sure to really listen."

So, I have been thinking a great deal about how everything is connected. And what I have realized is that on this relative level there is nothing that occurs in isolation. Whether it is anything we do, or think, or say, the ways we act, to the hummingbirds that visited while I was in Texas; to what I see in rather personal ways, and also in a larger sense in the nation right now with the political situation; and then in the global sense, as I think about the interaction between nations and also environmentally. So really, I am looking at the interconnection of everything, from ways we are not even aware of, to ways that are more obvious. So, I was hoping that you would address the interconnectedness of everything from very subtle levels to very overt levels. [Dan and students laugh together.] That's all. [Laughter again.]

Dan

A simple question. Every time she says, "I've been thinking about something," [Laughter] I brace myself. [Dan laughs.]

Okay. So, it is true that everything is interconnected. Everything is always right here, but in our ordinary mind we don't see it like that. And what clouds over the direct experience of the interconnectedness of everything are the conventional structures of mind, not the least of which is the convention of ordinary time. As long as we see things as coming and going in time, then there is a linearity to our experience—one thing, and then the next thing, and the next thing. There is a seeming temporal structure to things. But, that's not the only way the mind is capable of working.

What is unique about Mahāyāna Buddhism, in contrast to the older Theravāda Buddhism, is the development of emptiness practices specifically dealing with time and space. So, in the older Buddhism, if you get very concentrated, all of the thought elaboration of your mind will stop. And you will perceive everything very quickly in terms of what we call "mind moments," simple bursts of movement and energy, a hundred thousand bursts of movement energy in the blink of an eye.

So, for example, if you are concentrating on the breath, it's not solid anymore. It's all just bursts of movement and energy in a field—a very lively even, dynamic field. If you look at the arising and passing of those very quick moments of experience as they are called, and you hold the level of concentration at that level, the natural tendency, if you look at everything arising and passing very quickly, like a strobe light, is that after a while you start looking more at the going out rather than the coming. And you look at the going out more and more, and everything will start breaking up and disintegrating and dissolving. In the older Buddhism, the *Visuddhimagga*, (the path of purification, which is the stages of practice in the early Buddhism), that was known in Pali as *bhanganyana*, dissolution. It's not a very pleasant experience. And if you watch the simplest elements in the mind, which were called *dharmin* in the older practice, the simplest, observable elements of consciousness breaking up, then, what's left is a mirror-like awareness—a vast field of mirror-like awareness. So, it's said that that dissolution becomes the platform to awakening because you can then look more clearly into the nature of that mirror-like awareness, no longer obscured by all that activity of mind, which is a distraction.

But then Nagarjuna came along, and the Prajnaparamita literature, and said, wait a minute here. This idea that things arise and pass very quickly presumes the convention of time. What if that's its own illusion? What if that's just another empty construction? So, to test the issue he developed the famous dialectic on the emptiness of time.

You can use something like the rising of the breath, as you know. You can use the arising of a mind moment, if your mind is observing that quickly. It doesn't make any difference what you observe. You just need to observe a mental event. But when it comes in time, so, let's say you take the breath; when the breath arises in time, you take the view that it doesn't really come from anywhere because it's already here. And when the breath goes away in time, you take the view that it doesn't go anywhere because it stays here. Now, if you keep doing that for every cycle of the breath, that's going to screw around with your perception of time. Everything will seem to flatten out. And then in the interval between the breaths, when it's sort of quiet because there is no movement in the breath, if you keep looking into the nature of awareness, and then when the breath is happening, you are viewing it as it comes in time it's not really coming because it's already here, and when it goes away in time, it's not really going because it stays here. And you keep doing that, and each time in between the cycle of the breaths when it's quiet you're looking into the nature of awareness, what's going to happen is you are going to open up into your awareness a level of awareness that doesn't operate in time. You're stepping out of that convention of time. And that awareness is beyond time, it's changeless. And since time and space are related, it's rather huge. It's boundless.

So, you find yourself stepping into this ocean of still, changeless, timeless, boundless awareness, which is sort of nice, because once you do that, if you resolve this issue of the convention of time, how can you lose that awareness? Because it doesn't go away in time anymore. Now, essentially what you have done with that meditation, like a key, it unlocks a certain level of mind. You've opened up what in Tibetan Buddhism is called the very subtle level of mind. And there, everything is interconnected. And the awareness is a changeless ocean within the field of which everything arises in an interconnected way.

If you want a Western description of that, in terms of Western information processing, we'd say you shifted from temporal or serial information processing to parallel or simultaneous processing. The mind is built to process everything simultaneously. But we don't typically open to that experience. It remains a latent property in the human mind.

We tested that at one point with a tachistoscope, which is a high-speed electronic board that flashes events in terms of thousandths of a second, and we looked at the speed of the mind in meditating. And with normal people who've never meditated, you can produce what's called a masking effect. If I show you a target, like the letter "2," and if I randomize the amount of time, the duration I leave it on the screen, I can determine and calculate your recognition threshold. I can say, for example, that I will have to leave it on the screen for forty milliseconds; that's pretty quick. And if I leave it on the screen for forty milliseconds, you can recognize that target a hundred percent of the time. But, if I flash it quicker, you won't get it; only some of the time. So, now that I've determined your individual recognition threshold, conceivably if I show you a hundred trials of that letter, every time you should be able to recognize it. But here's the issue: if I flash you the letter, the target, and right after that I put a round disk, a black disk, the same size as that target, and I put them close together in time, but not simultaneously, then the subject can't recognize the target anymore. Putting it close together in time, it's what we call a summation effect. It gets collapsed with the perception of the target as if you're seeing those things together, and what it means is that you can't see the target anymore. We call that a backward masking effect. If I put the mask before the target, you still won't see the target. So, that suggests that the mind is able to read things both forward and backward.

Now, I can produce a stable masking effect in ordinary Western subjects every time I do this. But, when we repeated that experiment with lamas, advanced meditators who could shift to the very subtle level of mind, when they were in that level of meditation, we could produce no masking effect at any inter-stimulus interval, right down to the limits of the machine, which is five milliseconds. So, what does it mean? It's consistent with the idea that what they're doing is they're seeing everything simultaneously. So, if the structure of time is dropped out, it doesn't make any difference if you put it close together in time. Time isn't operative anymore. You're seeing everything all at once.

So, with these special meditations, human beings are able to shift to all at-once-ness mode. And from the mind side of the equation, that's a vast ocean of changeless, boundless awareness. And from the event side of that equation, it's the virtual interconnectedness of everything that could possibly be.

That's true in Buddhism. That's the heart of Mahāyāna Buddhism. That's why awakening is for the sake of all beings. But, if you would take a different system, like Patanjali's Yoga Sutras, and you read the last set of practices, book four, it's about the *vasanas*.[8] It's the interconnected virtue of the reality of everything. It's the same thing; a different language for exactly the same thing.

So, these meditations open up the direct experience of a mind that's operative outside of the convention of time, no longer clouded over by it. And as a consequence of that, you have the direct experience of everything interconnected and arising within the field of that boundless, changeless awareness. Now, once you have that direct experience, then what you're going to directly

---

8 *Vasana* is a Sanskrit term that refers to a past impression in the mind that influences behavior.

appreciate is what in Tibetan Buddhism is called *wang*. It's an unfortunate term. It's often translated in the West as "empowerment," and Tibetan lamas go around and give teachers, and teachings, and students collect empowerments, but that's not what the term means at all. The literal translation for the word *wang* is "influence." You're operating at a level of mind where you can directly perceive that since everything is interconnected, everything influences everything else. We're not operating in a vacuum.

When he was alive, I once had a chance to take a workshop with David Bohm, the physicist. And he had a mathematical formula for what he called "the implicate order," where everything is interconnected and implicates everything else. That was his whole contribution to contemporary physics. Where did he get his realization from in physics? He was a student of Krishnamurti. And his mathematical view of the universe came from his direct realizations in his meditation. Everything is interconnected, and everything implicates everything else. And the idea of "implicates" means that things influence each other in quantum, not Newtonian ways, not in any causal way. So, once you open up that level of mind, everything is always right here; and every thought, every action affects everything else. It has profound influence. Now, the more you develop that practice, if you shift to the next level of mind, which is awakening, the influence is much more profound.

If all structures of mind are just empty constructions, then that directly leads to freedom. If you understand everything as being empty constructions of mind, then the implication of that is that as much as we live in relative reality, some structures of mind are more useful than others. They're all empty. But that raises the question of what sort of structures of mind we want to intentionally develop, and which structures of mind are likely to have the greatest influence on the field around us. So, if negative states of mind eventually lose their grab and disappear, the intentional cultivation of positive space, albeit empty, has a positive influence, and it affects the field around you. How you act towards others matters. And what your client appreciated is that he could waste away in a nursing home feeling very miserable and isolated, which was his original tendency, but it sounds like the light went on, and he began to appreciate that he could have a positive effect on all those around. And that matters.

I was reading a book earlier this week from the positive psychology movement that speaks to the matter quite nicely. It's Barbara Fredrickson's work. She got the Templeton award for her work, which is sort of like the Nobel Prize for positive psychology. And what she discovered is that positivity breeds on itself, and that if you intentionally cultivate positive emotions towards others, the more you do that, the more it has a cascading effect. So, if you think about something like reflecting on what brings you joy, and times you've experienced joy in your life, and bring those times to mind; and then trying to find instances of bringing joy into your everyday life, simply by the intention in the systematic reflection on that, you will bring more joy into your life. And if you think about times when you were intentionally engaged in something with a kind of rapt interest, and you start cultivating that, you find that you bring a kind of rapt interest and vital engagement to whatever you're doing. And the joy makes it easier to develop the intense interest; and the intense interest then makes it easier to bring the joy into it—and, as we did last week, when we focused on the cultivation of gratitude. And they all affect each other. The times in your life where you felt a deep sense of serenity, calmness—think of moments in your life when you felt a deep sense of serenity. Was it in nature? Was it after doing something that you struggled with, and finally there was that quiet?

And then when people started to reflect on these positive emotions and bring them more into their everyday life, they developed it. She found that for most people, the ratio of negative to positive emotion states is about two to one. But she found an interesting thing, that when people intentionally try and cultivate positive emotions, each positive emotion that they cultivate reinforces the other, and you get a cascading effect. And when the ratio of positive to negative emotions reaches a critical tipping point, at about three to one in favor of the positive, and that's where you're operating out of, people fundamentally transform themselves, and they begin to flourish on every level. And everybody around them begins to change. And they're fundamentally different people. And the whole social field around them is influenced by that. And this is important because the earlier research on happiness suggested that happiness is relatively fixed. It's genetically determined in part, and the only thing you can really change is what you do with your leisure activity. But this suggests that that's not correct. Anybody who systematically cultivates positive feelings, at a certain point there's a cascading effect. They flourish. And it has a deep effect on everybody in the field around them. That's what you're describing with this guy. He figured it out, all by himself. And it was noticeable to everyone in his field. And when you cultivate those positive states, so they strongly outweigh the negative states, look what you're leaving behind, the wake of your influence. That's a person who in the last years of his life contributed to the greater good, and that's the legacy he'll leave behind. And anybody in this room could do the same thing.

Now, it sounds like he got some realization along the way. If you carry these practices beyond the convention of time, beyond the limits of individual consciousness, to awakened mind, and you cultivate and stabilize that awakening, that awakening shines like the sun that's always right here, as you know, and there is no possibility of dying. That's a stupid idea. It's not possible. The body decays. The brilliant shining like the sun of an awakened mind never dies with the body. And does the influence of that continue? Absolutely.

As you know, if you talk to Rinpoche, because he's now eighty and he's saying he's not going to be in his body that much more, some students say, "Well, what are we going to do after you're not here anymore?" And, he says, "I'll still be here, don't worry about it!"

The transmissions just come from mind to mind. They don't come from words coming out of a mouth and a body. Do you think that's really where they come from? You think it's the Dan in a body here that's teaching you this stuff? [Dan chuckles.] That's its own illusion. This guy understood that. He's saying loud and clear, nothing dies. The brilliance of that awakened mind shines forth because it's always right here.

So, you can see from the Western research with the cultivation of positive states, when you reach that critical point [they] give you profound influence. It leads to goodness for all around you. But the Western research doesn't know anything about awakening. If you're cultivating awakened mind, or fully enlightened mind, that's like multiplying those effects a billion-fold. Because if you develop that awakening to the point that everything arises spontaneously from groundless ground and then recedes without leaving any trace, it's what we call automatic awakened *dharmakāya* release. It will exhaust all negative states. Think about what it means to manifest a mind where it isn't a three to one ratio, because there are no negative states left, not even the dregs of negative states.

We call that mind *drima*—clean, stainless. There are no negative states whatsoever left. Think of the influence of that mind on the whole field around. Think of the influence of the deep strength of that level, the realization, on all those in one's social field. Then you'll understand why they translate the term "influence" as "empowerment," because it has a certain power to it, a very strong field effect. So, when you have a fully realized being, they engage in what we call *chingilap* in Tibetan. *Chingilap—lapa* is like a wave on an ocean, like a big ripple. And *chingwa* is the word for giving. So, what's being given is the gift of influence. It's like a wave. It ripples across an interconnected sea of beings, more like a tsunami I guess, and carries everybody in the wake of that influence in a positive direction. It clears away all the obscurations and clouds.

So, being in the presence of a fully realized being influences the unfolding of your own mindstream. It gives you a window of opportunity. It clears away the clouds just for a short amount of time, so that you could have a clear realization. But, here's the catch. It's sort of like a matching grant. You only get the influence if you match it with effort in your practice. If you just get the influence and you do nothing, the influence will fade in a day or two. That's why everybody goes around collecting empowerments from different lamas—what a useless thing to do, because they never practice anything.

You've got to put it into practice. Then the effects will be obvious. But, that level of influence goes beyond just creating the goodness. It creates realization. Not like in the place that you work where everybody feels the goodness of this guy's realization because he's tipped the balance to positive states. And everybody acts better towards each other. That's a very real effect. Imagine if his field of influence went beyond positive states to the influence of a buddha mind. Then, you see, the real issue here is people don't just act better, they become buddhas.

Student 2

They become what?

Dan

They become buddhas. You've got a huge field effect towards realization. At the time of Shakyamuni, how many buddhas in his lifetime were developed? There's the time of the second turning of the Wheel of the Dharma at Vulture Peak. The turning of the Mahāyāna. Look at the Heart Sutra. Hundreds of thousands of *bodhisattvas* showed up. That's a big field of influence.

A realized mind is not limited to this body. It's like the vast scope of influence that saturates all beings, out of kindness. The purpose of the influence is to help you out, so you don't keep getting in your own way. But, if you don't see the value of it and don't put it into practice, it means nothing. Or it's like the great master in the Sufi tradition said, "Great masters roam through the marketplace every day, and no one ever recognizes them." You have to appreciate the influence that's always given freely. But if you don't see it, it has no effect. [Long pause]

Good question. As always, it's a great question.

I would suggest one addition to your question. It's not necessary to talk about the letter you received, that you got it from that patient, or what you saw there. It's about time you started looking at your own influence on your work environment. It's the same. I know that you have appropriate humility with that, but be truthful. It's not different. And when you look at that squarely for what it is, with courage, then you'll manifest it more, because it does good. You understand what I'm saying. You're capable of an ocean of influence, but, it's not you, the person, just the nature of the realization. Good.

[Long pause]

So, what's the ratio of negative to positive states that you all feel in your life on a regular basis, today? If today is the sample, what's the ratio of positive to negative states? Look and see for yourself. That's your starting point. Then you must work to change that. And when you change it, your whole field of experience changes around you, and everybody changes, too. That's true for individuals and it's also true for groups of people. It's true for couples.

Gottman's work is pretty good with that.[9] If you don't know it, he did work on how couples communicate with each other. And most couples get into the blame game, and they spend a lot of time criticizing and trashing each other. What he found is that if the trashing ratio, if the negative things outweigh the positive things, when the negative things that people communicate to their partner outweigh the positive things by a ratio of five to one, the odds are extremely unlikely that that couple is going to make it over time. But, when the ratio was positive, the likelihood that that couple would stay together in the long haul was very clear. These are empirical findings. They work. When the findings first came out, people were upset about that. But it is what it is. I do a lot of couples' therapy, and I still don't get it. I'm sort of naive, I think. It's amazing to me that somebody that you loved enough to marry, you end up trashing so much. And couples do this all the time. And if there's anybody who

---

9 John Mordecai Gottman was a clinical psychologist whose focus was on stabilizing marriage, and well known for his cascade model of relational dissolution.

comes into couples' therapy, by the time they come into your office, they trash each other. Where does that come from? It never works.

So, in your close relationships, with your work environment, it doesn't make any difference where you are; within yourself, the starting point of the ordinary mind is suffering. The negative states outweigh the positive states. And your responsibility is to change it so the positive states outweigh the negative. That's considered a great feat, if you look at this positive psychology stuff in the West. Changing the ratio to a very positive over negative would be the starting point of meditation in Buddhism, just from a different perspective. The view is that you'd never be able to concentrate very well until you change that ratio.

If you are deeply positive and your mind manifests that, it will have a remarkable influence on the whole social field around you. But then there's another level of influence that's really interesting. See, in karma theory, there are three *tak*, three signs of the manifestation of influence. If you do something positive and you practice it over and over again, the first sign that you're getting somewhere with that practice is that you will see spontaneously emerging positive states. And they occur more frequently and with greater intensity. So that's the first sign. The second sign is that it begins to influence your behavior. You act more positively. But the third thing isn't something that we acknowledge in the West. It's really interesting. It begins to unfold when the positive effects of a practice are very strong. It begins to affect the unfolding of events in your life. The course of your life is changed by the practice. You begin to have good fortune. The fact that we're all doing this together tonight is good fortune. It's the accumulation of your own effort. Nothing is accidental.

For me, I've worked at this stuff for forty-two years. The fact that I have so many wonderful students is good fortune, the culmination effect. The whole field of the world unfolds, changes, and if enough people did that, you'd change the course of history. And if we don't, then the course of history continues to progressively get driven by self-interest. And that's not going to take us anywhere good. And we may not survive it. When you start developing positive states, they eclipse self-interest. Then you start to think more in terms of the greater social good, a message that's been lost by politics and the financial industry.

There's no place for selfishness.

August 29, 2012

Themes: Stages of Concentration; Meditation; Neuroimaging

Dan

Welcome everyone.

Generally, what we do is to open up the first hour here for questions, either about meditation practice or about spiritual practice in everyday life, and whatever topic gets raised we then try and translate into a practice. So generally, the spontaneity of that's sort of fun. But, given the fact that we have some new people tonight, and some people that are particularly interested in concentration, we'll do a concentration night. And for those of you who haven't been to retreats with us, this will be relatively new, or completely new. And for those who have, maybe this will be a refresher, because it is the foundation.

So, what's the starting point for meditation? The starting point for meditation is the dysfunction of the ordinary mind. When you try and concentrate on something, as soon as you try and concentrate, the mind jumps off to something else. We say in Tibetan, "it doesn't stay." [See Chapter 3 for Dan's teachings on *dukkha* and reactivity.]

If you look at the content of the mind in everyday experience, what you'll notice is what William James called the "buzzing, booming, confusion of the ordinary mind." It's filled with junk. And our mind scatters itself with lots of things going on, seemingly at once. The contemporary psychologist, Mihali Czikszentmihalyi, in his research on flow states, coined the term "psychic entropy."[10] The ordinary mind is entropic. It jumps around from one thing to another and there's lots of background noise. It's never calm. It's just filled with stuff. Mostly our mind wanders. We think too much about past stuff. We anticipate the future and worry a lot. And we get lost in our daydreams a good part of the day.

Modern neurobiologists do functional neuroimaging studies of the brain and have recently looked at what they call the resting brain, which they take, unfortunately, as "the default option."[11] And, when the brain is at rest, what does it normally do? It mostly spaces out, and it gets lost in daydreams. And there's a kind of a frontal parietal circuit, neurocircuitry, that gets activated when we're in our so-called resting state, as if that's the natural condition of the brain—because the neurobiologists don't know anything other than their own experience. That's not the natural condition, the resting state of the brain. That's the dysfunction of the ordinary mind. The mind wasn't built to get lost in daydreams, and to space out all day long, and to fill itself with junk. It's an incessant habit that we've learned. And along with that incessant habit, what cognitive psychologists tell us is that we spend a lot of that time in negative self-talk, putting ourselves down in one way or another.

I remember once participating in the Mind and Life dialogues with H.H. the Dalai Lama, and one of the faculty members asked him about negative self-talk. And he started talking in Tibetan with his two senior translators for almost forty-five minutes. He speaks very good English, and his senior translator has the equivalent of a doctorate in philosophy from Oxford and speaks perfect English. Why were they talking in Tibetan? Because none of them have any experiential basis to know what negative self-talk is. They don't have it. And after forty-five minutes, he sort of turned to us and said, "Why would you ever let your mind get like that?" He was very concerned. Because for them, the default option of the mind, when the mind is at rest, is the mind is at rest. And it's free of all extraneous content and doesn't wander. It's just alert and quiet. It's not filled with any extraneous activity whatsoever, certainly not daydreams.

---

10 Czikszentmihalyi was a Hungarian-American psychologist. He recognized and named the psychological concept of "flow," a highly focused mental state conducive to productivity.

11 Now commonly referred to as "the default mode."

It's clear, it's quiet, and it only stays on whatever you intend to put it on. That's the default option of the mind in its original state. So how do we get back to that? Because we've gotten very far away from that as the norm. You get back to that by training the mind with meditation—*gompa* in Tibetan.

It takes practice to meditate, repeated practice, over and over again, to train this mind. In the Indo-Tibetan tradition, in Mahāyāna Buddhism, the mind is likened to a wild elephant. Elephants are very smart and they're very strong. But they get easily scared. So, when they stampede, they cause lots of damage. The ordinary mind is like the wild elephant, stampeding.

There are two ways of training the elephant, and there are two basic styles of meditation. In the first style, concentration meditation, you tie the rope of mindfulness onto one object, the concentration object. Everything else is a distraction. So, there's only two possibilities, either you're on the concentration object, or you're off of it. The Tibetan word for concentration is *newa*, to stay. Either you're staying on the object, or the mind is distracted with something else, usually thought or sense experience, and sometimes emotions. Now, the other type of meditation is an awareness meditation. And in the awareness meditation, there's no object to concentrate on. There's no distraction. Whatever comes up next, you focus on that because the goal in awareness meditation is to develop continuity of awareness, and to correct for that discontinuity, so you are not having lapses of forgetfulness. So, you see, they're different skills; one trains continuity of awareness, the other trains staying for longer and longer periods of time on whatever you're concentrating on. Those are very different skills.

An example of awareness meditation would be Krishnamurti's choiceless awareness—just being aware of everything each moment. It's sort of hard to do—also *shikantaza*, the "just-sitting" style of Zen. No object. Now because awareness meditations are very difficult, if I just said to you, "Okay, just be aware of everything, track everything, every moment," it's not easy. So, therefore, a system that's become very popular now in the US is a system that developed in Burma with Mahāsī Sayādaw. In the West, we call that mindfulness meditation, or mindfulness-based psychotherapy now. And, that system is a hybrid of both pure concentration practice and pure awareness practice because its originator, Mahāsī Sayādaw, said, "Look, it's really hard to say, 'be aware of everything.'" So, what he did is he had people concentrate first, to calm the mind down, and once they got modestly concentrated, through following the rising and falling of the breath, then they'd open up the field of awareness. So, the second modification of the system was to use categories or labels; it helps you to approximate tracking everything continuously. So, you open up the field of awareness, and if a thought comes up, you use the label "thinking." As long as thinking is occurring, you say "thinking." You don't think about the content of the thought, just the fact that at that given moment, thinking is occurring. If you have an emotion, "feeling." If you have a body sensation, "sensing." And if you hear a sound, "hearing." Not the content of the sound, just the hearing is happening. They use these simple categories to approximate continuity of awareness.

What you need to appreciate is that the system that became very popular here in the West, Burmese mindfulness, is a hybrid of concentration and pure awareness meditation. It's a mixture of both. Therefore, it has both advantages and disadvantages. The advantage is you learn a little bit of concentration, and you learn some about mindfulness. That's not bad. The disadvantage is that you never see what these skills are like in their pure form. And within the tradition, this hybrid that Mahāsī Sayādaw developed is about a hundred years old. That's not very long. The tradition of Mahāyāna goes back fifteen hundred years as an unbroken lineage, and some of the Theravādin practices go back twenty-five hundred years in an unbroken lineage. There, the foundation is always concentration. But concentration isn't emphasized very much in mindfulness. So people don't really learn to concentrate seriously.

Therefore, we try and introduce to the West the correction for that, which is a system that comes from Asanga because it's the most widely used concentration practice in all of Indo-Tibetan Buddhism. It is the great tradition of concentration. The other great tradition is from the Hindu tradition, which would be Patanjali's yoga sutras, which is the other great tradition that emphasizes concentration. But unfortunately, the person who brought that to the West is Maharishi, and Maharishi watered down the concentration piece for Westerners and cut out most of the good stuff. It never got into the deep concentration that is the individual version of that in Patanjali. So, Westerners never had a chance to become familiar with what it's like to do pure concentration meditation, which is always the foundation. So, that's what we're going to talk a little bit about.

The central point is that when you concentrate, the mind stays on the object for longer and longer periods. The first thing you train is what we call continuous staying. Can you stay for longer and longer periods on the concentration object? If you first start, it doesn't stay very long. Many years ago, in 1979, a graduate student of mine at Harvard, Michael Forth, did his dissertation on meditation, and here's what he did. He took people that never meditated before and he had them focus on a candle flame in front of them for exactly twenty minutes. And on their baby finger, they had a little mercury switch so that every time they'd get distracted from the target, they would simply twitch their baby finger, and you could do a spectral analysis on the computer to actually do a pattern analysis of the patterns of distraction over time. And he did that, I think, for ten or twelve weeks. And he watched how people changed over time as they learned to meditate, and he found three phases. In the first phase, when you focus on the object, you constantly have to bring the mind back. The Tibetans call that "frequent enforceable engagement." You have to put in a lot of effort, and you have to keep bringing it back over and over again. Don't worry about the number of times you have to bring it back; the mind is a crazy elephant; it's going to wander all over the place. But there's a cumulative effect: the more you bring it back, the more you train it. If you wander a lot, so what? Most people do at the beginning. But, if you continue to bring it back, the cumulative effect of that over time will be that the mind will start to stay for longer durations.

The second phase that Michael found in his research was that if you get a run for maybe five minutes where the mind has stayed on the object, then you get an equal one that was completely lost in a daydream for five minutes. So, the duration of staying on the object increased, and the duration of being distracted increased. But there was a third phase, which is much more interesting, and that is that as meditators developed some skill, they stayed continuously on the object of concentration, and there were no more daydreams. And there wasn't a lot of thought activity to distract them. They had achieved one of the first things you achieve in concentration, and we call that "continuous staying." The mind stays continuously over time for longer and longer periods of time.

When I was in Burma learning from Mahāsī Sayādaw, the mindfulness person, ironically, they had a very strict recommendation for what deep concentration was, even though it was largely a mindfulness system. You could follow the rising and falling of the breath for an hour, have no more than five thoughts come up, and notice the thoughts immediately and dissipate them. That's staying, pretty continuously. Imagine what it would be like to stay continuously on whatever you put the mind on, for as long as you put it there, with no or very little extraneous thought activity in the background. Remarkable. But that's the goal of concentration.

The word concentration in Tibetan is a compound term: *shiné* [pronounced "she nay"], *newa* [pronounced "nay-wah"], means to stay. With concentration training, the mind stays for longer and longer durations on the concentration object. *Shiwa* [pronounced "she wah"] means calm. The more the mind is trained to stay, the more all the extraneous background noise calms down, and eventually it stops, and then the mind gets more organized. The more you train attention, the more you stop that psychic entropy that Czikszentmihalyi discovered. And more and more what the person who is systematically training attention discovers is it has an organizing effect on the unfolding of mental events. Hence in the Western research Czikszentmihalyi called this a "flow state," because flow implies organization, like a river flowing. It's not entropic; it doesn't bounce around anymore and get scattered all over the place. The more you concentrate, the more organized the mind actually becomes. That's a direct experiential effect. *Shiné*—the word literally means staying-calming meditation. It stays on whatever you put it on; the background noise gets calmer and calmer.

So, you can measure the progress of concentration from one of two perspectives. First is the duration of staying. A good benchmark that we use is for a given meditation session if, say, you're sitting for fifteen minutes, what's the percentage of time you stay on the concentration object? Beginners stay less than 50 percent of the time. A good goal for a beginning concentration is to see if you can train yourself to stay 80-100 percent of the time. There's a whole other set of problems that come up. But, 80-100 percent of the time staying on the object is good concentration to start with.

Another benchmark is what happens to thought. If you let the mind spin out—the wild elephant-mind—thought is said to become more and more elaborated. The Tibetan word for that is *trulwa*, to become more complex or more elaborated. Thought starts from simple bursts of movement and energy, and those become organized into fleeting thoughts. They happen so quickly that you can't recognize the content, but you know you're thinking. Those get more organized into specific thoughts. Now you know that you're thinking and now you know the content. Those get more organized into association, a series of thoughts in a row that are somehow connected with each other, though not necessarily in an obvious way. And finally, we get daydreams. We call that the continuum of thought elaboration. At the head, the simple bursts of movement in the mind, like a hundred thousand mind-moments in the blink of an eyelash. At the other [end] we get complex daydreams. The further along the continuum of thought elaboration, the more complex the product of thought. The further along the continuum from head to tail, the more awareness drops out. That's why we get lost in our daydreams. We don't even know we're having them, completely lost.

But if you train concentration, it reverses that thought elaboration cycle. It winds down rather than winds up as a byproduct of deep concentration. What does it mean? You get less frequent thoughts, which means rather than having thoughts seeming to be there all the time, there'll be times when thought is moving through the mind and times when the mind is quiet or still and there's no thought. The periods of stillness get longer, and the periods of the movement of thought get shorter and shorter. In other words, there'll be less frequent episodes of thought; it's not a constant thing. Secondly, the magnitude of thought elaboration gets simpler. After a while, all that's left is fleeting thoughts, very quick movements of thought to keep the meditation on track. All that daydreaming stuff, all the associations, or even specific thoughts, it all drops off, and the mind becomes calm—so, *shiné*, staying-calming meditation. You can measure it in terms of the continuity of staying, how complete your staying on the object is, or you can measure it in terms of a decrease in frequency and magnitude of thought elaboration. They're both legitimate ways of marking progress.

So, that's the general overview. Now, in terms of the object of concentration, it's not important. There's no right or wrong object for concentrating. In the Asanga tradition, the Tibetan name for this path is called the Semnegu, the nine states of the mind staying. Notice the emphasis. It's on degrees of staying. There's no emphasis in the title of that text in terms of what the mind is staying on because it doesn't matter. It's very important that you understand this because all that matters in terms of concentration practice is the refinement of the degree of staying on the object. Serviceability: whatever you put your mind on, it stays only on that, like a laser, for as long as you want the staying—even hours—and it doesn't go anywhere else; there's no extraneous thought in the background. That's a serviceable, concentrated mind. But we are so used to looking at the content of our mind that we lose the forest for the trees. It's the degree of staying that matters. So, the concentration object doesn't make any difference.

Some Mahāmudrā texts say, "Take a stone or a stick and put it in front of you and focus on that." What difference does it make? It's not like in Woody Allen's movie *Annie Hall* when at a party someone calls 911 because they forgot their secret mantra. [Laughter] There's no secret mantras here. It doesn't make one difference what you're focused on. It doesn't. And the reason why it's so important is that a lot of people in the beginning confuse experiences with the task at hand.

The task at hand is always the degree of staying. So, what does it mean? Don't think. If you are meditating for fifteen minutes, and you're spending 75 percent of that time thinking, "Ooh, these thoughts are really interesting," because finally—we're so busy—you get quiet for the first time. We never are with ourselves.

I used to teach this with Denma Locho Rinpoche, who was the head Abbott of Namgyal Monastery, the Dalai Lama's monastery in Dharamsala. One time, Denma Locho and I we were teaching in the West, and one of the students said, "What do we do about laziness in our practice, our everyday practice?" And he said, "Nooooo, laziness is for monks in the monastery. You Westerners, you're not lazy, you're busy. Busyness is your laziness." That's very astute. We're so busy that we're never quiet with ourselves so we sit down to meditate, [but] we don't meditate. We chase after interesting thoughts thinking, "Oh those are nice. I didn't know I was thinking that." [Laughter]

In Burma, at Mahāsī Sayādaw's center, there's a three-month retreat that I took many years ago in the late 1970s with Mahāsī Sayādaw when he was alive. Two thirds of the people who took that retreat over a forty-year span—which is a long time, big statistic—two thirds of those people reached first path, first gradation of awakening. In the same course taught in the U.S. … as a psychologist, we did outcome studies on those meditators for ten years, and a hundred and twenty people would sit that course each year. I followed 120 people a year for ten years.

In each course, out of a 120 people, we'd get about two dozen people who got modestly concentrated, and maybe one person every two years who reached first path. Same course. Sometimes the Burmese teachers came over and taught it. That's a lousy track record. So, I once asked one of the teachers who had taught in India and Burma, "Look, it's the same course. How come the Westerners don't get anywhere?" He said, "They don't meditate, they do therapy." And what he meant is that they spend all of the time chasing after thought. Either you're on the concentration object, or you're distracted. However interesting that thought is, if you chase after it, you're off the object. If during a fifteen-minute period you're spending 75 percent of your time engaging in thought on the balance sheet, you trained yourself to be skilled in thinking.

But on the balance sheet, if during that fifteen minutes you spend 80 percent of your time staying on the object, and when a thought comes up or other distractions you immediately turn away from it, on the balance sheet, you're training concentration.

So, when you're meditating, don't think.

You won't stop thinking, but you can stop engaging it, and that makes all the difference in the world. If you keep bringing the mind back to the concentration object, it stays. Then of course, there are lots of other interesting things to distract you because you're going to have a lot of state changes during the concentration. You're going to have all sorts of bliss, and you get luminosity and quietness. If you focus on the rising and falling of the breath, people think, "Well maybe I should focus here, or I should focus down there. Where do I focus?" We don't care where you locate it; just wherever it is, stay! Because the issue is staying. We don't care what you're staying on.

Asanga's smart. He called it Semnegu, Nine Stages of Staying, because he's trying to get you to train out of looking for experiences and because we are experience junkies. We're always looking for the content of our mind. As soon as you train yourself out of the content, and just stay on the object, and you disengage that content and just stay on the object, the elephant mind will settle down. So, don't cancel out the effects as you're learning to do this. Then the mind will really stay.

In the older Theravādin literature, there's all sorts of classifications in terms of how this type of personality should use this type of meditation object and how that type of personality should use that type of meditation object. It doesn't make any difference. We like to use the breath and the body because as Westerners, we think too much. So, if you take a sensory based or a kinesthetic based object, it will get you out of your head quicker. The felt sense of the breath, or the felt sense of the body, is a much better meditation object for Westerners because you concentrate more quickly because you get out of your head.

One more thing—the body itself. When you meditate, posture matters, okay? Many of you said you have a yoga background. If I asked you right now to all lie down on the floor and start meditating, what would happen? Think about the end of yoga class. You'd get sleepy. And what happens to your mind when you get sleepy? You wander more, not less, right? There's your default option that we talked about earlier. A resting mind wanders, and you get lost in all these daydreams; and you get sleepy and sort of drift into this reverie state. That is not meditation.

Unfortunately, in the West—because we like to reduce everything to things that we understand, but not necessarily understand accurately—some years ago in behavioral medicine, people began to classify meditation as a relaxation response. It's wrong from the body point of view, because if you relax the body too much, it's much harder to train meditation. The best studies on that were done a long time ago, in 1970 at Kyoto University by Akashige. And what he did is he took an EMG [electromyograph], which measures muscle activation in the big muscle groups of the body—striate muscle activation—and he wired up all the main muscle groups with EMG with beginning and very skilled advanced Zen monks from all of the monasteries in Kyoto. There are a lot of monasteries and Zen monks in Kyoto. And what he found surprised everybody, because it disproved the notion that, from the perspective of the striate musculature, that meditation is relaxing. A more accurate discovery was, from the perspective of the striate musculature, meditation is an even output of distribution of muscle work. If I use the big muscle groups in my body like the psoas and latissimus dorsi and erector spinae and things like that, and I sit like this [upright and cross-legged], it takes a lot of muscle work to hold up the upper trunk. If I take my hands and I put them like this [holding them up just below the navel] and I have to hold them up rather than flopping them down, it takes a fair amount of muscle work to do this. And I have to keep holding the body like this. What happens is if I keep holding the body like that for say the full meditation session, the cumulative effect of that is that it guarantees a certain optimal level of alertness, so I don't get too dull or sleepy. I stay more alert and awake just by holding the body posture, as opposed to lying down to meditate. And second, Akashige found that the more you hold the body posture firm, it was significantly correlated with less wandering of the mind rather than more. So, there's less of that background noise; the mind is calmer, and, therefore, easier to train the elephant. So, the posture matters.

You know, the first great tradition that developed meditation was Patanjali's Yoga Sutras. And there, for those of you that have a yoga background, that is where all those postures came from. Unfortunately, as Westerners, we forgot that the posture is only the first *āṅga*, the first limb. There are eight limbs to concentration. The posture was just preparatory for the rest of the limbs of this practice, all of which are involved in concentration practice, the different aspects that support concentration practice. But what we do is we make the postures things in themselves. So, we tack a little meditation on for the last five minutes when you rest. That's not meditation. Nobody trains the mind in yoga class anymore.

So, we've taken out the concentration practice from the great system of Patanjali. When Maharishi came over, he took out the posture. He thought it was too hard. So, you can sit in a chair and spin your mantra. And what are you training yourself to do? To get dull and sleepy? To weave your mantra in and out of a wandering mind? That's not good practice. I'm just being truthful. I'm not trying to be critical here. Just saying what is. We know better.

So, if you hold the body up—and you don't have to sit in a lotus posture—you can sit in the chair and hold it but lean against the back of the chair. You can stand up and meditate. Any one of those three positions involves an even output in distribution of muscle work. You've got to understand the basic principles here. So, if you hold the body posture so there's an even output in distribution of muscle work, and you keep tying the rope of mindfulness onto the concentration object, whatever that may be—in this case, the rising and falling of the breath and the body—and you keep bringing it back, the cumulative effect of that is the mind will stay for longer and longer periods. And all that background noise and thought elaboration will fade, and all that's left is a completely concentrated mind that stays. After a while, the concentration is so great that when you reach the last of the nine states of the elephant path of mind, it's like a laser beam, and goes freely. The mind works not with thought, but with intention, and intention is a property of awareness. It's much quicker than thought.

Whatever mind intends, it goes just to that and stays on it as long as you want, with no extraneous background. That's useful in everyday life. It's a fundamental skill, but you're not going to stop thinking.

I had an interesting experience with that because in medical school, I teach a course in performance excellence for athletes, and also for people in the work site; and more recently that course became popular with judges. So, after doing a kind of brief performance excellence course for the judges, some of the judges wanted to follow up with more extensive training just in concentration. So, we did a whole day on concentration. And about a third of the way through the day when thought activity was all fading and they had not very much thought, one of the judges raised his hand, very concerned, and he said, "Look, we never have our time, we don't have enough time to write up our findings. So, if I get more concentrated and all this thought elaboration stops, how am I ever going to think to get my findings done?" And I said, "Trust me. I'll answer your question experientially at the end of the day; you'll see for yourself. Just keep concentrating."

So, at the end of the day when they got very concentrated, I said, "Okay, now what I'd like you to do with a fully serviceable mind is I'd like you to think about something silently. You can't share it with anybody else. Think silently to yourself about some case finding you're trying to write up and try and see what happens when you use directive thought with a fully concentrated mind." And what they discovered—most of the group discovered—is that all that laser like property of a concentrated mind can be used in directive thought. But what's interesting is that there's no extraneous background noise. So, the thinking is clean and sharp and right to the point, because the only thing that goes is not the capacity to think. You can use that laser-like property once you train the mind, for anything, because the elephant mind is now serviceable. You have the full strength and intelligence of that mind. If you want to use it for directive thinking, that thinking is clean, laser-like, and right to the point. So, then it becomes a skill.

We use about 2 percent of what the mind is capable of. We waste it. It's a wonderful instrument. Train it. See for yourself. It's not even hard to do. At the beginning it takes some work.

So that dovetails us into the second part, which is the suggestion that learning to meditate is about as hard as learning to drive a car, which means that when you first start, it seems completely impossible and overwhelming. And not long after that, you're learning it and it's second nature.

Another metaphor is training a horse. If you hold the reins too loose, the horse will keep pulling away to eat things. Likewise, if you hold the mind—*trinpa* literally means, in Tibetan, to tighten—we call it "intensify." If you tighten the reins and hold it tighter on the object and closer on the object, it's not going to be able to wander off because you're not giving it any play; you're not giving any slack, so it stays more on the object. You'll train concentration much quicker that way. You don't have any trouble understanding that the steering wheel and the accelerator are different tools in a car. Now you have to come to see in your direct experience that directing the mind to the object, and then, once you turn away from other things, stay on that object, that's a different skill, engaging it more closely.

In neuroimaging, where we can take live action shots of the brain, there's an area of the frontal system called the anterior cingulate cortex, or the ACC. That's the area of the brain that gets activated when you have competing attentional demands and you have to decide between how to apportion your attention from one thing or another. So, the classic way of studying that in Western psychology is the Stroop test. I show you an index card and it has a text that says red, but the color of that text is green. So, you do a double take. Do you focus on the text, or do you focus on the color? This is an example of competing attentional demands. When you give people tasks like that, the ACC becomes activated because you have to put added effort into deciding to focus on this as opposed to that. The ACC is that area of the brain that's offline, it's underactive in adults and children who have attention deficit disorder. Ritalin selectively turns the ACC back on. It puts it back online.

When people are hypnotized, when they go into a trance state and they are constantly reminded what to focus on, all hypnotic inductions activate the ACC. When people train concentration meditation like you're going to learn tonight, it activates the ACC. The brain is an equal opportunity employer and doesn't care whether you use drugs or mind-body techniques. They all do the same thing. They all activate the ACC and turn it back on. Only long-term concentrators show an increase in the volume and structure of the white matter tracks [i.e., axons] that come into and out of the ACC. The brain is plastic. If you use it, you develop more of the structure. If you don't use it, it shrinks and atrophies the same way that muscles do. So, if you really train this, at a certain point, you're training new structures and it won't go offline anymore. It becomes a skill that you'll never lose at a certain point. Concentration training is about activating and training the ACC.

September 5, 2012

Themes: Buddhist History; Beyond Representation; Awakening Beyond Time

Dan

Welcome everyone.

So, here's what we're going to do tonight. Usually, we open up for whatever people raise, but last time we did a review of concentration that people thought, I think, was useful. And tonight, I'm going to give you an overview of the whole path, and part of that is … oh, I want to say, "Hi Britta." This is Britta. And Britta is a neuroimaging person, and she's done studies on functional MRI and the neuroimaging of mindfulness meditation and concentration meditation. So, she's one of the main persons looking at what happens with the brain during concentration, and particularly with mindfulness—some of the best studies.[12]

But Burmese mindfulness, I suggested to her, is a hybrid system that mixes … it confounds concentration and awareness training, and traditionally those are separated out. But what I suggested is that if she really wanted to get an understanding of these traditions, no one's doing neuroimaging of the heart of

---

12 Britta K. Holzel's published mindfulness meditation study: "How Does Mindfulness Meditation Work? Proposing Mechanisms of Action From a Conceptual and Neural Perspective."

this, which is awakening. So, talking about the nature of these practices and how it leads to awakening and the refinement of awakening up to buddhahood is the heart of this tradition. It's not about sitting still; it's not about becoming more mindful. The only reason to do these practices is because all of those meditation techniques will move you in the direction of an awakened mind. So, I thought we might talk about that tonight a bit as a way of emphasizing what these practices are about.

Historically, within Buddhism there are three developments, and they're referred to as the Three Turnings of the Wheel. And the first is associated with the Buddha Shakyamuni. Upon enlightenment, his first lecture at Sarnath was on the Four Noble Truths and the eightfold path. And most of that practice was about the nature of suffering. The first noble truth is often translated as "the truth of suffering." More accurately, in Pali, *dukkha* means reactivity. And what Buddha was describing is that there is a bias in our ordinary information processing. If you look carefully at your experience, whenever something comes into our field of awareness, if we like it, the mind moves towards it to make more of it. And if we don't like it, the mind moves away from it to make less of it. Or the mind can just leave it alone. Or the mind is oblivious to it. But whenever it moves towards it to make more of it or [away to make] less of it, it's reacting to it. And it's that moment by moment reactivity that Buddha saw as the source of what causes suffering.

But suffering is the end state description of that process. What he was really trying to get at is how you look at your own information processing system so that you can actually see the mind moving towards to make more of something it likes, or the mind moving away from something it doesn't like. I once studied with Taungpulo Sayadaw in Burma. And he had an interesting meditation. He used four categories: mind moving towards; mind moving away; something just happened, and you were oblivious to it and you noticed that after the fact, in other words, mind not aware; or mind being purely aware without reacting to it. Those are the four possibilities. And those first three possibilities are what were called the three poisons. Mind moving towards causes desire; mind moving away causes aversion; mind being oblivious causes confusion, ignorance.

But again, translated into an actual practice, if you're looking at your information processing system, Taungpulo Sayadaw's whole approach is, what do you do? You catalog everything every moment and there are four possibilities; and what are you going to find? Lots of moments of mind moving towards, lots of moments of mind moving away, lots of moments of being oblivious, and every now and then a moment of pure nonreactive awareness. And if you keep looking at it like that, it starts to shift the balance towards pure awareness, nonreactive awareness. And then the whole substrate of suffering that's built into how we process information subsides. That's the foundation of the first turning of the wheel of Buddhism.

The second turning of the wheel of Buddhism at Vulture Peak in India was the Prajñāpāramitā or the wisdom literature. There was the whole notion of emptiness. In the old Buddhism, the three insights were [first,] *dukkha*, the built-in reactivity of the mind. The second, impermanence: everything is impermanent, always changing. If you look at mind states, they don't ever stay the same. They're always changing. And the third, which is problematic, was *anātman*, no self. If you concentrate the mind long enough, the sense of your personal identity drops away. So, it's no longer Dan meditating, it's awareness itself that's guiding the meditation rather than Dan. And if you concentrate enough, that personal identity gets deconstructed temporarily. And that was in the older Buddhism, *anātman*, no self.

In the second revision of the teachings, that notion of no self got completely rebuilt into what was called emptiness practices. That's a very unfortunate term. If you want a good synonym for emptiness practice, it means that everything is a construction of mind. Mahāyāna Buddhism and the notions of emptiness are very much like modern cognitive sciences in the West where we see everything as constructions. Perception is a construction system. Memory is constructed. Thought is constructed. In other words, the nature of the mind is to make representations.

But what happens is that once we make those representations, we reify them. We actually think that we're seeing a world out there. What we're seeing is our own constructions because all we can be aware of is what we construct. You're looking at your own representations of mind. When we say something is empty, we're not saying it doesn't exist. We're saying it exists as a construction; we're de-reifying it. [And] if you look at it that way, it defines the way out. On the relative level of truth, everything seems to exist. We seem to have a world where we all behave as if we see the same thing, which isn't exactly true. But we see roughly the same thing because we all share the same perceptual apparatus.

But Buddhism isn't interested in defining what's out there like science is. Buddhism, and its interest, is a soteriological system. It defines the way out. It frees you. The whole idea is if you look at everything as a construction, two things happen. Things lose *dzin-pa*, grab. And second and more importantly, they lose *mümpa*. They lose the capacity to obscure. The sense of self is a construction. Dan-ness is a construction. I didn't come into the world with Dan. Self-psychologists in the West say that we construct a psychological sense of self at around eighteen months. We construct representations for attachment to other people around the same time. Why? Because between twelve and twenty-four months is when we develop representational thinking. The outcome of that is I have a sense of self. That's useful. It organizes my everyday life around Dan-ness. In relative reality that's useful. But then I take it too seriously, I reify it. I actually think that Dan exists beyond being a construction. And with that comes grab. With that comes the capacity to obscure.

So, emptiness practice is a way of seeing things just the way they are, to look into them. If I try and find Dan-ness, where am I going to find it? If I use my awareness—because awareness works at high speeds, much more quickly than conceptualization—and I roam everywhere through my experience, everywhere I look, I can't find any independently existing thing. Anything in itself that is "Dan" keeps slipping away. With all these complex discussions of schools of thought and theories of emptiness in Buddhism, His Holiness the Dalai Lama says it comes down to one simple principle, *nyedme*, unfindable-ness. If I roam around with my awareness everywhere through my experience, I can't find Dan-ness. And it starts receding from my awareness as the target I was looking for. It's kind of a negative search task in Western psychological terms. I keep looking for it; I can't find it.

But the outcome of that search is that something shifts in my experience, and if I do emptiness practice correctly, I start seeing something about the nature of awareness that wasn't clear before—*mümpa*. The construction of Dan doesn't get in the way because when I finished the emptiness practice, I've shifted my basis of operation. So, I'm now operating out of a kind of awareness that's cleaned up of the Dan-ness, as a structure or a construction of mind. It doesn't obscure anymore. So that refinement of seeing everything as a construction in such a way that it doesn't get in the way is the nature of emptiness practice, the second big discovery within Buddhism. And I don't have to get rid of Dan. Dan is pretty useful in everyday life—a central organizing principle. All I have to do is get rid of Dan's capacity to obscure. Then, if Dan's still there in the background, so what? It just doesn't get in the way anymore. So that's emptiness practice. The other practices that develop during that second turning of the wheel were all the practices of compassion, *bodhisattva* practices.

Then there was a third turning of the wheel, and that had to do with the Essence traditions. The Essence traditions were the traditions developed by a lineage of what we call the eighty-four *siddhas* or the eighty-four masters. And they were proponents of looking into the true nature of the mind and awakening to that. They wandered around. It was a popular movement. They sang little song poems as a way of teaching. People were sung into awakening. And they developed a way of looking into the heart of the matter, the essence of it. Because when you do emptiness practice, we say that emptiness practice is an affirming negation. You're negating this to affirm that. You're negating seeing this personal identity, Dan-ness in my case, as too solid. So, what will open up in your awareness if you do it correctly is you're affirming something about the nature of awareness. It's what's left after you do your search. It's far more interesting.

And that's the heart of the Essence traditions. And it's always about the nature of awareness. In the Essence traditions, the fundamental metaphor is that we all have buddha nature. It's part of our hard-wiring. And the way to understand that is like the sun. If it's raining out [with] very dark clouds like it was this morning and then suddenly the clouds clear up like it did this afternoon, we say that "the sun just came out." Is that true? The sun's always been out. It's always shining. But from our perspective, we couldn't see the brilliance of that sun because the clouds were in the way. In the Essence traditions, the whole idea is to clear away the clouds as obscuring the real nature of the mind, and the awakened nature of the mind shines forth here all the time. It's not a state that you discover. It's not anything out there. It's the heart of your true nature that's always shining forth with its brilliance all the time, but it gets clouded over by all these constructions of mind.

So, the path systematically clears away clouds until there are no clouds left. Essence traditions—examples of practices would be Mahāmudrā (great gesture practice or great seal), and Dzogchen (Great Completion practice), and the *tantras*; those are the three Essence traditions.

Now, if you divide this practice into stages, the first stage of practice is to concentrate. Concentration does two things. The Tibetan word for concentration is *shiné* [pronounced shee-nay]. It's a compound term; it means … *newa* means to stay. *Shiwa* means calm. It means to keep focusing on a single concentration object like the rising and falling of the breath, and that's all you do; and every time the mind turns away to some distraction, either by thought or sense experience, you turn it back, much like steering the steering wheel in a car. The Tibetan word is *semtong*, which means to steer or to direct the mind.

And then once you direct the mind away from all that stuff towards the concentration object, you then engage the concentration object even more. We call that *chugpa*, to intensify on the object. Direct, intensify; direct, intensify, like using a steering wheel and then an accelerator in the car. You don't have any trouble understanding that the steering wheel and the accelerator are different tools. But in concentration, you need to use both of these things. In concentration, intensifying is the key to quick concentration. You find that well-developed in the Asanga tradition in Buddhism. You find intensifying well-developed in the great system of Patanjali's Yoga Sutras. You won't find any concept of intensifying in Burmese mindfulness or in Zen. And that's why these systems of concentration are more refined and quicker.

If you keep steering the mind and concentrating, the mind will stay continuously on the meditation object for longer and longer durations and ultimately will stay on the object without ever going off it. And it will stay on it a hundred percent. There's a concept in Buddhism called partial staying. Let's say this is the rising and falling of the breath. [Dan raises and lowers his arm] And when I train my concentration, I direct the mind towards the rising and falling. And after a while I can pick up the rising breath and I can pick up the falling breath continuously. And we call that continuous staying.

But you see, watch what's happening. After a while I get pretty good. I can stay with every cycle of the breath. But after a while what I'm noticing is I start to see that I'm picking up a piece of that rising breath, and as it's continuing to happen, I go back and engage in all that background noise of thought, and I pick up a piece of the falling breath and then I go back and engage in all that background noise. I'm apportioning my attention between the object of concentration and the background noise. Maybe 20 percent is on the object. We call that *neycha*, partial staying. And only 80 percent is still engaged in the background noise. So, at that point in concentration, I have to do additional practice that would allow me to stay, not only continuously over time, but cross-sectionally at any given point of time 100 percent. So, look at the difference between this and this. [Dan lifts both arms, first in opposing movement and then in parallel movement.] That we call complete staying. And when I get fully concentrated, I have both continuous staying over time and complete staying at any given point in time. Okay?

And the more I get concentrated, after a while, all that background noise drops away. There's an idea in Tibetan theory of mind called *chuwa*, which means to elaborate. Thought is said to occur along a continuum. Everything starts as quick bursts of energy and movement called mind moments, and those get constructed into fleeting thoughts where I recognize that I'm thinking but I can't tell the content. And those get constructed into specific thoughts where now I know I'm thinking, and I know the content. And those get constructed into associations where I get a series of thoughts that are loosely connected. And then I get complex reveries and daydream states. [Dan holds first one arm out to his side, then the other arm out to the other side.] This is called the tail end of the thought elaboration continuum. [He moves one hand.] This is the head. Where do we spend most of our time? [He moves the other hand.] In the tail. The further along I go along that continuum, the greater the degree of thought elaboration, the more complex the products. The further along, the more awareness drops out. That's why I get lost in my daydreams.

So, here's what happens. As you get very concentrated, after a while, thought elaboration will decrease in frequency and magnitude. So, after a while I get long periods where there's no thought-going activity at all. And then a little burst of thought rather than a continuous background noise, and the magnitude will get … The elaboration will wind down so I get simpler products. All what's left after a while is just fleeting thought, no daydreams anymore. And even that stops. All that's left are mind moments, one hundred thousand bursts of energy in the blink of an eyelash.

So that's called, in *shiné*, that's the calming component. All that background noise becomes calm. So now I'm staying fully on the object. In time—continuous staying—I'm staying completely, at any given point in time, cross-sectionally, and there's no background noise. The mind is laser-like. Whatever you put it on, it just does that. It does nothing else. We call that making the mind serviceable; it just does what you intend to put it on. For as long as you put it on that, it doesn't do anything else. There's no background noise. That stabilizes the mind. That's the first stage. You're no longer lost in thought.

And when all that thought elaboration winds down, you'll probably find that your sense of self, which is also an elaboration, will get deconstructed. So, the problem of who's doing the meditation will come up, and what you'll begin to see is that awareness is more involved. You'll get this taste of pure awareness, separated out from thought. You'll see that awareness is not the same as thought. In our waking state, we confuse awareness with thought. Nevertheless, you'll still at that point—the mind will be quiet and stable and you'll operate out of pure awareness. But that's still confused with personal identity. So, if I do emptiness of self practice, I clean that up. And I shift my basis of operation to awareness itself.

Now, awareness itself is doing the meditation. Dan isn't doing it anymore. Dan's sort of there in the background. A very important word in Tibetan Buddhism is *chöyul*, which I translate as "basis of operation." Where are you operating out of? In all these practices you learn to shift. In our waking state, where do we operate out of? We operate out of thought mode. When I get deeply concentrated, I learn to operate out of awareness mode, *rigpa*, rather than thought mode. When I do emptiness itself, I learn to operate out of what we call *rang rigpa*, awareness itself, rather than Dan mode. I'm cleaning up the clouds, you see?

But that awareness will tend to fluctuate because another huge construction of mind is time. Nagarjuna came along and did a whole complex meditation on looking at the nature of time so we can see it as just a construction. We tend to make it too solid, just like out-there-ness is too solid. Time as a construction develops late in childhood. The calendrical structure of time where we sort events into episodes in a calendar doesn't develop until concrete operational thinking develops. It's at about eight or nine years old. Young childhood is rather timeless. But once we develop time as a construction of mind, it's a mixed blessing. In relative reality, it's useful because we organize everything around time; it becomes a central organizing principle. But in ultimate reality, we reify it. We forget that it's merely a construction of mind. We make it as an outside thing. We think there's an externally self-existing time clock, a cosmic clock, we even locate in Greenwich. It's a complete fiction.

And with that comes *dzin-pa*, grab. Time has its own tyranny like the rabbit in *Alice in Wonderland:* "I'm late, I'm late, for a very important date." We developed the disease of hurry sickness. What if it's all just a construction and I can see it just the way it is by doing emptiness of time meditation? If I do it correctly, I'm no longer making time too solid. I'm not going to get rid of it. Things will still seem to come and go in relative reality, but I'll get rid of its capacity to obscure. I'll move beyond the convention of time, and that's huge—because what will open up is a level of awareness that's beyond time. And what is that like? Well, because time and space are interconnected, that awareness will suddenly seem huge and boundless, and it will be absolutely changeless.

Now if I make that my basis of operation through emptiness of time, that's rather convenient because once I lock onto that boundless, changeless awareness, I can't lose it, because it can't go away in time, you see. And I've cleaned up the cloud of the convention of time enough so it doesn't obscure. And now I know changeless, boundless awareness. And that's the heart, the beginning of the great vehicle. And along with that timelessness, everything that appears within the field of that boundless, changeless awareness is all interconnected. In Western information processing terms, we've shifted our temporal processing mode to simultaneous processing mode. Everything's here all at once. Everything hangs together all at once. And you learn to operate out of that just extraordinary different state. That's the starting point for the great vehicle of the Mahāyāna. It's the starting point for all the Essence traditions.

Now there's a point in there where I open up a field of awareness that's boundless and changeless, and I let everything arise within that field of boundless, changeless awareness, and it all is an aspect of the very field of awareness itself. See in the Essence traditions, it's all about awareness. And awareness has a knowing aspect, and awareness has an expressive aspect. We call that the liveliness of awakened awareness. This whole thing here is a dance of awareness, expressing itself to itself and knowing itself through its lively expressiveness. So, when I practice that meditation beyond the convention of time, everything that arises is viewed from the vantage point of an ocean of changeless, boundless awareness. Sometimes we use the metaphor of Ocean and Waves—an ocean of changeless, boundless awareness viewing its own waves. And whatever arises is just another momentary dance with no substance. And there you get a taste of what we call spacious freedom because whatever arises has absolutely no grab left to it. It comes and goes, and you learn to operate out of that boundless, changeless awareness all of the time.

Now that's where you get into the realm where what we call mental pliancy, or the quickness or the speed of that awareness, will definitely deepen. So much so that if you start looking at how everything comes up in this, like waves in the ocean, you start noticing the waves more and more at the very moment of arising, and everything is seen as an empty momentary appearance as soon as it begins to express itself, and the whole thing gets automatic. We call that automatic emptiness. Everything comes up of its own momentum, and everything just releases itself as empty with no grab. On and off the pillow, it goes on all the time. That automatic emptiness is the starting point for all the instructions for awakening.

Why? Because if you get the instructions for awakening before that point, you'll harden the mind through conceptualizing about awakening. Conceptualization is like a huge cloud. Anytime you conceptualize about state or outcome, it makes it cloud over even more. Every time you're operating out of self, it clouds over even more. The self doesn't awaken. Awakening happens to itself by itself. It's the wisdom of your own intelligence, innate intelligence. All you have to do is clear away the clouds. Now, when everything gets automatic, you see, as soon as you notice a tendency to conceptualize it, it releases itself. So, conceptualization can't get in the way if you have that as your foundational state. As soon as you want to focus on something, the tendency to focus or make anything happen or look at anything, that's empty too.

But here's the last big cloud. The last big cloud is your information processing system. Here's why. We can classify levels of operation. The slowest part of our information processing system is conceptualizing. Quicker than that would be directing our attention to something. Even quicker to that is a term that we don't even have a term for in the West. In Indo-Tibetan Buddhism, it's called particularizing—the tendency of the mind towards something, the outcome of which is to pick out something particular. It's like an action potential. It's the quickest movement of our information processing system. You want to understand particularizing? Take a panoramic view of the world right now. Try and take in everything at this room. And if you're really careful, you keep noticing the mind going this way and that to pick out things. It's impossible to hold the whole thing at once. That's particularizing. Okay?

So here's the issue. Your information processing system as it operates is your biggest cloud. Right here, all the time, is an ocean of boundless awareness-love, which is your true nature like the sun that always shines. But every operation of your information processing system, every moment operates in such a way that it clouds it over. And here's why. Every moment of conceptualizing delineates. A great Dzogchen scholar says the function of conceptualizing is to delineate. When I say it's this, it's not that. So, every moment of conceptualizing partializes this boundless wholeness of awareness-love that's already here, and it clouds it over in that instant at a quicker speed of our information processing system, directing attention towards something. As soon as I direct the mind towards this, I'm missing the rest of it. I'm partializing again.

And at the quickest operation of our information processing system, the tendency of the mind towards something—the outcome of which is to pick out something particular—that very tendency, as quick as it is, clouds things over because as soon as I'm moving in this direction, I've missed the whole of it that's always right here. What are called crossing-over instructions in Mahāmudrā, they're called *gomaypa*, non-meditation instructions, or what are called *trekchö*, thoroughly cutting through instructions in Dzogchen—they're all specialized ways of helping you to see through the operations every moment of your information processing system so that you are operating out of that unbounded wholeness of awareness-love that's always right here.

And that whole path is captured in the mantra of the heart sutra, which is why it's so popular in the Essence traditions. In Sanskrit it goes like this: "*Gate gate pāragate pārasamgate bodhi svāhā. Gate gate pāragate pārasamgate bodhi svāhā. Gate gate pāragate pārasamgate bodhi svāhā.*" And here's what it means in Sanskrit. *Gate*: gone. *Gate, gate*: "gone, gone." *Pāragate*: "gone beyond." *Pārasamgate*: "gone way beyond." *Bodhi svāhā*: "oooh, what a realization." That's the literal translation. And here's what it means in the Essence traditions. I'll unpack it for you.

The first cloud and the biggest cloud is we get caught up in thought, the default option of the dysfunctional mind, our thought and reverie states. Through concentrating the mind when the mind stays continuously and completely, the outcome of that also is calming. All that thought elaboration stops and winds down rather than winds up. And then in my direct experience, I can directly get a taste of what it's like to operate out of *rigpa*, awareness, rather than thought mode. I've separated out those things that we confuse so much in our waking state.

Gate, the first gate, *rigpa*, is awareness gone beyond thought. I've now shifted my operation, my basis of operation, out of thought mode into pure awareness mode through all the concentration training.

The second *gate. Gate gate.* But still I'm operating out of the construction of self, personal identity. I still think that Dan's doing the meditation. So then if I do the emptiness of self meditation, I'm not going to get rid of Dan, but I'm going to get rid of Dan's capacity to obscure. And if I do the emptiness correctly, I'm going to shift my basis of operation out of Dan-ness, and I'm going to shift it into rang *rigpa*. Now I'm going to mark it with the *rang* and say "awareness itself" to show that it's a different level of awareness.

So now I'm operating not out of awareness, but awareness that's freed up of the cloud of Dan-ness. That's the second *gate*. I've gone beyond personal identity to awareness itself as my basis of operation. That's where I'm operating out of. But still that awareness would tend to fluctuate within the convention of time. So with the emptiness of time meditations, I clean up that construction. I don't have to get rid of time, I just have to get rid of its capacity to obscure. And by doing that, I then shift to a boundless, changeless awareness, which is huge and absolutely changeless. And we call that *rangi rang rigpa*, awareness in and of itself, or sometimes we call it *mahkiwa*, ever-present awareness, always right here awareness.

And if I look into the nature of that awareness, and that's where I'm operating out of, and I'm beyond the convention of time, and I look at everything arising within the field of that awareness, and as an expression of that awareness, that awareness will turn to nonduality. Everything here is a field of awareness, and all this is the lively expressiveness of that very field itself. There is no duality.

Now I know nondual teachings are very popular. Do not confuse nonduality with awakening. There's a lot of false teaching out there about this. Nonduality is a nice state, but it's not awakening. It's a precursor, because you see, even though I have this boundless nondual field of awareness expressing itself to itself and knowing itself through its expressions—and that's huge, and there's a lot of spacious freedom within that—I'm still operating out of individual consciousness.

But then, if in that process of letting all the waves arise in this ocean very quickly and spontaneously, everything automatically becomes empty, I don't have to do anything anymore. So, all conceptualization releases itself right on the spot, in an instant, in a millisecond. All tendencies to focus the mind in this way and that way release itself. Automatic emptiness is the foundational state, it's like a clearing agent, it gets rid of all the tendencies to cloud over. The only last cloud is particularizing. And there is a certain way to set up a view that will get you beyond that so you start seeing the particularizing not as something you're going out to, but you learn to view it as all the liveliness of the awakening so all that activity of your information processing system doesn't cloud over. It's none other than the liveliness of that awakened state.

So after a while with the right view, you can't see anything but awakening. And if you hold that view the right way, without a sense of self getting in the way, without thought and conceptualizing, this awareness opens itself to itself, awakens itself to itself. The self—Dan—doesn't awaken. Awareness happens, awakens to itself once you get those structures out of the way, clears them away as clouds. And then you shift to this boundless, changeless ocean of awakened awareness that's very distinctly different from ordinary awareness. It's awake, it has awakeness, *hrige*. It has intensity to it, every moment, *gnar*. It's bright, *dangpa*; soft, *bole*. It has a spacious freedom to it and a stunning wonder. And if you develop this awakening so you have it all the time, you end up with *hedawa*, a state of chronic wonder. *Hedawa*. And nothing that arises within that ocean, that field of experience, has any grab left to it. You've cut to the root of all suffering.

Now, all of that has to do with shifting levels of awareness. I know that Burmese mindfulness is very popular in the West, but there's no concept of levels of awareness in Burmese mindfulness. The idea of levels of awareness are the heart of the Essence traditions like hyperspace, comes from Rechung. Rechung was the main student of the great Saint Milarepa. He's Milarepa's mini-me because it really means Little Mila, Rechung. [Gentle laughter by students.] So the original mini-me was Mila's mini-me. And Rechung was the one who put forth this notion of levels of awareness.

So let's unpack the Heart Sutra. We're clearing away the clouds. *Gate*: through concentration practice, you go beyond thought, and your basis of operation becomes awareness. *Pāragate*: through emptiness of self-practice, you go beyond personal identity as a cloud to awareness itself as your basis of operation. *Pāragate*: the bigger shift. Through practicing the emptiness of time, you go beyond the convention of time to a level of awareness that's boundless and timeless. It's a bigger shift, that's why it's *pāragate*, awareness in and of itself; ever-present awareness, changeless, boundless awareness; always right here, gone beyond the convention of time. And then through the practice of the crossing-over instructions, you go beyond the constraints of your information processing system to awakened awareness. That's a huge shift. Huge shift. So *pārasaṃgate*, gone way beyond the constraints of your information processing system to awakened awareness as your basis of operation. Oooh, what a realization.

Each one of these practices clears up the clouds so there's nothing that gets in the way of what's already right here. Or as the Sufi poet, says, "It's not hard to find a door when there are no walls." These emptiness practices clear up the boundaries, clear up the walls, the veils, the clouds. And when there's nothing left to get in the way or it's like a thin veil, this awakening happens to itself by itself. It's always right here. If you experience that, how do you know it's not conceptual? How do you know it's real? It's more authentic if it's likely to be accompanied by spontaneous compassion, spontaneous gratitude, spontaneous devotion. But as Rinpoche, who teaches with us, says, put yourself in difficult life circumstances. If the awakening deepens, you're likely to be on the right track. If it falls apart, it was likely to be conceptual.

Now there's a whole other map that takes those little flames of awakening—and so you develop them on the pillow for longer duration and more frequently—those are called *chungwa*, you have to nurture it. You keep setting up the conditions that open up that awakening so you'll operate out of it for more time, for longer duration, and greater frequency on the pillow. And then when you can open up on the pillow more of the time than not, most of the time, then you intentionally take it off the pillow. We call this *drewa*, mixing practices. Try and hold the awakening as your basis of operation without having it cloud over while you're out in nature, while you're moving. Try holding awakening during conversation. That's interesting. Try holding the awakening when you're working on your computer, when you're in deep sleep, when you're in dream sleep. And through mixing practices, you develop the awakening until you have it all the time. Never goes away. And after a while it possibly can't go away. That finishes the second map.

And the third map begins with [or when], you are now operating out of a boundless ocean of awareness-love. We call that the groundless ground of your being. Everything that arises within the field of that boundless, changeless awareness will arise very quickly and immediately dissipate, leaving no trace if you hold that view of awakening all the time. I call that automatic *dharmakāya* release because what happens is that when everything arises spontaneously within groundless ground and releases itself, you are no longer making new karmic impressions, because what makes karmic impressions is attending to it and fixing on it. Everything just comes up and leaves like writing on water; it immediately disappears. And because you're holding that state all the time, 24/7, automatically, you are not making any new karmic impressions.

So, the only thing left is that all previous karmic impressions will unwind, your whole database for lifetimes unwinds at an accelerated rate. We call that process *dharmadhātu* exhaustion. And the outcome of that is there are no negative states left. *Triwa*, the mind gets clean, more and more clean and bright, and at some point it will dawn on you that there are absolutely no negative states left in your experience. And what will flourish is all the positive states of your buddha nature. There are eighty positive states of a buddha mind. The flourishing of all the positive states; and there are absolutely no negative states left. That's one thing that happened. That third map we call buddha training.

The other thing that happens is all perception; there's nothing solid in the world anymore. Earlier it was dreamlike. Now everything changes to light—light, energy, and vibration. You see the whole world in those terms. It's all infinite variations on the theme of light and vibration and energy. And it gets very magical. We call that the practice of the wisdom energies.

The third thing that happens is the body gets transformed; the body loses its solidity. The body is just a field of energy. We call that clear light body. And no bodily states will have any grab. That's the hardest one to work with. If you really refine that, eventually the very elements of the body go into the hopper, too. You end up with rainbow body. Nothing is left except light.

And lastly and more interesting, there's a certain point along this whole path where you start to get a sense that this bubble here is just one bubble in an infinite sea of bubbles in this ocean of awareness-love. And the mind will naturally begin to express its limitlessness. And there'll be a kind of pervasion of the mind in all directions, beyond this bubble, to include all bubbles.

If you look at some of the original sutras, the degree of buddhahood is measured into the hundreds of thousands of worlds you'll open up all at once. This is called cracking the eggshell, the all-at-once-ness mind. And the scope of a full buddha mind contains all realms and times all at once with a mind that acts with enlightened activity for the sake of helping others in all planes of reality simultaneously, the ultimate of simultaneous mind. Then there isn't anything beyond that. Full buddhahood. Game over.

Now, please understand me. In the original turnings of the wheel, the first noble truth was about the truth of suffering. All of Theravāda Buddhism is about stopping, getting beyond suffering. That's not where the Mahāyāna goes with this or the Essence traditions. Stopping suffering is only the beginning of this. What's more important is the flourishing of all positive states, all the enlightened conduct of a full buddha, the flourishing of all eighty positive qualities of a buddha mind; the pervasion of the mind so its vast limitlessness encompasses all of reality—*thigle chenpo*—the one great sphere of a fully awakened mind; and it encompasses all realities at once in its boundless wholeness, its infinite scope of awareness-love. We call that the omniscient component of awakening. It doesn't open up in the older Buddhism practices because it doesn't open up the key of time, doesn't move beyond some of the clouds. So these refinements opened up a whole different thing here.

That's your path—stunning. Know what you're getting. The heart of the practice is awakening to your true nature. And when you know it? "*Bodhi svāhā*"—"Oooh, what a realization." That, my friends, is why we do the practice. And if you refine that awakening, the ultimate authenticity of that awakening is always and necessarily *choepa*, conduct. It's how you live your life, and how you act towards other people. That's the only thing that matters. That's the heart of this. If your practice is deep, you act differently in the world. If it's not, it's just conceptual. The only mark of authenticity is *choepa*, conduct.

Something that William James, the great American psychologist, said over a hundred years ago in his book—great book, *The Varieties of Religious Experience*—when somebody asked him, "How can you tell then genuine spirituality from all this religious institutional stuff?" And his answer was, quote: "By their fruits, ye shall know them." End quote. It's how you live your life. It's how you live your life towards others. Awakening to your true nature, and you live a good life, and a life that contributes to the greater good of others. That's the heart of this practice.

October 24, 2012

Themes: External and Internal Refuge; Positive States; Virtue

Dan

Welcome everyone. You have a question?

Student 1

During the Level 3 retreat, at one point, with Rinpoche, there seemed to be a distinction that was drawn between just taking refuge, and between doing it externally or internally. But Rinpoche seemed to be showing us the way to do it internally. At the time, I understood it, but since then I conceptualized my way out of that, and I wonder if you could speak about the difference.

Dan

Are you sure you can't conceptualize your way back into it?

Students

[Laughter]

Student 1

Maybe with your help. [Laughter]

Dan

Okay. So, the question is, what is the difference between external and internal taking refuge in the Indo-Tibetan Buddhist *dharma*? So, let's begin with external refuge. In the Indian Mahāyāna, you do three things: you take refuge in the Buddha, the *dharma*, and the *sangha*.

What does that mean? It means that you begin your practice by taking refuge in the Buddha, who is the exemplar of what's possible with your own spiritual development—a fully realized buddha. So, if other people can do it, then maybe you can do the same thing. And although we sometimes make reference to Buddha Shakyamuni—in the West we tend to impose our own ideas on that, like there's only one historical buddha that's like Buddha Shakyamuni, like there's one historical Jesus … It's not like that. There are many buddhas. And there are, if you look at some of the sutras, there are thousands and thousands of buddhas at certain times. Because anybody can do this. So, from that point of view, the buddha serves as a kind of model for what's possible with your own spiritual development and realization.

And then, in terms of external refuge, you take refuge in the *dharma*. And what that means is that the *dharma* means the set of teachings. These teachings have been around for a long time because they work. And they work for generation after generation in the same way. So, unlike science, which is forever innovative, Buddhism is somewhat conservative. It doesn't change around the techniques once they work. So, you use them the same way, each generation, if they work. You modify them in small ways, according to the needs of that particular culture and time in history. But the essence of it never changes, the heart of it, because it works.

The Western equivalent would be, in therapy, in medicine, we talk about evidence-based treatment. We use these methods instead of those methods because these methods are empirically supported. They tend to work better. And to take refuge in the *dharma* is something similar to that. It's a body of teachings that's worked to get people there, over many generations.

And then thirdly, you take refuge in the supporting community, the *sangha*. You don't practice alone. You practice with the support of others, and sometimes you're behind and sometimes you're further along. And everybody supports each other, without competitiveness, because collaboration means better practice. You're not doing it alone, and you share with each other your discoveries and the things that you learn because Buddhism is an entire world. And a good way of understanding the *sangha* would be—well, since I teach in a medical school, I think of it in terms of the fundamental change in the way that interns and residents were taught when I first started, almost over thirty years ago, to the way they're taught now. Because in those days the model of teaching interns and residents was essentially a surgery model. You teach by shame and humiliation. Highly competitive. And somewhere along the line people realized that that was a wasted model. It never got anywhere good. And the reason why it changed was—with great resistance to change it—quite honestly there was just too much stuff for people to remember. So, they shifted more to a collaborative model, where each member of the team was responsible for a certain domain of information, so that's your stuff.

My kid is now in medical school and just finished his cadaver. And each of the team had a different piece of the cadaver that was their responsibility. And you can't do it alone. It's too much to remember and memorize. But as a team, each shares with the rest. You came in that generation, some of you, when it was much more collaborative. That wasn't the way my generation was. And it's similar in Buddhism. When you have a *sangha*, this is a huge and profoundly deep world, the *dharma*. You can't master it all. So, when you take refuge in the *sangha*, you take refuge in the people you're doing this with who are going to share with you things that you won't know, because you can't cover it all.

So that's the original model in Indian Mahāyāna Buddhism. Now, when it got transferred to Tibet, they changed it a bit. We say in the Indian Mahāyāna that there are three refuge objects: Buddha, *dharma*, *sangha*. But, in Tibet, there are four refuge objects: lama, Buddha, *dharma*, *sangha*. And in Tibetan Buddhism, the lama is revered as the embodiment of the other three. The lama is the Buddha. The lama is the messenger that conveys all the teachings, through his knowledge base. And the lama is the source that inspires the entire community. So, in Tibetan Buddhism, the idea is that all three refuge objects are wrapped into one, rolled into a ball, as we say. They're all included in the embodiment of the lama.

Now, that's a very restricted definition of lama. See, in the oldest layers of the tradition, lama was not a title that was given out easily. A lama was somebody whose life course of teaching and conveying the *dharma*, after a lifetime, would be nominated to get that title because the value and how they were with others was shown through lifetimes of work. So only great masters would be given that title. That was when the model was originally set up. That was all pre-monastic. Then in the monastic tradition, you've got a traditional structure that evolved, [including] twelve years of philosophical training, three years of a retreat. So, you had to at least put in fifteen years before you could get that title. But that's not the same as the original use. You had to be a buddha. Now, you just have to clock fifteen years. And what began to deteriorate over time is that, you know, we know that from Western schools. You can put in your time and get a degree, but that doesn't mean you know anything.

So, you get the term being somewhat watered down, because there's no test of competency there. At least it depends on the monastery. Some have more rigorous tests than others. But where that became even more watered down was when the Shangpa tradition, when the previous incarnation of Kalu Rinpoche began to convey the titles of lama on Westerners just by virtue of taking a three-year retreat. No test of competency of what you got out of the retreat. You could sit there in a dull stupor for three years, but because you clocked your time, you can call yourself a lama. Be careful with that.

So, particularly the ones that might call themselves that in the West—does that mean that they are realized buddhas? Or is that a title of self-importance? It's about as far from being a real live buddha as one could imagine. And that was a huge controversy among Tibetans. Kalu Rimpoche's rather loose conveying of that title was a source of great concern for many Tibetans. Now the term doesn't mean anything. In the old years it meant a lot. It meant somebody who embodied the full realization of a buddha, a lineage holder, who not only had the full realization, but the full knowledge of how to teach it for all the people of different capacities and who can inspire a whole community of people to move along with their practice. That's the original model. Rare to find that these days.

So that's external refuge. But that's really Tibetan. Why do we call it refuge? Because the world sucks. We suffer. And it's a nightmare if you look at the amount of suffering and all the stuff that goes on. But the teachings will give you a safe haven. It's like a safe house. You can hide within it and develop your practice and come out fully realized. Meanwhile, you get away from the nightmare long enough to evolve yourself, free of it.

Now that's the external version of refuge. In the Essence traditions, the basic idea is everybody has buddha nature, but we don't realize it because we've clouded over with layers and layers of ordinary mind stuff. So, given that, in the Essence traditions you have to develop the mind and clear away the clouds so that its awakened nature is like the sun that always shines. You have to clear away the clouds before you can see the sun.

So, the internal version of refuge is very unique in Dzogchen, the Great Completion practices. And you take refuge not in the Buddha as an external person; you take refuge in your own buddha nature. You have faith in the fact that buddha nature is part of the hard wiring. Everybody has it. And that you have all the necessary ingredients. You have the innate intelligence, and you have the resourcefulness to master the entire practice, from beginning to end. So that kind of internal refuge is kind of similar to what, in Western psychology, we call self-efficacy—the actual conviction, a belief that has conviction, that you can actually do this thing because it's within you.

Then, rather than taking refuge in the body of teachings as something out there, you take refuge in all the internal ingredients of your own mind: your metacognitive intelligence, your innate intelligence, all your inner resources, all the positive ingredients that you've been endowed with in this lifetime that will support the practice. And the fundamental assumption in there is you've got what it takes—the opposite of the "I can't do it" thinking, or "I'm not capable of it."

And lastly, rather than taking refuge in the support of community, you take refuge in all of relative reality, because in the Essence traditions we use relative reality as the vehicle of awakening. There's nothing you have to get away from. In the Essence traditions, we don't have the view as is true in old Buddhism that everything is suffering. It only appears to be suffering because you don't see it correctly. But ultimately, all of relative reality is here because it serves a purpose. And in Dzogchen, every moment of the awakened mind is said to have *gongpa*, [enlightened] intention. And the intention, every moment of experience, seems to be relative reality, the intention of wisdom, or the intention of compassion. They're both the same thing. This whole display is here for a purpose. Every moment is an invitation to get it right, to see it just the way it is. That's why we call it Mahāmudrā—the great gesture, the great invitation. And relative reality will actively display itself with its own intention every moment until you get it right. You get a lot of opportunities—a great gesture.

Or, every moment is the intention of compassion. This whole display has the purpose of compassion. It appears as a suffering reality to train and foster our own authentically compassionate response. This is your training ground. So, in internal refuge, you take refuge in all of relative reality, which is the training ground for ultimate reality. So, that's what we call internal refuge, and it's very unique to the Essence tradition.

Now there's another aspect of this because, as I said, what's unique to the Tibetan tradition is that there are four refuge objects. So, let's look at the internal version of the four.

Buddha, *dharma*, *sangha* would be the external version. Buddha nature and all the inner resources of your own mind and all the relative reality would be the internal version. And we take refuge in the lama. But when you take refuge in the lama, with the internal version of refuge, it's not like he's the embodiment of these other three things we talked about as external refuge. When you take refuge from the internal perspective, the lama is the source of *chingjilap*. That's a hard word. It's often translated as "blessing." I don't like that translation. A *lapa* means wave, and *chingwa* means to give. So, it literally means "waves of giving." And what's being given is the gift of *wang*, influence, a term that's often unfortunately translated as "empowerment." That's not what it means! It means that if you call forth the refuge object, as embodied by a lama, that these are not ordinary beings. They come forth from the intention of awakened *dharmakāya* space. And when you call them forth, they have the potential to directly influence your unfolding mindstream. Because your unfolding mindstream is layer upon layer of awful habits, which keep clouding over ultimate reality or awakened nature, which always shines forth right here. So, when you call them forth, they are compelled to come. But in addition to calling them forth, you have to *solwadeb*, which is often called praying. But that's not what the word means. The literal translation of *solwadeb* is "to throw out a request." You have to make a formal request to this non-ordinary being you called. And what you're requesting is the gift of influence. You're requesting that this non-ordinary being is going to directly intervene in your mindstream and do two things: clear away obscurations, clear away the clouds; and to activate buddha nature. Both things have to happen. And if you call forth a non-ordinary being and make the request, they are compelled to do what you ask. But it doesn't work unless you then follow it up by putting it into practice. It's like a matching grant. They'll make their influence, but you have to match that within a reasonable time after you get the influence.

Now the Western thoroughly misunderstanding of that dynamic is "empowerments." Lamas come to the West, they do a weekend, they give empowerments, you get the requirements; they go up and do all these prayers, you've got no idea what they're doing. And you say, "I just got an empowerment!" And then you go home because it was a complicated visualization, and you do absolutely nothing with it. Cause you got nothing out of it. Unless you put it into practice, that influence will wane like the moon within a few days after you get it. [If you did the practice,] it opens up a window of opportunity and your unfolding mindstream might be a little different than it usually is if you start practicing it that way. It's not being empowered. It's sort of like cleaning house in your mind, clearing away the clouds, and activating buddha nature. And that's all that it does, which is a lot; it increases the probability that you'll actually get the gain in the right direction for the practice.

Now, that's unique to this Essence version of internal refuge—to ask for the gift of influence. That's what we do when we do guru yoga, say with Padmasambhava or Doprje Chang, or Vajrasattva. Okay. Vajrasattva is the Buddha who clears away obscurations and negative states. And what you do is you call on Vajrasattva and you put out all your negative states, like a confession. And then you imagine Vajrasattva directly intervening into your unfolding mindstream and clearing it all away. It's gone. If you do that as a regular practice, it's going to be hard to conjure up negative states after a while.

Student 2

Why does the lama have to clear away clouds and activate buddha nature if buddha nature's always there, hard wired into everyone?

Dan

Because … it's true, when you clear away enough clouds on a very cloudy day, you can probably see the sun. But, if it's really cloudy, and dark, and rainy, you're going to have to do a lot of cloud clearing and still probably won't see the sun because there's so many layers of clouds. So that's part of the problem, where we have layers of clouds for so long that clearing away the clouds isn't enough. Because what we've lost in the process is access to all the positive qualities that are part of our true nature. So, we have to activate them.

If you look at the *Abhidharma* theory of mind, in other words, they say something that's very different from Western psychology. And I like it, I've used it a lot, and it's influenced me a lot in my Western clinical work. But in the *Abhidharma*, what they basically say is, "Look, the techniques that you use to work with negative states and the techniques that you use to work with positive states complement each other, but they're not reducible to each other." So, let's translate what that means. If you develop effective means to work with negative states, then their effectiveness will mean one of two things. Either you have reduced the negative states, or in the case of the most effectiveness, it's a relative absence of those negative states.

But the absence of a negative is not a positive. It's just the absence of a negative. And that's the position in Buddhist psychology that's very different from the West, because if you look at our great profession of psychotherapy, almost every school of thought is designed to work with negative states. The psychodynamic tradition works with intrapsychic conflict—a negative state. Behaviorism works with maladaptive behaviors—a negative state. Cognitive therapy works with negative self-talk and irrational beliefs and schemas—negative states. Developmental therapy works with developmental deficits—negative states. And what's virtually absent, except recently in the positive psychology development, is there's almost nothing in psychotherapy that deals with the development of positive states.

Now in Buddhism, it's very much the opposite direction. Most of the complex visualizations that you do aren't designed to clear up negative states. The great majority of the visualizations that you do are designed to cultivate positive ingredients because they potentiate spiritual development. So, you see, here's the issue: If the overlay has been so strong for so long then it doesn't mean just clearing up negative states. You're going to have to clear up negative states, and you're going to have to cultivate the positive states, and those positive states have been offline so much you're going to have to give it some oomph, which is where the gift of influence comes in. Try and activate and get those positive states back online.

But in the West, it doesn't really occur to us that we have positive states that we need to activate. So, you see that's different. It's important to cultivate these positive states because they lead to positive ways of being with others and contribute to the greater social good that way. There are many positive qualities. Take the buddha, the Menla, the medicine buddha. I like to call him the Buddha of Behavioral medicine. [Laughter] The blue one—of course they're all blue. [Laughter] The last retreat I was doing, Gretchen and I were doing the *tsa lung* practices where you have to do the vase breathing. And one of the students said, "That's why all the buddhas are blue—they hold their breath for a while." [Laughter]

So, Menla represents a quality that we don't even have a word for in English—human concern. It's a prerequisite to be a Tibetan doctor. In other words, before you can even go to Tibetan medical school, you have to evolve your state of mind so that you have strong human concern, which means that when you're present with somebody, you convey with your presence authentic concern for their physical wellness and their psychological wellbeing. It has to exude from you.

The opposite of that is sort of the distance and indifference of the surgeon in the West. Whatever the total opposite of that is, that's human concern. You can't even get trained to be a Tibetan doctor unless you develop that quality.

So, what do you do? You visualize Menla doing this kind of thing and get familiar with the quality, and then you imagine taking it into your own heart. You do the visualization over and over again until you successfully approximate having that quality as your own. And when you develop it strongly from the process of learning, practice, then that quality is part of who you are. And then you want to take another quality. And every one of these buddha figures represents a certain configuration of qualities, and you can develop all of them. They want you to develop the whole deck, not just one. Can you imagine being in therapy for five years and what your therapist did is give you a series of assignments to develop positive qualities? And that's all you ever did in therapy? It's so alien to us. "So, for the next months, we're going to practice gratitude. Then we're going to practice forgiveness. Then we're going to practice wisdom. You're going to practice compassion." People don't go to therapy to practice those kinds of positive things. You go to church for that. We split it down the middle, you see. But you can't have one without the other. The whole point is to reduce the negative states and complement the positive states until you tip the balance—more positive states than negative states.

So, when you do guru yoga and ask for the request of influence, you want both of those things. You want reduction in the negative states, you want an activation of the positive states, and to get the help of a non-ordinary being to tip that balance because we're so weighted in the other direction. It's just too much work. We'll never get through it. So, you imagine you get some sort of help from your friends here in non-ordinary reality. Even if it's all just a metaphor, it still works. That's the idea.

And finally, in the idea in both external and internal refuge, there's the idea of protection. That's what refuge means. The world of the *dharma* becomes a safe haven to protect you from all the potential harms of the everyday world so you can develop your practice with that protection, and with that guidance, with that help. It's a sanctuary, to do the practice with.

In Buddhism, there's an implicit contract, a tacit agreement. As long as you're serious and motivated to do the practice and your motivation is sincere, you're protected, and you'll always get what you need along the way. But rarely in ways you expect. But that is the deal.

Good question. Anyone else?

Student 3

That song ran through my mind, what is it … It begins with: "accentuate the positive, eliminate the negative …"

Student 4

Latch on to the affirmative.

Dan

I don't know the song.

Student 3

It's from years ago. "You gotta accentuate the positive, eliminate the negative." [Students comment and laugh about the lyrics.]

Student 4

Yeah. You know every other song there is. You know every song …

Dan

No, I just know rock video, that's all. [Laughter] I pride myself that I can keep my wife in rock video. [Laughter]

Okay. Just one more. Yes.

Student 5

I think that for me at this point one of the most surprising is … I don't know how to accept positive. You know, I've been a very angry person, so all I want to do is remove the anger. It's hard to believe, just to move into something that's so truly unfamiliar.

Dan

That is part of the Western disease, isn't it? Either we feel we're incapable of doing this, or we feel that we're not willing to, and those are big issues. I found nobody that teaches this stuff in the West. But it goes on all the time; those are our limiting beliefs. It's all about self, and it would be the incapacity of the self or the undeserving-ness of the self.

And the Tibetans, since they have a reincarnation model, their limiting belief is that this takes eons and lifetimes, so they're not going to put the work into it because why bother, because it will take so long to do anyway. It's just an idea; these are all ideas. Ideas don't define ultimate reality. So, what you're talking about, you're in good company. Most everybody in the culture has different variations on that same theme.

Student 6

[Inaudible question about virtues]

Dan

I think that this is something that we've lost. The Templeton Foundation, in the early '90s, threw a lot of money into revamping the research on virtues. What came out of that was a book by Chris Peterson and Marty Seligman called *Character Strengths and Virtues*. Chris Peterson just died last week at the age of sixty-two.

Students

[Sounds of surprise at Peterson's age at death.]

Dan

But that was a remarkable piece of work; it's a very thick book. And what they did with their grant was they looked at all the cultural systems around virtues. They looked at Aristotle's text on virtue, they looked at Plato, they looked at Confucius, they looked at the early Taoist literature, they looked at ethics and virtues in Buddhism, in Hinduism, and Islam. They looked at the virtues espoused by Charlemagne and the Knights of the Round Table. They looked at the list of virtues in the Boy Scouts and the Girl Scouts; they covered all sources. And the task that they set about was to define virtue and then to see if they could come up with a cross-cultural, universal list of virtues.

They defined virtues as qualities that never diminished. They do not diminish. They're immediately recognized as positive qualities by anyone. Most people can immediately come up with a historical example of each virtue. Everybody knows what you're talking about. And they don't diminish other people. They contribute to the greater social good as well as of personal development and social development. Those are the main forms.

And they came up with a list of six core virtues and three subtypes in each group, so it was a list of twenty-four virtues. Some of the main categories would be humanity, justice, wisdom, transcendence, temperance. I'm leaving out one of the six.

Student 5

Honesty?

Dan

Oh, dangerous—courage. So, those are the big six and there are three subtypes in this group. They could find evidence in almost every culture to support that. The idea was to write a detailed description of what these virtues do in terms of self-development and the greater social good, to give examples of moral exemplars in each of these, and to put it out as a counterpoint to psycho-technology in the West.

This is the counterpoint to the *DSM, the Diagnostic Statistical Manual.* What they call the "manual of the sanities." It's a very good book. And what I like about it is that it's a good model of the assessment of virtues. But what they don't have in the book is anything about treatment, or the development of this. The idea is that we have moral exemplars of this and we should be more like this, but there are almost no tools in the West for how we develop this stuff, where in other traditions, most of the emphasis is on how you develop it. And my point is the project is incomplete in that sense. They should have developed a process of quality development.

How can you develop virtues of mind? The first method is apprenticeship. You develop them from people in your life with whom you've had what you would call a fiduciary relationship—people whose duty it is to us to put aside their own personal means for our development and welfare. That would mean somebody like a mentor who is tirelessly there helping you to develop and grow, despite yourself. And they don't want anything bad, so that would be a clinical mentor or a teacher that you had, a big brother, or somebody in your life who gives of themselves for your development and growth.

What do we get from people like that? It's not the content. It's who they are. In the 1940s and '50s during the heyday of psychoanalysis, in those years, unlike Freud—his analyses were two, three months long—by the 1940s and '50s, most analyses were ten, twenty years. Like the Woody Allen film where he says he's been in analysis and he'll stay in another ten years to see if it works. That's what was common in the '40s and '50s. But if you had an analyst who's a decent analyst, so that they are interested in everything about who you are, and they see you four to five times a week for ten or twenty years, they probably know you better than anybody that's ever going to know you in this lifetime, and they probably would've done you a good turn and you got better.

Roy Schafer, when he was at the Menninger Foundation, talked about what he calls selective identification. With somebody who spent all that time tirelessly being there for you, we don't just change in the process, we don't learn things. In addition to all that, we become like them. We're grateful for what we got, and we pick up—hopefully—good qualities. So, we become more like our mentors in the good things that we have in mind about them. Plato got it right. In his essay on the education of the state, he said that teaching is always and necessarily about character development. That's what we teach. You see, if people are going to get that in law school it's not because you're conveying a certain content to them as part of a curriculum. It's who you are as a person and the quality of caring for your students. They're going to be taking part of who you are. That's always good.

I had the great privilege of having many good mentors in this lifetime. And what I remember from them isn't the clinical content. What I remember from Erika Fromm, who was my main clinical mentor, was how nurturing she was; and I spent thirty-five years in a relationship with her. We taught together until she died in 1992. She was in her late eighties and we were still traveling around teaching [inaudible]. She was tireless but she was very nurturing. She was there basically for my development until I graduated. So, what I got from her was who she was and how brilliant she was. It wasn't about what I learned from her in the clinical space.

I remember once when I was a graduate student, and I was poor, I was sick, and I came back to Boston to visit some friend, we ate in one of these cheap Indian restaurants and we got hepatitis C. And I basically dropped out of most of my classes, and I was just trying to stay alive. One day, there's a knock on the door and there's Erika. She had all these baskets she put on me; it was about two weeks-worth of cooked food. [Inaudible few words] And my other clinical mentor—Karl Menninger—he was, I think, key. He wondered about everything. Everything was exciting. I'd go for walks with him. He'd stop and look at these flowers and wondered about these plants and wanted to know about their medicinal properties; and we'd talk about politics, we'd talk about Native Americans, and we'd talk about clinical stuff. [Inaudible few words] He was inexhaustible, his energy, and always wondering about everything. And what I got from him wasn't about clinical skills. It was his infectious curiosity about looking into everything. So, you see, that's what you get when you have a mentor. You become like them.

Now, if you don't have the fortune of having that kind of mentorship, then you do a visualization practice. You make up exemplars. But the point is, if you develop these characters, these virtues … See, we have a huge literature on peak performance and fluid states in the West, how to be on top of your game, but all of that literature is about doing good in short durations of time. It doesn't change anything. And the difference is if you add virtue training to what we know about the ingredients of peak performance and flow, then you don't have short duration states. You become a master in everyday living. That's what all the spiritual traditions figured out. The virtue training is what makes you live your life in a good way, and be the master of every moment. [Inaudible] Not just scoring a lot of points for a given game. Virtue training makes the difference.

When I ran an internship for ten years at a medical school, we drew some of the best young talent in the country. We had a pool of about five hundred applicants and we probably interviewed a hundred, which is more than most programs. And out of that, we had about fifty applicants who are all very well-qualified. They all have glowing recommendations. How do you tell the difference between them? They're all going to present their tanned faces; they're all going to have positive recommendations; they all have great friends—so how can you tell the difference?

I wasn't interested in any of that stuff. The only thing we were interested in was the young and talented of good character, because that's what we train. It was who we wanted in the field, not what we would teach them. And the best way of seeing that was having them all together for lunch, [inaudible] to see how they'd interact with everybody. Who's competitive? Who's selfish? Who is kind in humility? That was much more important. Let's see that naturally in a setting. See where they really are; then they'd reveal their real character. And we would tend to try and select people who maybe weren't quite as stellar on paper, but they had good character. And I'd go the extra mile to get them in. [Inaudible few words.] So, that's what we looked for.

When I was in Chicago, when Kohut went, and learning analysis of self, it wasn't about narcissistic patients. The group was all about the residents because they couldn't do squat with narcissistically vulnerable patients because they were young, narcissistic, full of themselves, self-important—they thought they were god's gift to medicine. They were so filled with themselves they couldn't be present for the patients, so they did a terrible job. But they thought they did well. It was really a hidden calamity against the field of selecting the wrong people. [Inaudible few words]

Virtue development is important. It's what becomes the difference between having some peak performance when being on your game and being an asshole off the field. I say, "Remember that"; or when you have a genuine master who lives his life and every moment that way. How many sports figures do we have in the West that you can think of like that? It's really hard to think.

Student 7

[inaudible] Oh really?

Dan

On the other hand, if you develop the character, then you would be great at everything you do, including during the day. And the same rules apply to meditation. People can have great meditation states, I mean, these great yogis, they're basically assholes because they never developed character.

So, who cares about what your meditation states are like. Who remembers? But, if you develop the character, then maybe it starts to influence your everyday life, because you're being different with people. It makes all the difference in the world.

You see, it's the same when we talk about meditation or sports. Character development makes all the difference in the world, but you've got to train it.

November 28, 2012

Themes: Karma Theory with Levels of Mind; Virtue Training

Dan

Welcome everyone. You have a question?

Student 1

In yoga, I find myself entering meditative states. [Inaudible]

Dan

Somehow, in the development of yoga in the West, it got somewhat dissociated from the mind. So, the postural stuff gets emphasized and we forget the great tradition, which is Patanjali's Yoga Sutras, which have eight limbs, or eight *áṅgas* for the practice of which the postures are only the first. And the next seven are all about meditation. So, they're just preparatory for meditation sometimes, at least as it was originally practiced. It's important to learn about training the mind in yoga because that's what Patanjali's great system did.

Anybody else?

Student 2

Dan, I would like for you to talk a little bit about karma. What I've been noticing is that there's something really shifting for me in my limited understanding of karma, and there's something that's shifting a whole lot due to my meditation practice. So, what's shifting is that everything is getting less and less conceptual. I've always had very strong personality. I've always had a very … sort of like My World. There's Carpet World, and there's My World. At one, you buy carpets, and in the other, everything centers around Me.

Dan

Like *Wayne's World*?

Student 2

Yeah, like *Wayne's World*. [Laughter] This is much more scary though, I'm afraid. [Laughter] So, for example: concepts of right and wrong, concepts of how other people should act, concepts of when I've been hurt by another, those concepts. Concepts of the old way of kind of putting a spiritual band-aid on all of that, and thinking, "Oh, I'll just look at like this it's my karma," and etcetera, etcetera; and putting those old solutions onto it, finding that they didn't really work for me.

But what's happening lately is, in my meditation practice, what's shifting is even the concept of "I" and "you," "I" and "other." If I'm thinking that somebody else hurt me, that really starts to shift. Then I start thinking of, okay, I wouldn't be experiencing *this* unless I had done *this*, at some point, done this to another—kind of like my old understanding of karma. It's like when you get into how time and space are just conceptualizations, that shifts too. Concepts of forgiveness involved like, "I have done this to other," or "Other has done this to me," and that's really shifting too.

So, it seems to me that there must be just layers and levels to this, and I just wonder if you can speak to that some. I don't want to get too much more …

Dan

That's a great question, but it involves a long answer here [Laughter] because you see, the answer to the question is different at each level of mind. So, in the Indo-Tibetan theory of mind, there are different levels of mind. There is coarse level mind, which is the realm of mental content, specific thought content, emotional content, perceptual content, specific sights, sounds, tastes, smells, sensations. That's the coarse level of mind.

The subtle level of mind is the burst of movement and energy in the mind, prior to its being constructed into content—the "mind moments" in Buddhism. That's called the subtle level of mind. The third level of mind is the very subtle level of mind. And at the very subtle level of mind, that's the level of mind where the awareness doesn't operate within the construction of conventional time.

Awareness is timeless, and since time and space are related, awareness is rather vast. We call it timeless, boundless awareness. And the content that arises within that field of changeless, boundless awareness contains the potential storehouse of everything that could come into fruition. So, it's like the level of virtual mind, where everything is interconnected but not yet manifest, necessarily. That's called storehouse mind. And the fourth level of mind would be the mind where you're operating out of awakened awareness, awakened mind. And then the fifth level of mind would be the mind of full enlightenment, or buddhahood. So, the answer to that question is completely different in each one of these levels, so let's start at the beginning. All right?

At the coarse level of mind, karma theory is very much in Buddhism, and not just in Buddhism. Karma theory is very similar in Patanjali's Yoga Sutras. So, it's sort of pan-Indian. And karma theory is comparable to what in Western psychology we would call learning theory. Okay? Karma theory isn't this thing where when bad things happen to you, say, you have an explanatory model for it: "It must be my karma." That's a rather unsophisticated and somewhat popular folk culture of karma. But actually, karma theory in Buddhist psychology is quite sophisticated. It's at least as complicated and as dense as Western learning theory in Western psychology. And the first principle is that if you engage in any kind of action, the engagement in that action produces karmic traces—memory traces, or karmic traces. In Tibetan, they're called *bagchag*, habitual tendencies or karmic traces.

Now, actions can mean behaviors, but in Buddhist theory of mind, actions also include mental action. What you think, every specific thought, creates karmic impressions. So that's the first principle of what are called the laws of karma. All actions have effects.

The second principle of the laws of karma is that those effects proliferate over time. In other words, they ripen. The Tibetan word is *minwa*. You don't see the effects right away. The effects ripen slowly over time. It may be months, it may be years, it might even be lifetimes. But there will be effects. All karmic impressions eventually release themselves and ripen, and they ripen in three successive stages. First, they ripen in terms of spontaneously emerging states of mind; that is, the content of your mind is all determined by ripening of previous karmic impressions. From where, it's difficult to say. You can't trace it to the given action that caused that particular mental state. Second, it ripens in terms of behavior. And thirdly, it ripens in terms of the unfolding of events in one's life.

So, the next principle in the laws of karma is that different actions have different weights. The word is *tok*, strength, power, or *chu* in Tibetan. So, for example, if you have a moment of anger as a thought, that has less weight than killing somebody. So certain actions have much greater karmic weight than others. In classical Buddhist thinking they are called the seven restraints; in other words, you just don't go there. No killing, no stealing, no sexual misconduct, no abusive speech, no deceitful speech, no divisive speech, no meaningless speech or gossip. Those are the big seven. Four of them have to do with speech. We just don't go there, because those events have great strength and cause a mess for you and everybody else.

Now, the next principle in the laws of karma is that if you don't engage in an action, there's no ripening effect. And the last principle of karma which was incorporated into Buddha's discovery of the Four Noble Truths, Buddha Shakyamuni, is that it's possible to stop karmic effects.

Now those are what are called the laws of karma, just like we have general laws of learning theory in the West. And you see, it really is a kind of learning theory. If you will, it's Buddhist learning theory applied at the coarse level of mind. Because if you think of the implications of that in positive terms, what does it mean? If you engage in spiritual practice, the intention and the actual practice of that is going to produce positive karmic impressions, *bagchag*; and those will ripen in terms of spontaneous positive states of mind. Eventually, if you put a lot of practice into that, the force of that karmic impression—the cumulative force of that, which is called merit in Buddhism—the cumulative force of that will ripen.

If you catalog states of mind in daily life, most people will discover that there are far more negative than positive states. But if you do a cumulative spiritual practice, the accumulating strength of those karmic positive impressions is such that after a while the balance tips. So, at the coarse level of mental content, more positive content comes up than negative content. At that point it's easier to meditate because not all the stuff gets played out on the pillow. Cause there just isn't as much negative stuff. And in terms of karma theory, if you produce an effect because of your strength, the outcome is guaranteed sometime over time. So, that means if you do your practice and you do it with some diligence, it will shift to positive states. If your practice is very strong, after a while it will begin to affect your behavior; you'll act differently. And if your practice is very strong in a positive sense, it will affect the unfolding of events in your life, and the whole interpersonal field around you, which means you'll start to have good fortune. The fact that we're all together is good fortune. It's the ripening of previous karmic impressions. The fact that you get these teachings is good fortune. Nothing is accidental.

So, karma theory is an explanation for why spiritual development actually happens. The word for spiritual progress in Sanskrit is *bhāvanā*, like in Kamalashila's *Bhāvanākrama*, the very text that His Holiness the Dalai Lama gave his talk on when he came to Boston recently. The Tibetan word for *bhāvanā* is interesting. *Gompa*. And phonetically, it has an affinity with the word for "becoming familiar with." To meditate means to become thoroughly familiar with your own states. That's the Tibetan word for meditation. And to develop something. And what you're developing is the ripening of positive karmic impressions so your whole mind shifts its balance towards something positive. That's why a synonym for meditation is *genjor*, which means virtue practice. And a *genjorwa* is a practitioner of virtue, which is a name for a meditator, because it shifts the balance to virtuous states as opposed to non-virtuous or negative states of mind.

Now that's all karma theory in application as it applies to practice and meditation. The more you practice, the greater the strength, the greater the development. It's not very different from learning theory, and it's sort of a caricature of the very sophisticated laws of karma theory that say, "Well, that's just my karma," and use it as an explanation for bad things that happen in our lives. That's not what it means at all. That's a Western, distorted, somewhat insulting view of karma theory. But then again, karma theory is complex. If anybody ever took learning theory in Psych 101, it's boring and it's difficult. Buddhist karma theory's the same way. But you have to learn it because it's the foundation of learning, East and West. So that's what we would say at the coarse level of mind. It's the understanding of why you learn and develop your mind in a positive way through meditation.

Now, let's go to the very subtle level of mind. The very subtle level of mind opens up in the Mahāyāna practices, not in the Theravādin practices, as you know. And the difference is how you deal with the convention of time, because in our ordinary experience, it seems like things come and go in time. And it was Nagarjuna's Dialectic that changed all that. If you watch things coming and going in the older Buddhism, everything actually starts to break up and disappear. It was called dissolution experience. Not very pleasant. You watch the simplest elements of your mind dissolve and disappear, usually accompanied by fear or disgust. However, the positive result of that is it clears away even the subtlest activities of the ordinary mind, so what's left is a kind of mirror-like awareness. And there's a window of opportunity there to look into the real nature of that awareness, which is limitless and changeless. And that's why dissolution experience in the older Theravādin Buddhism is said to be the platform for awakening because you can come to appreciate the nature of awakened awareness as different from ordinary awareness and all the stuff of the ordinary mind.

However, Nagarjuna came along and said, "Look. When you watch everything go, arise, and pass very quickly, how do you know that that arising and passing isn't its own illusion?" That's the whole notion of time as another illusion. So, he developed this weird thing called Nagarjuna Dialectic. When things arise in time, take the view that they don't really arise because they're already here. When things go away in time, take the view they don't go anywhere but stay here. And then in the interval between the arising and passing, look squarely into the nature of awareness, and what will open up is a level of awareness that's beyond the convention of time. Always right here—changeless, boundless awareness. You know the instructions. So, by taking that view, it sort of flattens out time enough so that if you look into the nature of awareness, you'll see that always right here is a rather vast, limitless, changeless awareness that has nothing to do with the convention of time. And once you open it up, it's hard to lose it because it can't go away in time, because it doesn't operate in time. Simple.

If you open up that very subtle level from the mind perspective, that awareness will be like a limitless, changeless field. Like an ocean of awareness. And the events that occur will all be the expression of that very awareness. They all occur vividly, but they're insubstantial. Everything arises as insubstantial and everything arises as interconnected within that field, because that field is a storehouse of everything that could potentially be—past, present, and future—and because it's beyond the convention of time, so it contains the *kunji*, the basis of everything. *Kunzhi namshay*, it was called. Storehouse mind—*ālaya-vijñāna* in Sanskrit.

Now, if you enter that very subtle level of mind, everything that comes up is just another momentary expression, another construction; empty, yet it occurs. But it's where you're viewing it from that makes the difference. In the mind perspective, you're viewing it from the perspective of being an ocean of boundless, changeless awareness viewing its own waves. Two things happen when you're operating out of that boundless, changeless awareness viewing its own waves. One is that whatever comes up loses grab. We call that "spacious freedom." And after a while, everything's just another expression of emptiness. It's all the same taste of emptiness. So, if you just hang out in that ocean of waves from the vantage point of being the ocean of awareness, after a while, things start to lose distinctions. There's no good, there's no bad. There's no pleasant, there's no unpleasant. There's no hope, there's no fear. All states are just another momentary expression of emptiness. And there's great variability, but all that variability has the same underlying sense of all being momentary constructions—mind, the dance, the play of awareness itself. What we call [in Tibetan] the *tsal*, the liveliness of awareness.

Now, you know about that practice, and that's the level of mind where everything loses distinctions. And as you practice that and learn it, something else happens. The distinctions that are made from karmic impressions as good, bad, or any kind of polarities all dissolve. And the outcome of that? Every moment is the same emptiness. All distinctions go; all reference points go. And if there's no distinctions, you're not partializing. Always right here is an infinite ocean of awareness-love, the totality of this boundless, limitless awareness-love. Like the sun that always shines. But anything that the ordinary mind does to partialize, that clouds over the wholeness, the totality of that. That's why you can't conceptualize about awakening because every conceptualization when you say it's this [Dan points his finger to one side] it's not that [he points his finger to the other side]. Every time you pay attention to this, you're not paying attention to that.

So how do you directly experience the totality of this boundless, limitless awareness-love in its totality? The first way that you're going to get to directly experience that is you have to get rid of all distinctions, which naturally comes from this level of mind. That's why the famous quote from the Third Chinese Patriarch's *Hsin Hsin Ming* is "the Great Way," which is the way of awakening. "The Great Way is not difficult for those who have no preferences … Make the slightest distinction between this or that, and Heaven and Earth are set infinitely apart." As soon as the mind goes in this direction towards this, you're missing the totality of what's always right here. The habit of ordinary information processing is that in every moment the mind's doing this or that; it misses it every moment. But what will happen at that level of practice, at the very subtle level of mind, is you will collapse all distinctions.

Are you still making karmic impressions? Yes. Now, if you have no distinctions and no partialization, and you can directly allow this awareness to manifest itself to itself in its totality, then you'll shift your basis of operation. You're no longer operating out of the constraints of your individual consciousness, the limits of your information processing system. All those movements of the mind are just part of the dance of that ocean of the boundless, limitless awareness-love. But now you're looking at it from the perspective of being that. So, whatever comes up is none other than the liveliness of that awakened awareness. It can't get in the way anymore. It clouds over because that's the habit of karmic impressions. And it will keep clouding over in certain ways, and you have to set up the conditions to open it up again. After a while it doesn't take much work to open it up again. It stays open for a longer duration, for greater frequency on the pillow, and ultimately off the pillow. Then you practice until you stabilize that awakening and have it all the time, 24/7.

Now, a very interesting thing starts to happen. If you have that awakening most of the time, what happens is that as you're operating out of being that ocean of changeless, limitless awareness-love, whatever comes up in that as the seeming event—whether it be a thought or an emotion seemingly inside or a perceptual event seemingly outside, like a sight, a sound, all of those things, every one of those—you begin more and more to see as *tsal*, the liveliness of that awareness, because awakened awareness is very lively. It's dynamic. It's not a static thing like empty space. It dances. It's alive every moment. Everything that you see is this liveliness, it's all the same feeling of awareness. Awakened awareness. And after a while, you can't see anything other than liveliness of awakened awareness. Everything. It's a continuous flow of liveliness, or as you know in the Lion's Gaze book, they call it "the ups and downs of the *dharmakāya*." Everything is the same ups and downs, the same lively, awakened awareness. It's very awake, very bright, crystal clear and lucid.

So, the first map is how you get from ordinary mind to awakened mind. The second map is how you refine that awakening until you have it all the time. And then something begins to happen that's interesting. Because that infinite, vast expanse of empty awareness space you begin to see as *kunzhi*, the groundless ground from within, in which everything arises in an unconditioned way and then disappears back into it, leaving no trace. Now that's ultimately the fate of karma. If you refine your awakening so you have it all the time, you're going to initiate a whole new process of what we call *dharmadhātu* exhaustion. Everything will be groundless ground. *Kunzhi* is the structure of being. It's the groundless ground from which everything arises and disappears. But it's where you're looking at it from. There's no duality. It's all the liveliness of the same field of changeless, boundless awareness. But where you're looking at it from is from the perspective of being that ocean of limitless, changeless awareness-love. And it will start to appear more and more as the groundless ground, the structure of being from which everything dances.

But here's the key, okay? Particularly in Dzogchen, they talk a lot about *langdor mépa. Langwa* means to take something up, to accept it. *Dorwa* means to push it away, reject it. *Langdor mépa* is a negative. It means do not accept anything, do not reject anything. What's the common factor in there, in Western terms? Mental engagement. Whatever comes up in the field, as soon as you engage it with even the slightest impulse of mind, either to bring it forth more and process it more, or to not process it and turn to something else; if there's any activity of the mind at all, at that moment of engaging, in either direction, at that moment of engagement, that's what creates a karmic impression. Okay?

So, when you are practicing what's called groundless ground, as your view, *dharmadhātu* exhaustion, what happens is that you can operate from the perspective of being that infinite vast expanse of awareness space as groundless ground. And within that field everything arises in an unconditioned way, disappears without leaving any trace; and in every single moment you are no longer making any new karmic impressions for the first time in your lifetime. And if you hold that view uninterruptedly, something funny begins to happen. Since you're not forming any new karmic impressions, the only recourse for the ordinary mind is to ripen all the previous storehouse of karmic impressions across lifetimes in an accelerated way. Hold the view, watch everything arise and disappear; it disappears immediately, and nothing leaves any trace. We say it's like writing on water. Or we say it's like a gust of wind—it rises up and disappears back into the atmosphere. Everything is like a gust of wind or writing on water. Hold that view uninterrupted when you're on and off the pillow, or waking or sleeping, you do it all the time. And all previous karmic impressions will unfold, release themselves, until there are no negative karmic impressions left. The whole storehouse empties out. The average time, if you do it with holding the view uninterruptedly, according to a certain text, is six years. If you do it part time it takes much longer. If you accelerate it with the *tögal* practices that use the secret energy channels, you can get the whole thing done in about two years.

I've been doing that practice now for about a year and a half, continuously. What happens after a while is *drima*, stainless mind. I like to translate it as "clean." Because what happens is that after a while there are very few and infrequent negative states of mind left in your experience. [A student sitting next to Dan makes a clumsy gesture of some kind causing laughter.] That's one of those ripening karmic impressions. [Laughter] That's one of the negative ones. [More laughter] A gust of wind rises up and leaves no trace. [Laughter]

Now you see, what happened just then—you got a chance to see what mental engagement was. Look at the impression it leaves. But you see, the difference at the third map, when you're doing *dharmadhātu* exhaustion is, if you hold the practice of … what are we going to call it [Dan pauses to reflect] " leave-it-alone-ness." If you practice with the perspective of leave-it-alone-ness every moment, which is the opposite of any kind of engagement of anything, it just arises and disappears in the field. There's no self that's reacting to it; it's just the field expressing itself and releasing itself.

If you hold that view uninterruptedly, all karmic impressions release themselves from the storehouse until there's nothing left. And the outcome of that is what we call *dharmadhātu* exhaustion—you have exhausted all karmic impressions of the storehouse across lifetimes. And the only thing that's left is the *kadak*, the original purity of the mind.

The subjective experience of that as you're going through it? The practice will get cleaner and cleaner. Awakened awareness gets brighter and brighter, and it's just clean. You're cleaning out the mind and body completely. Everything is clean and bright all the time, and it's not possible after a while for negative states to arise; and at some point, it just sort of dawns on you that there aren't any negative states anymore—which is rather nice.

The full fruition of that? The exhaustion of all negative states. That's the liberation component of awakening. No suffering. But what's not emphasized in the older Theravādin practices, and very much in Mahāyāna is the flourishing of all positive states. There are eighty positive states of a buddha mind. All those are part of your original nature; they're all right here. You don't see that because it's clouded over, but when you have *dharmadhātu* exhaustion there's a flourishing of all eighty positive qualities of the buddha mind. I'd recommend it, it's nice.

And that's the word in Tibetan for buddha. In Sanskrit the word for buddha is *budh*, which means the realized one. That's not how the Tibetans translate it. The word for buddha is *sangyé*. It's a compound term, *sangwa* and *gyeywa*. *Sangwa* means purification; *gyeywa* means to flourish. What does it mean? The word for buddha means the purification and eradication of all negative states, and the flourishing of all eighty positive states of a full buddha mind.

That's at least part of what happens with full enlightenment. There's more to it than that, but that's the piece relevant to this. The difference at that level of practice is you're practicing with a certain level of awakened mind, and a certain *dawa*, a certain view that will eradicate the entire storehouse of previous karmic impressions at an accelerated rate until there's none left. Then you are completely free, not just in not having any grab to current states, as is true of Ocean and Waves as they come up. But there isn't anything left that could possibly cause any negative states to develop. Your mind is completely clean. Or you've restored it to the original condition of buddha nature. That's the way it was in the beginning, before you crudded it up.

So, you see, it's an important question. But the last level of mind is the profound one, because there is a level of practice that's beyond all karmic impressions. That's also the level of the *gunshes*, the supernormal powers. If you're not bound by the ripening of previous karmic impressions, then the mind has infinite scope. You can make the events the way you need them to be for the sake of serving beings. That's useful. But it's not as simple as saying you're beyond the effects of good and bad karma so you can act any way you want. That's another one of those misunderstandings about being free of karmic traces. Awakening and the development of awakening … the only test of true awakening—to make sure it's not conceptual, the only true test of awakening is conduct. It's how you act in the world.

And the full fruition of buddhahood is *trinlé*, enlightened activity across all levels of reality for the sake of helping beings. So, beyond karma doesn't mean you can do whatever you want. Beyond karma means that you have a degree of awakening, if not enlightenment, that shows you that the intention of the mind, the fully awakened or enlightened mind, every moment, is the intention of compassion for the sake of helping all beings. There isn't a moment of exception to that. There's no place for selfishness. That's gone a long time ago.

Good question.

Student 3

Can I ask a follow up?

Dan

Sure.

Student 3

Last retreat I've been thinking about karma a lot, and you just offered this fairly elaborate description, but I had a simpler version, so can I just like share that and see if it's …

Dan

It's wrong, Larry. [Laughter]

Student 3

Okay. [More laughter]

Dan

It's a shred of grab that's left. [Laughter]

Student 3

It's funny because you said, is there grab, and I was like, no, Dan's just playing with me, like, you know … none. Which is good! Yeah, so you're not supposed to hear it. It's for the video folks, right?

Student 4

It's for Europe.

Student 3

So, if I understand this correctly, just reducing things to the simple formulation of *rigpa* versus *marigpa*?

Dan

For those of you that don't know the terms, or new people, *rigpa* means awakened awareness and *marigpa* means non-awakened awareness. Every moment there are only two possibilities: either you are operating out of awakened awareness, or you're operating out of non-awakened awareness or ordinary mind. Every moment, the entire path of *saṃsāra* and *nirvana* is created depending on which you're operating out of.

Student 3

So, thinking about it through that lens, it seems that if *rigpa* is present, there is no engagement. Like the definition of *rigpa* is no engagement and I guess …

Dan

No, no, no. That's not true. I understand your reasoning.

Student 3

Okay.

Dan

But, if you have developed *rigpa* and you're operating out of awakened awareness, you still have to refine it. You have to clean up the mirror, as we say. Because first you have to develop that, so you're operating out of awakened awareness more frequently and for longer durations on the pillow and then off the pillow. But, throughout that whole process of that second map, when you're sort of developing *rigpa* to the point where you have it as a continuous flow all the time, there are what we call *nyigma*, the residuals or the dregs. And those clouds that still come up as the residuals are variations on the theme of subtle habits of subject-object duality. They'll still come up. And some of the stronger karmic impressions will still come up and cloud it over. It won't completely cloud things over. It's like a thin veil. Sometimes all you need is the intention and you're back in awakening.

Student 3

But I think that's helpful, because that's the other piece. You know, I think I'm being too reductionistic in defining *rigpa* as just the utter absence of self, and you're saying that in that second map there's still dregs …

Dan

In Western terms we'd say this is all-or-nothing thinking. It's not like that.

Student 3

Yeah.

Dan

Okay?

Student 3

Yeah. But if there's absolutely no self, if you get past …

Dan

You can have no self and still have dregs.

Student 3

So, subject-object …

Dan

The subtle versions of subject-object duality.

Student 3

So, any subject, how about …

Dan

Any kind of distinction is a dreg.

Student 3

So, any time there's a subject-object, that's going to produce—

Dan

Even in the subtlest way.

Student 3

In the subtlest way, but as soon as that's gone there can't be any …

Dan

Well, you see, if there's the slightest subject-object duality then the mind has something out there to engage.

Student 3

Right.

Dan

But if there's not even the slightest dreg of subject-object duality, there's nothing that can be engaged.

Student 3

Right. And it just arises and then disappears.

Dan

And you're in *dharmadhātu* exhaustion.

Student 3

So, anything that has ever happened where there was a subject or a self, you have to bring … that stuff has to come back up.

Dan

When you refine the awakening, you have enough mental pliancy.

Student 3

Mm-hmm [affirmative].

Dan

So that there's a kind of quickness, with no more than the speed of intention which is like the speed of light.

Student 3

Instant.

Dan

Which is a property of awareness. With no more than that intention it will clean up that thing. That's when you can do much more refined practices like look at the moment that subject-object duality recreates itself. That's very quick. Look and see *marigpa* as an instance of *rigpa*. Those are profound practices, but you can't do that unless you're awakening is pretty stable. You want to introduce them at the right time. Can you understand what I'm saying?

Student 3

Yes. Thank you.

Dan

That was a good follow-up. There's a whole practice; there's a whole domain in Dzogchen called dregs practices. [Laughter] There are texts about, just about that.

Student 4

Given the fact that the process you described is years in the making, for those of us who are still in the coarse level …

Dan

That's a limiting belief. It's not measured in time.

Student 4

Okay.

Dan

You can do it in an instant.

Student 4

All right. [Laughter]

Dan

Clean up those clouds. [Laughter]

Student 4

The voice of conviction.

Dan

Doubt is the biggest hindrance to spiritual development. [Dan laughs.]

Student 4

It's not easy to make a politician speechless. But the question …

Dan

Good! [Laughter]

Student 4

In the meantime, until time goes away … for those of us who are in the coarse level of mind, or the very coarse level from time to time … [Laughter]

Dan

The extremely coarse level, but you better classify the other direction. [Laughter] There are varying degrees of density. The eight levels of dense mind. [Laughter]

Student 4

That's right. So, while it sort of percolates, it's the opportunity to do something useful, and you hope for the benefit of others without necessarily getting all the way to where you do it as an expression of awareness. You got any guidance for the folks that …

Dan

Yeah, if you're working on simple concentration, every intention to direct the mind, that's learning. It may seem slow to you, even the learning effect is clear. Thought elaboration gets less frequent and less developed over time. And the mind stays more and more on what you intend to put it on in terms of the concentration object. All of that is learning theory, or karma theory, depending on what you want to call it, East or West.

Student 4

What I was asking a little differently was the shape of conduct. In other words, if you say the manifestation of awakened awareness is a positive conduct, but you want to aspire to positive conduct on the way there, that's what I'm trying to understand.

Dan

At the basic level of practice, you develop the virtues of mind. The positive ingredients of service support the development of awakening—trust, mindfulness, lightheartedness, balanced energy. You know the list. And then [you know] the six perfections—generosity of spirit, patience, etc. You develop those qualities. It not only supports the more rapid and clean development of your own practice, but they're beneficial in everyday life, as you know. It affects how we are with other people, in a positive way. So, either what are called the seven factors of awakening in the older Theravādin Buddhism, or the six perfections in Mahāyāna Buddhism, that's the virtue training at the beginning of practice, at the coarse level. And there's lots and lots written about that.

December 5, 2012

Themes: Staying Awake in Sleep & Dreams, Night and Day

Dan

Welcome everyone. You have a question?

Student 1

You know sleep is just not of interest to me …

Dan

Such a waste of time. [Laughter]

Student 1

And then, every once in a while, I have these [inaudible] and we're practicing—and I did have one dream two days ago. And it's not me. You know, you're there, and then you're teaching, or we're sitting together and we're practicing, and I did have one dream two days ago.

Student 2

Uh-oh. [Laughter]

Student 1

No, I just had to mention this because this was so cool. I dreamt about a *garuda*.

Dan

Oh. Dreamt about a *garuda*?

Student 1

Yeah, which was really cool.

Student 3

You know what that means, don't you? [Laughter]

Student 4

Uh oh.

Student 1

That's the problem. I have no idea what that means, but it was this huge bird. This really big, golden …

Dan

I think this is for general viewing. [Laughter]

Student 1

I think I'm going to stop here, [Laughter] but the serious part of it is … knowing the interweaving, I guess, of whether that's … I mean, I do need my sleep …

Dan

Well, that's a great question.

Student 1

And I guess I also don't know if other people have that experience.

Dan

It's a great question.

Student 1

Thank you.

Dan

Okay, good. The question is: how do I get to sleep, if I practice before I go to bed?

Okay. Well, let's just talk about sleep. Let's just talk about the Western view first, but then we'll talk about the Eastern view.

In the Western view, you have diurnal rhythms, and you cycle through those diurnal rhythms, so during the waking part of the day, you have, in terms of bandwidth, you have largely fast wave activity. You take the bandwidth of EEG: the fast wave activity, which is beta; very fast, which is gamma; somewhat slower, which is alpha; much slower, which is theta; and then very slow, which is deep sleep, which is delta. That has to do with the frequency of vibration in the electrophysiology of the brain.

And generally speaking, when you go to sleep, you transition out of the relative distribution of largely fast wave activity to progressively slower activity. The first stage of sleep is what's called stage one descending, otherwise known as the hypnagogic state. And when you're in the hypnagogic state, you're shifting the relative distribution away from mostly beta to alpha, theta; and there are two sub-bandwidths with theta. The lower frequency theta is associated with getting a lot of spontaneous imagery that's usually fragmented imagery.

So, when you're in stage one descending sleep, there's a point where there's a lot of spontaneously emerging fragmented imagery that will come up. Then sometime thereafter, you'll just fall asleep. Then you go to stage two, stage three, and stage four. And in each of those stages of progressively deeper sleep you get increased slow wave activity. The distribution of those is there's always some beta, always alpha, always theta, but there's more and more delta, so the distribution shifts, as you go into deeper sleep, to slower and slower wave activity.

When you're in stage two, three, and four, progressively deeper sleep, the body, in terms of the motor system, is still active, but the mind is shut down. So, when you toss and turn, you tend to do that in deep sleep, but there's no mentation pattern. There's almost no content, relatively speaking. The content is very infrequent. So, when you're in deep sleep, there's no content.

Then when you finish stage four—the deepest, the slowest activity, mostly slow wave delta activity—then you shift to what's called rapid eye movement sleep, REM sleep, and that corresponds to dreaming. When you're in REM sleep, the activity, the waves are much faster, but the body is inactive. You cannot move while you're dreaming. It's a kind of sleep paralysis, but the mind, in terms of its content, is very active. So, a simple thing that you might remember to understand is, in deep sleep body is active, mind is at rest. In REM sleep, mind is active, body is at rest.

And then you go through a period of rapid eye movement, dreaming, which lasts, on the average, fifteen or twenty minutes. Then rather than coming back up to waking, fast wave activity, you come back up somewhat, usually to stage two, go back down two, three, and four to deeper sleep. Then you have a second round of REM sleep, and after finishing that for fifteen or twenty minutes, you then go back up to stage two, three, four, down to deeper sleep, and then to another REM. Basically, during the night, if you were to sleep, say on the average of seven hours, you would probably go through, on the average, four to five REM dreaming cycles per night.

And the last thing that you do before you wake up is usually dream. So, when you remember your dreams, typically, what you remember is the last of four or five cycles of REM dreaming because it's the last thing you do before you wake up. You don't usually remember the content of the previous ones unless you were staying in a sleep lab and they woke you up in the middle of the night. So that's the architecture of sleep.

And then during the day, you still go through the same diurnal rhythms. Throughout the day, you're still going to cycle down to slower activity, progressively, and then up, and then back down, but the threshold is set differently. So, when you cycle out of it, you're in fast wave activity. You're alert. But during the day, you will get periods when your energy level clearly dips, but you're not falling asleep, and you're not dreaming. But is the activity of the brain slowing down at those periods during the day? Yeah, but the threshold is set much higher, so that through those dips in energy during the day, you're not really asleep. You're not dreaming. You understand what I'm saying?

So then, from a Western point of view, the question becomes: what are the functions of dreaming and deep sleep? And generally, from what we understand, the deep sleep is the maintenance of the body, and dreaming is the maintenance of the mind. So, in deep sleep, what we know is we go through stage two, three, and four progressively. Deep sleep is kind of like the body's workshop at night. Whatever cell repair is necessary from the wear and tear of the day, it gets done at night during deep sleep, while the mind remains pretty much suspended.

[Bad buzz making quite a bit inaudible for a few minutes] People who have so-called fibromyalgia usually have a stage two sleep deficit. What does that mean? It means that because of that sleep deficit—which may be genetic, we don't know—they are much more vulnerable to things like muscle tissue pain because they're not cleaning the stuff out the way that would usually be expected. You see what I'm saying? And as we get older, the architecture of sleep changes as we get older. So, when you get to your sixties, between sixties and seventies, the amount of time you spend in deep sleep drops off. So, you tend to shift to lighter sleep. And then when you're between seventy and eighty, it drops off much more, and between eighty and ninety it drops off much more. So, I don't know what the biological, evolutionary significance of that is, but what we know from an observed, scientific point of view is that it means that as you get in your sixties, and then seventies and eighties, all of the tissue repair and growth regulating hormones progressively get limited. And then you die. [Laughter]

That old Zen saying: "Life sucks, then you die." [Laughter] This is the "then you die" part. The system shuts itself down progressively, over these decades. Why? We don't know.

But that's the function of deep sleep—it's growth regulating and cell repair. The function of REM sleep, dreaming, is essentially the maintenance of the mind, not the body. So, dreams are sort of like abstracts. We encounter so much information during the day that what dreams are is they sort of consolidate and aggregate the fundamental themes of the day, and then they compare them to previous themes, mostly emotional. And then the content of the dream, or what Freud called the dream work, is about solving conflicts and unfinished business. We tend to see dreams as problem solving. Whatever is salient to our experience, whatever is unfinished, the dreams successively make a stab at solving that. When you have recurrent nightmares, it's because there's some issue that's not being solved. Think of something like recurring nightmares associated with trauma. People sometimes have them for years.

About seven or eight years ago, in the *Journal of the American Medical Association*, somebody introduced a re-dreaming procedure. Someone has a recurrent nightmare about trauma; you have them in the waking state in your office re-dream it. Revisit the dream, and then come up with a different ending. And then re-dream it again and try another solution. And you stimulate the problem-solving ability. What they found is that people who had ten, twenty years of nightmares were usually resolving them in two or three sessions, without medication, which I thought was significant; it was published in the *Journal of the American Medical Association.*

In other words, what does it tell us? It tells us that dreams really are successive problem-solving stabs at whatever is unfinished. And if you set up the conditions by which people can review it and keep trying to work at solving the problems, they settle down. So, dreams sort of maintain the mind the way that deep sleep maintains the body. We can understand from an evolutionary point of view why that would be the case.

So that's the Western point of view in what we've learned in fifty years of sleep research. I used to work in a sleep lab, so I know some of that research firsthand.

Now, from a meditation point of view, there are two issues here, or three. The first issue is the effects of meditation on sleeping-dreaming and, from a certain perspective, we could say that the effects of meditation, particularly regular practice and especially retreats, are disruptive of that sleep-wake cycle. So, it's not infrequent that people who, if they come and they do the seven-day retreat with us or they even go on longer retreats, will go through a period of time that they are not sleeping well and they tend to have lighter sleep than deeper sleep.

There's no study that's actually taken people in the middle of a meditation retreat and then put them in a sleep lab at night. So objectively we don't really know what the sleep architecture looks like, but the subjective report is that they're sleeping lighter and the total sleep time is less. Now I have to say that with a caveat, and that is that what we know from comparing an ordinary waking mind—people in the sleep lab when you're measuring their EEG and then you ask them the next morning—most people, particularly people who see themselves as sleep disrupted or outright insomniac, most people fundamentally underestimate the amount of time they slept. "Oh, I had an awful night. I only slept two hours." But then you find in the sleep lab with objective measurements, they actually slept five, which is less than what we'd expect, but it's not two. So, people tend to, when they think they're not sleeping well, they tend to catastrophize it, and they over evaluate the degree to which they haven't slept. That's well known.

I think that that over evaluation is probably operative in retreats, too, that when you are in a retreat, you probably think that you're sleeping much less than you are. Objectively, it is the case probably that both your deep sleep is reduced, the total time in deep sleep I think is probably reduced; and I think that people in retreats tend to have at least lighter sleep, and if you're really humming with your meditations, the likelihood is you're going to have substantial reduction in overall total sleep time. So, that's said.

Now, that's the negative spin [saying] that retreats, from just an empirical observation, tend to disrupt sleep and dreaming. But one could take a positive spin on that same theme and say that maybe the reason for reduced depth of sleep and total sleep time may have to do with the fact that whatever the functions of sleeping and dreaming are, that you're getting those met through the meditation. Because there's a lot of literature that suggests that the so-called relaxation response is associated with calming the cascading of stress response hormones.

There are three studies, one in the U.S. and two out of the National Institute of Mental Health in Bangalore in India showing that controlled breathing—that is, good old *prāṇāyāma*, like say alternate nostril breathing and things like that, or nine-round breath—if you do that for a minimum of twenty minutes, it causes a significant uptick in metabolism of catecholamines and other stress response hormones. So you're cleaning the stuff out of your tissue.

So, in terms of the maintenance and repair of the body, it's likely that the way you regulate the posture and the way you regulate the breathing and the way you concentrate the mind is having beneficial effects on cell repair and growth, and are accomplishing some of the functions that one would get out of deep sleep, which would be a positive argument on why you're not sleeping so deeply.

And secondly, because you're letting all the … depending on what kind of meditation you're doing … if you're doing Ocean and Waves and letting everything come up from the view of a changeless, boundless ocean and whatever comes up comes up with no grab, what are you doing there? It's spacious freedom, right? And from the perspective of spacious freedom, if you're doing *lokagambhe*, reverse *samādhi*, and letting everything just come up, and you're reviewing it very rapidly, aren't you doing the same kind of rapid review and processing that is really what dreaming is about?

So, one would expect that those kinds of meditations would lead to a significantly reduced need for the mental regulating effects of dreaming. You'd probably have reduced REM time based on the fact that you're accomplishing some of that on the pillow while you're still alert. I think in a positive sense that's what's going on. People when they first get the sleep disruption in retreats, they tend to interpret it negatively. But, you see, the tipoff is that we have, in the West, extensive research on sleep deprivation. And if you keep waking people up in the sleep lab night after night, they start to get pretty miserable and their behavior deteriorates. And their capacity for problem solving and organized behavior and all these wonderful things that we associate with getting by in everyday living go down the tubes.

But you see, it's been the case that when people are on long retreats and they're claiming a fair amount of sleep disruption, what we *don't* observe in them is the usual effects of sleep deficits. It's absent. So that would be a compelling argument that probably what you're doing is getting some of the same body and mind regulatory effects of sleeping and dreaming from the meditation, which is why you don't get a sleep deficit. Whereas, if you just wake people up at night (non-meditators) and keep waking them up in the sleep lab night after night, that probably explains why they have a sleep deficit, because they're not doing meditation to compensate. Or maybe even do more efficiently what you're doing at night. See the difference?

Student 1

Mm-hmm (affirmative).

Dan

Because what's striking is that most people who have lighter sleep or less reduced time in sleep as a function of meditation don't report sleep deficit. That's the first thing I would say. Okay?

Now the second thing is you're opening up a whole other world here about what's called sleep and dream yoga. And the second level of this, the answer to this question, has to do with what would otherwise be the normal sleep and dream cycle and how that's affected by the awakened mind. Not just by meditation practice.

But let's say you have a taste of awakening and, more than that, you develop, or you nurture that awakening so you have it more frequently and for longer durations first on the pillow and then off the pillow. Then we need to look at the effects of awakening on sleep and dreaming. And essentially awake means awake. So from the perspective of an awakened mind, what begins to happen spontaneously is that the nature of awakened mind—*rigpa* or *dharmakāya* or whatever you want to call it—if you train it and nurture it so you have it more frequently, so you're operating out of awakened mind rather than ordinary mind, then what's going to happen is that that's going to drift over into sleep and dreaming so that there will be times during deep sleep, which has no content, where you will be awake during deep sleep. You don't wake up. But the awakened mind is operative during deep sleep. Awake means awake.

And you will find times during dreaming spontaneously that you'll actually be awake enough to know that you're dreaming without waking up. In the West we call that lucid dreaming. Okay, now that's spontaneous, and depending on the magnitude of your awakening and how frequently you nurture that awakening, you can expect that the effects of awakening will drift into deep sleep and to dreaming more and more. Okay? Awake means awake.

Now, the next part of the answer is that there are practices which intentionally allow you to train this. And those are called sleep and dream yogas. You can find them, and there are two sources for that. In the Kagyu, Karma Kagyu tradition, you find dream yoga in the Six Yogas of Naropa. The Naro Chodrug is one of the Six Yogas of Naropa. And there aren't six yogas. These were sets of practices that all the yogis knew and sometimes there were three yogas and four yogas; and the one that sort of got popular was the sixth version of this. It also includes *phowa*, consciousness transfer at the time of death. So these are a bunch of things that yogis found interesting. And one of those that was necessary in all ways is sleep and dream yoga. So, a good source for that would be Naro Chodrug, the Six Yogas of Naropa.

The other source for that is that these sleep and dream yogas are very well developed within Bonpo Dzogchen. So, you tend to find them in the Akhrid and the Shangshung Nyanjyud lineages of Bon. And of course, the lama who teaches that in the West is Tenzin Wangyal. And he has probably the clearest book on sleep and dream yoga. I've done the Akhrid practices and the Bonpo. So those are the ones that I know the best. They're not easy.

Now, in the actual practice that you do, these practices are not taught until you have pretty much stabilized awakening. So that means that you can, on the pillow, set up the view so you can shift your basis of operation to awakened awareness. And you can sustain that throughout your meditation on the pillow. And then you can bring that awakening off the pillow and *drewa*—you can mix it into everyday activities—so that regardless of the nature of your activities, you're always operating out of awakened mind in the midst of everything. Mixing practices, you learn to mix it into whatever. You learn to mix it in conversation. So, I'd have to mix it into lecturing, what I'm doing now. But if I'm working on my computer, I have to be able to sustain the awakening while I'm on my computer. Those are called "mixing practices."

Once I can reasonably sustain that awakening in everyday life—not always, but more than not—that would be the starting criteria for the introduction of sleep and dream yoga. And when you do sleep and dream yoga, what you do … the visualizations are rather elaborate but they're not necessary. The main requirement is that just before you go to sleep that you are operating out of awakened mind. Usually, you go to sleep in what's called lion's posture. In lion's posture you lie on your right side like this [Dan leans his head as if propped up on his right hand] with your feet out somewhat bent, like a sleeping lion on one side.

And then you do practice. You do the energy channels. You open up the central channel. But what's more important than *tsa lung*—the *tsa lung* practices are just to help you—if you open up the central channel, then the awareness is really bright and awake. So it makes it more obvious how to recognize awakened awareness, which is much brighter and "awaker" than ordinary awareness. So that's your starting point.

Then, what you train yourself to do is you train yourself to try and have that awareness and carry that awakened awareness with you into stage one descending sleep, the hypnagogic state. You can train yourself to get closer and closer to that point where you find there's a threshold where you drift right into sleep.

Nothing to do with meditation, but years ago in the 1980s when I was doing research in this area in the West, we used to do a little thing where we went … If you want to work with people with guided imagery …—some people aren't very good at imaging—but everybody has strong imaging during the hypnagogic state. So if you ask a person to lie down on their right side, and they deeply relax themselves, and you have them hold up their arm like this [Dan lies on his right side and puts his right hand up by his head] with your legs stretched out "like a sleeping lion"; if you're holding up your head like this [Dan wonders if the camera can see him, which it can't so he sits back up and holds his hand up so it's limp, hanging down]; you see, if you're holding up your hand like this, you train them to get more and more profoundly and deeply relaxed. Then what's going to happen is, if they go over that edge [Dan drops his hand quickly, making a sound effect like "phht"], they immediately get the feedback that they've gone too far and drifted into sleep. But, as long as the hand is up, they're not really asleep. And you can train them to get successive approximations of finding just that threshold where they drift off.

Now, in the sleep and dream yoga you do something like that. You don't have to do this. [Dan holds up his right hand with it hanging down from the wrist.] But I'm saying that we had done something like that because we taught people to find that threshold where all that spontaneous imagery comes up, and it's so vivid but it's somewhat fragmented unlike dreams, that they at least, they lend access to their own natural imaging capacity which they didn't think they had, and then once they've learned that, after three or four or five sessions of training, then they're pretty good at imaging. So that's how we used to train poor images to be better images, by using stage one descending hypnagogic training.

And then when I was taught the sleep and dream yoga, it was surprising to me to find out that they were doing something very similar. You learn to carry awakened awareness into deep sleep and to get successive refinements of finding that threshold so you can find just that threshold. And it's like threading the eye of a needle. You can actually, with awareness, pick out the point that you drift to on the other side of that threshold, and you're asleep but you're still aware. And you learn to carry the awareness right into deep sleep because that's the first thing that comes up, then stage two, three, four.

And then you learn to carry that awareness into dreaming. At first, it's a little choppy, but then after a while you get to be able to carry it more continuously. It's a kind of learning. You don't wake up. If you wake up, you screw it up, and then you have to go back to square one and then go back to doing your meditation, set up your awakening as your basis of operation, come back in the sleep preparation, try and find that threshold, and draw your awareness from stage one, descending right into stage two, where you're on the other side of that looking glass now, and you're actually asleep, but you're awake.

And you keep doing that, until you train yourself to carry it continuously. And sleep yoga is one half of the equation where you learn to carry the awakened awareness into deep sleep, stage two, three and four, in Western terms. And dream yoga is when you learn to carry that awareness into the time that you're actually dreaming and having all that content going on, and in Western terms we call that lucid dreaming. And when you can carry that awareness to deep sleep and then dreaming continuously, without waking up, you've mastered the first stage of this training of four stages.

This is, you'll see it's a little humbling. That's the first stage. Now, it's considered better practice if you can carry the awakening into deep sleep rather than into dreaming sleep. So, awake during deep sleep is superior to awake during dreaming. So, awake during deep sleep is superior to what we call in the West, lucid dreaming. There's no literature in the West on lucid deep sleep. Most of the Western literature—Stephen LaBerge and others have done a lot of research on lucid dreaming—is about dreaming. And the reason for that is because the strength of awakening is stronger if it drifts into deep sleep than into content related things. You follow me?

Now, I had a friend who's a psychophysiologist wire me up at times in the day because I was curious about this, and he had a sixteen channel EEG; and we found something that was surprising, but it made perfect sense to me. We found that I cycle through, just as I said, fast waves to slower activity, the way one would normally expect. The bandwidths, the frequency bandwidths, are not any different; they followed the reasonable pattern for normal diurnal rhythms. But what was striking is on any bandwidth—beta, fast wave activity; alpha, more relaxed activity; theta, more slow wave activity; and even delta—that the amplitude was off the charts.

And, I suppose, that is a good explanation from a psychophysiological point of view of what the sleep and dream yoga looks like. Awake means awake, which means that even though you're cycling through sleep-wake cycle, there's a lot of energy; there's a lot of energy in the mind in all those bandwidths. So it doesn't make any difference whether it's fast activity or slow activity—the mind is awake so it's got a lot of energy. Because awake means that all those neurons are still active, even though the frequency of their firing follows diurnal rhythms. You understand what I'm saying? And that makes perfect sense to me. But that's the sample size of one, [Laughter] so I don't know what it really looks like, but I thought it was fun to play with.

So that's the first stage. Now the second stage is when, in addition to carrying continuous awakened awareness into sleep and dreams—the second stage is when you can then gain voluntary control—so while you're asleep it's not enough to have lucid dreaming. While you're asleep you have to be able to voluntarily alter the dream content. And they use that to train supernormal powers. So, if you want to be a *dharma* superhero, you have to do this part of the training. So, what you have to do—and you're told ahead of time that when you dream what they want you to dream is supernormal ability. Because we know in the West, that if you tell people in the waking state to contemplate a certain target, and then you test them in a dream lab where the people are collecting their dreams at night, they wake the person up when they're having REM sleep and the lab techs are blind to what's being asked for. We know that if you suggest to people to dream about a certain topic during the day, there's a good likelihood that they will actually dream about that topic at night. So this isn't a hard thing to do. We know that in Western terms. So, if you have the meditator, you give them an assignment to dream about supernormal abilities. Then the task of that second stage, in this case dream yoga, is that they have to be able to change around reality at night.

So, jumping over mountains with a single leap, flying through walls, these are the typical assignments that you're given—super normal assignments. And as it's explained in the commentaries that all of us have buddha nature and all of us have supernormal abilities—there are twelve *gunshes*, supernormal abilities—but the reason why most people never manifest the supernormal abilities is that our deep-seated beliefs about reality prevent us from seeing that we can do this stuff. Because we really don't think we can, and those are really hardcore beliefs. So, the reason for having you change around the dream reality is that it starts to change around those deep-seated beliefs about the nature of reality, because in the dream you can make anything happen. And what you make happen is all these supernormal abilities because it changes fundamental core beliefs about the nature of reality. So, you do the second level of practices without waking up, where you have voluntary control of the content and you try and change the content in supernormal ways. That's stage two.

Stage three is you reverse the practice. And in stage three, you don't focus on dreaming; you focus on everyday reality as a dream, and you have to view everything as a living dream all day long until you meet the test criteria, which is there's absolutely no difference between waking dream and dream at night. You're awake continuously during waking dream, and you see it as a dream; and you're awake during dreaming sleep and you see it as a dream; and there's no difference. And you have to do this thoroughly until it's all one dream, whether you're asleep or whether you're so-called "awake." Understand what I'm saying?

And then the fourth level gets pretty interesting. The last, the fourth level then you have to change around ordinary waking reality the same way you changed around the dream. And you have to manifest the same supernormal abilities in waking realities. So, you have to jump over mountains in a single leap, and you have to walk through walls, and do other things just as you did in the dream. And if there's no difference at that point, since you've completely eradicated all the karmic impressions of these limiting beliefs, you should be able to do all the psychic abilities at that point. Easy. [Laughter] So that's the second answer to your question.

Now there's one more, okay. This is a fun question. Thank you for asking. There's a lot to this.

Student 1

Yes, there is.

Dan

The third answer to your question is that, irrespective of sleep and dream yoga, it is the case that as you deepen your practice, it's said that the practice will deepen to deeper levels of the mind. So, we look for signs of progress. Okay, so, if you, in terms of karma theory, which is Eastern learning theory—the more you practice something, the more it has effects, and we tend to see those effects in three stages. The first stage is that if you practice positive states through your meditation over and over and over again, then you should expect the *tak*, the first signs of that to be spontaneously emerging positive states. Spontaneous positive states will come up in your experience as a result of the cumulative effect of all your spiritual practice. Now, those spontaneous states you'll experience during the day and also during your meditation. But as the practice really deepens, there's a second stage to this. You'll notice that it will start to affect your dreams. So, when you start getting positive dreams, particularly where the content of the dreams is deeply positive and about your practice, then that shows you're integrating your practice at the deepest levels of the coarse level mind, content-level mind. Understand what I'm saying?

So, when you start reporting positive dreams, then that's a *tak*—that's a sign that you're integrating the practice at the deepest levels of your mind. And a lama would be especially interested in the content of your dream in that case. So, you've done a lot of work on Ocean and Waves, and sealing practice, and automatic emptiness, and tastes of awakening. And that whole range of practice is the range of what we would call spacious freedom. So, it's not an accident that you're dreaming about a *garuda*, because a *garuda* when he flies—which is the mythical bird of prey—the *garuda* has vast, infinite scope of his view, and pinpointed focus on his target. So, the *garuda* is the symbol of King of Samādhi—the infinite, vast scope of awareness; the ocean of awareness; limitless, boundless awareness; and pinpointed focus.

So, if that's the range of your practice, you see, it's not accidental that you're dreaming about a *garuda*. But if you have a taste of awakening, even if you lose it and it clouds over, which is typically the case, it changes everything. And the *garuda* symbol is very specific because it's a mythical bird. But *garudas*, like chickens, hatch. It's the way chickens and dinosaurs hatch, right? But what's said about a *garuda* is … what's unique is that when a *garuda* pecks out of the shell and it comes out, it's already fully formed, unlike a chicken. A chicken comes out with a lot of blood and a lot of very beginning feathers, and it takes a while to grow the feathers and grow the wings. The *garuda* is not like any other egged animal. The *garuda* comes out already fully formed. The only other mythical animal that does the same thing is a dragon. And so, in that sense, *garudas* are like dragons; they come out already fully formed even though they might not look fully formed.

And buddha nature is like that, too. If you get a taste of awakening on the deepest levels of mind, all of the eighty positive qualities of a buddha mind are already fully formed. And even though you don't know it, you already know it, and that's why you're dreaming of the *garuda*, because you know where this is going to take you. Understand what I'm saying? Okay. That's why you're dreaming about a *garuda*.

Now, if you dream about a lama, that's considered to be very auspicious because it tells that you have the heart connection, and that you don't need the physical presence of your lama to show you things because you already have that form, that connection. So as the practice spontaneously unfolds, if you hold your view, because the view is the meditation; then at various points when you tend to get a little off, spontaneously the lama's image and a reminder of that will come up in the field of vast awareness space, and then it's self-correcting. You understand what I'm saying.

So, the content of the dreams matters in that sense, you see, because it's a kind of indication of the degree to which the positive effects of all your cumulative practice is *minwa*, ripening. The first that ripens is spontaneous states in your waking state and in your meditation, then spontaneous positive states in your dreams, and then as you deepen and integrate the practice, it ripens in terms of spontaneous behavior. You start acting better. And then when your practice gets really, really strong, it ripens in terms of changing the unfolding of life events. It affects what you experience, so you start having good fortune. The fact that we're all here is good fortune together. That you have an opportunity to hear these teachings is good fortune. It's all the ripening of your own karmic propensities—the very fact that you can take this in at all, that would be a Tibetan explanation for this.

December 19, 2012

Themes: The Sun; Enlightened Buddha Bodies; Confession and *Tonglen*

Dan

Welcome everyone. You have a question?

Student 1

I asked Rinpoche about [the sun and moon symbols], and one of the things that he mentioned was the elements, where he talked about the sun and the moon representing wisdom and compassion, but he also talked about the elements. And I said, well what do you mean by the elements. He said okay, so this is the earth, where we are. The sun is the fire. Here's air. This is all space, and the moon, he said, well, the moon is clearly water. And so it just started opening things up for me about, you know … just there's something here I'm sure about how it's all right here, and yet I don't ever see it. And yet it's all right here, it's all, like, so obvious, and so I just would like you to talk about that.

Dan

So, there's not one answer, but the traditional use of the symbolism of the sun is the manifestation of ultimate reality. Sometimes it's used for ultimate reality in general, and sometimes it's used as a symbol of the compassion aspect of ultimate reality. But, the sun, no matter whether you see it or not, it always shines. It never stops shining. It's like that line from Tilopa that for thousands of eons the sun has shone every day; it never stops shining. The awakened mind never stops shining, but like the sun, when it gets clouded over and it rains or storms, and then the clouds clear away, we say the sun came out, which isn't correct. The sun doesn't come out, the sun's always out. What happens is the clouds go away enough so you can experience or perceive the sun shining forth in its full radiance.

So, the sun symbolizes the nature of an awakened mind. Everybody has buddha nature, everybody has their own sun, and, like the sun, that buddha nature always shines; the nature of an awakened mind always shines forth all the time right now, always. And it has, awakened awareness has, a certain, we say *dangpa*, brightness. We say *gnar*, intensity. We say *hrige*, awakeness; *bole*, softness. And those are descriptors of the nature of *rigpa*, awakened awareness. And all of those are qualities of *selwa*: lucidity, the lucidity of awakened awareness, like the lucid brilliance or radiance of the sun. And like the sun, awakened awareness, or *rigpa*, never stops shining, so it's ... we call it *yeshe*, primordial; it doesn't have a beginning and it doesn't have an end. It's always shining. True nature, always shining.

And awakened awareness has a kind of, it's not just an ocean of empty awareness space. It has a kind of dynamic energy to it. The energetic dynamic manifestation of awakening is like all of the energy of the sun. And it shines with a certain inexhaustibility. It never stops shining. It shines with *Ma Gag Pa*. It's unobstructed, it shines everywhere. *Ma Gag Pa* means the rays of the sun shine everywhere equally. And in the compassionate aspect of the sun as a metaphor, it doesn't decide who to shine on. Ultimate compassion is superior to relative compassion because if you're acting out of ordinary mind and relative compassion, you can decide who you want to extend that compassion to. But, in ultimate compassion, when you are being that sun of awakened awareness, it doesn't decide who to shine on. It shines everywhere equally.

So, usually the sun is a symbolism for *rigpa*. And another aspect of the sun is that the various aspects of the sun symbolize the three enlightened buddha bodies. I mean the ultimate attainment in becoming a buddha is the manifestation of the buddha bodies. There is a boundless wholeness that extends in an unbounded limitless way, like vast empty space. It's the groundless ground, the structure of being. And that's *dharmakāya*, the embodiment of all the teachings. *Kaya* means body, but in this case, they don't use the word *lu*, which means ordinary body, they use the word *ku*, which is honorific. So it really means the embodiment, *dharmakāya* literally means the embodiment of all the teachings. If you awaken to *dharmakāya* space, and you are that unbounded wholeness, which contains everything that could possibly be, then you have embodied all the teachings. It's the one point! All 84,000 baskets of the *dharma*, and the thousands of skillful means, all lead to the same end. That's the attainment.

But that space-like groundless ground is always right here. It also has a kind of dynamic energy of manifestation, or has a liveliness to it, and the brilliant lucidity of that energy—knowing itself and expressing itself, and knowing brilliantly, knowing every moment what is expressed—that brightness of the energy of manifestation is where the entire world is energy, knowing itself. That's *saṃbhogakāya*. And that lively energy is wondrous, and deeply satisfying, every moment, which is why *saṃbhogakāya* means enjoyment body, *longku* in Tibetan. It's like *hedawa*, which means a chronic state of wonder. That's *saṃbhogakāya*. It's the energy of manifestation brilliantly known by an awakened mind every moment.

Then, the brilliant display of the details of what's seen is *nirmāṇakāya*, but seeing it as two ways different from ordinary perception. One is that this whole display is very vivid but insubstantial; it's like a dream or mirage, so nothing has any solidity to it. It's all light, but it's light that seems to take the ethereal form, and sound, and thought and motion, and none of it's real, but it's a wondrous display. The second aspect that's different from ordinary perception is that this bubble is just one bubble. The mind that manifests the buddha body manifests all the bubbles, all the universes that could possibly be—past, present, and future—all at once, because it's all contained within this unbounded wholeness. The scope of that awareness has now become limitless.

So, if you have an awakened mind that shines like the sun all of the time, at some point, that awareness by itself begins to display entire worlds. And you see that awakened awareness, *rigpa*, not only has liveliness, it has organizing capacity, it has intelligence, and it will present all worlds and buddha fields. None of them are real, but you watch with utter awe, wonder, the display of all the worlds, every moment, simultaneously, multiple worlds. Then, you see, the scope of that awareness is said to pervade and saturate everything in this unbounded wholeness. Then you move beyond the doctrine of two truths, the relative and ultimate reality. There's no division between ultimate reality and relative reality. It's all the same unbounded wholeness, in what's called the *thigle chenpo*, the great sphere, the one great sphere of reality.

And the mind is that. The awakened mind is the buddha mind, is that. Now that goes beyond a taste of awakening, because when you lock onto the very structure of being, to all the bodies at once, you know right away it's not like even a little taste of *rigpa*. You're locking into the structure of being itself, in a way that inspires deep awe.

And what do you say about it? It embodies everything. That's why it's called buddha bodies. So, we can say that the three buddha bodies are also captured in the metaphor of the sun. The vast unified sphere that the sun is, is like the *thigle chenpo*. It's a huge reality. It's so vast, like the extent of *dharmakāya*. And it's always radiant and alive and inexhaustible in its energy, like *saṃbhogakāya*. And it's constantly emitting rays in specific directions, in all directions, an entire display of rays of energy and color and light, and seeming form, like the rays of the sun. So, the sun itself, its energy of manifestation, and the rays of the sun are the three aspects of the buddha bodies. And I don't know whether you'll always get somebody sitting on the sun, but the reason why they're sitting on the sun is because they're firmly implanted in buddha nature. It couldn't be any other way. But what you always get, whether or not you get the sun cushion, what you always get is the depiction of the buddha bodies. [Dan stands up to face a *thanka* hanging on the wall.]

So, here on our *thanka*, see this round sphere, that vast space? That's *dharmakāya*, unbounded wholeness. Every *thanka* has the buddha bodies. And, it's right here, this empty space. Brilliant like the sun is *dharmakāya*, the space-like, unbounded wholeness, the structure of reality. And then, you see all these wavy lines? All those wavy lines, that's *saṃbhogakāya*. That's the energy of manifestation, brilliantly knowing itself through its own liveliness and energy. And, everything around that is the display. And usually, they have one bubble—like the bubble we're in now—and then, you have the background bubbles, to illustrate the limitlessness of *nirmāṇakāya*, where there are many manifestations. One may seem more in the foreground. But if you hold all of it at once, like so, the rest of this area is *nirmāṇakāya*, many buddha bodies. Every *thanka* has that. So … [Dan gets seated again.] Now, that's what I would say about the sun. There's a lot to it. So, in the narrow sense, it depicts awakened nature. In the broader sense, it's the aspects of the sun that depict buddha bodies.

Now the moon—sometimes we use moon and sometimes we use water moon. If you look at the surface of the ocean, like I was just on the West Coast, so if you watch the sun go down, on a night where there's a good moon, you can watch the dance of the reflections on the surface of the water. So, all of relative reality is said to be like a water moon. What you're seeing are the representations, the constructions. You're seeing the reflection of the moon. You're not seeing the moon itself. And all of this is a reflection of the energy of manifestation.

We don't see the energy of manifestation in ordinary mind. All we see are the reflections, the constructions. We don't even see them as empty. We take them as too solid. So, to say that you see things in terms of the reflections in the water is to say that you see them as empty—visibly appearing, yet insubstantial. When you look at the dance of the reflections on the surface of the water, you don't have to stop and say, "They're not real, but they're vivid, brilliant." You come with emptiness practice; you come to see all of perception like reflections in the water.

But then, the same also applies to the moon itself. When you see the moon, what you're seeing is a reflection of the sun. So, the moon or the reflections on the water of the moon … the moon itself is also like a water moon. Sometimes, in Dzogchen we say it's like seeing the reflections in the mirror. Everyday reality is like seeing the reflections in the mirror rather than looking at the mirror itself. When you look at true nature, the true nature of this boundless wholeness, this infinite expanse of awareness, you're looking at the mirror—except it's a pretty big mirror—rather than looking at the reflections in the mirror.

So, to be seated on the moon is to be firmly grounded in emptiness. It's to understand that all reflections, everything that we see, from all five senses—sight, sounds, smells, tastes, sensations—and all seemingly internal thoughts and emotions, are all like reflections of the water moon. You vividly see them, and they're all insubstantial. They're just constructions because the mind constructs. And they have no substance to them, but they're vivid. So when you're seated on the moon, you're firmly grounded in the perception of emptiness.

Now you see in this picture, [Dan points to a *thanka* behind him] that you see a lotus. And the symbol of the lotus is that the lotus is a beautiful flower, which thrives by growing in mud. And the blossoming of an awakened mind grows in the mud of relative reality. You use the mud of relative reality, all the stuff of what you experience, as the vehicle for insight. And when you see all the mud of relative reality just the way it is, as empty yet appearing, so it no longer clouds over, what will blossom is an awakened mind. Like a beautiful flower in the midst of the mud. So, that's the reason for the sitting on the lotus. You don't have to get rid of relative reality to get awakened. You use the relative reality as the vehicle of awakening. It best shines forth or blossoms by looking into seeing relative reality just the way it is. So that's usually the lotus symbol.

Then, sometimes, it's the sun, the moon, the lotus, and then they're being held up by the five animals. There's a horse, there's an elephant, let's see, what am I missing? There's a dragon, a *garuda*, and a lion. Those are the five animals that hold up the lotus, the sun-moon seat. And those are pretty much obvious what they mean. The horse is very fast—the speed of your mental pliancy. What's going to hold up your realization is your mental pliancy. The lion has great physical strength. What's going to hold up your realization is physical pliancy. Remember the lion from Tilopa. And with awakening you seem to have the strength of a lion.

The elephant you know, it's the elephant path. What's going to hold up your realization is the stability of a fully concentrated mind. Only here it doesn't mean ordinary concentration; it's King of Samādhi. Because what happens is that by maintaining concentration … you see, at this level the practice, the view is the meditation. The view is the meditation, but you have to hold the view undistractedly. So, concentration training is what reinforces the view. And because you're holding the view, the emptiness aspect of holding the view eradicates all the grab and all the things that get in the way of being able to hold the concentration. We call that the yoking of concentration and insight—that concentration reinforces the view, the view reinforces the concentration, so you can technically hold the view correctly every moment, day and night, waking and sleeping. That's why it's an elephant.

And then the dragon symbolizes with the realization comes the *gunshes*, the super normal abilities of the buddha. There are mythical creatures that have super normal capacities. A buddha needs super normal abilities to teach—especially for Western students because Western students are difficult. [Dan laughs, and students, too.] A lot of mud here.

And the last is the *garuda*. The *garuda* is a mythical bird and there are two unique aspects of a *garuda*. Sometimes we use the word *garuda* for King of Samādhi—pin-pointed focus every moment against the backdrop of the infinite vast expanse of an awakened mind. So, what makes it different—when you're concentrating when you're doing elephant path, you're concentrating from the perspective of your ordinary mind trying to keep concentrating on whatever the object is, like the rising and falling of the breath. But when you're practicing King of Samādhi, you have the scope of awakened mind with the infinite vast scope of awakened awareness. And that's where you're concentrating from. So, if you want to concentrate on the body, the body will immediately … with no more than a moment instant of intention, the body will hang in space. But it won't be solid. We say like an empty glass bottle filled with light. Then if you do no more than put the intention on finding the breath, then the body, the movement of the breath will be perfect every moment. All against the backdrop of viewing it from being that ocean of boundless awareness, awakened awareness.

So, the difference is where you're concentrating from. And if you're concentrating every moment from an awakened mind, then we say that you're practicing King of Samādhi. It's like a great bird of prey, like a *garuda*. A great bird of prey has infinite scope of the horizon when it's flying, and then a pin-pointed focus on its prey at the same time, like a *garuda*.

There's a famous Dzogchen text called *The Flight of the Garuda*. It has two translations. One by Keith Dowman, and one by Tony Duff. And, it's a good book. So, flight of the *garuda* means the practice of King of Samādhi. And then the second is, what's unique about *garudas* … Oh I remember when my kids were young, and we would go to the science museum. And of course, one of the favorite things that the kids loved to do and it was true of most kids, I think, is to go watch the chicken eggs in the incubator. And if you come back two or three times a day, somewhere during that time frame, there's a good likelihood that you find the egg cracking and a pecking, the beak pecking its way out. And you watch these remarkable birds come to life. But, you see, when a chicken breaks the shell, it has almost no feathers. And it's not very well formed. But *garudas* aren't like chickens. The mythical *garuda*, when it breaks the shell and hatches, it's already fully developed. And the *garuda* is a symbol of buddha nature. You don't have to develop buddha nature. It's already fully developed.

So, to have the *garuda* holding up the seat of your practice is to have the view that there's nothing you're developing here that isn't already known. It's better that you take the view that you're activating what you already have rather than something you're looking for, in some remote concept of what you think you're finding. People search for awakening and that's a problem because the search doesn't lead anywhere. And it can't be found by a self because the self can't awaken. But if you get out of the way, then awakening happens to itself by itself; and with the point of awakening then, and deepening that awakening, you discover that this has been there all along. It's all part of, it's your nature. So in that sense, you discover that you are a *garuda*. That's the symbolism. And our buddha here [Dan points to a snow globe by his side that has a buddha sitting in the snow] is one sphere of reality—infinite, brilliant, energy of manifestation. In it, everything appears like a magical display that is not very real. There's our buddha bodies.

Anybody else? [Long pause. Dan chuckles.]

No, come on, everybody else has responsibility to what's important in your practice. Go ahead.

Student 2

The whole concept of time, emptiness of time, is something which I've sort of worked with over the years. It's been something that—it's sort of come up and I sort of worked with it. And last week a teacher was doing a meditation of *tonglen*. And as part of that meditation, it was going to … one part of it was going to various parts of your life that had been problematic. In going to those and using *tonglen*, breathing in, breathing out, basically telling yourself, you know, it's okay. And …

Dan

Well, but if you're looking at the parts of your life that are problematic, and you're not operating out of time, then those problems have always been there and always will be.

Student 2

Yeah … [Dan laughs along with others.] Well, here's sort of what happened to me, is I went to a couple of points in my life—the worst parts of my life had been points where, to make a long story short, I really thought I'd screwed up my life. I thought, man, I really … I made such horrible decisions and there's nothing I can do about it and I totally messed up my life. There were two times when that happened. So I went back to those as I was meditating last week doing the *tonglen*, and went to a guy that was there, you know, to just tell him it's okay, it's alright, don't worry about it because I was in such agony at that time. And, the part that was … I felt on this really strong level at that moment when I was doing that, remembering back to those times in my life when I was in the midst of all of that turmoil, and I felt this sense of all the turmoil that was going on; it was almost sort of this sense of, "Oh yeah, it's alright. Things are going to be alright." So, I mean, I wonder if—and this defies all of my preconceived notions, that I was last week really going back to those times; and what I felt at those moments was myself last week going back and assuring myself that everything was going to be okay.

Dan

Okay. Well, let me just start with a Western answer. Then I'll contrast it to the Buddhist answer. In the Western literature, there's a genre of what are known as the confession studies by the work of Jim Pennebaker and his associates. And in the confession studies, the instructions go like this. I want you to think here now about something in your life that you feel deeply, emotionally, unfinished about, something deeply, emotionally unfinished. It may be a loss. It may be something traumatic or deeply upsetting that happened to you. It may be something that you felt deeply ashamed or guilty about. Reflect now on whatever it is that feels most emotionally unfinished. And bring it to mind repeatedly. With all the thoughts and feelings you have about it. And if you're finding yourself wanting to avoid it and get your mind off of it, all the more reason to bring it to mind even more. And keep reviewing it with all the thoughts and feelings about it.

Now that was the experimental instruction. The control group was to just think whatever comes to mind. But the instructions were not for processing unfinished emotional business. And in the experimental group, they tried different formats. Some people talked to another person about what was emotionally unfinished. Some people talked into a tape recorder. And some people were given instructions to journal, and write about it in a journal, for twenty minutes, four times over four weeks. Not very long. And what they found were strong psychological and biological effects of this. Not only through processing unfinished emotional business were people having high reports of psychological well-being, but they were also showing improvement of immune function. And they were more resistant to illness proneness.

So, confession maybe good for the soul, but it also happens to be good for the body. So these studies became known as the confession studies. And in the trauma field—at least for single incident trauma, not extended trauma—but for single incident trauma, the best studies we have in the West are studies about what we called exposure-based treatments.

And the early studies were mostly done with rape, single incident rape. Bring to mind the experience with all the thoughts and feelings you had at the time. And if you find yourself wanting to avoid anything because you're uncomfortable, keep bringing it to mind all the more. And keep reviewing it and keep reviewing it. Then people like Edna Foa and others found that roughly in about eight sessions with that kind of review, in the hour and at home, there was a significant drop in post-traumatic symptoms. So, one is what exposure-based work told us on the one hand, and the confessions studies on the other hand told us that what gets us from a Western point of view; what gets us in trouble is, when something happens to us, we don't process it. When the going gets tough, the tough avoid it. And there is cognitive avoidance, which means we keep it out of our mind and don't deal with it. And there's behavioral avoidance, which means we avoid situations or people that would stir it up.

And avoidance has long term consequences, including, if we keep putting it out of our minds, we can actually block the mind's access to it. That's where this whole stuff about dissociative amnesia or repressed memories comes in. Now I have neuroimaging studies showing if you ask people to intentionally forget something, after a while they don't have access to it anymore. And if you look at what's going on with neuroimaging during the time that they're given instructions to intentionally forget, they're activating top-down control. The dorsolateral executive system is activated. But then if they're told after ten sessions of trying to intentionally forget it, they can try and remember all of it as much as they can, they actually remember less after that. And the hippocampus, which contextualizes the retrieval of the memory, is shut down. So, it's like if you try to avoid too much, it tends to deactivate the neurocircuitry and goes offline. So then you have, if you will, a neurobiological disadvantage to putting it back online again.

So, we all do this to some extent, and failing to process things that are upsetting has long term consequences for physical and emotional health. And so, all this exposure-based work comes down to rather simple principles, and I think why Pennebaker struck gold on his simple studies was that it was the wording of things. If you give the instruction to intentionally look for what's most emotionally unfinished and process it, it's going to give a high clinical yield. It nearly works for everybody, because all of us can find things that we didn't deal with. And just by providing the context to finish the processing of it so it settles down, it unhooks you.

So, that would be the Western equivalent of what you're doing with *tonglen*; but the instruction you got [from your teacher] is not actually how it's done. I mean there's nothing wrong with what he's doing. It's just that usually when you do *tonglen* you're taking the suffering of others, you don't look at your own suffering. [Inaudible comment by someone] But if you look at your own suffering, then what you need to do is make a context to process what's unfinished until you're settled with it. It's not a hard procedure, but that's the first part of it.

From a Buddhist point of view, I suppose you could include processing the suffering of self along with the processing of others because the mind includes both; there's nothing wrong with that. But the second part of *tonglen* is not the taking in of suffering from self and others, it's the giving out of loving-kindness. And if you are practicing giving out loving-kindness then it's going to … it does something beyond just the confession. It leads to psychological well-being.

The Dalai Lama, in his book that he wrote with Howard Cutler, the book on happiness, he says, "For me, compassion practice is what makes me happy." You feel good after it. We know from modern neuroimaging studies that part of the frontal system, the medial orbital system, is the area of the brain when it's activated that gives emotional significance to things, and it's the area of most of our positive emotions. And so, if you're practicing loving-kindness, you're activating that orbital frontal system. And since that has top-down control over negative feelings, if you're activating your positivity, at some point it shuts down all that negativity.

And Richie Davidson—who's a long-term meditator and probably the best neuroimager in this country, in Wisconsin—he looked at lamas who had a career of practicing loving-kindness and other compassion meditations. And when they looked at the activation of the orbital frontal system compared to people who don't do those practices, theirs was far more developed. The capacity to activate the orbital frontal system was significantly developed in these lamas. So, you see, if you're not just confessing the negative, but if you develop the positive, we know in this generation of neuroplasticity that the brain isn't a constant organ. It changes size and shape depending on demand. If you don't use an area of the brain, it gets smaller. If you use it, it gets bigger. Well, the hippocampus is spatial memory. So there's the so-called taxi study. In the UK, taxiing is a noble profession. You have to memorize all the streets for two years and you have to take an exam on it. So, they took people who were just at the beginning of going to taxi school, and they scanned them at the beginning, and then six months later after spending six months of cramming all these memories of the streets in their mind; and what they found was about an 8 percent increase in the size of the hippocampus after six months. It changed the structure. We also know there's about an 8 percent decrease in the size of the hippocampus in some people with chronic PTSD, who have poor memory for their trauma.

So, the brain increases and decreases structure. There's a study on concentration meditation [showing], if you practice the elephant path, the anterior cingulate cortex, which is the attention center of the brain, shows an increase in its volume and an increase in structure. There's more white matter; you're laying down new tracks. So, the brain isn't a constant organ. And if you use it, you develop it. If you don't use it, it remains underdeveloped, just like muscle structure. It gets either more developed or it gets atrophied, depending on the use and lack thereof. No different. So, what these lamas are doing is they've really got a great deal of skill in altering the brain structure of the orbital frontal system. What does that translate in terms of everyday behavior? They're far more positive all of the time, and most of the time. You can see that, they're happy lamas, because that's what they do for practice.

So, you see the giving, the taking in and the giving out; although it's one structure of practice, the two components of that are not equal. They do very different things. But each is necessary. And we have a very good understanding of emotional processing and the positive benefits of that both to mind and body in the West. But we don't have much in terms of developing the positivity until this positive psychology movement that's been popular in the last twenty years. You need both components. And *tonglen* has both of them, you see.

[Inaudible comments from another student to which Dan responds briefly.]

Dan

Did you what?

Student 2

Did I jump back into what I experienced when I was twenty, when I was thirty-five—was that me?

Dan

It's never going back. It's never going back when you retrieve your memory of something. You're never going back. It's always reconstructed, at least partially. So, you went back with a different sense of yourself. That's important. So, you ended in resolving it, you see. This is something that got lost in the critical literature for years. But, one of the grand old masters in the trauma field was Pierre Janet, in France. And he developed a thing called Substitution Procedure. When somebody had something traumatic, he would have them revisit the trauma and keep going over it until they could come up with a better solution, a better outcome in their mind.

Now people have rediscovered that around recurrent nightmares. People who are traumatized often have the same nightmares every night. And, of course, the pharmaceutical industry has put a fortune into research trying to develop drugs for this because they think they'll make a lot of money off of it. But there's a rather simple procedure that came out in the *Journal of the American Medical Association* a few years ago, called the Re-dreaming Procedure. If a person has a recurrent nightmare, in your office, you have them go over the nightmare, the content of it, and keep reviewing it; and it's a processing model again. They keep reviewing it with different solutions until it settles. The average time is three sessions, after years of nightmares.

So, it's the same model. If you process it, it settles down. And what we know about all exposure-based treatments in the West is the greater the avoidance the more exposure works. The greater the avoidance, the more likelihood, if you deal with it, it will work. If we've learned anything in four decades of exposure-based research, that's the simple principle. But, the other part of this that's more important is that in the course of reviewing it you have to come up with a different sense of yourself. And you have to stop dissociating from it. Janet called those personification realization. You have to make the experience real to yourself. That's what realization means. You have to review it in such a way that you're not disconnecting. It has to be made real, and you have to review it in such a way that you actually change your sense of self as who experienced it, like becoming a different person. He called that personification.

Now, this is stuff that's written almost a hundred and forty years ago. And you can see how relevant it is. He got it right way back then, but we're sort of just now rediscovering it all. So, what you're talking about is that in the course of reviewing this you changed your sense of self about those times in your life that were most difficult. You actually experienced yourself looking back on those times differently now, in a more positive sense.

Student 2

[Inaudible comment.]

Dan

You're a different Robert.

Student 2

Yeah.

Dan

That's part of the key of why it works.

Student 2

I guess.

Dan

It's not just reviewing it, you see.

Student 2

So have I … Did I change my memory of the event then?

Dan

Of course. Yeah, you changed your memory of the event, you changed your sense of self as how you experienced the event, and you've brought into that a more positive experience of the whole thing. All those things changed.

Student 2

[Inaudible comment]

Dan

I don't think the time has much to do with it. That's why I didn't include that. You went back and you revisited it. You revisited it and processed it, number one. You processed it in a way that you altered your experience of yourself and had a different sense of yourself in the process, number two. And number three, you processed it in a way that brought greater positivity into your experience, number three. All three of those are mechanisms by which this works. The time thing is basically irrelevant. That's why I'm leaving it out. I'd rather have you appreciate what works. You're going off on a red herring with that. It's not necessary.

Student 3

So, if, as you say, the Western approach now is to focus on the event, and process it intensively, why …

Dan

You're encouraging, you're setting up a context by which you can finish the processing of what's unfinished.

Student 3

Right. So why is the use of beta blockers such a hot topic now around people who experience traumatic events? Because …

Dan

But you've got to understand … I don't want to go too far off on that, but … so why do we use beta blockers? Because look, the pharmaceutical industry is, what can I say? When Bill Clinton came into office, within the first weeks he raised a question which he got really slammed for; and the question was: "What kind of industry can boast 25 percent or higher quarterly profits every single quarter for decades? There's something wrong with this picture."

Student 3

But beta blockers are cheap.

Dan

Well, but what the industry makes is huge, and they are hell bent on pushing their reality. In the *Journal of Anxiety Disorders* in 2006, there was a special edition on PTSD; and all of the researchers had been doing research to do away with the diagnosis of PTSD, to say that what we should do is reclassify it as nonspecific anxiety disorder because, they were arguing, you can get post-traumatic-stress-like symptoms without having a traumatic event. So, the category A of the *DSM* defining PTSD in terms of having to have a traumatic event was irrelevant. And there was a strong push in all of that research, all pharmaceutically funded, to do away with PTSD. The only dissenting voice in that journal special edition was by Bob Spitzer, who was the grandfather of the modern *DSM*. Okay? Now, at the same time, there was a strong push to do away with the dissociation disorders chapter in the *DSM*, in *DSM-5*, which is the new edition which will come out shortly. In fact, the lobbying was so strong, the American Psychiatric Association actually tabled the committee for the diagnosis. We were going to wipe off the map all the dissociative disorders. And I call this scientific fundamentalism. It's scientific fundamentalism.

But what happened was the neuroimaging stuff came out and it gave a rather strong neurobiological base to things like dissociative amnesia, and dissociative identity disorder, and depersonalization disorder. So, given the experts who cited this research and did field trials, they were convinced that leaving this chapter out would be scientifically unsound. And still there was great resistance to putting it in. And I'm happy to say that it went to the board of trustees, and they ratified it. And now the people who tried to block it are now calling foul and saying it was aggressively pushed through, and they're putting a certain spin on it the way that fundamentalists do; and the committee is saying no, everybody was participating in the field trials, you had a chance to submit your research and your objections, but you didn't have any evidence for it and we had strong evidence, so you guys lose.

So, PTSD and dissociative disorders survived, but we almost completely rewrote our diagnostic manuals based on huge amounts of money, and most of those monies come from two sources. One is the pharmaceutical industry. And you can see that if they wipe out PTSD and dissociative disorders then there's no competition from trauma therapists. Everybody gets drugs.

Student 3

Right.

Dan

So, that's clearly what was going on politically. And a lot of the lobbying for getting rid of dissociation was through the Catholic Church because if there are no repressed memories or dissociative amnesia then the statute of limitations is run out and they don't have to pay all these claims out. So, you've got to believe there's huge amounts of money that went behind trying to rewrite our scientific history here in favor of political interest groups. So, the fact that it actually didn't go through, given the amount of lobbying that went into this is, I think, a victory for modern science over and against these remarkable trends. But it almost didn't make it.

Student 3

So, the positive thinking, is that like people forgiving the rapist? I mean is it more to act on a day-to-day basis, positive thinking in general, right?

Dan

No, that's a whole other topic. I don't think we have time to go into that now. No, it's not like that. No.

Student 3

Restructuring the brain with positive thinking is the basic ...

Dan

I wasn't talking about positive thinking. I didn't say anything about positive thinking. I talked about the experience of positive emotions. It's not like saying new-age affirmations to yourself. It's the activating [of] positive emotional states, like compassion.

Student 3

Right.

Dan

Like gratitude.

Student 3

Right.

Dan

Like altruism. There's nothing about positive thinking in that.

January 9, 2013

Themes: Mental Constructions; Four Levels of Realization

Dan

Welcome everyone. You have a question?

Student 1

How can you best protect yourself from subtle negativities? Aside from cultivating positivity in one's life, attempting to have a positive life, maintaining a positive life. Are there any other ways to at least protect oneself from deep negativity?

Dan

Can you describe a little more … I should have maybe given you the talking stick. The question was, how to protect yourself from subtle negativities. What are subtle negativities? Why subtle?

Student 1

Emanating from people, for example, or taking on the suffering of others, the patterns of thought of others, and lived emotions of others.

Dan

So, you're specifically referring to negativities within the seeming outside field rather than things evolving within your own mind, is that right?

Student 1

Yes. Well, things are being manifest in our mind from sort of microcosms as well. Things that may be strong in a particular time that may almost saturate our awareness with negativity. For example, around New Year's, there's a very significant feeling.

Dan

Okay. Understood. So, the answer really depends on the level of mind you're answering it from, and that's very different. I'm going to have to answer this in terms of some background, in terms of karma theory.

Karma theory in Indo-Tibetan Buddhism means that if we engage in certain actions—and actions are not just behaviors, they're also mental—then those actions form karmic traces, and those karmic traces over time develop and ripen, and they appear in three different ways.

First, they appear in terms of spontaneously emerging mental states. So, whatever your mental state is at the moment, it's a product of previous karmic influences that are now ripening. Second, if karmic influences have great strength, they ripen in terms of behavior, how you are in the world. And thirdly, when karmic influences have very great strength, they ripen in terms of events. In other words, in karma theory, which is very different from the West, all the events that unfold in our life and how they seem to us are the results of karmic unfolding. They're not occurring apart from us—apart from mind.

And those same karmic rules apply whether the original actions that caused the karmic traces are negative or positive. So, we can think of engaging in negative actions that ripen over time in terms of more negative states of mind and negative behaviors and ultimately, misfortune in our life, but the whole of spiritual practice is based on the positive basis of that. If we engage in positive actions repeatedly, then those result in a shift to more positive states of mind over time, and ultimately to acting differently and more positively, and ultimately to good fortune emerging in our lives. So, the same rules apply whether the original karmic traces are negative or positive.

Now, why that's important is because from that perspective, all of our experience, whether it seems outside or inside, is all derived from mind. So, we have developed this enormous habit of seeing the world as out there, existing independent of us and our construction of it. And in Buddhism—the fundamental idea in Mahāyāna Buddhism is the notion of emptiness, and emptiness is an unfortunate word. It doesn't mean that things don't exist. It means that they're just empty constructions. So, a good synonym for emptiness is that everything is a construction of mind, because the way the mind works moment by moment by moment is to make constructions.

We make representations. We have visual representations; we have auditory representations. We have tactile representations. We have olfactory representations, gustatory representations. We have representations for thought and representations for emotions, and it's all constructions. There's nothing wrong with the idea that the way that the mind works is to construct things. Western psychology says something very similar to that. The grandfather of modern neurobiology, Karl Pribram, said, "The function of neurons is to make their own models of the world." Neurons work by making maps. Everything here is a map.

So, external reality is a construction. Our sense of self is a construction. Kids don't come into the world with a sense of self. You weren't born with a sense of your self-ness; I wasn't born with Dan-ness. The psychological sense of self develops roughly, or peaks, around eighteen months, right smack in the middle of when children develop the capacity to represent. Our representations for connection to other attachment representations develop around the same time. Everything is a construction. That's how the ordinary mind works.

There's nothing wrong with constructing the world—it's the way the ordinary mind works. Where Buddhism differs from Western psychology is the idea that we tend to reify those constructions. They become all too real. A Tibetan word for that is *nozhin*, to grasp things as too solid, too real. We forget, in other words, that they're just constructions. I actually think that Dan exists other than a construction. Now, in Buddhism there's this notion of the Two Truths. There's relative reality, relative truth, and ultimate reality. Relatively speaking, we dwell within the world of constructions. They're useful. Dan is useful to me, because Dan becomes the central organizing principle for my everyday life. But Dan, ultimately, is just a construction.

Time is useful. We all can behave according to some time clock. We can arrive at class on time because we all share the same construction of time, but the trouble is that all of these constructions work in relative reality, and we pay a price for that. We make them all too real. We reify them. Grasping things as too real, this English word reification is very similar to the Tibetan word *nozhin*.

So, the Buddhist criticism of constructivist theories of mind is that we make two mistakes. One is that once we hold these constructions as too real, comes the issue of *dzin-pa*, grab. Things have grab. So, once I develop a sense of self, if I take that sense of self too seriously, then if I organize everything around Dan-ness, things that Dan likes or don't like have grab. So, think about ... do an analysis of your everyday experience. You can look for grab, it's perceivable. What has grab? Somebody criticized you. That's grab. Somebody praises you, grab. You want something, grab. You don't want something, grab. You can see infinite variations on the theme of grab in everyday life. The self is the central organizing experience, but also is the central organizing principle for grab and therefore for suffering.

Think of another construction of mind, time. There's nothing wrong with organizing anything around time, but we forget that it's a construction. We make it too real. We actually think there's an external existing cosmic time clock located in Greenwich. We forget that it's just a construction—useful in relative reality, but as soon as we forget that it's a construction, it leads to grab. Think how much time not only becomes a useful organizing principle, but then there's the tyranny of time. Like the Rabbit in *Alice in Wonderland*, "I'm late, I'm late for a very important date." You run around like crazy trying to meet deadlines, based on some fictional notion of time.

So you see, all these structures of mind get too solid, and they have grab. Another construction of mind is external reality. Grab. We actually think there's a world that exists out here, and not even Western psychology believes that anymore. What you're seeing is your own representations, because you can't see beyond that. What you're hearing is your own representations of sound. What you're tasting, smelling, touching; all representations, all constructions. There is no "out there" apart from the mind's perceptual apparatus that constructs it. If there is, we don't know what it is, because our perceptual apparatus and our brain isn't designed to tell us anything beyond the constructions that we see. We're seeing our own constructions.

So you see, if you look at it from that perspective, every construction that is too solid runs the risk of having too much grab and therefore suffering.

But the second thing is *mümpa*, and it means the capacity to obscure. When the constructions of mind are too solid, they become like clouds that obscure true nature. Ultimately, all that you can perceive is your own brilliant lively awareness that creates this whole show. Everything comes down to this field of boundless, timeless awareness, its brilliant liveliness showing itself to itself and knowing itself through its own expressions every moment. This whole thing is about awareness—brilliantly awakened, sacred awareness.

But we don't see that, because every structure of mind that becomes too solid clouds it over. And we get layers and layers of clouds. Thought clouds it over. Thought becomes too real. We live in our thoughts as if they're real. Emotion becomes something that clouds it over big time. "External reality" clouds it over—the idea that there's an "out-there-ness." Time clouds it over. Our sense of self clouds it over, and all that we see are all the clouds.

But you know, in terms of everyday weather, when all the clouds and rainstorms clear, the sun's always been shining. The brilliant lucidity of an awakened mind always shines like the sun that never stopped. It's always right here. But as long as it's clouded over, then you can't see it. And when the clouds clear up, we say "the sun came out." It doesn't "come out"—it's always been "out." You've just got to clean the clouds up enough so you can see it.

So, more important than just grab, is the idea that all of these constructions of mind, when they're too solid, cloud things over. That's what matters. And all of these practices are cloud-cleaning practices. They clean up the clouds. Okay. Until there are no clouds left. And the brilliant lucidity of the awakened mind is shining forth all the time. In that sense you see it's simple.

But as long as we're dwelling in the clouds, we get lost in the clouds and things have grab. We don't think there's anything other than the clouds. If its pouring rain outside and you're in the midst of a rainstorm, it's hard for me to convince you, if you're standing in the midst of it, that the sun is shining at that time. In reality, ultimately, it is. You just can't see it. The awakened mind's always shining like that sun. But in the midst of the storminess of our everyday coarse level experience, always seems stormy … can't convince you that this awakened lucidity is always right here.

So, you see, now in terms of practice, how do you clean up the clouds and how does that, in your words, protect you? Ultimately, all of these clouds come down to the habit of duality. We make a distinction between what seems to be here and what's out there. But what we perceive, if that's the liveliness of this dynamic awakened awareness and what knows what's perceived, is the same awakened awareness, ultimately there is no duality. But as soon as we create that habit of duality, we create all the clouds again. Ultimately that's true.

Now, what practices will help you to get through this? Depends on the level of mind you're operating out of. If you're operating out of what we call "coarse level mind," the level of ordinary content, then that's the level of mind where you have content. You have seeming internal content, which is thought and emotions, and seeming external perceptions, sights, sounds, tastes, smells, touch. And if that's the level you're operating out of, within the domain of duality, then there are practices that are designed to help you with that.

In the Bonpo—the indigenous Tibetan system which is derived from shamanism—there are protection practices that you do. There are nine levels of Bonpo practices, and the first five of those are all about various kinds of protections. Based on visualizations that you have somebody else do, visualizations that evoke a non-ordinary being to evoke protection; to practice that, you do [it] within yourself to protect yourself. And if you're operating on the ordinary level of mind, which is clearly right smack within the duality of the mind, then those practices, in a relative sense, could be useful. Usually, you evoke non-ordinary beings to protect you from subtle influences around you. And they can work, relatively speaking. They tend not to be terribly stable. But in the short run they can give you some relief.

Now, if you train the mind in concentration, then when you do a visualization practice, then that visualization has great stability. Therefore, from a karmic point of view, it has much greater strength. So, the protection you derive from visualizations with a mind that's trained and disciplined is much stronger, karmically speaking. So that would be a better kind of protection practice. The trouble is, concentration and visualizations only clear up what are called the coarse propensities for suffering. They don't get at the subtle propensities. And here, subtle doesn't mean it the way you mean it—it means that they're not obvious at the coarse level of mind; they're more deep-seated habits.

The only practices that will clean up those are emptiness practices. So, ultimately, these afford the best protection. Emptiness means seeing it the way it is, as just a construction. Those practices are said to "cut to the root." If you want to cut to the root, and you have weeds, and you pull off the top of it, it's going to grow back. But, if you cut to the roots, the weed won't grow back. If you do visualization practices, it's like cutting off the top of the weed and it growing back. But if you do emptiness practices, which is the insight practices, it cuts to the roots so it doesn't grow back. That would be a superior practice. So that would be a pretty good practice.

A third type of practice is that you could intentionally visualize whatever those negative forces are and hold it in your awareness with a structured visualization, until you could see that visualization that you're creating in elaborate detail, with all the fear associated with it, as just an empty construction. That's the way the practice is done in the *Tantras*.

And then the superior practice would be to see all of that as just the lively manifestation of awakened awareness in a way that has no grab and no duality to it. That would be the superior practice. You see, then those negative forces are no longer outside of you, nor are they inside of you. They're just the dance of awareness. And they arrive within the vast expanse of this awareness in such a way that they have no grab, they just come and go. And we call that "spacious freedom." Because from that level of mind they can't possibly interfere.

Sometimes Rahob Tulku, who we teach with, tells a story about these different levels of practice. And the story is about a poisonous plant in the back of someone's house. And they are concerned about getting rid of the poisonous plant. So, they bring in people who cut the plant off, but it keeps growing back. Those are your protection practices. They work only with the coarse level of mind, but never to the root. So it keeps coming back. So, the idea is that you will repeatedly be afraid of these negative influences around you. But do they give you temporary relief if you cut the plant off? Yes, just like cleaning weeds in your garden. However, they grow back. So that would be concentration and visualization practices around the theme of protection. That's the first level.

Second level is the way that you can get rid of that poisonous plant is you could have somebody come in and cut the roots, right to the heart of the roots of it. And that's the insight practice. Now you see all of those negative influences as just empty constructions of your own field of mind—they're not out there. The Tibetan version of what you're calling subtle influences would be influence of gods and demons. Are gods and demons, the operation of gods and demons—mountain gods and wind gods and river gods—as important in Tibetan Buddhism? Absolutely. But ultimately, they'll tell you that superior practice is to see all those influences, positive or negative, as just constructions of mind—elaborate constructions of mind that in that culture and belief systems have enormous grab. But ultimately, there are no gods and demons except for our own mind. It's the mind that constructs them around the theme of fear and then they have huge grab.

So, you see, when you use emptiness practices, it goes beyond weed whacking. It's cutting to the root of that poisonous plant. So, the results of that are more lasting.

A third way of practicing would be you could take the plant and try and extract the poison from it; and using various elixirs you could try and transform that poison into some positive elixir. And that's what the *Tantras* do. You eat the poison and transform it. You intentionally visualize your worst fears. You put it right out there—your worst fears, not just as they come up seeing them as empty, but intentionally creating elaborate fears in your mind as a way of getting rid of them. And then at some point they're not out there anymore. You're transmuting them.

I remember once when I was younger, working on that, and what I did is I went out, on a moonless night to a forest, rubbed myself with sage so the animals wouldn't be able to smell me, and I sat in the forest in the pitch dark all night. And I watched what my mind did with all of the sounds of the animals approaching me. It was a remarkable movie show of fear until there was no fear left. So, you intentionally create the vehicle to bring this on and elaborate it until it's gone.

I remember when I was a kid watching *The Night of The Living Dead*, the zombie movie, which terrified me. I had nightmares for months after watching that movie. So, one time after a retreat I got *The Night of The Living Dead* and I got the sequel, *The Dawn of The Living Dead*, and I watched them in a state of mind of perfect clarity, and it was hilarious. I couldn't remember what all that fear was about as a child. Instead, I felt compassion for this scared child, terrified child. But I had to revisit it to see that. So, see, that's the third level of practice. You invite it on with all of the stories and elaborate on it, all seen as empty, until there's nothing left of the grab of it. And then it's done. Completely done. That would be taking the poison out and transforming it to something positive, which is *tantra* practice.

But then there's the fourth level of practice, which is what you get in Dzogpachenpo, the Great Completion practice. And here, it's all about the view. The view is the meditation. And the view is that whatever arises is an infinitely boundless field of awakened awareness, expressing itself every moment through its liveliness. All sights, all sounds, all emotions like fear, all thought, and self, is all the dynamic, lively expression of this awareness. And what knows it is the brilliant knowing of an awakened mind. There is nothing beyond this boundless wholeness, this infinite, vast expanse of awareness space that expresses itself in its dance every moment and knows itself through that very expression. Awareness expressing itself to itself and knowing itself every moment, without a shred of duality. And when you view it like that, nothing can possibly have any grab. And something different will happen. If you hold that view every moment, you're not forming any karmic impression anymore. Because everything arises spontaneously and leaves, leaving no trace. If you hold that view continuously, 24/7, you enter a path that we call "*dharmadhātu* exhaustion."

You see, what causes karmic impressions is mental engagement. Something comes up into your field of experience and you either go towards it or move away from it. And as soon as you make that act of mind, in an instant, you've formed a karmic impression. You've fixed it, and that impression will ripen over time. But what if everything comes up in the field of groundless ground, comes up in an unconditioned way, disappears back into groundless ground, and your view is holding that infinite groundless ground? And the stance that you take towards whatever comes up is what we call leave-it-alone-ness—*rang sang nyi*. Then, if that's your stance all the time, it forces the mind to release at an accelerated rate all of its previous storehouse of karmic impressions, not just for this lifetime, but for all lifetimes, until you exhaust the depository. Then there are no negative states of mind left. There is no fear. There is no anger. There is no sadness. There are no negative states. And what flourishes are all the positive states of a realized mind.

There are eighty positive states of the realized mind and there are no negative states. That's profound.

So, you see there are these four levels of practice. How you protect yourself? You can do visualizations, and those visualizations will cut the visible part of the plant. You can cut to the root with emptiness practices. You can go beyond emptiness practices and intentionally visualize their whole construction around fear—all of the stories that go with that until it has no grab at all. Or, you can hold a view of spacious freedom like a mountain, unshakably, and let everything arise as the play, the liveliness of an awakened mind that has neither negativity nor positivity. It leaves no karmic trace if you hold the view right. That would be the superior practice. And that's why it's the story of the peacock. Because what the peacock does, is the peacock eats the poisonous plant and experiences nothing negative from it because the peacock sees that there is no negativity.

So, the issue is, what level of practice do you use? See, all four are very different. Sometimes you do them in stages. If you're very afraid, then protection practices and visualizations are a good start. But as you refine your capacity and train your mind, the emptiness practices would be superior because it will get rid of the grab that goes with that fear so it doesn't keep coming back. But ultimately, the Dzogchen practice is the best because then there's no outside, there's no inside, there's no self that needs to be protected from outside forces because there are no outside forces, and the forces are neither positive nor negative anymore. It's just the lively dance of awareness. There's nothing to be afraid of anymore.

That level of mind, that level of realization is very powerful. Sometimes we say that level of realization goes beyond the gods and the demons. They don't exist anymore. The mind's more powerful than that. Then what can affect you? Not possible. At that level of realization, knowing goes beyond the influences or the seeming external influence of gods and demons, or negativity from people. It goes beyond the influences of birth and death. That level of realization can't go away when your body dies. Always here. So, that would be the superior practice—for obvious reasons. It's okay?

Student 1

The first level's dualistic. The second level …

Dan

Is also dualistic. But it includes seeing everything as a construction that's ultimately empty, so it loses grab.

Student 1

It's dualist?

Dan

The first three are still dualist, but they're different gradations of dualism. The third level goes beyond emptiness to actively creating the whole show, the whole story. What the Sufi master called "the whole tiresome project of self." And the fourth level goes beyond all dualism. The mind's operating out of an unbounded wholeness itself.

Student 1

How can one best view it in the beginning?

Dan

Well, why don't we answer that question later; this is a good start. Maybe after the break we'll do a visualization on all four of these levels. We'll practice on all four of these levels; see for yourself. That would be the best way of handling it. Answer is to do it, okay? So, we'll revisit this after the break.

Student 1

Of course.

Dan

The Peacock Practice: the four ways of mastering the poisonous plant.

Anything else? We have a little bit of time left.

Student 2

To take the point to the other side of the case, we talked a little bit about it in the past—about trying to train virtue and whether there are levels of mind including that.

Dan

Oh, good question. The question is, are the levels of mind in terms of training virtue? And the answer is yes, [the] same four levels apply.

At the first level of practice, you can do visualizations around virtue; we call that "exemplar method." So, think of a virtue—like, say, patience—and then think of who might be a figure that best exemplifies the practice of patience, the virtue of patience, which means being able to move beyond all states of aggression. In Buddhism patience mean something very particular—seeing the nature of aggression and anger-related states and moving beyond them.

Anger is said to cause a deterioration of all positive states. There's no place for it. In martial arts it makes you off your game. In meditation arts it makes you off your meditation practice. In modern western sports it's no different—you want to throw somebody off their game? Trash-talk them. We saw that yesterday with the Celtics and the Knicks, right? Kevin Garnett trash-talked Carmelo Anthony; he couldn't put a basket after that, and the Celtics beat a superior team, because the trash-talking got him pissed off and he couldn't shoot. Anger causes a deterioration of all good states.

Let's say we want to cultivate patience. The first level of practice would be a visualization practice; you cultivate the virtue of patience by thinking of who best exemplifies that. Maybe you want to take a historical figure like Gandhi, or the Dalai Lama, and then the first thing is you visualize around the theme that's called "becoming more familiar." And becoming more familiar, you imagine that exemplar, like Gandhi, practicing patience and being the exemplar of a strong manifestation of that patience in various contexts. And every time you imagine the details you're becoming familiar with the quality in somebody else who's the best exemplar.

Then you visualize "in front": you imagine that Gandhi is here with you. You familiarize yourself with how that quality is woven into the very fabric of his being. Then you dissolve Gandhi into a bubble of light, and you bring him into your body right down through the space of your body and into your heart. Then you imagine rays of light bursting forth in all directions, and the stronger the light emanates, the stronger the quality grows within your heart, and you keep the visualization going until you can actually feel him in your own heart.

You do these visualizations every day, until you actually successively approximate having that quality as part of your own feeling experience. And when you master it and your quality of patience is very strong, you start work on another virtuous quality. You keep doing these until you collect the whole combination. Each of these *thankas*, or paintings, is a configuration of positive qualities. You collect them until you have the whole set. Just like merit badges to the boy scouts and girl scouts. You collect the set of virtues. So that would be the first level of practice at the coarse level of mind.

Ultimately, having developed all those virtues—and we have to actively cultivate them, because unlike the negative qualities of mind, if you observe what comes forth in your mind, if every moment you were to catalogue every state in terms of positivity and negativity, most people would find that the spontaneously emerging states throughout the day are much more negative than positive. So, unlike the negative states that we want to reduce, the positive states need to be actively cultivated, so, they take more work. You have to do much more work on these kinds of visualizations to counteract all the negative stuff and to eventually tip the ratio of the balance of your mind so there's more positive than negative states [that] come forth in your daily experience. That would be the first level of virtue practice.

If you develop these virtues, the superior practice would be, once developing them to see them as empty constructions of mind, just like any other state. So, the virtues don't have grab then, you have to clean them up of grab. You have to clean them up of the capacity to obscure; you have to clean them up of the construction of self. Otherwise, you walk around being a mighty righteous person. And it's all about self-grab and self-importance. Activating virtuously for the sake of self, that's not virtue, that's self-importance.

So, you see a superior practice would be to then clean up the virtues of self and grab and the capacity to obscure by coupling the virtue training with emptiness practice. Then why do you do these things? Because they contribute to the greater good, not because you're getting anything out of it in terms of self. You do them because it's the best way of being in the world, but not because it's self-important.

The third level of practice would be to create entire scenarios in your mind—the tantric practice—of virtuous qualities and elaborate stories around those, until you can see that all those elaborate stories are just that—just stories we create for ourselves in the subtlest ways to create some sort of self-importance until the virtues that we do become natural ways of being in the world, cleaned up of even the subtlest propensities towards self-importance.

But the superior practice would be that fourth level of practice. Just as we can, like the peacock, eat the poison and not be affected by it, the peacock will eat the medicinal plants and not be affected by them. Because you're beyond all karmic impressions, beyond all imprints of good or bad at that point, because you've gone beyond; you have a level of practice that goes beyond karma. You're not forming karmic impressions anymore; you're cleaning up the depository of all karmic impressions good and bad.

Now, that's interesting because that's often misinterpreted in the West. Does it mean if you've got that level of mind where you've achieved, relatively speaking, *dharmadhātu* exhaustion, so the mind manifests mostly of all pure states and no negative states—technically you are beyond all karma—does that mean you can act in any way you want? Absolutely not. Because if you have that realization, and it's authentic, the scope of that mind is always oriented towards the greater good for all beings and the behavior doesn't come from self. It comes up spontaneously from an awakened mind, as the best fit to what's needed in that situation. You don't even have to think about how to think or act because your behavior's spontaneously manifests the realization.

Because at that level of practice the ultimate test of realization is conduct. And conduct is always naturally arising from groundless ground and an awakened mind. So, can you act anyway that you want? Technically you could, but the question would never come up that way with that level of realization. It's just not something you would think. You act in accordance with your realization; there's no choice in the matter. It just is the way it is. That's the superior practice.

So, you see the same four levels of practice apply to virtue as they do to the negative states of mind, like fears, do they not? Same four levels of realizations.

January 23, 2013

Themes: Processing Grief; Making Sense of Unfinished Emotions

Dan

Welcome everyone. You have a question?

Student 1

I was talking with the son of one of my patients recently, and he was telling me about how his father had died some years ago, and about four years ago his wife had passed away, and then six months after that his dog died. And so, he was there tending to his mother in her nineties who'd just suffered a really terrible stroke, and I was thinking to myself, "What about this sounds so familiar to me?" It sounded like something I'd heard before, and then what I realized was that it was the story of suffering. And so my question to you is: how can we best be with people in their suffering?

Dan

Well, there are two questions here. One question is how to best be with people in their suffering in general, and the second more specific question is how to be with them in their grief, because the example you're bringing up is specifically about loss and therefore grief.

So, let me start with the more specific question, because there's a lot to this. And the specific question you have talked about is a man with multiple losses in a short period of time. So, we have here overwhelming grief. And, how do we best approach the issue of grief? And I'm going to answer this both East and West, because from a western point of view the main approach would be to resolve the grief.

The work on grief in the west goes back to the 1940s, the work of George Engels. And he developed a stage model for grief. When we experience a sudden loss and the coordinates of our relationships are suddenly gone, the underpinnings of them drop out from under us, and it's a crisis in meaning—how do we make sense of the loss? How do we move on from there? And, Engels had a kind of information processing approach to loss. You have to process it and make sense of it. And until that processing is complete and you integrate the experience, then the consequence of that is you remain symptomatic, and there are classic symptoms of grief that people experience. How long do those symptoms last? They can last weeks, months, years, decades. How long do they last? They last until you can find a way of processing the experience and integrating it. So, from a western point of view, the question behind your question is, "How can you be with somebody who experiences a loss in a way that helps them process the loss and integrate it?" And what does integrating it mean anyway?

Well, first it means that you make sense of it. Particularly if a loss comes suddenly, then you have to make sense of, why did this happen when you had no warning, and you have to have some explanatory system in your mind about what really happened. So, I remember saying to someone who had a child … As a couple they had great difficulty having a child, and finally she got pregnant and they had one child because it was their last shot; and she was clearly over-involved with this child. And when the child was now sixteen, she got news that he was driving along a country road and the car went off the road and hit a tree and burst into flames, and not only was he killed suddenly, but the body was burned beyond recognition.

Her whole world was shattered. She became suicidal. So what's the task of being with somebody like that? And there are two things. The first is meaning-making. You have to help them make sense out of what happened in a way that explains the suddenness of this loss, and even if the explanation is not exactly accurate, we all need an explanation, because the explanation finishes something about the processing of it. So, part of what you do with grief is help the person talk it through and come to their own way of making sense out of what happened. That's the first thing you do.

In her case, what she came to was that there were layers of meaning. The first she probably thought that he reached down for a CD or something like that and was distracted, and it was a winding country road and [he] just wasn't paying attention. But on a deeper level of mind that's not what was going on. She knew that he was drinking a lot and didn't deal with it, with him or with herself. And since the body was burned beyond recognition, there was no way of getting an alcohol level. But what she settled with was the likelihood that he was drinking and that's what happened. But after she could put it together and make sense out of it, which is basically making sense of the senseless, then it could settle down a little bit. And that's especially the task of when the death is sudden.

Now, if the death is not sudden, if it's a slow evolving decline and deterioration either physically or mentally in terms of cognitive capacity, if you watch your parent slowly lose their body or slowly lose their mind, for example, then part of the process of making sense out of this whole thing is to deal with the discrepancy between their current decline and how you know them in your head, as vital of both mind and body. And you've got to deal with that discrepancy because it gets bigger and bigger. So, helping them to make sense out of that discrepancy is part of what you do with slow decline leading to death. That's the first layer of how you work with grief in terms of meaning-making.

But, the field of grief really started here in—I think it was 1944 or roughly around '44, and that was the beginning of the modern grief and trauma field. And it started with the famous Coconut Grove fire. And the Coconut Grove fire is now the—I think it's the—what hotel is it? Is it a Ramada or something like that? It's on Stewart Street. There's a hotel there that is at the original site of the Coconut Grove fire. And if you go to the hotel you'll see on the wall, on the outside of the building there's a little plaque. And in the Coconut Grove fire, it was a nightclub, and in those days, there were no fire exits and they had a revolving door, like the lazy Susan kind of door, with different panels. That was the only door for in and out. And there were over two hundred people sitting at tables having dinner at the nightclub. And one of the waiters in the kitchen tried to change a light bulb that went out, and it turns out that the wallpaper, which was one of these early plastics, was highly flammable. The glue was highly flammable, and no one knew that. So, when he put the burned-out light bulb that was hot down on the paper, it immediately lit up and the whole kitchen went up into flames, and there was this very dense black toxic smoke. And of course, everybody panicked and pushed each other out of the way, and they all made a beeline to the door, but people got crushed on the floors wedging the door so you couldn't open them, and since that revolving door was the only way out, everybody was trapped inside. And I think over a hundred and fifty people died.

That was the first early mobilization of crisis trauma teams to deal with the victim impact on family members, because of all the huge loss. You know, we've seen that more recently with the fire in Rhode Island. It's not so different. It's very similar. And there it was because the band was using pyrotechnics that lit up, and they didn't have adequate escape routes and safety.

So, in that generation, most of the work was helping people make sense out of a sudden loss that was unexpected, explaining what happened with the fire, working out the details. We go through this ritual unfortunately once a week around shootings now in schools around the country. And, you know, a month or two later we come up with some explanation of who the shooter was and what happened and all this kind of stuff, and how many people got killed and all that kind of stuff, and it's becoming a …

Student 2

[Interrupts with an only partially-audible comment about the role of mental illness.]

Dan

Oh, if that's the case, and, you know, it's become like a cultural ritual of grief for the entire population. And it's all about meaning-making, and all the new stuff is about meaning-making. And you can see how important that is for human beings because in the early stages of something like in Aurora there was a lot of reporting about what was going on inside when nobody had any idea. And most people watching the news got angry, because they wanted a better explanation. But there wasn't any yet. And that's always the case, because that anger comes from the human need to have it make sense. So that's the first tissue.

And, the second issue is really … something that Freud said way back when. And Freud wrote a classic paper called "Mourning and Melancholia." And he noticed the remarkable similarity between chronic melancholic depression and mourning following a loss, because the symptoms seemed very similar. But there was one important difference. He felt that in acute grief reactions versus chronic melancholia, and he noted that chronic bereavement is like chronic melancholia, the difference between the two situations has to do with conflict. And where grief is "complicated," when it's complicated by conflict, it's much more difficult to go through the normal stages of making meaning and then integrating the experience and putting it behind you, because the person that you lost you had significant conflict with. That makes it more difficult, you see.

So if you, for example, had a very complicated relationship with your father but not your mother, who do you think you're going to have more difficulty with the loss about? Not with the mother, the father. And that's again human nature, because it's hard to process something where we never really worked out the conflict in this lifetime. And there's a lot in the clinical literature about how one works with that second piece of this problem. How do you process grief when the person had significant conflict with the person that they lost?

And we have rather simple methods for that. I will show you a visualization for that, that you can do with some loss you had in your life. It's remarkably simple and it's not Buddhist, but it developed in the West and it's very, very, very good. It originally developed in Australia, and the average time to treat complicated bereavement was three sessions. And they noted twenty, no sixty-three cases resolving complicated bereavement in three sessions or less. That opened my eyes. I said, "You know, look into this." But as was the case in a lot of clinical reports, they didn't tell you the details of what they did. So, we repeated it here and tried to develop more elaborate protocols for it, and I found that it was remarkably easy to do.

And, there are two steps to it. The first is finishing unfinished emotional business. One of the things when people suddenly lose a person, we know that the phenomenology of this is that for weeks and months and sometimes years, the person that suddenly was lost seems to appear like a presence in the room. So, it's not hard to visualize them as a live presence because most people who are in grief can feel that. So, you start by putting them as a live presence in the room. That's the setup for the visualization.

And then what you do is you ask the person to imagine that they have one last chance to really talk with this person who's now dead. And the way you word it is in terms of, "This is your one opportunity to give voice from the heart about whatever it is that seems most emotionally unfinished still about the relationship." Now, if you follow what people do with that instruction, the first thing they want is meaning-making. They want an explanation from the person who's dead about why they died. It doesn't have to be accurate. It has to be an explanation that's coherent. And oftentimes it's remarkably accurate, because we know more than we think we know. So, for example in the case of that woman, she sort of knew that he had a problem with drinking and that might have contributed to the accident. So that's the first thing that comes up.

Having done that, the second thing is to see what else comes to mind. And you do that until the person feels settled. So, you set up the relational conditions by which the person can give voice to whatever feels emotionally unfinished, and they keep exploring that until they feel finished with it. Sometimes it takes one, sometimes two, sometimes three sessions. Rarely does it ever take more than that.

But the third part of the protocol is the most interesting. I can't exactly explain why it works, but it works remarkably well. In the third part of the protocol you say, "Now this person"—the person who died—"has some things that they want you to know. They can see how much of a conflict this has been for you, and they have some things to tell you that will help you to settle with that." And you let the deceased other be the one that gives voice to the solution to the conflict.

Now, what's really going on is that you're tapping your own inner resources. But if I say to you, "You know how to resolve this conflict," most people say, "No, I can't, I haven't a clue." But if you do it through the metaphor of the other who knows how to do that, most people will resolve it because it gets by our limiting beliefs. Bypasses all of that stuff and it gets right to the chase of the matter. And it works.

So, for example, with that boy, I asked her to imagine what she needed to give voice to that would make her feel more emotionally finished with this process, more like, "Why did this happen?" And he talked about the drinking and then she said, "I sort of knew that." At that point she felt settled, and her own suicidality stopped. But it didn't resolve. And it took three sessions with her. And in the third session I said, "He has some things that he wants to tell you in a way that will help you to feel more settled with the conflict about his death." And what he says to her is, "Ma, you were always in my face. Get a life. You wanna kill yourself and be in my face again? It's not gonna happen. Get your own life." [Laughter] You see what I'm saying?

Now where did that come from? He's not saying that. It's a metaphor for what we call "the displaced other." But through the voice of the other who can see into what she needs, he gives voice about what she really needs, which on the deepest level of her mind her own inner wisdom is telling her. She knows that. That's why she wanted to kill herself, because she wanted to join him. And as soon as he gave voice to that you could see everything settle down. The suicidality cleared up.

Student 3

[Inaudible comments.]

Dan

Yeah, he needed that. It was a little bit late, you know. But it would have resolved it. But that's the whole point. And in her case, it completely settled the issue. And then she tried again with artificial insemination and had twins the next time around. And raised them very differently the second time around. This is somebody in the field, so I know her well. I watched her kids grow up. They're healthy kids and now they're healthy adults. The entire time was three sessions.

So, it's a remarkable protocol. I'll show you it with any kind of grief if you're past it; it really gets right to the heart of the matter. And it does two things. It makes meaning, and it identifies, unhooks, and resolves the conflict. In the West this is the best of what we know. So, that's what I would say about how to be with people in grieving, help them resolve the grief.

Now, from a Buddhist perspective, it's a little different. Because it's not content-oriented. What you want to do, from a Buddhist perspective, is help them to use the tragedy, the loss, as a vehicle to understand true nature. And whether it be the loss of someone else or sitting with someone who's dying, it's no different. We talk about hospice, where, what do we do? I mean most hospice care in the West isn't hospice care. It's palliative care. We try and make them comfortable, which often means making us comfortable by giving them a lot of medications, if we're truthful about it. But some hospices get the view that if you sit with them and you meditate with them and you calm them, then they'll have a better journey. And there's nothing wrong with that, but it's not essentially Buddhist.

It might represent a kind of being mindful, and we take mindfulness as an end in itself, but if you look particularly in the Mahāyāna tradition, and the teachings in *The Tibetan Book of the Dead*, there are two things you want to do. The superior thing to do is to be with a person in such a way that you help them understand their true nature. How can they use the dying process itself as an occasion to awaken? Because when all the physiological systems in the body shut down, all the stuff goes. So, you are much closer to understanding awakened nature. So, if you look at the structure of *The Tibetan Book of the Dead*—well it's not really one book, it's like an anthology; but the famous chapter four, that's a complete set of teachings by Padmasambhava. It's a pointing out instruction for the true nature of awakened awareness and how you can recognize awakened awareness that's always right here. You can recognize it at any moment in daily life. You can recognize it in the nature of the dying process. He didn't write that just about dying. In fact, that chapter is a book in itself that's been disseminated as one of the main pointing out teachings on how to open up awakened mind.

So, the best answer, in the Buddhist Mahāyāna sense, is how do you be with somebody who is dying in your work, geriatrics? Or how do you be with somebody who has experienced multiple losses? How to use all that as occasions for awakening into true nature. How can we use our strongest emotional states as a way of being free from all emotional grab? And here we get into emptiness practice. Roam around in the grab until it has no substance. Now that's not easy to do. And this is where I think the East and West complement each other, which is why I'm giving you two answers. Because if you try to do what Buddhists want to do with this and say to them, "Roam around in the worst of grab that you have from the multiple losses," your patient would see that as remarkably insensitive. Right?

But, if you help them make sense out of the losses, and then you help them work through the conflict of this so that the sign of success is that the symptoms of grieving mostly are resolved, then you can go back and revisit this issue. And [that person] can look at all the constructions and stories about those relationships that have created an enormous grab in his life from the perspective of emptiness practice, and if he would be more amenable to do that, then, because it's like handling the residuals, then, from that perspective, you see, he might be able to experience a level of mind that has what we call "spacious freedom," where the worst emotional states that cause the greatest grab are the ones that set us free the most. That would be useful. And if he got that sense of spacious freedom, free of all the grab and all the constructions and stories about those relationships that he was still holding onto, then his mind would be more naturally oriented to look deeper into true nature. And at that point, if he used the pointing-out instructions for the nature of an awakened mind, they might actually make some sense.

Now, with the dying process, we either prepare people with these practices well in advance of dying so they've got the meaning system down and they know the practices so they can actually ... if they practice them a lot, they can actually use them during the dying process itself. You can actually do simulations with certain kinds of *phowa* practices; you can actually get simulations of the states you go through dying. It's like an analog practice. So, you're so well-versed in going through those states of body-mind and the subtle consciousness and the very subtle consciousness that revolve around that, that when you actually go through the real dying process, you're well-versed. I remember His Holiness the Dalai Lama saying it's sort of like surfing. You go through these practices many, many, many times, the *phowa* practices, and then when you actually die, he says it's like getting the perfect wave and you know how to ride it.

Now, that's being well-prepared in advance. But most people don't have that belief system. So, your second opportunity is that most people when they die, they get religion. Right? There's a window of opportunity that they might actually listen to and be open to understanding the pointing out instructions for true nature, because they got nothing to lose any more. And that's the time that you might be able to, even when they're close to death, prepare them not to just be calm with them so they have a safe journey. But if you want to cut to the chase, prepare them for getting off the wheel. Prepare them for awakening in the dying process, and there's no more recycling. That would be the superior approach. Or, to take a person who's grieving and to use the worst of the grief as a way of seeing that they can be free from the most severe of our life's human pain, which is often around loss and attachment.

That's good practice. And, you know, grief invites a sort of peculiar paradox because it reminds us that we are attachment creatures, and that the depth of attachment is so much the part of our human existence, and yet we don't get to take that with us. So, it cuts to the heart of what's human here, our biggest attachment and our biggest pain, and to looking squarely at the face of that; that is the breeding ground of genuine compassion because we're all attachment-related beings.

Dan

Okay, say your version again.

Student 3

Well, the Sufi said, "Don't go and fly off into the blue sky of perfection, but stay and nourish your grief seeds, and water your grief seeds so they sprout into heart." Because it's all too easy as practitioners, of course, to pull back and to hold a vast expanse beyond and outside of those grief seeds. We need to find it inside of those seeds. I know that you know that, but.

Dan

Good.
Yes?

Student 5

I wanted to follow up the question about sense-making. What about a very specific set of multiple griefs, like Holocaust survivors? And I have encountered it a lot, obviously, and what I've found except for the few of them who managed to find meaning … and always, Victor Frankl always comes …

Dan

Yeah, Victor Frankl comes to mind.

Student 5

I didn't meet Victor Frankl, so mainly who I encountered were people … somehow, they made a living on top of the grief, but, whenever deeper conversations happened and I just sometimes touched upon it, and I would say that for myself I want to figure out, this was years ago, what is real and meaning. And I would invariably get this answer, or it would come out, "There's no meaning, nothing is real. What I know to be real is that we got slaughtered. That my children got killed and my relatives are dead, and it was so huge." I would never, I mean one can't possibly project a wish that you would want them to resolve it, it's just so, so big. You can't come the other way either, because there's no meaning making. Very often, it just doesn't happen.

Dan

I think it's the same process when you have grief of that cultural magnitude. It's still the same process. What that means is that that individual, saying there's no meaning, has deep conflict about the magnitude of what happened.

Student 5

About surviving.

Dan

They have to resolve the conflict to resolve the grief. And the approach isn't any different.

Student 5

Do you resolve it with two hundred family members? It's just huge. It seems endless, how could you go there?

Dan

Yes, you still do it the same way. That's the legacy of Victor Frankl. The ones who find deeper meaning, or wider meaning, in the midst of that tragedy, are the ones that become psychologically healthy and leave that behind. And often they get a larger, wider vision of life, which is deeply spiritual, as did Victor Frankl, or Elie Wiesel. Or, we have studies of POWs in tiger cages in South Asia. And the ones that survived pretty much unscathed of the usual effects of torture are the ones that in the midst of the worst of that developed some larger spiritual meaning system.

And there has been work with, in Dharamsala, torture victims from China, mostly Tibetan lamas. And the lamas who had an absolute conviction in their faith don't show the usual expected things that we see of torture. It's the same thing. You have to arrive at a larger, usually spiritual meaning in the process, and you have to work through the remarkable deep-seated conflicts that get stirred up around the worst of human nature. How do we resolve the face of sadism and evil? Because you come face-to-face with that in these situations.

Student 5

The people who mostly resolved it, let's say the very orthodox people who had a spiritual context for it—but that is really a rather crazy explanation. Excuse me, but, you know, they found reason for it and they live better, but those are the only ones that I ever met; and there are few examples who manage to do this.

Dan

But, there, I think that when you have, you see I think that Nelson Mandela had some wisdom here. And what we know about trauma, if it's not worked through is it goes down the generations. And Mandela, from his years in prison, foresaw that. And that's why he developed the Truth and Reconciliation Commission.

And what he did was so unique, is take perpetrators of human rights violations and the surviving victims and families of those human rights violations from the same villages, and put them all together face-to-face in small groups. In a very structured way. And the victims had to say to the offenders, in a heartfelt way, the impact of their behavior on the entire village of victims. And the perpetrators had to hear that without being distracted from that. And they had to look squarely at their own behavior.

And what came out of that was something truly remarkable: the possibility of freeing future generations from the transgenerational effects of trauma. That didn't happen after the Nazi Holocaust, except in small groups, but mostly it didn't happen. Nor did it happen in the Killing Fields in Cambodia—which is why the wars are still being played out—because that required a single individual, who spent decades in jail developing that spiritual vision. It was a vision of compassion.

And think of how many victims in future generations have been saved by that one vision that came out of one human being's suffering, transformed into compassion. We need to do that with every trauma. But, we don't, because it's

Our impulse to be there, the natural impulse to be there for someone who is in grief, comes from our deepest attachment need. It is not hard to be compassionate about that, because as humans we all share that need for secure attachment. We all share the recognition of what it's like to have that threatened or to never have it. As Bowlby and his work on attachment I think clearly showed, it's part of our hardwiring. And therefore, it goes right to the heart of our deepest pain.

So, if you want to muck around in *samsāra*, then immerse yourself in life's grief. And, therefore, what you're doing is very much part of this whole experiment of bringing the *dharma* to the West. It's not hard to imagine the ease of trying to practice in a monastic setting, but it's not an accident that all of these monastic cultures have disintegrated, because that's not real practice. It's lazy practice. Real practice of these teachings is right in the thick of the hell of *samsāra* and all of its pain. If you can do that, then you've mastered the practice. And that's why all these teachings are now coming to the West, but it won't be a monastic tradition. My Root Lama used to say, "Time for monks is history. Now find it in everyday life."

So, you're trying to sit with someone with multiple losses in a compassionate way to ease their pain, to resolve the grief; and to use that as maybe a vehicle for them to look deeper into human experience, into the real nature of the mind, is living *dharma* practice in the West. And the best thing that one can do. Good question.

Student 4

Do you know the line … the *dharma* poet laureate seemed to … I forget the poem itself, but he says something the extent of, "Don't go fly off into the blue sky of perfection, but nourish your grief seeds, because those are the ones that sprout heart."

Dan

Oh, that's a good one. Nice. Nice. Thank you. Say it again.

Student 4

Well, this is my version of it. [Hearty group laughter]

just too damn difficult. Myself and some of my colleagues that through the U.N. were scheduled to go and work on something very much like that in Rwanda, but the U.N. canceled the trip because it's still too damn dangerous to do it there. So, the war goes down the generations.

And there it's deeply tragic because the average age of the troops was twelve years of age. Because you see what some evil mind figured out is that kids who are eight to twelve years old don't have cognitive or brain controls over violence. They haven't developed those areas of the brain yet. So, kids that age, if you take them out of their families and train them to be soldiers, make the most violent soldiers you can get. And that's about as ugly as it's ever going to get, when you have a war of eight- to twelve-year-olds. But that was really the legacy of Rwanda. It's staggering.

Student 6

In the case of intergenerational trauma, would the figure that one imagines, would it be an ancestor, or who would be ...

Dan

What do you mean?

Student 6

The person, the external meaning-maker. For instance, if a person dies and we're grieving them, the person making meaning is the person who died.

Dan

No, in another student's case, if you have a Holocaust victim, they need to bring present the offenders.

Student 6

The offenders?

Dan

Yes. They need … and it's the same process of grieving. It's better if you can do it live presences. But if you do it in imagination then what you have to do is bring forth the Nazi perpetrators, and they [the survivor] have to give voice to all that is emotionally unfinished about that first. Then they have to let the Nazi perpetrator be the person who sees into what they need to unhook the conflict, so it doesn't go down the generations. It's the same process and it's damn powerful. But you've got to do it right. And it can be done. And if it's not done, it will do down the generations.

Student 6

I imagine the same sort of thing can be done with—

Dan

Anything.

Student 6

Okay, divorces, breakups.

Dan

Yeah.

Student 6

Even if the person's still around.

Dan

Okay, one more. Go ahead.

Student 7

I think often it's really important to separate the issue of explanation or meaning in terms of—why has something happened from the issue of what you do with it from here? Because I think that's often where the sense of meaning develops.

Dan

I think what you're saying is true, and if you look at the grief literature, the steps are: meaning-making, resolution of conflict, and then moving on. And that needs to be addressed so the person who's living moves on.

Student 7

There's a wonderful local example to us of a family whose daughter was killed in an earthquake in Haiti, who've developed an orphanage. And it was just—it was funded and constructed and just had a big ceremony down there. A very powerful process.

Dan

Yeah, I'll give you an example of all three of those. I saw a woman who grew up in a violent, alcoholic family where the father was physically abusive. There were two boys and I think three or four girls. All the girls were sexually abused. The boys were physically abused a lot. And she had a twin brother. And the twin brother died by what seemed to be suicide. And for a twin that's a very difficult loss.

So, the first part of it was meaning-making. And the meaning-making part of it was why he decided to kill himself. He was a very talented athlete in high school who never did anything after that. His life went down the tubes and he got very drug-involved, mostly with opiates, heroin. And when she evoked his presence and brought forth what was emotionally unfinished, she first brought forth her outrage of being abandoned, and they were so close, and how could he do this? Then it evolved into making sense of it.

And the making sense part of it was, why he seemingly overdosed. And, she remembered a time, the last time she saw him was at a family gathering. She remembered being really pissed at him because he was high, and she could tell right away. So, she finished the family gathering, she said, "I want to go outside and talk to you." She told him how angry she was for him getting high. And then she understood that drugs were somehow involved in his suicide. But then when I asked her to imagine what he wanted her to know, what he told her is that he had contracted AIDS from needles and he was in the dying stages anyway. And he thought this was compassion to spare everybody in the family a slow decline. Then she shifted her meaning about his death, and it was no longer the violation of the suicide. But she could see this was something that he was giving to the family.

And then the second level was the conflict which had to do with essentially survivor guilt. And what she then said to him was that she wanted to express her gratitude. And he in this fantasy said, "What for?" And she said, "I knew that you often provoked Dad, and took the brunt of the beating to protect the girls." She was the only one in that family who was functional. High-functional. She had a good marriage. She had two healthy kids, and a good profession. And she was the only one that got out of the family. And as part of working through the conflict of the survivor guilt, she had to tell him—face-to-face as she evoked the images in the presence of him—she had to tell him her gratitude, express gratitude for sacrificing himself so that she could become free. That somebody in the family could get out of hell.

But the third part of it is what you're talking about. All three steps are necessary. How is it she can then move on from there? And the missing ingredient was that now she had healthy kids, and he would never be able to share in knowing them. So, what she did was she made a playroom for the kids in the new big house that they bought. There was like an altar that had his picture there. And for her, he was always looking over the kids playing, and that's how she could have him participate in her getting out and raising a family because he gave her that. We call that, in the field "a linking object." The picture linked the two of them, and linked him to the family. And that's all it took for her to move on and resolve it. In that, you've got all three steps. Clear enough?

February 6, 2013

Themes: Bases and Treatment of Depression; Positive States; Neuroplasticity

Dan

Welcome everyone. So, it's open for questions. Whatever you want to do. Yes?

Student 1

Dan, I mentioned to you briefly before class, I unfortunately relapsed into a very severe, full episode of depression. And it seems to have been triggered by a back injury that left me unable to do most of the things that I do to maintain my health, along with therapy and medications. I have a vicious breed of bipolar depression. It destroys my concentration.

Dan

And confidence.

Student 1

And confidence. Ruminations are relentless, and I don't sleep. It's my greatest fear, is to be in this state, and as part of that, for obvious reasons, it impacts my practice. And, you know, the greatest fear is that I don't—when I'm in this state and it's so disorganized and fragmented—I don't have a healthy sense of self to work with as part of these practices. I do find relief in taking refuge in Guru Rinpoche, and now that my back has gotten better, I can start to do the *tsalung*, which is a very good practice for me.

Dan

That will get your energy going. It will address the vegetative symptoms of depression.

Student 1

It'll address the what?

Dan

The vegetative symptoms of depression. The puddle stuff—that you can't get out of bed, the inertia.

Student 1

Yeah. But when I try to do … you know, I was very happy with the progress, how my practice was going after the 3B [retreat]. The emptiness … I haven't been able to open up in the *rigpa* in a long time, and my emptiness practice, I think, suffers because as soon as I get any relief from the emptiness and the negation, and things opening up, I'm grasping at that relief, and reifying myself and the state that I'm in. So, it's heartbreaking. So, what would you recommend in terms of my practice, especially as far as compassion and emptiness?

Dan

Well, let's answer that East and West. From a Western point of view, what is it that constitutes depression? First, it is the dysphoric mood you feel—emotionally blah, or ultimately between feeling nothing and feeling sad. Most of the feeling states or mood states are distinctly dysphoric or negative. And the negative mood state is the primary criteria. Associated with that is the nature of thought pattern. So, it is when you get into a depressive state, there's a tendency to systematically distort and bias the thinking in the direction of negative. So, you tend to highlight the negative things in your experience and selectively mis-attend to the positive. And you tend to amplify and catastrophize the negative. You tend to personalize everything, so there's an incessant patter of ruminative, negative self-talk about the self, and it's specifically negative about the self.

Student 1

And it's also about, how am I getting out of this? There's a constant effort. I feel so …

Dan

Well, that's part of the hopelessness. What's called a depressive triad is helpless, hopeless, worthless. Those are the big three. Helpless, hopeless, worthless.

So, the negative self-talk is another important part of what happens. And negative self-talk is a kind of moment-by-moment negative evaluation of a state. But the deeper structure of that cognitive distortion is kind of underlying, maladaptive beliefs and dysfunctional attitudes, which are more stable, like seeing yourself as worthless, or the kind of negative beliefs exemplified by Eeyore's thinking[13] about the world. And those can be relentless.

So, the third is what happens to the sense of self. When you're in the depressive state, there's a kind of inability to conjure up positive aspects of the self. Mostly, you focus on the negative self. And fourthly are the "vegetative symptoms," which means that you don't feel much. Your movements either alternate between slowing down or getting agitated, and in the height of those vegetative symptoms, you just get inert. You just don't want to come out from under the covers, and you sort of withdraw from all interactions with the world.

So, those are the main issues: The dysphoric mood, the changes in distorted thinking, the negative self, and the vegetative symptoms. And here's the issue: from a Western point of view, a lot of the treatments focus on trying to counter

---

13 Eeyore is a depressive stuffed donkey in the Winnie the Pooh children's stories.

the negative states. So, you can counter negative self-talk by trying to see how it's distorted and test it against the evidence. That's what cognitive therapists do.

Student 1

I work closely with a therapist on CBT.

Dan

So, you do CBT work?

Student 1

Sometimes.

Dan

But … all well and good, but from a Buddhist perspective, the criticism of Western psychotherapy for depression, as much as it's useful, is this: In the *Abhidharma*, originating from Vasubandhu and Asanga in the sixth century, what they say in Buddhist theory of mind is that the techniques to work with negative states and the techniques to work with positive states complement each other, but they're not reducible to each other.

So, if you develop a set of methods that primarily work with negative states and they're effective, then what we could reasonably expect is a relative reduction of the negative states, or in the best sense, maybe thereafter. But the absence of the negative isn't the positive. It's just the absence of the negative. So, if you use cognitive methods and correct or minimize the cognitive distortion to the extent the cognitive distortion drives the dysphoric mood, then you may reduce the dysphoric mood and the cognitive distortion. But the absence of that isn't the positive. You see the difference here?

And that's what I think is fundamentally different about the approaches with something like depressive state in East and West. How do we develop the positive? And that's important.

Now, not to minimize what cognitive therapy and things like that do, because as you know, you can get so trapped in the negative states, and all the negative self-talk around that, it's like a maze where you can't get out. And it does provide tools to give you some perspective on how you get locked in all that stuff, and that's useful. But something far more robust would be to directly approach cultivating the positive. And maybe we'll translate that into a visualization practice.

You can practice affirming self-talk, but when you're in that state, it seems rather wooden.

Student 1

You lose the vastness.

Dan

Yeah, you can't do it very well.

Student 1

I've always said the backbone of my recovery of mental illness is the spiritual practice, because that stuff's all well and good, but …

Dan

Well, I think there are things you can do from a kind of Western perspective using what we know from this *Abhidharma* approach, and that is that one of the main dimensions of depressive states is the negative self and the inability to conjure up a positive sense of self. So, if you systematically focus on bringing into your awareness the positive felt feelings of that positive self, and you keep doing that, it sort of overrides the depression at a certain point. Like, okay, what's healthy self-esteem? The best work on that from a Western point of view I think comes from Joe Sandler's work at the Hampstead clinic in London. And he has sort of a developmental model for self-esteem. Self-esteem is the, quote, "developmental linkage of positive emotional states for the self-representation." [Dan repeats:] "A developmental linkage of positive emotional states for the self-representation."

So, what does it mean? It means that if you have healthy esteem, the older child or the adult who has self-esteem, it means when they go about their everyday life, and during the day, you evoke your sense of self—if I evoke Dan-ness (as you evoke Bob-ness), I evoke Dan-ness against the backdrop of a whole network of positive feeling states. Experientially, that's what self-esteem is—the feeling good about the self.

If you were to not be depressed in your best moments, as you went about your daily life, and you evoked Bob-ness, you would evoke Bob-ness against the backdrop of good feelings. And when you're depressed, that's what shuts down, okay? And you can't conjure up what we call in Western terms, "evocative memory." You can't evoke the memory of the positive memories of self–experience, the positive Bob-ness, and all the qualities that go with that.

So, some years ago, we put together a protocol for how to do that. And in the visualizations, I'll show you how to do that. The first step is to imagine a scene where you feel really good about yourself. Now, if you're depressed, that's the hardest thing to conjure up, but you can do it if you work at it; and then to evoke that with the feeling, and bring out the feeling more, in any situation. So, the task is to remember times you felt really good about yourself, especially good about yourself.

If you really lost touch with yourself totally, we don't just go for the good feelings about yourself, we go for the self. And there the instruction would be, "Imagine a situation where you're most you. What are the qualities that come out that are most you, that are uniquely you." So, the first is defining the self and its positive qualities and then to get you to reflect on that scene and articulate the qualities so you're actually living in the moment, and the task is very direct. It's to actually generate the positive feelings about the self and to hold that in any situation, and then another situation, and then another situation. And the second is to then imagine scenes where you can hold a good feeling about yourself around other people. That's harder. You take it in steps. And the third is what we call "skill development." After you can hold a good feeling about yourself in any kind of scene, see how quickly and immediately you can bring it up. See how long of duration you can sustain it. So, the task is to bring it up upon demand, and you get skills with the visualization, and to sustain it for longer and longer periods of time.

Then we give you homework assignments to go home and do the visualization at home and then to try and bring it into your everyday life and report how long you can actually sustain it, until you can get to the point where you can hold the good feelings about yourself more of the day than not.

And the fourth part is what we call the challenge. Then, operating out of the good feeling about yourself, we then have you imagine the situations that you don't feel that in and try and bring that good feeling into those situations, first as you imagine it, and then we give you a homework assignment and do it in real life. And then, to evoke that good feeling about yourself, and then to try to bring it into the situations that are the most difficult to feel that in. First in fantasy and then in real life, you're given an assignment to put yourself in those situations and hold the good feeling about yourself.

So, if you go through all the steps of that, after a while you're pretty much evoking and holding a good feeling about yourself most of the time, and it doesn't get challenged or lost in certain situations. You just keep it. And then that emphasis on the positive experience of the self, the positive affective emotional experience of the self, is the core of this. And it tends—because the emphasis is squarely on developing the positive that's missing—it tends to work more effectively with lower relapse rates for depression because I think it goes to the heart of the matter. It's not so much how much you're caught up in the negative states, it's the absence of being able to generate the positive states that's more of the issue. You know, good treatment consistently focuses on what the issue is, until you get it.

From a neuroimaging point of view, what happens during depression? Well, there are two issues. One is that when people are depressed, they show deactivation of what's called the caudate nucleus, which is part of the basal ganglia system, top of the brain stem. It's the first gate. And what the basal ganglia system does in the caudate nucleus is it gates out extraneous stimuli, like extraneous self-talk. So, when that system is offline, you relentlessly get an onslaught of all that negative stuff that would normally be gated out.

So, how do you treat that? Well, there's, in neuroimaging terms, there's a top-down and a bottom-up way of treating that. SSRI, antidepressants, essentially activate the caudate nucleus. That's what they do. So, they put it back online so you filter out all that negative self-talk and dysphoric emotional states more efficiently. To that extent, the symptoms of depression clear up. There are studies, scanning studies done on cognitive psychotherapy, and those studies show that the cognitive psychotherapy doesn't affect the caudate nucleus at all directly. What it does is it activates the dorsolateral prefrontal cortex, which is the executive control system of the brain. What happens is that you look at all that stuff and you say, "Hey, what am I doing here? This is pretty disordered. My view of myself is pretty imbalanced." All that—what we call, in neuroimaging terms, top-down control—all that increased metacognitive capacity, all that executive control actually puts the caudate nucleus back online because the neurocircuitry is reconnected.

So, what's been amazing about the neuroimaging studies on psychotherapy versus drug treatment of depression is they both work, but for completely different reasons. And we now know something of the neurocircuitry that affects each. So, there are different pathways here.

But that's the Western approach. But what's missing in that approach? The same thing that I started with. Okay. And that is the positive. The orbital frontal, medial frontal cortex, the OFC, is the positive emotion center of the brain. That system is sort of underactive and offline when people get into depression. And there's no studies of psychotherapy that have addressed that issue because of the bias in Western psychotherapy towards working with negative states rather than working with positive states.

There are some exceptions to that in Western psychotherapy, but they're rare. For example, if you look at the literature that's now coming out in positive psychotherapy, Giovanni Fava's work—he calls it "Wellbeing Therapy." And what he asks you to do is actually bring to mind instances of wellbeing in your life and rate them on a scale, from say, how much wellbeing you experience on a zero to one hundred scale. And then you're given the assignment of, in your daily life, to keep track of every episode of wellbeing, and to rank it in terms of the number.

And what do you think happens if you give a person an assignment to look for episodes of wellbeing in their everyday life? At first, they say, "What?" They're so depressed they can't do it at all, but it doesn't take very long before they start finding it and bringing it to mind more and more. And Fava found that as they did this, with no focus on the negative stuff, the depression clears up in a much shorter time, because what are they doing if they're evoking episodes of wellbeing? In neuroimaging terms, we would hypothesize that they're activating the OFC. They're putting that positive emotion center back online, which is something you really want to do.

I think when we do our self-esteem protocols, when we ask you to imagine the episodes of feeling really good about yourself, it's doing the same thing. Both the self-esteem, self and self-esteem protocols that we develop, and I think the wellness episode protocols that Fava developed, both are OFC generated. They're focused on that even though there's no imaging studies to show that because we don't spend the money on imaging studies on the positive because we don't think that the positive is important.

But we do have one imaging study on the OFC, and it comes from Buddhism. And what Richie Davidson and his cohorts at the University of Wisconsin did—and Richie is an old friend. Richie is probably the best neuroimaging psychologist in the country. He has a big lab of functional MRI studies in University of Wisconsin. But Richie's background is that he's a meditator. He trained at Harvard. He and Danny Goldman were both students together under Gary Schwartz, the psychophysiologist who was at Harvard and Yale and is now in Arizona. And in the years that he [Richie] was learning psychophysiology, which was the precursor to neuroimaging studies, he was a very serious meditator, and he trained both with mindfulness and concentration meditation, both kinds.

And he's done some of the best imaging studies on both mindfulness and concentration. But in one of Richie's studies, because a lot of his neuroimaging is mapping out the emotional brain and the neurocircuitry of emotions, including the OFC stuff, one of the most definitive findings was taking Tibetan lamas who were doing *tonglen* practice, compassion training, and they had done years and years of compassion training; so they compared the brain regions of interest in the lamas who were trained in compassion training to normal brains, and they demographically matched the brain. And, in comparison studies like that, you can see which areas of the brain are being either over or underactive compared to what we have for statistics of normal brain activities in those regions of interest. And what Richie found was that what compassion training particularly does is it trains the OFC. It develops the positive emotion center of the brain. It makes it very strong, puts it back online.

You see, this is the generation of neuroplasticity. We no longer think that the brain is a stationary organ. Just as we know that muscles build their mass and decrease their mass depending on vigorous use or lack of use. You either build muscle mass or it atrophies. The brain does the same thing. So, if you use certain areas of the brain a lot, those areas of the brain do two things: they increase in volume, number one, and number two, they actually increase in white and gray matter. They actually change their composition and add more cells and more circuitry. So, that's what's called "neuroplasticity." On the other hand, if you don't use it, you lose it. So, one of the areas of the brain that's been extensively studied that way is the hippocampus, which is spatial memory. It provides the contextual cues of how we remember things.

It's well documented that people with chronic post-traumatic stress show lower size of the hippocampus, about 8 to 10 percent lower than would normally be expected. So, not only is their contextualization of retrieval cues offline, it makes it harder for them to remember important aspects of the trauma; but after a while the structure actually atrophies. That's on the one hand.

On the other hand, there was an interesting study called "The Taxi Study." What they did, because the hippocampus is also about spatial memory, is they looked at London taxi drivers. In London, taxi driving is [and at least in 2013 was still] a noble profession. They took people who were just starting to learn who have to memorize streets for two years. And they have to know all the streets by heart anywhere in London, which is a very difficult task. So, they have to cram, they have to overuse the hippocampus, the spatial memory system. They scanned the taxi driver students at the very beginning of the class and six months later, and they found about a 10 percent increase in the volume of the hippocampus.

So, you change brain structure by use. Lyle and I were reviewing articles on meditation for this thing that we're writing on meditation training for law students, attorneys and judges. We reviewed all the neuroimaging studies and found several studies on concentration training that show that persistent concentration training not only increases volume of the ACC, the anterior cingulate cortex, which is the concentration center of the brain, but also increased both white and gray matter in those areas. So, concentration changes the volume and the composition of the neurocircuitry of the concentration area of the brain.

So, you see, we could say the same thing about the lamas who trained for years in compassion training. What does the Dalai Lama say about compassion training? You'll find that in the book that the psychiatrist, Howard Cutler, did with him on happiness. Howard did a series of interviews with him about what constitutes happiness, and he said, "It's two things. One is training the mind—that's concentration and emptiness practice—contributes to happiness. And the other thing is, compassion training breeds happiness." He says, "I practice compassion all the time and that's why I'm happy. Because when I'm always compassionate and giving to others, that makes me happy."

So, you see, whether you work with evoking positive feelings about the self, as in the protocol I suggested to you, on the one hand; whether you give task assignments to look for and develop an increase in episodes of wellbeing; or whether you do any one of an infinite variety of compassion practices, in my opinion, the common factor is you're activating the OFC, and you're putting positivity back online. Then it doesn't make so much difference how much all that negative self-talk and all that other stuff comes up, because it overwrites it—it sort of positively remaps all that. And it's more positive. That's one thing I would say is important that is kind of a blind spot in the Western stuff on depression.

But there's another one. And that is … what do people do when they start feeling badly? Not when you slip into the intensive depression. You get out of it. They get more behaviorally active. When the going gets tough, the tough reorganize their environment. They go out and do things. They more actively engage. They go shopping. And the common factor in all of that is that the tendency of when you get more and more depressed is to sort of disengage and to become more and more passive. And it's very clear that when you work to get yourself more active, it counters that tendency, particularly if the activity that you are engaging is one, engaging, and two, if it engages you in a positive way.

So, the positive opposite of that passive withdrawal from everything about life is what? It would be what Jeanne Nakamura calls "vital engagement" in everything about life. It's the last thing you can possibly think of when you're depressed, right? And therefore, it's one of the most important because when you start doing that it draws you out of that state. So, developing the positive emotional quality associated with the self and active engagement are the most necessary active components to … of getting out of that state and preventing it. That's what I would say from a kind of a Western point of view, [a] critique from a Buddhist point of view.

Student 1

Should you, if you have like these family members that are very active and loving and engaging, actually …

Dan

Oh, but you use that against yourself when you're depressed, right?

Student 1

No, but around them, they just sort of …

Dan

Okay, but you can turn that into a sort of negative self-talk because it's a nice thing, and you can think of all the things, why they shouldn't be. That's the problem with depression because it's that kind of distorted thinking. Why are they doing that? I mean, sometimes it makes you feel worse about yourself. But if you're using that to draw you out of yourself, that's great. Look, the very fact that you came here—you're being proactive, you talked about it, you took the lead here. That's not passive withdrawal. You're enacting what it takes to work your way out of this right on the spot.

Student 1

Trying.

Dan

This is resourcefulness, even if you don't see it. It's being really resourceful, in the best sense. And knowing you, I see that in you as one of your clear senses, your strength. It's your resourcefulness. But you vary in your ability to see that about yourself. So, I think that you have to sort of see this on the spectrum approach. You have to work with these methods to get out [of] the state, reasonably so, before you can use any of the purely Buddhist methods. But ultimately, when you get out of that enough that you can get some perspective, then I think, focusing on emptiness of self, and roaming around and finding the solidness—because the self gets pretty solid when there's a crack in the ice and it's like an iceberg. A rather big iceberg. [Dan chuckles] And it doesn't seem like it's ever going to melt. But, roaming around with your awareness, it's like a … because awareness has the speed of light, and there's a softness to it. Awareness that … roaming around through all that solidness of self with that awareness is like a flame thrower. It melts all that.

But you can't start with that. It's very difficult. I mean it's not impossible, but that's the best I can say about it honestly, is that you can't start with that. But if you get some perspective on that as you're coming out of it, what's going to really reinforce getting out of that is to do emptiness of self. Particularly to look at the grab of the negative self. That's a big one. My teacher used to call it the "pride of lowliness." To think of yourself as that bad is remarkably proud and arrogant. "I am the worst person in the entire world." I mean, that's pretty arrogant. And everybody who is depressed thinks like that. They used to call [that] the "pride of lowliness."

So, looking at all that stuff and all of the stories that reinforce that, there's a whole fabric in there. There's a whole world in there. Roaming around through all that stuff and cutting through it, that would be a very strong method at a certain point in time. What you're doing is you're squarely addressing and seeing it for what it is—they're all stories. And the stories don't define the ultimate nature of yourself because in the ultimate nature of yourself, there are no negative spaces—*kadak*, everything good. But you have to roam around [in] what the Sufi master Hafiz calls "that tiresome project of self." And it's pretty tiresome when you're depressed.

So, from an East and West perspective, I would say from all that we've learned about depression in the West—which is considerable—in my read of all the outcomes literature on that, the best approaches are what focuses on positive emotion associated with the self and developing that, positive episodes of wellbeing in everyday life, and loving-kindness and compassion towards the self and others, including the self. You know, we have a lot of students who take the Level 1 course; they get incessantly into their negative self-talk about themselves during the meditation. And what Gretchen likes to do with that as a teacher is to give students compassion practice—not about others, but to do visualization, compassion visualizations about treating the self compassionately. And they're very powerful. As you know, I like to do that with the attachment stuff.

You see, you have to step back with all this research on outcome studies and this generation of evidence supported treatment—you have to step back and read all that with a kind of critical eye because science isn't what you think it is. You know, we all trained in the philosophy of science. [Dan speaks here with a mock serious, authoritative, or dogmatic inflection:] "There's a scientific method. Scientists are objective and they go through this disciplined process of testing their hypotheses." Well, that's total crap. Okay? I mean we'd like to believe that but it's really a Western mythology.

I think the best studies on science are the studies on the sociology of science. And what sociologists say is that science is about "interest group behavior." And the name of the game in science is if you have a particular interest group, and somebody else has a different interest group, and they're pushing certain hypotheses, that you have a lax methodological criterion for your own research, and you criticize the hell out of the other guy's research. But you don't apply that same standard to yourself. And then you put forth your hypotheses in a way that is basically in order to push power interests.

We market, we market science. We market science. It's not necessarily accurate. And who does the best job with marketing? Look, I, as an expert witness around memory and trauma issues, have gone up against Rebecca Loftis, who is world famous. I was on the stand two weeks ago and the other side was trying to say, "But she's world famous." And I said, "So what?" You know, it's not a voting contest here. If you look at the methodology, what I call her "slash and burn" research studies, the research design is really poor. A graduate student wouldn't get away with it. But she markets herself well. And this stuff is garbage.

And when I worked on the war crimes tribunal as a rebuttal expert to her, I had a chance to sort of sit there and dismantle her research designs. So, I took her four most important research things, showed the judges in a common-sense way how she designed the experiments, what was wrong with the research designs, and how she wildly overplayed the results, and they just rolled up their eyes because nobody's ever done that. And as a result, the defense pulled her as an expert; after she'd testified in front of the whole set of experts, because we essentially destroyed her position.

But I'm not saying that to single out one individual. I'm saying that happens all the time in science. We market it. That's true for outcomes research. If you look at the comparative outcome studies of cognitive therapy, drug therapy, and psychodynamic psychotherapy, what people report is not what the studies show. If you read the reports of the drug studies, it looks like they came out the best, but that's not what the studies show.

[In] the NIMH [Treatment of Depression] Collaborative Study, which is the biggest study, actually it's psychodynamic or what's called interpersonal therapy, did as well as the drugs, and over time, when they looked at it with a six-year follow up, the dynamic therapy did better than the drugs, with lower relapse rates, and it worked better for so-called endogenous biological depression. But the analytically trained people don't market themselves, so nobody knows that finding.

What the drug companies say about the research, that their stuff did okay relative to wait-list control, is not incorrect, but it has spin. And the cognitive therapist didn't do well in that, so they don't talk about it very much. They cite other studies showing that cognitive therapy works terrific. But if you reanalyze the meta-analysis there, you'll find they only work terrific for people who believe in cognitive therapy. If you factor out the experimenter's bias, the results, the statistics, go to chance. So, what I'm saying is you can't just accept the interpretation of the findings because it's all about spin in this country.

We saw that there was the embarrassment with *The New England Journal of Medicine* where there's a drug that caused serious cardiac arrest. And they knew that when they reported the study. And the way it slipped by the peer review is that they simply said, "There is some question about this to be reported in a later study." They had no intention of reporting a later study. They put that in to cover their butts because the lawyers told them to do it, and it slipped by the reviewers. And a lot of people died. Why? Because there's a vested interest to push this stuff. That's not science. But if you sift through the stuff, you can come up with certain, what we call active treatment ingredients, and focusing on the positive self and focusing on active vital engagement, in my opinion, having looked at this stuff pretty carefully, are the things you want to do. Okay? We know from a neuroimaging point of view why that works in Western terms, and we know in Buddhism why that works. So, there is some common ground here, and to stay consistently focused on what's going to work, that's what you want to do.

May 1, 2013

Themes: Four "Discoveries" of the Turnings of the Wheel; the Essence Traditions; Conduct

Dan

[Just back from a teaching trip to Australia] Hi everybody—nice to be back. Obviously, I didn't get eaten by crocodiles. It commands respect, being there. We went with Aboriginal guides through the Outback, and they know the animal, so, when you're with them it's pretty safe. But when you're not with them, it gets pretty dangerous pretty quickly. But, in the country where we were, there were many thirty-foot long crocs, like giant dinosaurs. Thirty-foot long crocs! They can leap about ten feet out of the water, and they can jump about thirty feet. There's one river you can go on where they have these thirty-foot crocs, and they hold a chicken up and the crocs will come out of the water. It's just really, it's a wild country.

It was interesting, being with the Aborigines, because they don't talk much. But the key to opening them up to talk in a very honest and open way is if you talk about lineage. Because they understand lineage—absolutely understand lineage. And as soon as they know that you know something about lineage, they're completely different with you, because the land that we were at, they'd been living on that land for fifty thousand years. Can you believe that? Fifty thousand years! The same land. It's just remarkable. And everything is interconnected. It's remarkable. It's a great view of the world. I'm happy to have been there and to really get into being in the Outback and the land; it was truly extraordinary. We went to places that you had to fly in to. There's no way of getting there other than that. It was good.

Student 1

So, this is something I've been thinking about for a while Dan, and it's not urgent, but I'm guessing other people might share this struggle or concern. It's more about talking to others about this practice; talking about Buddhism in general. When people ask what I do on retreats, or what my experience is, it feels delicate, how to talk. Particularly that people know that I go on retreats fairly regularly.

Dan

That's a good question.

Student 1

And so let me just add one more piece to it. Also, as you well know, and you speak about this frequently, the difference between Mahāyāna tradition and Theravāda, most of the people who are Buddhist in my personal world kind of fall into a Theravāda tradition, or they're going to IMS or CIMC; that's much of the literature out there. And so, they ask, well what's different? And that feels delicate for me. It feels really delicate about how to articulate some of those differences. So, anything that you can offer to help me, I'm guessing, talk about this stuff would be great.

Dan

Okay. You've got two questions here. And the first, which is your second question, is about the differences within the tradition itself and then any level of that tradition, how do you talk about it? That's a lot. Let's take the second question as the first because it sets more of a context.

In traditional descriptions of the history of Buddhism, the levels of the traditions are described as the Three Turnings of the Wheel of the *Dharma*. And so, as Westerners, you can think of that similar to what we in the West talk about in terms of scientific revolutions. In the history of science, at some point there's enough anomalies that accumulate and then you get a discovery of a whole new paradigm. So, there's a significant rethinking of previous paradigms. And you can think of the Three Turnings of the Wheel in those terms if you like. There's the original Buddhism, and then there was a significant number of things that were either not explained and/or there were significant revisions of old concepts that people were not happy with, and then a whole new form of Buddhism, a paradigm shift, occurs.

So, there are three paradigm shifts. The First Turning of the Wheel was the teachings of Shakyamuni Buddha. And his first speech after full enlightenment under the *bodhi* tree that he gave at Sarnath was on The Four Noble Truths and The Eightfold Path. That defines the First Turning of the Wheel. The first [Truth] is, *dukkha*, which is often translated as the Truth of Suffering. But it's not a good translation. *Dukkha* means reactivity. It means if you look at your mind very carefully, every time something comes into your field of experience, if you like it, your mind moves towards it to make more of it, to amplify it. And if you don't like it, the mind moves away from it to make less of it. And that constant reactivity of moving towards or away is the root of suffering. It's like—in Western terms, it's a bias built into information processing, so that moment by moment we don't leave our experience alone, we're always trying to change it. And the outcome of that is suffering.

But from the level of practice, what Shakyamuni Buddha was talking about was being able to observe the mind in its operation so you could see how that worked, or better, how it didn't work, because it creates suffering. And the path was the path of meditation that led to liberation or freedom from suffering. And if you did the meditations then it led to the way out of suffering.

Now, that path in the older Theravāda Buddhism was the most detailed model for that, stage by stage, and was called the *Visudhimagga* in Pali. And it's translated into English as "The Path to Purification." It was published twice in English as the first text by the Pali Text Society in the early part of the twentieth century, and then republished more recently by Shambhala in the, I think '60s or '70s, by Nyanaponika Thera. And that's a stage-by-stage model of the path in Theravādin Buddhism that led you to awakening, and in that awakening, what stopped is that reactivity. So, if you have the first of what are four gradations of awakening, nothing about the content of your experience changes; what changes is you stop that moment-by-moment reactivity and you just let things be there the way they are. So, in that sense you cut to the root of suffering.

But what you need to understand is the First Turning of the Wheel is mostly about liberation from suffering. That's the main thing. The three major insights in that tradition are what are called the three signs of existence: reactivity or suffering; everything is impermanent (because if you observe the mind, it changes all the time—nothing's stable); and the third was much more problematic: *anatta*, no self.

And what it meant was if you concentrated long enough, all thought elaboration would stop, and at some point in the meditation, your sense of self would drop away, so it would no longer be, for example, me doing the meditation. It would be awareness itself doing the meditation, which would probably do a better job than I could, because I get out of my own way. And that temporary deconstruction of Dan-ness would come about because if I suppressed the tendency to elaborate thought during deep concentration states, I also suppress the other constructions of mind, like the construction of the sense of self. So that drops away, too. That would be what the description of no self was in the older Buddhism.

Now, why that's important historically is that what's now become very popular in the West is mindfulness meditation, and that pretty much is about the nature of suffering and freedom from suffering. But it doesn't have most of the later developments and new discoveries in Buddhism, if you will. I like to call them new discoveries.

The Second Turning of the Wheel was Mahāyāna Buddhism. And that's complex. But there are three things that are important in Mahāyāna Buddhism that are "new discoveries." The first has to do with 500 years of revision around this notion of *anatta* or no self, because it became rather controversial, and some people within the tradition rightly criticized the notion of no self because it can lead to nihilism—the idea that we're trying to get rid of your sense of self, which is extreme, and represents the practices of ascetics. And what came out of that is a reworking of the notion of no self into the notion of emptiness, which is a terrible term because it doesn't really define what it means. But since every Western textbook on Buddhism defines [*tongpanyi*] in Tibetan or (*shunyata* in Sanskrit) as emptiness, we're sort of stuck with the term. But if you want a good synonym for emptiness, the phrase "just a construction of mind" would be a good synonym.

In other words, emptiness is about the constructive nature of the human mind. The way that the mind works is to make representations. And in that sense, it's very similar to modern cognitive science, the so-called modern cognitive sciences revolution, because it used to be that we thought that the eye would make a mirror image of what was out there, and then the brain would make a representation which was a mirror image from what the eyes made. And now we don't believe that at all—we don't even know if there is an "out there."

In other words, most constructivist theories of perception in the West have gone to holographic perception—that what we see is all representations. The mind makes representations, and even the grandfather of modern neurobiology Karl Pribram at Stanford said, "The function of neurons it to make neuronal models of the world." That what we're seeing is our own models. This "out there" is our own construction. And for social convenience, we like to create the idea that we all see the same thing. But that's not the case at all.

But, do we see something similar? Yeah. Why? Because we all have a similar perceptual apparatus. We all have similar brains. But what we see is just the mind's representations. We're seeing our own constructions. So, perception is constructive. Thought is constructive. Our sense of self is a construction.

Infants don't come into a world with a psychological sense of self. I didn't come into the world with Dan-ness. Western self psychologists tell us that the psychological sense of self develops at about eighteen months, concurrent with the development of representational thinking. When you can represent, you can represent self. There's nothing wrong with doing that. As a representation, it becomes a central organizing principle for everyday life—useful. But what we forget is that it's just a construction. The Tibetan word for that is *nozhin*, taking it as a thing, or taking it as too real. We take the world as independently self-existing apart from ourselves. We forget that it's all a construction based on a perceptual apparatus. We think our sense of self actually exists independently. I actually take "Dan" way too seriously.

So, once we make constructions, we take them as too real. The English word that comes close to *nozhin*—meaning to take as too real—is reify. And the consequences of reification are two things. One, in Tibetan, is *dzin-pa*, things have "grab." So, we go about our daily life organizing experiences around grab. You can go through your life and catalog the infinite varieties of grab. If you don't like my talk, you criticize me—grab. If you like it, you praise me—grab. I can't win either way, you see? [Dan chuckles] It's all grab. Fight with your partner—grab. When you get defensive, you can observe grab. It's perceptual.

And the other part is more serious, *mümpa*—when you develop the construction say, of self, it has the capacity to obscure. It clouds over our real nature—so that we start dwelling within the constructions rather than operating out of our real nature, which is an awakening that is always here. We just don't operate out of it because we're lost in our own clouds of constructions of mind. So, the idea of emptiness practice was to look into seeing things just the way they are, and what they came up with is this notion of two levels of truth: relative truth and ultimate truth.

Relatively speaking, we make constructions all the time. Some of them, like sense of self, are useful. The sense of time is a construction and it's useful. We organize so we can get here on time, except my sense of time didn't work very well tonight, so that's why I was late. But usually, it operates effectively in relative reality. But ultimately, we forget they're just constructions. As long as I'm operating out of self, I'm not operating out of true nature. As long as I'm operating out of time and I'm lost in time, I'm not operating out of the timeless nature of boundless awareness—timeless, boundless awareness space that's always here. So, this idea of emptiness means that the constructions of mind we mistakenly take as all too real. And that has very clear consequences. On the one hand, by creating suffering; and on the other hand, by clouding over true nature.

The second revision of the path in Mahāyāna Buddhism was an emphasis on the construction of time. And that's a big one because in the older Buddhism, if you really develop good concentration at the so called "subtle level of mind," you get to the level where you don't perceive solid forms anymore. Everything is reduced to very quick bursts of energy and movement in the mind, called "mind moments." Everything pulses like a stroboscopic light. And if you watch everything pulse, after a while everything will start to disintegrate, and you focus more on the going out of things rather than the coming forth of things in time. And at some point it all starts to break up. It's not very pleasant.

And what you're observing is that what in the older Buddhism we call *dharmin*—the basic operations and elements of consciousness—begin to disintegrate. It was called *bunganyana* in Pali or dissolution experience. If through concentration you reduce consciousness to its simplest operations and even those disintegrate, then what's left is a kind of field of boundless mirror-like awareness. And you have an opportunity there to look into the nature of that field of awareness for what it is. So, dissolution was described in the *Visudhimagga* as "the platform for awakening."

But then Nagarjuna came along, who was the main proponent of the emptiness practices of the Mahāyāna, and he said, "Look, when you're looking at things coming and going in time very quickly, that presumes the convention of time as a structure of mind. Maybe that's just another cloud, another structure that we reify." So, he developed this funny thing called The Nagarjunan Dialectic: when something comes forth in time, you look at it as if it doesn't really arise because it's already here; and when it goes away in time, you look at it as if it doesn't go anywhere but it stays here.

That's going to screw around with your notion of time. And if you keep looking at things that arise and seem to arise and pass away in time like that, it busts everything open. And you experience a level of *samādhi* called "the very subtle level of mind" or "extraordinary *samādhi*"—*tumomyempa* in Tibetan. And that is often described as "simultaneous mind." In Western information processing terms, by doing that funny thing with time, what you're doing is shifting from temporal or serial processing, from where you process things sequentially in time, to simultaneous mode, where you process things as being here all at once.

Those experiences are described in terms of levels of all-at-once-ness. It's hard to describe that in language. But it's a remarkably different experience. Think of an experience where everything here that could potentially exist across all realms and times is here all at once and it's all interconnected. It's a pretty big shift.

And that notion of opening up levels of all-at-once-ness, is the starting point of the Mahāyāna vehicle. So, what people don't often realize is that from a meditation point of view—in terms of meditation experiences—what you're actually experiencing is a whole different function of operation of the mind that you just don't get in the older Buddhism. That's a huge shift.

And that was the foundation for the other main discovery of the Mahāyāna, which is *bodhisattva* activity—people who devote themselves to helping all beings, but it comes from this direct experience of simultaneous mind. Because if you experience a mind where everything is here all at once and interconnected, it will change your ethics. Because you then have the direct experience in an ongoing way that every thought, every movement of your mind, every action of your behavior—what's called *choepa*, or conduct—affects the entire interpersonal field.

That's why in the Great Vehicle it's called the Mahāyāna; your practices are for the sake of the awakening of all beings. And the main notion is what's called *wang* in Tibetan (which is often translated as "empowerment," which is not a good translation)—*wang* literally means influence. It's like a "field effect." If you meet a non-ordinary being, a full buddha, they have *wang*.

If you call forth in Guru yoga a great master like Pabmasambhava, they have the duty to come forth at your calling. But then, when they come forth, you have to *solwadeb*, you have to make a request. And if you put the intention into making that request, they respond with *chingilap*, which literally means "waves of giving." *Chingilap* means that the gift they give you is the gift of influence, which means they can directly intervene in your unfolding mindstream. Because your unfolding mindstream—if you really look at it, is going to have many more spontaneously emerging negative states because of karmic ripening than positive states. And, they can directly intervene in your mindstream to do two things: they can clear away the clouds, and they can activate your original buddha nature, and put the positive aspect of that online—they've been offline for a long time. So, when you ask for the gift of influence, you're getting a direct jump-start to your mindstream in a way that's more likely to make your meditation practice come to fruition. Otherwise, you're going to play out the same old same old patterns on the pillow that you're playing off the pillow, and you don't get very far.

The other part of that is what you do has influence. Not to the same strength as a non-ordinary being. But it means the more you develop your practice, the more it has a positive influence-field to it. And you sort of pull the entire interpersonal field along through the influence of the strength of your own practice. It's not like if you awaken everybody on the planet, they wake up at the same time. But it is the case that that has force or influence. It's like planting seeds that will eventually ripen in the entire interpersonal field. So, you're having a positive influence on everyone.

Out of that comes the idea of *bodhisattva* activity: that how you act matters because it has direct karmic influences, either positive or negative, on your entire field. So, things like acting for the benefit of sentient beings, practicing things like the Six Perfections—those all come out of that realization. That's the Second Turning of the Wheel. And part of what they were trying to do was correct for two different, what Nagarjuna called "extreme views." With the notion of no self, they were trying to correct for this idea of nihilism that you're trying to get rid of the self—you're not. In relative reality the self is rather useful. You just don't want to take it too seriously. And the other was the extreme of eternalism: thinking that things are independently existing out there somewhere.

So, they did five hundred years of very sophisticated revisions of that, most of which are not at all appreciated by Western practitioners. Many people think that all Buddhism is the same. So, I remember somebody sending me a cartoon.

And it says Dalai Lama's birthday, and he's holding up a box that he's opened up and there's nothing inside it. And the caption says, "Just what I wanted for my birthday, nothingness." People don't understand that that cartoon would be perceived by the Dalai Lama, or anybody who is a proponent of Mahāyāna Buddhism, as an insult—it negates 500 years of careful revision of this notion of *anatta*, or no self. And it represents a nihilistic position that they developed all this stuff to get out of.

And more recently, he was insulted by a journalist for the eternalist position. I don't know if you saw that one on YouTube. But a journalist goes in and he's interviewing the Dalai Lama, and he tells the Dalai Lama a joke. And he says, "Your Holiness, here's a joke. The Dalai Lama goes into a pizza shop and says, 'make me one with everything.'" And then the journalist starts laughing and laughing and laughing and laughing. And the Dalai Lama is sitting there clueless about what this guy's doing, because "make me one with everything" represents an eternalist position. That's not funny to the Dalai Lama. It's a complete misunderstanding of all of the years of trying to correct for both eternalism and nihilism, to create what's called a "middle path." But as Westerners we don't understand anything about the sophistication of that, and it's insulting. Okay, so that's the second revision or Turning of the Wheel.

The third revision, or the "new discoveries," came with what are called "the Essence traditions." In the Essence traditions are The Great Seal of Mahāmudrā or Chagyachenpo in Tibetan, Great Completion or Dzogchen in Tibetan, and the *tantra* practices of the Vajrayāna. And they all share a similar world view or theory of mind.

And the idea here is that we all have original buddha nature. We are all fully awake. But through habitual karmic tendencies, we put layers and layers of reified constructions of mind on top of that, so we can't realize the awakening. And the metaphor to understand that is the clouds and the sun, which many of you have heard before. But the idea here is if it's raining outside and the clouds clear up and the sun comes out, we say, "the sun just came out." But that's not correct. The sun's always been out. But when we cleared away enough clouds, we could actually perceive that the sun has always been shining.

Right here is an infinite ocean of awareness-love, which is your true nature. The lucid radiance of that always shines forth like the sun that never stops shining. But in our ordinary mind we have layers and layers of clouds, and every reified structure of mind clouds it over. So, the idea in the Essence tradition is that you all have buddha nature—part of the hard wiring is that you have an awakened nature—you're always awake, you just don't recognize it. The clouds prevent us from recognizing what's always right here. It's not a state we're going to find at some point, remotely, and in some distant point in our practice. It's always here every moment. Immediately you have *rigpa*—you recognize awakening in this moment—or you have *marigpa*, you don't recognize it. Every moment.

So, in the Essence traditions, the idea is you clear away the clouds and discover and recognize what's already here. But if somebody points out what to look for, you're more likely to find it, because it cuts through the bullshit. So, that's one thing that's unique to the Essence traditions—they're quick path traditions. And most of them involve a "direct introduction" or "direct pointing out," whatever you want to call it. And the instructions that open it up are very precious and they're often kept as guarded secrets.

And the reason for that is because if you're given instructions [when you're] not in the right state of mind, you tend to try and conceptualize about awakening, as you know—been there done that one. [Dan laughs] It hardens the mind and makes it harder to awaken. But if you do all the preparative practices, which clean away the layers of the clouds, then if you're given the instructions, in the right condition of mind, the probability is very high that it will open up. So, they're kept secret, to be given out to certain students who are having certain states of mind, that have "built the vessel" we say, and "made it fit for the nectar of the teachings." Then the realization is pretty easy in the right state. So, that's one of the contributions of the Essence traditions.

The second contribution of the Essence traditions is an emphasis on the positive qualities of mind. There are eighty positive qualities of a fully-ripened buddha mind. And when you clear away the clouds, it's not like these qualities are something you develop over time. You have all these eighty positive qualities as part of your *kadak*, your original nature. So, when you clear away the clouds, all of these just radiantly shine forth. The positive qualities of the primordial wisdom of the mind shine forth. So, there's much more emphasis on a better recognition of those positive qualities that develop from awakening.

And thirdly, and this is important, is that if you look at the Essence traditions, they did much more development on what was called "the mind beyond the three times"—meaning past, present, and future. If you read most any Buddhist book, it would say "beyond the three times." What it really means is that you've done emptiness of time practice and moved beyond the convention of time to a level of awareness that's changeless and timeless. And since time and space are related, it's vast, huge awareness. And it's convenient because, of course, once you've experienced it, it doesn't ever go away, because it's not in time, so it can't go away.

But if you start developing that level of awareness, way along the practice, once you have stable awakening (awakening that you have 24/7), at some point in the practice what will start opening up is you realize that awakened awareness creates everything. We call that "recognition of the liveliness of awakening"—everything is the liveliness of awakening. All sight, all sound, all thought, all touch, all smell, all emotions, all are liveliness of awakening.

But at some point you discover that awakening has something else. Awakened awareness has organizing capacity—it organizes entire worlds. In Dzogchen it's called "cracking the eggshell." This bubble that you see is only one bubble of millions of bubbles. At some point that awareness becomes so pervasive and vast that it busts through this eggshell and starts to extend out to many realities simultaneously, because in Mahāyāna when you open up simultaneous mode, it really does mean that. You open up layers and layers of simultaneousness. So, the mind operates on thousands of levels at the same time—thousands of realities at the same time. In fact, in some of the older Indian Mahāyāna sutras, they measured degrees of buddhahood in terms of how many millions of realms you opened up. And they would have contests with each other. In terms of how many realms you opened up.

That's pretty inconceivable, but they really mean that. So, the key to understanding all that is directly perceiving the organizing nature of a fully awakened awareness: all the descriptions of entry into buddha realms and [buddha] fields; you can get complete downloads of teachings at that point (but they're not "out there")—there is no duality; and you don't need a live teacher anymore. The path has its own intelligence and shows itself to itself at that point. That's why I can teach you some of this stuff. It's like the Cliffs Notes[14] of higher realizations; you just enter into *samādhi* and download what you need. I'm not joking with that. And then the *tögal* visions in Dzogchen—four levels of visions all about this organizing principle. So, you just watch the show without a watcher. And the path has its own intelligence and unfolds itself to itself.

The ultimate thing that comes out of the Essence traditions is that once the mind opens up on multiple levels of reality, with that vast grasping directly of

---

14 A well-known series of student study guides.

the interconnectedness of all beings, then there is *thinle*, enlightened activity. You work inexhaustibly like the sun on many levels of reality simultaneously to help beings; and all practice comes spontaneously, it doesn't come from self—it all comes from awakened *dharmakāya* space to help beings. So, the ultimate test of your realization is always conduct.

Now, you see, because we have Buddhist practices that have become popular in the last thirty or forty years, as Westerners we have no clue of the remarkable differences in these things. It's the luck of the draw what comes over here. Mindfulness is very popular but it only represents that First Turning of the Wheel. I have old students of mindfulness who now are all teachers in that tradition that I've known for forty years or more. I went to one of my old student's talks today; it was a student of mine almost forty years ago. And after forty years he's still talking about suffering; there's nothing about positive states, nothing about conduct. Because it doesn't exist in that level of tradition and I haven't seen any evolution of his ideas in over forty years. It made me very sad.

So, you see, not all paths within the realm of Buddhism lead to the same outcomes. You ought to know what you're getting. It's very different. They're all useful, so it's not that one is superior and one is inferior, but it is the case that certain paths will open up far more than other paths. All of them will lead to the liberation of suffering, but in addition to that, opening up the emptiness so that things lose grab and things lose the capacity to obscure so that you can open up simultaneous mind? That only occurs in the Mahāyāna. And the focus on opening up all the positive qualities of the mind that just flourish—positivity of the mind that flourishes—that's only in the Essence traditions. So, you ought to make clear what you're getting, because if you're going to spend a lot of time on these practices, they lead to different ends.

Personally, I have a bias. I think focusing on simultaneous mind and the positivity is the heart of this tradition within Buddhism. Those were the later discoveries; those were the new discoveries that were considered more valuable than just ending suffering; and as Westerners as we ought to appreciate the profundity of that, which we're mostly clueless about. So, that's the first answer to your question it's important.

The second has to do with how do you talk about it? And I suppose the main issue there is, what's your motivation for talking about it? You've got to look at your own motivation. Within Tibetan Buddhism, as opposed to Indian Mahāyāna Buddhism, the etiquette is one never talks about personal attainments. And the reason that they developed that is that they thought that if you started talking about personal attainments, there are two problems that come out of that. One is the reification of the attainments, so you make them into things and then they're not empty, and you create more clouds—the attainments become clouds rather than things that liberate you from clouds. The second is that if you talk about them it leads to spiritual pride.

It's fairly explicit in the Tibetan tradition, but I've seen it more clearly in the early Christian Desert Fathers when Johannes Cassianus wrote his list of seven deadly sins. He added an eighth, and the reason why they're listed as "seven or eight" is the eighth is only for practitioners who've gotten somewhere in the practice, and he called it "spiritual pride." And what Cassianus correctly said is, "the further along you are in the path, the more spiritual pride becomes a problem, not less." So, you're always having to look at that, and there are many stories in the Tibetan tradition about that.

For example [with a student of] Tsongkhapa—the great revisionists who started the Gelugpa, the lineage of the Dalai Lama—he had two students, Kyedrupje and Gyaltsap. One of them was a devoted student for many years, but the other one was a newer student, and he went there because he was jealous of Tsongkhapa. What's the motivation? Because he [Tsongkhapa] had become very famous with his teachings, he wanted to challenge him. So, he did what one never did. When Tsongkhapa was going to give a talk to a rather large audience, he went up before Tsongkhapa arrived and sat on Tsongkhapa's seat.

Tsongkhapa thought it was hilarious, but to teach him a lesson he picked him up by the ear and threw him off his seat. He told him honestly that he didn't think he could teach him until he overcame his spiritual pride. And they worked it out over time, and he became one of the two lineage holders, which is the beginning of the entire Gelugpa lineage, which is now the Dalai Lama's seat. But it started with a remarkable showing of arrogance at a young age towards the senior teacher, something that we do all the time in the West.

Another example was at the beginning of a [major] Bonpo lineage. Tapihritsa was an Indian master, and he was the first human to develop that Bonpo lineage. He had very well-developed miraculous powers much like Padmasambhava did. And he decided that the best person to transmit his teachings to was a Tibetan, a Tibetan master who was a great Tantric [Gyerpung Nangzher Lodpo, aka "Nearpo"] who had mastered many supernatural abilities and was filled with pride about his spiritual accomplishments.

So, he [Tapihritsa] decided to teach him a lesson and he manifested himself as a sixteen- year-old boy who showed up and said he wanted to be Nearpo's assistant. Nearpo said yes, and let him collect firewood, build the fire, and cook for him. And then they would have these *dharma* talks, where Tapihritsa would ask these penetrating questions that would anger the *tantra* master because he was being showed up by the penetrating nature of the questions. Nearpo kept getting pissed off at Tapihritsa who was only a sixteen-year-old boy, and finally he got so enraged at the boy that he did what one should never do. He lost it, and then challenged the boy to a public debate in front of the king (and in those days whoever lost [such a debate] basically got beheaded).

So, Tapihritsa laughed at him and said, "I can't debate you because you're too conceptual." And Nearpo thought that Tapihritsa was avoiding the issue, so he was yelling at Tapihritsa when Tapihritsa put his hand on the table like this [Dan puts his right hand to his temple and leans down as if he's going to rest his elbow on a table] and then put his elbow right through the table [Dan leans further and further down] and then put his head right through the table so it was half in the table and half out of the table. At that point the master stopped, realizing that this was not an ordinary kid, decided that he'd been set up, and apologized. And then he started learning from the kid, as did the king. Tapihritsa then changed himself into his original shape and the whole point of showing what's called a *chotrul*, or miraculous display as a teaching, was to counter the spiritual pride in Nearpo who eventually became a lineage holder for the Tibetans of the Bon.

There are many, many stories like this because both in the Christian Desert Fathers and in the Indo-Tibetan tradition, the idea is that the biggest hindrance to practice is spiritual pride. We have many Western teachers with self-professed realizations (and I'm not questioning anything about the nature of their realizations), but I've looked at the websites of a lot of the people who're teaching nonduality and what you see is remarkable descriptions of their own realizations with great pride and great self. Why? Because when you have self-realizations, there's no checks and balance because it's not a lineage tradition.

I have the great fortune at my age of having a senior teacher. You know he's got good credentials—he's the Dalai Lama's senior teacher. One time I was with him, and because he reads minds, I walked in and he said, "Watch the spiritual pride, you're teaching too much." I said, "Busted, thank you." I find that useful, and that's what you get in a lineage tradition as nothing is ever done by an individual, no teaching comes from self, can't, self can't teach this thing.

So, you see, in the Tibetan tradition customarily noble silence is what you practice—you never talk about it. The exception to that is [within a *sangha* with] a pointing out style. You have to talk about it to your teacher, and to the *sangha*—people who share the same experiences—because that's how you get corrections, that's how we can tell you're off track; that's how we can tell if you're getting it right so we can help to reinforce that. So, in a relational style of teaching, which the pointing out style is, you have to talk about it. But that's not how you talk to others about it outside of this *sangha*.

If you talk about practices, what you have to watch for is, what's your own motivation? Are you talking about your own realizations or the nature of what you learn to make the self important? And if you have, your realizations have gone astray. If you're talking about it with a genuine motivation that maybe somebody could learn something, not conceptually, that might help them see the preciousness of these teachings, that's a useful thing to do. But how to do that and the skill of that matters a great deal. I'm fairly negative about people who want to talk about awakening. We don't do that. We certainly don't talk about full buddhahood which we use the term enlightenment for before full buddhahood—that's a formidable achievement. But I don't like it when people try and talk about awakening because it leads to spiritual pride on the one hand in the person who's talking about it, and in the recipient it's going to lead to spiritual greed.

If you do that, the people who are going to come to these teachings are going to be all the wrong people because they're coming for the wrong motivation. They're going to grasp at states out of greed and self-importance. That's not the right motivation to do this. On the other hand, if you can talk about it in the way that people can grasp the preciousness of this, then that's a useful way of talking about it. I think that what's most useful in that capacity is to say very little. The ultimate test of these practices is always conduct, *choepa*, live it.

The first great Western book on mysticism was William James' *Varieties of Religious Experience*. And somebody asked him while he was writing it, how does he tell the difference between genuine spiritual practice and inauthentic practice? James had said that religious institutions are the biggest impediment to spirituality (and I agree with that). And his answer to the question was interesting. He said, "By their fruits ye shall know them"—how they lived their lives. And in Tibetan terms the answer to that question is *wang*, influence—the mark of a teacher who has realizations is the field of positive influence they create on others. The mark of what you do with your own practice as a teacher (or not—as just a practitioner) is no different—is the positive field of influence you develop on those around you.

That's the only true measure of the authenticity of your realizations and it's the only thing you get to take with you. Your wealth, your self-importance, and how people perceive you when you die, you don't get to take any of that with you. The only thing that will follow you is *wang*, influence—good or bad. That goes with you. So, the depth of realization ultimately is the appreciation that conduct matters.

I'm reminded of when we were teaching once in Israel. It's a good story and a sad story. One of our students, who was a well-to-do businessman, after taking the course several times brought his two big investors. They were big finance people who had never meditated a day in their life and they really worked dedicatedly at the course even though it was a completely alien world for them. And one of them had a pretty good awakening. And then Gretchen and I were resting in Tel Aviv three or four days after the course and after four days we met with the local students in Tel Aviv because they wanted to form a local *sangha* for the teachings that we represent. I went to the *sangha* meeting to support them.

At the *sangha* meeting he told me the story of how he went home after the retreat with his awakening, didn't say anything about the retreat to his wife, and just went about his business being with his family, and there's a couple of kids. And about three days later his wife came up to him and said, "I have no idea what you did at that retreat but whatever it is keep doing it." That's *choepa*, that's conduct, and that's the best statement of what you can tell others, live it.

Unfortunately, I found out that shortly after that he died of a heart attack suddenly. He died with an awake mind. That changes the whole game plan … because if you have the realization, at some point along the way the prospect of dying seems ridiculous; it's not possible. Only the body goes, goes on to recycling. You'll just get a new one in the recycling process.

Good question.

May 8, 2013

Themes: Opening the Great Sphere; The Importance of Intention; *Bodhicitta*

Dan

Welcome everyone. You have a question?

Student 1

Well, how does one best communicate with someone who is not physically present, and also how does one best communicate with someone who may be disembodied?

Dan

That's an interesting question. [Long pause as Dan ponders the question] Well, we have to talk about the nature of the organization of reality for that one. [Dan and others chuckle.] We can talk about different levels of mind.

In Indo-Tibetan Buddhism there is "the coarse level of mind." And the coarse level of mind is the ordinary mind as you know it that has content—thought content, emotions, sights, sound, sensations, smell, taste, specific content. And that's the level of mind that we ordinarily dwell within.

Then, if you concentrate and look deeply into the nature of things and you quiet all that thought through concentrating the mind on a concentration object, over and over again, then you shift to what's called "the subtle level of mind" where everything is just very quick bursts of energy and movement prior to its being built up or constructed into content. In Buddhism that level of perception is called "mind moments."

If you [go on to] practice the ordinary emptinesses—emptiness of self, emptiness of out-there-ness, but particularly emptiness of time—you open up a level of mind that's beyond the convention of things seeming to come and go in time. You open up a level of mind called "the very subtle level of mind" or "extraordinary level of mind," and since time and space are related, you open up a level of mind where everything is here all at once. And the field within which all that occurs is a kind of boundless field of empty awareness space, within which everything is interconnected. That's the gateway to the Mahāyāna practice when you open up the level of mind where everything is here interconnected. But you're still operating out of your ordinary consciousness. You still pay attention—your mind goes to this; it goes to that. And those operations of the mind going to this and that becomes your locus, where you operate out of.

If you continue the path to awakening, the next level is awakened awareness. And with awakened awareness you open up a level of mind that, what you come to see is, that always right here is the boundless ocean of, on the one hand it's empty awareness space, contains everything, on the other hand it's a boundless ocean of love. And the difference is where you're operating out of. When you open up awakening you're operating out of being that ocean rather than operating out of the locus of individual consciousness trying to find that.

Nevertheless, at the beginning that awakening isn't terribly stable, and you have to keep setting up what I call nurturing practices to increase opening to that awakening more frequently, for longer duration on the pillow, and then off the pillow, so you have it all the time. Then, if you have it all the time, whatever arises within the field of what we call the "groundless ground" of your being will arise and pass and you don't do anything to it anymore. You take the stance of "leave-it-alone-ness," as we call it. And everything will arise as spontaneously present from groundless ground and disappear into groundless ground and leave no trace, "like writing on water." At that point you stop making any karmic impressions. So, it forces the mind to begin automatically to release all the storehouse of previous karmic impressions. And if you do that all the time, without doing, then the mind will eventually exhaust all negative states, so they no longer cloud over the positivity of the mind, and what will shine forth is the eighty positive qualities of a realized buddha mind. And there are no negative states left. There're all pure states.

Now, during that process, you'll open up what in Dzogchen are called the *tögal* visions. The *tögal* means, is often translated as "bypassing," sort of like the equivalent of what we would call hyperspace. And it works with certain secret energy channels in the body. And if you open up the *tögal* visions, as they're called, then this reality that you perceive right now is just one little bubble; and that awakened awareness will begin to, in Dzogchen what's called, "crack the eggshell," and it will begin to *kyep*, it will begin to pervade or saturate all possible existences across all realms and times. It sort of explodes and expands out in all directions. And then you will hold a very awake perception of simultaneous multiple realities.

And then, if you persist with those visions, because at that point awakened awareness has its own intelligence, it shows itself to itself, and has its own … what you discover is it has a kind of organizing capacity. And it organizes and displays worlds after worlds after worlds. And because none of the worlds are out there—they're all in the field of awake mind—at some point, a couple of things happen. One is that each of those worlds has its own knowledge base, so it's like getting downloads of complete bodies of teachings, but there's no out there to be downloaded from.

And there's another point where as all these worlds emerge and disappear; you get the direct perception that everything across all these worlds is interconnected. There are, if you will, loving threads of energy that connect everything and everyone across all times and space. Sometimes in the Dzogchen literature it's called "Indra's net." You can directly perceive the loving threads of energy that tie us all together—they're soft, gentle, sweet. And the endpoint of that process of visions is what in Tibetan Buddhism is called "*thigle chenpo*," the one great sphere of ultimate reality that contains all worlds and all beings; and your awareness at that point is expanded to encompass, express all of that.

Now, so you see, from that level of reality, the great sphere of ultimate reality, from that perspective, then, there is no dying. If there is somebody that you have known that is no longer in physical form, then every imprint of every being is contained within that ultimate reality, like an imprint, like a computer chip.

Now here's the point, and this is important. Beyond the coarse level of mind, each one of those levels of mind operates out of an intention. We only have one word for intention in the West. And intention is a property of awareness and it has great speed to it. Whatever you intend, the mind does that and just that. So, for example, at the subtle level of reality where you have gotten very deeply concentrated through concentration practice, at some point, whatever you intend to put the mind on, it stays on that and only that with no distraction. There's no extraneous thought and no reactivity. No extraneous activity, no reactivity of mind. And you can see for the first time there's this laser-like property of awareness. Whatever you put the mind on it just goes to that. It doesn't do anything else, like a laser beam. That's the first level of intention. We call that making the mind serviceable. Whatever you intend it does that and nothing else. You train the wild elephant mind so its full intelligence, its full strength is available to you with no more than the simple intention to place it on something.

When you get to the very subtle or extraordinary level of mind, attention is much more quick than that, like lightning speed. When you're looking into the nature of things as being empty constructions, how quickly you look into that has to do with this whole thing about intention. So, we call that "nailing the realization." Just like with the word in English, *cherbu*, nailing in Tibetan, is used with a double meaning: we can pound a nail in with a hammer, but we also use it to refer to sports performance. Somebody does really well in their performance we say "they nailed it." The Tibetans use it much like that—nailing it means you nail it quickly. You catch the realization and look into the true nature of things as empty, not after the fact of something having already arisen, but you catch it at the head, not after it's already become a big, elaborated thing. And you catch it more and more quickly. So, what you learn there is the intention of awareness has a kind of lightning speed to it, not just directionality.

Now, at the level of awakening, then everything spontaneously arises. So, then you nail the realization, not at the point that something begins to arise; it's already expressed in its true nature. You don't even have to put the intention into it; intention is an aspect of how it expresses itself. Sometimes we use the word *lung gi drup*, spontaneous presence, for that. And, at that level of mind then, the directionality and intention of awakening is what we call *ma gag p*a, unobstructed. No matter what level of reality, whatever you look at or intend, the mind goes only to that, right through anything, and there is no solidness. So, you see, if at that level of mind, if you wanted to communicate across time and space, then, the intention will do that. It's possible.

Now, if you open up the ultimate sphere of reality that everything is contained within, this great sphere and the interconnection of everything through these loving threads of filaments of energy, then, there's no need even to use the intention. Because, whoever it is, embodied or disembodied, you already know the connection. You realize the connection already, contained within the loving filaments. There's no need to intend to look for that connection—you're already manifesting it, to all beings. Unnecessary. In terms of the map of the nails, we call that *yecherbu*, way nailing it. [Dan chuckles] That's literally what it means in Tibetan: way nailing it.

So, you see, how it looks changes at every level of mind. And, only at the more solid levels of mind, like coarse level of mind, where you have content, does it seem like there is this disconnection. But, at the higher levels of realization, the connection has always been there. And, if you are at the ultimate level of realization, there's no need to make any contact with what everything is here and everyone is here all at once. So, you see, there's no problem. But, at those intermediate levels, the key to making the contact that you want comes through intention. As you refine the mind, you get more familiar with how to exercise intention.

Now, intention is very much tied up with motivation. So, you have to ask yourself the question, if there's somebody that you're not with, who lives in this plane of reality, and you want to contact them, which was your original question ... or, somebody who's disembodied ... what's the motivation for contacting them? Look at your motivation, honestly. Is it to be of benefit to them? Is it to reach out, in a loving way? Does it come from some need, of self? Look at the motivation and see what that is. Only you can answer that, for yourself. But, if the motivation is a pure motivation, out of compassion, and loving, then the mind has *shinshong*, it has more flexibility; so, that connection is easier to make through intention. Good question. The answers change, depending on the level of mind you're looking from. Good. Thank you.

Anything else? That's a hard one to follow?

Student 2

You were saying that if your intention is pure, then …

Dan

If the intention is pure, then the mind has greater pliancy. So, it just goes to whatever you intend. It finds its way. If the intention operates in an impure way, if it comes from something selfish, then those structures of the mind seem solid. But intention doesn't go very far. Light doesn't pass through solid things. But, the light of intention, when the mind is flexible, it passes through everything. Motivation matters.

Why do you want to make the contact? Important. [Long pause]

Remember, I just got back from Australia. When you look at the rock art, say in Arnhem Land, it's really interesting because there's a lot of rock art about magic—not necessarily good magic. The themes are pretty transparent. Motivation's not good. Sometimes, very good. And how the mind transmits in each case is very different.

Student 3

Going along with that theme, of intention, how about if we talk a little bit about [*bodhicitta*]?

Dan

Oh, that's a good question. Well, Tibetans like to classify everything. And, one of the conventional ways of talking about *bodhicitta* is the difference between what's called causal *bodhicitta* and resultant *bodhicitta*. But I have to explain the word first. And, *bhodi* means realizing [or awakening]. And, *citta* is the intention of mind. The root "*buddh*" is "realize."

I like the way His Holiness translates it. He calls it setting the intention towards awakening, as if it's an ongoing process. And, you've got to set the intention. But, the translation in Tibetan is a little bit different. And, I think, useful, because, in the Tibetan is *changchubsempa*. *Sempa* is like *citta*, it means *du*, the mind, the intending mind. But *changchub* is a compound term. And, *sangwa* means to purify.

So, you're setting the intention towards realization. It is that. But in Tibetan Buddhism, it specifies more clearly what the nature of the realization is. You're purifying all negative states and you're causing the flourishing of all positive states. That's more important than just realization. It captures more clearly the fundamental transformation of the mind that's going to take place: the eradication of all negative states; the flourishing of all positive states. But it begins with *sem*, in Tibetan, or *citta*, [in Sanskrit] which means to intend—setting the intention towards awakening.

So, what does it mean? It means that when you start your practice, you set the intention towards where it's going to take you. Because, if you set the intention towards awakening before you sit, it becomes a kind of central organizing principle for your sitting. So, that you're always doing the sitting against the backdrop of that—in the background of your awareness is the reminder of what you're doing this for, or where it's going to take you. It's about awakening, and, don't settle for anything less.

Now, unfortunately, most people don't sit that way. They just sit as if sitting becomes something of an end in itself. I mean, look how popular Mindfulness is these days. But Mindfulness isn't an end in itself. But how many people talk about practicing Mindfulness with not at all being mindful of the mindfulness as just a vehicle, for awakening? Most people who sit, sit as if the meditation is an end in itself. It's just a vehicle for awakening. So, you want to start by being clear within yourself where it's going to take you.

I remember, many years ago, with my Root Lama, Geshe Wangyal—and I liked being with him because I lived with him summers, in college and graduate school. And, here's a guy who, in the old Tibet, one of the main teachers was Ling Rinpoche, and Ling was the senior tutor for the Dalai Lama. And, Ling had three students. He had the Dalai Lama, he had Geshe Wangyal, my Root Lama, and Denma Locho Rinpoche, who is now the head of the Gelugpa. My teacher was much older, so he died in the late '70s. Denma Locho and I then taught together for twenty years.

What I liked about him [Geshe Wangyal], was here's a guy who was one of the main players in this tradition, who came to the US in 1955, before Tibet was overtaken, and he lived in the Delaware Water Gap area [of New Jersey] in the mountains until he died. He had maybe a dozen, dozen and a half close students, and, no one ever heard of him because he never played the guru game (which I found enormously refreshing).

He gave one public talk. It was at the first International Conference on Yoga and Meditation. I think it was in Chicago, a big hotel, somewhere in the mid-'70s. It was a bit of a circus of all kinds of yoga demonstrations and meditation workshops, and, he got invited as one of the token Tibetans. And, he actually accepted the invitation. I remember his talk—everybody did meditation demonstrations and talked for about an hour—he talked for three minutes. [Laughter]

He got up there, and he said, "There's lots of people here who are teaching you how to meditate. I'm not going to repeat anything. There's lots of people here who want to show you how to meditate." He said, "Just ask yourself the question, when you sit down to meditate, 'What's my motivation? Why am I doing this?' Clarify yourself, honestly, what the motivation is. Thank you." And he walked off the stage and that was the end of the talk. [Laughter] And, it made a point. Because, no one was talking about why they were doing this thing and where it takes you. And, what he was really doing in his behavior is showing *bodhicitta*, pointing it out: "set your intention towards awakening."

Now, what happens at the beginning of your practice is either one of two things. You forget to do that, so your practice is aimless. It's not going to take you anywhere other than maybe being quiet. But, so what? [Laughter] Or, why do you want to be quiet? The world's busy. [Laughter]

Student 5

There's some people that could benefit. [Lots of laughter]

Dan

Your kids, for example? [More laughter]

So, the second thing is that when you try and set the intention towards awakening as a central organizing principle, the first thing you bump across is your negative belief. And, you know, there are various versions of them. One that we see all the time trying to teach this to Westerners is, "I don't deserve it." Or, "I can't do this." That's our stuff, it's all that negative self-talk. The Tibetan version of that—because they are into recycling down lifetimes—is it's going to take you a million lifetimes to do this. So, they're slow! [Dan laughs with others.] Because it's, whether you think you don't deserve it, or whether you think it's going to take you millions of lifetimes, they're just ideas. And ideas don't define ultimate reality. Your awakening is always here—all the time. So, the ideas are stupid. [Laughter] Don't let them get in the way.

So, if you set the intention towards awakening, and you set aside your negative beliefs, it means taking yourself that seriously. It means every moment of this practice you do carefully, with great care. In the *Abhidharma*, that's one of the fifty-one qualities of mind, it's one of the positive qualities of mind. It's called *bakyapah*, great care. We practice with great care every moment because it matters.

Then, you don't sit there and space out or chase after this interesting thought. You work at concentrating your mind, or you look into things more deeply when you're practicing emptiness meditation. You don't waste it. And it's always, always because it's taking you closer to your home, which is your true nature. Until you know that, and even if you know that, then you have to develop it, and nurture it, so you have it all the time.

That's the first aspect of *bodhicitta*. But as I said earlier, since intention and motivation are connected, the other part of *bodhicitta* is why are we doing this? Why do we want to be awake? And if you understand this in terms of the levels of mind, each level of mind opens up an awareness which is more encompassing of the previous, where everything is interconnected. Particularly if you open up the very subtle level of mind, you're operating out of an ocean of boundless, changeless awareness, and everything comes up and everyone is interconnected within that field. And then you understand what the Tibetan's talk about with *wang*. *Wang* literally means influence. Every thought, every intention of your mind, every behavior that you engage in has influence. It's like a field effect—and the greater your realizations, the stronger the field effect.

So, it's not like if you awaken then everybody in the planet wakes up at the same time. But it is the case if you open up those levels of mind where everything is interconnected, if you awaken, that moment of awakening and its development has strong influence and great strength. It's like planting seeds in the sea of influence. It will eventually ripen into the eradication of all negative states and the flourishing of all positive states in an interconnected sea of beings. So, you move everyone along with you. That's why it's called The Lofty Vehicle of the Mahāyāna—it has influence.

The more your realization, the stronger the influence. If you're operating out of non-ordinary reality as a full buddha, then you can influence [countless other beings]. Thus, if you call forth such non-ordinary beings—we've talked about this before—the Tibetan word for their gift of *wang*, or influence, is *chingilap*, which literally means waves, like on an ocean, waves of giving. If you do guru yoga, you call forth a non-ordinary being, and they come from awakened *dharmakāya* space. It's like a Buddhist *Field of Dreams*[15]—"if you build it they will come," you know? They come forth out of curiosity for being called forth. Then you have to *solwadeb*, you have to throw out a request. You have

15 *Field of Dreams* is a popular 1989 American drama film.

to put the intention into requesting the gift of influence. If you don't intend, you don't get anything.

And then the third thing is you have to put it into practice. But what you get as a gift of influence is two things. One is that non-ordinary beings can directly intervene into your unfolding mindstream and clear away the clouds. Your practice goes better, easier. And second, they can intervene and activate your buddha nature and all the positive ingredients of mind that go with that, and put it back online. So, that's why we start all retreats with the gift of influence. We call forth our non-ordinary friends to sort of give you a jumpstart, so you get out of your own way and maybe you can actually get to awakening more easily.

So, influence is something that you develop through your practice, but it's also something that you can request from non-ordinary beings. It's an exchange. But the further you develop your own practice, the stronger the influence. When you drop your body, that's the only thing you get to take with you. The field of influence goes with you, with your subtle body, what we call "the indestructible essence" that survives human death. You can't take your wealth, can't take material things, can't take your family and friends. The only thing that goes with you is the influence. And that has a big effect.

So, how you live your life, and what you do with it, and the kind of influence you have matters. Ask yourself the question, "What sort of influence do I have on the field of those around me? Is it positive? Am I contributing to the greater social good?" And you start thinking of, and start viewing the world more in terms of developing positive influence, not selfishness. Then maybe we can all find a way out of this mess together, hmm?

I remember years ago when I was just starting my professional career, and I applied for a job to teach a basic clinical type of psychopathology course. I thought it would be useful to do. And I taught it at Simmons, the Social Work school, for twenty-five years. And I remember considering whether I was going to do the job, because there's a lot of work to prepare a new course, and it's a live interview course, which means I had to collect patients to interview all the time. So, it was really a lot of work, and finding just the right patients to illustrate the stuff. And so it was a huge amount of work to get a course like that to work.

And I remember sitting down with the section chair at the time, who was Sophie Freud, Sigmund's granddaughter, and she said to me, "Look, we can't pay you very much. The pay really sucks. And it's embarrassing, but you've got to think of it this way if you want the job." She says, "This is the core course for how they think clinically, and you'll have an opportunity to influence how most of the young social workers in this city will come to view their clinical work. It will form everything about how they view it." Because, since it's their core course and the main exposure to clinical thinking, it had great influence.

And when she put it like that to me, I had no doubt that I would do the course despite the huge amount of work it would take. Because that influence would affect how they saw things, which in kind would affect all of the patients that they saw, for twenty-five years of social workers. And she taught me something about what it means to think about your life in terms of influence. It was a good thing to do. I didn't make much money to contribute to retirement on it, but so what? Does it really matter? Influence matters. And the more you open your mind up to each of these more organized levels of reality, the greater the sphere of influence. And that's why you're here.

But it's not my influence. It's what you develop that matters—each of you, through your own practice. [Dan pauses.] Elephants move mountains. So, practice like an elephant.

May 22, 2013

Themes: Shifting Your Basis of Operation; the View Beyond Concepts; Compassionate Conduct

Dan

Welcome everyone. You have a question?

Student 1

All too often I'm still going back and forth, struggling between resting in the *dharma* and just wanting *samsāra* to work out better. [Laughter] I feel like an alcoholic who still wants to drink, and then every once in a while I get very clear about it: there is only one answer.

Dan

Yeah. That's right. Neural bliss does it all, but how do you "rest in the *dharma*?" Please educate us. I didn't know it was a resting place. Is it like a bed and breakfast? [Laughter]

Student 1

It feels like that, compared to my *samsāric* involvements.

Dan

You mean taking the view, is that what you mean by that? Is that a fair way of restating it?

Student 1

Yeah.

Dan

Okay. If you were to look at Padmasambhava's Kuntuzangpo Prayer (as presented in *Discovering Infinite Freedom*)[16], there are two parts to that book. The first part, which is unusual, has all the positive descriptors of operating out of awakened awareness. What is the awakened mind like? There are few texts that describe that. And the second part of it describes what we might refer to as a two-pathway model. One path is *rigpa*, awakened awareness. That is being able to recognize that awakening is always right here. In any moment that you recognize awakening, so that you're operating out of that, that's *rigpa*.

In other words, there's a boundless ocean of, on the one hand, empty awareness space, on the other hand, love. It's always right here shining forth with brilliant lucidity. Like the sun that always shines. And either you recognize that in any moment or you cloud it over. And if, in the instant that you recognize that and become that so you're not operating out of the constraints of your narrow individual consciousness, you shift your basis of operation, as we say, so that you're operating out of that awakening, so that you are that unbounded wholeness in that moment, however long that lasts; you're operating out of being awake.

And in the moment that you forget that and it clouds over again, then that's called *marigpa*, often translated as "the moment of ignorance," when it really means that you've lost the awareness of your true nature in that moment. And I think that's the distinction that you're making, what you are calling "rest in the *dharma*." You mean, I think, taking the view. And if you hold that view

---

16 *Discovering Infinite Freedom: The Prayer of Küntuzangpo* by Khenchen Palden Sherab Rinpoche and Khenpo Tsewang Dongyal Rinpoche, Dharma Samudra, 2010.

continuously, it will shift your basis so you're operating out of being that unbounded wholeness with a brilliant lucid awakeness. And in the moments that it clouds over, then you're operating out of the narrow constraints of individual consciousness or the even narrower constraints of the construction of personal identity. You're operating out of you-ness.

So, as Padmasambhava says, every instant the pathway diverges between *samsāra* and *nirvana*. Either you're operating out of being that wholeness without any grab or any reactivity to anything in the infinite empty awareness spaciousness of that spacious freedom, or, you create the entirety of cyclic existence, *samsāra*, in that instant that you forget. And the habits of the mind are so strong that we continue to cloud it over.

The Dzogchen Ponlop in Seattle, a Tibetan lama who has very much understood Western culture and Western humor, one of the things that he likes to say is that "most people, when they wake up, put the snooze alarm on many times." So, every time that you get a taste of awakening you put the snooze alarm back and roll over and go back to sleep—*marigpa*—it clouds over again. So, what you're talking about ultimately is the conflict between the very strong pull of the habitual tendencies to go back to our normal way of viewing things, and we're caught up in the realm of *samsāra*.

And, the opposite of that is that the more you develop the practice, the more what that view opens up is wondrous and breathtaking. So, even when it clouds over you long for that. And the more you develop the practice the stronger the longing. Longing is a state of duality. Longing only happens insofar as you've clouded it over, because if you have that unbounded wholeness as your way of being, there's no point looking for something else. There's a final state. You just are that. So, there's no longing. Longing only happens from the perspective of the constraints of our individual consciousness.

I like one of the newer songs by Leonard Cohen. There's a passage in the song "Come Healing" that goes "longing is love confined." If you're operating out of being that ocean of love, there's no confinement, there's no partializing wholeness. You just are that. But as soon as we cloud it over, we're partializing. And then we think there's a state out there that we need to get to that we're longing for. So, you see, there's a rent here, a bifurcation. As Padmasambhava says, "At any given moment, either it's *rigpa* or *marigpa*."

And those two worlds seem separated, the awakened mind and the ordinary mind. And either you're operating out of ordinary mind, or you're operating out of awakened mind. Now, there's a little trick to that. At the stage of practice that you're at, what you try and do is set up the view and establish just the right conditions that will open up awakening. You can't make it happen, you can't grasp after it, because that's making it into a thing. But you can establish the right conditions, which is a way of saying, "You're establishing the exact view."

So, what do you know about that? The foundation is always automatic emptiness—the natural state of the mind. Everything arises spontaneously unfolding, every moment is automatically empty. So, then you don't have to do anything. As soon as it comes up it's empty. So, no doing gets in the way, because any doing partializes, and in that instant that you're doing, that masks over the unbounded wholeness that's always here.

Conceptualizing masks over that unbounded wholeness. As Mipham says, "the function of conceptualizing is to delineate." So as soon as you say, "This is it," it's not that. So, any tendency to conceptualize partializes the unbounded wholeness. But if you have automatic emptiness, as soon as you attempt to do something, it's automatically expressed as empty and it dissipates. As soon as you have a tendency to conceptualize about state our outcome, it comes up, you see it for what it is, immediately it arises, and it doesn't get in the way anymore. And the mind unfolds by itself to itself. We call that *nelu*, the natural state. With that as your foundation, then for the first time you're not going to conceptualize about awakening, it can actually happen. Then you set up your view. You see everything as a single unified field of awareness, and everything that arises is that field. Whatever knows the events that occur in the field is that field. It's all the same lively awareness without any duality. Then you take your view, like an infinite vast expanse of space, and you orient the awareness towards the totality of awareness, and you're holding every moment uninterruptedly, until the awareness opens itself to itself and awakens to itself. You know the routine. And if you hold it just right, awakening happens to itself because it has its own intelligence. "You" doesn't awaken.

Well, if you keep setting up the view, just right, what will happen is you'll open up that awakening more frequently on the pillow and for longer durations, so that you're operating out of awakened awareness on the pillow more than you're operating out of non-awakened awareness.

In the Akhrid Bonpo system, there's a wonderful description of ordinary mind cognitive activity that's required to maintain awakening. But first it's a lot of cognitive work of the ordinary mind. Because you have to do all these steps to set up the view just right, and if you get it just right it will shift to awakening. But if you've done that many times and you know the routine, after a while all that's required is what the text calls "a subtle cognitive activity of the ordinary mind," and all that's required is the intention to maintain un-distractedness of your view. Because the view is the meditation … the view is the meditation, you know what I'm talking about?

And then if you keep doing that, shifting your basis out of ordinary mind to awakened mind will happen more frequently and for longer duration, and it doesn't take any more than the simple intention to look, and it opens up. And if you keep doing that, the awakening will last for longer durations and more frequently on the pillow, and then off the pillow.

And then finally there's a third stage where it's said that awakening takes over its own operations to maintain itself to itself. At that point it becomes relatively automatic. Even with the habitual tendencies to cloud over an awakened mind, the habitual tendencies become like a very thin veil. So, if you put the intention to look as what your basis is at any given moment, it just opens up. And at that point you develop what's called *dengwa*, confidence or reassurance. It's never very far away. And in fact, you'll get the confidence that it's impossible it could ever really go away. Then you have it all the time, or most of the time, and even if it clouds over, it's like a very thin veil that, like a thin mist that suddenly evaporates when you look at it, with no more than the intention to look. The mist evaporates and you are that unbounded wholeness and its brilliant lucidity and awakeness. So, you see, it's always right here. And then, it will seem perfectly ridiculous to you that you could ever possibly lose it. Then it's not so much work because it maintains itself to itself. It doesn't really ever go away, even in the most difficult of life circumstances.

So, it keeps going on and on and gets brighter and brighter. Tashi Namgyal, the main commentator on Mahāmudrā says, "Then what you've done is you've taken the little flames of awakening and made them into a raging forest fire." So, the radiance of awakened mind just flames up all the time. Now, when you get to that range where it's much more frequent, there's a little trick. And all you need to do at that point is be reminded that *marigpa*, that moment of non-awareness, is *rigpa*. If you try and do it too early it won't work at all—it'll be too conceptual. But at that point in time, what you can begin to see is the very instant that it seems to veer off, because you know you're never going to lose it because you're confident, you see; the very instant it veers off, it's not really veering off, because the tendency to veer off into creating *samsāric* existence is just the intention of an awakened mind displaying itself to itself for the benefit of compassion and wisdom.

The very intention of the veering off is to invite you to get it right. It's the invitation for you to not get hooked. Don't take the bait. Just see it as all the show of an awakened mind. And then, the very tendency to veer off and to create *samsāric* existence, that moment you see all of that as an invitation to you to deepen your realization and wisdom.

Now if you take that view at the right point in time, how can it possibly ever veer off? That's what the word Mahāmudrā means: the Great Gesture, the Great Invitation. Every moment is another invitation for you to get it right and to develop your wisdom. And, secondly, every moment of this miraculous display is the intention of compassion. The whole seeming suffering mess looks that way to train your mind to develop its softness and its compassion—to be touched by that. Once you train that compassion, game over. There's no suffering. You won't see it that way anymore.

Since wisdom and compassion are two sides of the same thing, you see, ultimately, it's the same intention built into the way the system works. So, the way you describe it, there's these two paths like Padmasambhava described. But, as you train, the Tibetan word is *chungwa,* to nurture it. Once you develop even the slightest taste of awakening, you've got to protect it, you've got to nurture it, you've got to take great care with it to develop it, and it comes more frequently and stronger. Then at a certain point when you develop *dengwa*, confidence, you're never going to lose it. And if you look at the times you seem to lose it, those times will just be the expression that deepens the realization that it's not possible to lose it. Then you're on your way, you see. You're on what we call "path." Then you're a "path walker" because you can't ever be off the path.

So, when you're setting up the view and you're trying, yeah, you're "resting in the view," but better to be an active path walker. Because the path has its own intelligence, and at that point the rest of the path shows itself to itself by itself. Enjoy the show. A good question. But it's a more advanced question. It's not a basic question about ordinary practice. But for the level of what you're talking about it's a great question.

Student 2

Is there a … I'm very new to meditation. This idea of being still and feeling this vast emptiness. Can you be doing things and be there at the same time?

Dan

Well, you have to do a lot to set that up. Even being still is an activity. You're not just sort of emptying out your mind. That's not what we mean about emptiness at all. It's a rather sophisticated set of procedures you're developing. And all those procedures are a hell of a lot of work. Once you set it all up right, then you don't do anything. But to get to that point where you can set up the conditions just right, that takes a lot of work. So, if you just sit down and you say, "Okay I'm going to empty my mind," what that's going to train you is to be dull. You'll be very still and very dull. And that will get you nowhere because dullness of mind doesn't lead to awakening. It just leads to quiet dullness. It's useless. So, there's a lot to this, you see.

You can hold the view all the time. You do it in the midst of all the relative activity of daily life. This isn't designed for sitting on a pillow. You sit on the pillow enough to get the view right so that you can awaken and then you take it off the pillow.

When I was working with His Holiness Menri Trizin to develop awakening, I spent a month with him in retreat. But I suppose saying "in retreat" was a bit of an illusion because other than a few times a day that we did short inner fire practices to brighten the radiance of awakened awareness, each of those times being about fifteen minutes four times a day, the entire month was off the pillow.

What we did was called *drewa*, mixing practices. The task is to open up awakening on the pillow, then immediately get off the pillow and mix it [awakening] into everyday activities. So, most of my time was sitting outside of his place, and because his schedule is as busy as the Dalai Lama's (he's the Dalai Lama's meditation teacher), there's a stream of people all day long. My task was to converse with them and mix my awakened mind into ordinary conversation.

Or working on the computer and translating and mixing awakening into working on the computer; mixing it with texting, until every activity of the day is mixed into. So, there's not a distinction between meditating and not meditating. The mind is here all the time, and either you work with it or you don't. Either it's awake or it's not. So, none of this is designed for being on the pillow. It's not about states. So, if you do this practice, you immerse yourself in all of everyday life.

I remember years ago when, of course it's a different kind of meditation, but when Jon Kabat-Zinn put out his first book on mindfulness, he called it *Full*

Catastrophe Living. And he took the term from a line from *Zorba the Greek*.[17] Full awakening is when you embrace the full catastrophe of everyday life and all that it is.

Some of you know the famous *Song of the Delights* by Milarepa, and one of the final closing lines is, "And when the whole thing's just not working, and everything's a hodge podge, sheer delight." That's the best time for your practice. And Rahob Rinpoche who we teach with says, "How do you know when people describe their experience whether their descriptions of awakening are authentic or they're just conceptual? If they're just conceptual they'll describe mostly about states. They're likely to be more authentic if they're accompanied by strong compassion, strong gratitude. But ultimately, one of the best tests is," Rinpoche says, "if you put yourself in the most difficult of life circumstances, and the awakening deepens, it's likely to be authentic. If it falls apart it was likely conceptual in the first place." In other words, you have the need to see yourself as awakened. But ultimately the best test is conduct. The only real test is how you live your life.

When I first started over forty years ago, and I had the occasion to live with a lama, summers between college and graduate school, over a nine-year span, that was the biggest lesson I think I ever got in those years, and it changed my life. He was one of the main players in the Tibetan tradition, and came over to this country before Tibet was taken over. We'll never know the full story of why. And he never played the guru game, which I found enormously refreshing. He lived his life, he had maybe a dozen or a dozen and a half students in thirty years. And the whole lesson was how he lived every moment. Because it's about conduct.

We have lots of non-lineage based Western style gurus who have their own discoveries of realization and, not to doubt the authenticity of some people's realizations, the trouble is if it doesn't come from lineage tradition, where it's passed down from generation heart-to-heart, then it leads to spiritual pride. There's no corrections. So, we get people who will talk a great deal about their states and realizations but it's not matched by conduct. So, conduct matters, I say.

So, what does that mean? It means that whatever I tell you about these realizations or states doesn't mean squat unless I can show you how to do it.

---

17 A popular 1964 film starring Anthony Quinn as Zorba.

That's conduct. Because if I tell you about how these states are, that just leads to self-importance. So what? If you learn anything in spiritual practice, it's that self-importance isn't terribly important. But if I can show you yourself how to do it, that matters. That's conduct. Anything else?

Student 3

To pick up on conduct, Dan, the question that occurred to me when you're talking about conduct: is conduct a path to awakening in reverse? Or, is it only that it manifests itself afterwards?

Dan

Both. It's a good question. The question is, if you didn't hear it, is conduct a path to awakening or is it the outcome? And both are true. See, from an Indo-Tibetan perspective, every moment of your experience ... You see if we ... How to describe this? ... I'm going to try something this way, okay?

If we look at theories of mind in Indo-Tibetan Buddhism there's several models for how the mind works or how information processing works. I'm going to combine three different models in Buddhism to make it simple here. But the very first thing that happens is, prior to recognizing a stimulus is what in Indo-Tibetan Buddhism is called "particularizing," the tendency of the mind towards something to make it something particular. It's like an action potential. The mind going in a particular direction. Okay? The outcome of that is you recognize something particular, but as soon as the mind goes in any direction, you're already partializing it, it breaks up this unbounded wholeness. So, the quickest part of our information processing system already is biased to obscuring the wholeness—every second, every millisecond. The next thing that happens in our information processing system is "contact." We recognize a stimulus, *rekpa* in Tibetan. We would call that in Western psychology "stimulus perception."

But note that the Buddhists recognize a tendency prior to stimulus perception. The closest thing we can come to in the West is an action potential. The best thing I could find in the West wasn't in psychology, but in the poetry of John Keats, who describes it as "reaching irritability." The mind reaches out, it's irritable. Not in the angry sense, irritable in the biological sense—it's stimulus irritating. It's irritable towards developing new experience. And that "reaching irritability" is what causes us to actually have [as a second step] stimulus perception—to pick out something particular.

The third step, if you'll look at Dzogchen texts they'll talk about *malangdor*: *langwa*, to engage something to make more of it, and *dorwa*, to engage something to make less of it [with the *ma* in front meaning neither[18]]. They're both forms of what we might call mental engagement. That third step, according to Dzogchen, is what causes us to form karmic memory traces. Whenever something comes into your mind, as soon as you do anything to engage it, either to make more of it or to make less of it, at that point you fix it as a memory trace. It's going to be part of your storehouse mind, and then it's likely to make further karmic impressions.

The fourth step in your information processing system is what, in Western terms, we would call hedonic tone, *chorwa* in Tibetan. *Chorwa* is sort of like feeling tone. In psychoanalysis we talk about pleasant and unpleasant. In Buddhism they talk about pleasant, unpleasant, and neutral. At that point the first thing we do once we make contact with a stimulus is at very high speeds in terms of milliseconds, we've already classified whether we like it, dislike it, or whether we're neutral about it.

That's true for stimulus perception and it's true for people perception. Social psychologists tell us as soon as we meet somebody, we've already decided whether we like them or dislike them—even with no information about them. It's all based on a "snap judgment" and after that we're not likely to change it. However wrong we may be, we don't change it. So that's the next step.

Then the next step after that is whatever process goes into creating perceptual categories. So, if I take in the entire visual field at the moment and my mind goes towards something, that's particularizing. And then I'm aware of making contact, I know there's a something there, that's contact. And then I decide if it's pleasant, unpleasant, or neutral, so, I decide it's pleasant. And then I develop perceptual categories, [all] high speed processes. I decide that's a bowl. And that's *dushe*, knowing it as a particular thing. And then I can pair that to my memory database and it has more meaning. And that's *duje*, acting upon it, analyzing it and pairing it to my database. And the overall sense of it is *nambashepa*, often translated as part of the aggregates as consciousness, but it really means knowing it as a very particular thing, and as a type of thing.

---

18 Altogether often translated as "neither accepting nor rejecting."

Now all those levels and information processing happen at a very high speed. But if you understand that information processing system, what it tells us is at the point that we engage anything, in any way, we're forming karmic impressions. And there are two kinds of karmic impressions: those that lead to negative mind states, and those that lead to positive mind states.

Then, if we look at the ordinary mind and the years of bad habits, or in the Tibetan sense, lifetimes of bad habits, the karmic impressions that we form are said to *minwa*, they ripen over time. And they ripen first in terms of spontaneously emerging mind states, then in terms of behavior, and then thirdly (which is interesting) they ripen in terms of how events seem to unfold in our life. Those are the three stages in the ripening of karmic impressions.

Now if you let everything be, the dysfunction of the ordinary mind is such that if you observed your mind and the content of your mind, what mostly unfolds would be many more negative states than positive states. And more negative behaviors than positive behaviors. And a lot of events in our life make us unhappy. We have misfortune.

But if you embark on spiritual practice intentionally, intentional practice, intentional actions have greater karmic force, greater strength. If you engage in any kind of good spiritual practice, if you get it right and it's not misguided, then what you're doing is forming a depository of positive karmic impressions as a result of that practice. The more you do it, the more positive the practice is, the greater the strength. So, you're making a bigger and bigger depository of positive karmic traces. In Buddhism that's called "merit." I like to think of it as sort of Buddhist frequent flyer points because you can cash them in. But typically, the etiquette is you symbolically offer up all the merit to all other beings for their benefit. You don't keep it for yourself. But of course, the more you offer it up the more merit you get. So, it keeps compounding itself. You can't get rid of this thing even if you want to.

If you develop merit then it should emerge over time that the cumulative effect of that in your practice is that you will notice a shift in the ratio of negative to positive states. In your daily life you will have more positive states than negative states. If the merit is very strong from your actions, then you will develop positive behaviors towards other people. You will serve the benefit of other beings more than you are being selfish, despite yourself, and [even with] whatever selfish tendencies [remain], you'll serve the benefits of beings more than you're being selfish. And then very interesting things happen. If the merit, the force of that merit gets very strong, it starts to affect the events that unfold in your life. And you start to have good fortune. Like the good fortune of us all being here together.

Like me trying to teach this stuff and struggling with it for many years and then my old friend Rahob Tulku Rinpoche calling out of the blue. And then he sort of offered to teach at the level that we had our students. That's good fortune. The fact that at that time he was not known as a teacher and was living basically in the West in relative poverty. Now he has many, many students all the time and his teaching is flourishing. So, we both have good fortune. Or then meeting Menri, His Holiness, and then his agreeing that he would teach the more advanced stuff, and that we could make it available to the students. That's good fortune.

So you see, getting back to your original question, along the path, at the beginning, and throughout the path, conduct matters. If you do conduct that's beneficial for other people, compassionate acts, "*bodhisattva* activity," usually what you see in the Mahāyāna is these *bodhisattva* actions, acting for the benefit if others; or actions like the Six Perfections. And if you intentionally do that kind of stuff and that becomes your MO, how you operate in the world, you're accumulating a huge depository of merit—positive karmic impressions. And that will help bring about the ripening of your own realization.

That's why traditionally, although I don't agree with the structure, that's why Tibetans ask you to do one hundred thousand preliminaries before they will teach you anything worthwhile. And the reason for that is they've calculated, however correctly or not, that that's how many repetitions you have to do of positive behaviors before the merit that comes from that is big enough that you can actually reroute this dysfunctional mind in a positive direction so that the realizations will actually make sense. Of course, many people could do it quicker than that, but that's the traditional way of viewing it.

So, conduct matters throughout the practice and it sets the foundation for what you do in the future with your realizations. If your conduct is flawed, the likelihood is that your meditation experiences will be flawed. And the likelihood is that your realizations will be flawed.

On the other hand, once you develop the realizations and nurture them, the stronger the realizations, the more that leads to conduct, spontaneously produced conduct that's always for the benefit of other beings because it comes from compassion. The difference is that at a certain level of stabilization of realization, the conduct that comes forth is always spontaneously emerging from awakened *dharmakāya* space, awakened awareness space. And it always emerges spontaneously as the best fit for the situation at hand. So, it's not like Dan thinking to act a certain way. That's what you do earlier in the practice. Now the conduct comes forth always as the best match of the situation. And since it doesn't come from self, it's basically, like we say of the energy from the sun, "it's inexhaustible." It's always for the benefit of others. So, that would be the ultimate expression of what you would call virtue.

So, the answer is both. Conduct is necessary to develop the realizations and the realizations lead to a whole different level of conduct. And the ultimate outcome of that in Tibetan Buddhism is *thrinle*, enlightened activity. A buddha works inexhaustibly over many levels of reality because the mind opens up the simultaneous levels of reality, all inexhaustibly, for the sake of helping other beings along the way. And there are twenty-one types of inexhaustible conduct that are unique to a fully enlightened buddha. But I won't go into the details of that at this point. But good question.

June 19, 2013

Themes: Ethics at Work; Energy Practices; Release Karmic Impressions

Dan

Welcome everyone. You have a question?

Student 1

Something has been going on at work, which has affected me, and the Lamps retreat helped with that. But I'd also like to talk about it a little bit and get further clarification. We have a new nurse who has been training with the nurse with whom I share the office. And he is new to us, he isn't a new nurse. But what he does is he makes a lot of jokes about the patients. And I've noticed that it really bothers me, it really offends me. And it's sort of been in the back of my mind, it's sort of reignited whenever he is on, in training, because he spends a lot of time back there, which is where I'm on the computer doing my notes.

And so some of my thoughts about it that have arisen are, one of them is that I've looked into the ways that I've been disrespectful to other people. And one of the things that arose for me this weekend, or this past week, was something that Rinpoche said that for me brought up the understanding that everyone needs recognition. They need to be seen; they need to be heard. And sometimes they don't do it in the best way; sometimes it has terrible consequences; sometimes it has wonderful consequences. But I did, in my recognition of that, I felt a softening towards him. Although, for me, the issue is still there around right conduct. So that's what I'm throwing out.

Dan

You really have two questions here. One is what you might do with respect to his disrespect. And then secondly, what your practice is within yourself about the reactivity that gets stirred up by his disrespect. It's more complicated because if you saw that kind of disrespect in the general public, that would be one thing. But when you see that kind of disrespect in the health profession, then you have a duty, in Western terms. And I agree with you, there's no place in the health profession for that kind of disrespect.

Disrespect used to be very rampant in medicine. And it was best seen, or worst seen, in surgeons. There's the famous Beached Whale case. And surgeons and anesthesiologists assumed that when people were given a general anesthesia, it sort of snowed them so they didn't hear anything. And there was one famous lawsuit where a woman weighed over three hundred pounds, and she was having surgery. And after they gave her a general anesthesia and assumed that she'd be knocked out they, throughout the entire course of the surgery, made derisive comments about her weight, calling her a "beached whale," amongst other things.

After she woke up from the general anesthesia, she remembered everything verbatim, and filed a lawsuit, and won that lawsuit for a number of millions of dollars. And that sent a sobering message to anesthesiologists that they shouldn't assume that people are out of it. And it changed medicine.

One of the ways that it changed medicine over time is the whole way medicine was taught, being a lineage tradition of sorts. And the original lineage tradition was teaching by shaming, where the surgeon model was the dominant model. You put down the students constantly about what they didn't know. And partly pressed by lawsuits like the famous Beached Whale case, and others, and partly pressed by the sheer volume of what medical students needed to know, what emerged was a completely different model of teaching medicine, a collaboration model; and that students were no longer competitive, because competitive was dysfunctional.

And what instead needed to happen is that each student was part of a team, and they had the responsibility to research certain areas and then share that knowledge openly with the rest of the team so that everybody was dependent on everybody else in the team to learn the massive amounts of knowledge they had to learn. And the team only was effective to the degree to which everybody did their job.

That … at a peer level there was a lot of pressure to make sure that everybody was doing the work and not being lazy. And what evolved in the last fifteen, twenty years in this country is a replacement of the surgeon shame model of teaching to a kind of collaborative model that's much more effective. And that is the dominant model now. But it doesn't mean that certain individuals don't still do the old thing, mostly because of personality issues. But that's more the exception than the rule in most areas of medicine now.

So, from a professional point of view, if you take any code of ethics, be it psychology or psychiatry or medicine, or social work or nursing, all those long lists of ethical principles come down to one simple principle, that if you're in the health field you have a duty to put the patient's needs over your own interest and welfare. That's your duty.

Disrespect of the patient, for whatever his needs are, is a fundamental breach of his duty. So, as much as it may or may not do any good, the correct conduct here as a health professional, irrespective of the *dharma*, would be to try and educate him about the fact that there's no place for those kinds of comments. Whether he makes them in the staff room or to other staff, or to the patients directly. Try and educate him in a kind of open, nonjudgmental and patient way about curtailing those behaviors.

And if you still don't get any place, then find out who the supervisor is and discuss it with the supervisor, because he needs to be educated that there's no place for that. Being in the mental health field for a long time, and running an internship at one of the Harvard teaching hospitals for a long time, we didn't tolerate that kind of crap. And sometimes we would can students because character in the health field matters. There's no place for it.

Student 2

We've sanctioned and …

Dan

(The person speaking is on the social work licensing board.)

Student 2

What's coming from the Board is that with conduct like this, we've actually sanctioned and required CEUs for this behavior. We take it very seriously.

Dan

Well, it's good to hear that. Yeah. So, it's actually actionable, is what she is saying. Because the field is built to protect itself in that sense. It should be taken very seriously. There's no place for it.

Student 1

If I might add another comment. That in general in this field we encounter a lot of really ill patients, and many very difficult families. And when families persist in ways to get what they want, whether it's skillful or not, a lot of times staff say, "Oh, she's crazy, or he's crazy," that sort of thing. And so that's a rather generalized opinion around people trying to get their needs met around their loved one's needs, or what they perceive them to be, or what they want to happen. And then this particular example is one that I really haven't seen in this particular school facility. And I guess for me the complication, or maybe I'm making it complicated and it isn't, so, I have to do some thinking about this. And maybe some counsel on this. That I'm obviously not in charge of him because I'm …

Dan

Well, you can on a peer level, you can patiently try and educate him. And if you don't get anywhere, or the other option is that you can talk to whoever the supervisor is. Supervisors are only as good a what they know. As you know, people in clinical supervision, sometimes don't present the full story, and then the supervisor is compromised. And I'm sure if you tell that to the supervisor, it's likely if the supervisor does due diligence, the supervisor's going to get an earful from other people too. Then there's a problem, and the supervisor has to address it.

Student 1

He's also the friend of the director of nursing.

Dan

Yeah, but, so what? I used to deal with that all the time when I was at Cambridge because the city and the state were notorious for political appointees. So they would impose people on us that they wanted to train to be a psychologist, and they were completely incompetent. But we were told we couldn't do anything about it. My position was, if they're bad, we get rid of them. And if you want to fire me over a political appointment, then go ahead and fire over a political appointment. I'm not going to compromise myself. And I never did. Because I'm responsible for who comes into the field.

So, that's the Western point of view. From a Buddhist point of view, the issue is around right speech. The Seven Restraints are (restraint means just don't go there): no killing, no stealing, no sexual misconduct, no lying or deceitful speech, no harsh speech, abusive speech, no divisive speech, which means speaking in a way that causes deterioration of one's practice or another's practice. And lastly, no meaningless speech or gossip. So, this would fall under the category of harsh speech. His speech is disrespectful, and in that sense it's violent—it violates the patient's dignity. There's no place for it. So you try and educate people in terms of there's no place for this.

Now, the other half of your question is what you talked about in terms of your own inner stance towards this. And at the same time, you can take a certain stance towards his behavior, you can practice forgiveness. And there's a lot of Western literature that's come out on forgiveness practice. I'll just summarize it briefly.

Forgiveness practice always starts with a transgression. Somebody has to transgress normal moral principles towards you or to someone else that you know. It always starts with a transgression. And as a result of that transgression, some harm has been done. And if you're going to practice forgiveness, the first step is an acknowledgement of what the transgression is, so you don't minimize it. You have to see it just the way it is.

The second step is you have to see the harm. In this step, if you're going to do that in yourself, is you've got to look squarely into the feelings that are caused by this. And the easiest feeling to access is anger, but anger is always a secondary emotion. If you look deeper, there's always something else with that anger. There'll be hurt, betrayal, shame, fear, indignation. The underlying feeling in this case is likely to be disgust. Disgust is the emotion that comes up when there's some sort of violation of a basic moral principle. So, you're disgusted with his behavior. So, before you can forgive, you have to be able to look into the emotions and process the feelings.

Then, having done that thoroughly, which is your work, then you have to step back and contextualize it. You have to look at what might be going on for this guy and why he's so limited that makes him act this way. And contextualizing means looking at where he's come from and his own limitations that cause him to be this way. If you knew his history and his family background and things like that, or things that happened in his life, you might have some explanation for why he is an asshole. And, if you could come up with a contextual explanation for it, that softens it. That's the first step in softening it.

The second step in softening is more difficult, and that's where the Western literature on forgiveness and the research on that interfaces a lot with Buddhism. Here you have to step back and see that you and this guy have a common humanity. And that means two things. It means, number one, that you both want the same things out of life, even though you're remarkably different in your approach in general to life, and certainly to your patients. But secondly, then you can also look at ways and times that you've acted not so differently, without beating yourself up, just truthfully.

And then that requires a certain kind of metacognitive honesty to really see yourself in times that you've done something similar. And you might be struck with a kind of deep pain at that point, knowing in yourself that that didn't work out very well for you. And it's not working out very well for this guy. Then you're sharing a common humanity. When you forgive, it's an emotional process that allows you to take a different view that will soften that disgust.

It doesn't mean you don't hold him responsible for the behavior. But if you take a two-pronged approach where on the one hand you're trying to find a way that he can hear, of educating him differently, and on the other hand you are going through the steps of the forgiveness process as we now understand it, then you end up feeling like you've done everything you could here. And you're free of it, even though the pain of how he's behaving may linger. But that's not a bad thing. The best forgiveness is when you can see common humanity and see that, you know, we can all be like that.

As one of my trauma patients once said when she had worked through her trauma and abuse and was seeing how she had internalized the perpetrator in some ways, and she gave a number of examples of how it worked, she did things that were very much like what was done to her, with some dismay to be that honest. And her famous line that she told me was, "It's hard to fight the enemy when they have an outpost in your own heart." That's honest. All our enemies have an outpost in our hearts. It's the common humanity view that allows you to see that.

Now, it's easier to do what you're saying in a private setting like a health clinic, because it's partly the duty of a health professional to bring it up. It's harder to do that in general public, because there we don't have a connection. And even though you're not really connected with this guy, you work together, so you have a connection that allows you the context to be able to bring it up. But what if we see something on the street?

I always struggle with that if I am in a supermarket or some other store and I see a mother being abusive to her kid, dragging him along, yelling at them. It just breaks my heart. At what point do you say something? You know? It's not an easy call, because sometimes if you say something they'll get more harsh and violent. And in some ways the well-meaning thing on your part actually makes it worse for the child. So, it's not an easy thing.

You're on safest ground in that situation if whatever you say, whatever your speech is, whatever your conduct is, arises from awakened *dharmakāya* space —it doesn't come from self. And trust the wisdom of the mind to come up with a response verbally and in conduct that's the best fit for the situation, and don't worry about it. That's the ideal, but it's not so easy.

Good question again, thank you.

Student 1

Thank you.

Dan

There's another question over here …

Student 2

I was wondering about the energy around loneliness, and particularly two kinds of loneliness. One, I think is a feeling I've often had in my life of just being lonely, disconnected from other people. And the other is a kind of loneliness yearning. Yearning. And it feels like that's shifting for me in this practice. And I'd just like to hear more about the energy, the possibility of the transformation that sense of loneliness or longing.

Dan

Well, they're quite different things. The question is from a practice point of view, how does one deal with loneliness? And she's talking about two kinds of loneliness. One is loneliness that comes from self, where you feel lonely and longing for a connection with people. And the other is a kind of longing, a spiritual yearning. Is that fair to say?

Student 2

Yeah, that's it.

Dan

They're quite different, so, I'm going to handle them as separate, and try and say why they're separate.

With respect to loneliness ... from a Western point of view, loneliness is very much related to disconnection in attachment issues. If you feel it very strongly, it's a disconnection of the dismissing attachment issue. And the visualizations on secure attachment, if you did them in a regular way over time, would help you to develop that. I'm not going to go into the details of that, but if you go on our website, and go under supporting materials, there's a meditation called "Cherishing." And there's a lecture about cherishing, which is about attachment. And if you listen to the lecture and do the visualizations over time, it will soften all that loneliness.

We just analyzed the data from my orphanage study that I did a couple of years ago, and the data clearly show that there's a relationship between attachment issues and loneliness, amongst other things. So, from a Western point of view, working psychologically on that, so you develop a better internal positive map for secure connection, softens that loneliness. It doesn't take it away, but softens it.

From a Buddhist point of view, you would handle the loneliness the same way you handle any emotion. You do emptiness practice. So, you roam around and look for the loneliness in areas of the body and physiological systems until the substance of that is unfindable. And that what's left is the pure energy of manifestation. And the pure energy of manifestation of loneliness is connection. So, in that connection, that quality of connection, is a property of lively awareness. So, that will transform it.

Now the other thing is a little bit different, and that's longing. The further you go along the path, up to a point, you activate longing. The more you clear away the clouds of the mind, and the closer you get to awakened awareness, the more you know where you're going—on some level of the intelligence of the mind's innate buddha nature. And the closer you get to that, the stronger the longing gets.

So, you don't feel longing at the beginning of spiritual practice. You tend to feel it as you get further along because you can feel that this is taking you somewhere back home, and that longing will come up. But longing occurs when you are still operating out of your ordinary mind, and operating out of duality. So, as long as you're seated within individual consciousness and duality, then you're longing for something you think is outside of that duality and outside of individual consciousness, but it's still framed within duality.

But, if you step out of that, and you're operating out of being this unbounded wholeness, this vast, boundless, awakened awareness-love—if you're operating out of being that rather than operating out of this localized little individual consciousness looking out towards that, then there's no more longing. There's a wonderful passage in one of Leonard Cohen's recent songs about that. "Longing is love confined."

If you take love and you package it and confine it within the constraints of individual consciousness, then it's longing for something beyond that. But if you are that, and not stuck in the narrow confines of individual consciousness and its localization, then there's no longing anymore. You just found your way home. Longing is when you know that that exists strongly, but you haven't got it yet. So, your realization is incomplete, still confined.

One of the first written statements about spiritual longing is *The Song of Songs* written [some say] 5,000 years ago. And every November we teach a course in Israel, in Ein Gedi, in the very site where *The Song of Songs* was written—Ein Gedi's even mentioned in the song. And there they cast spiritual realization in terms of an intimate love relationship, when your lover is so close but not with you—you can feel their presence, but they're not with you. That's not complete, you see. But if you are that, there's no longing anymore.

Now, once you have a taste of awakening and you develop that awakening, there's not only no more longing, but if you live in a reality where every waking moment you are interconnected with everything else and everyone else [Dan chuckles], loneliness seems pretty ridiculous at that point of view. It's not possible. Can't be possible.

And if you develop a heart connection with your teachers, they're always there in that space. So, couldn't possibly be alone. For me, whenever I'm practicing, if something new is developing, there's Menri's mind appearing, reminds me to keep on track. So, not only am I never alone, but it goes back to that first question. If you're always connected with your heart-connection with your lineage, then all your behavior is mindful. Because you don't do anything to disrespect the lineage. And that gets back to the previous question—it changes your conduct. Good conduct is a way of expressing gratitude for what you got. How you act towards others is gratitude in action.

At a certain point, loneliness doesn't exist anymore. And at a certain point, if you get to the process of *dharmadhātu* exhaustion, there just aren't any negative states left anymore. That's useful. We get so caught up in the negative states, it's perfectly ridiculous, a waste of a life. All that is not necessary. And the practice is to find the way out of that mess.

Yes?

Student 3

In terms of practicing on the cushion, something came up at the end of this past week about the *tsa-lung* in connection with practicing for, among other things, for the benefit of *dharmakāya* release when waking in the morning from a dream. And I'm wondering if I become more routine in doing the *tsa-lung*, will it not feel as it did feel like doing that was an interruption of my going right from sleep to …

Dan

Oh, that's a good practice. Good question, really good question. I'm going to say there are two separate practices here. One practice is *tsa-lung*, in Tibetan, that means the practice of energy channels, *tsa*, and energy currents, *lung*. And there are many kinds of energy meditations. In the ones that we did last week in The Six Lamps course with Tenzin Wangyal Rinpoche, that is called *rushen*. And it uses five of the main energy currents in the body—upwardly moving current, the life force, the downwardly moving current, the all-pervasive current, and the fire current. Those are the big five.

It's not the central channel, but they regulate the activity of the central channel. If you do those practices, then the effect is that it will brighten awareness—it will leave you with a kind of lucid bright awareness. And it will clear away a lot of the conceptualization of the mind. So, if you do those practices, it makes it easier to appreciate the nature of awakened awareness. That's useful. Cleans up the issue if the field of awareness gets brighter. There are other central channel practices which are more dangerous and need to be guided, so we didn't do those. It's a little bit harder to do in a group. But those practices that we did, the rushen practices are fairly harmless, and they're useful.

The other thing you're talking about is very different, and that is it's hard to ... You're asking me to cover the whole map here. But there are three maps, for those of you who don't know this. There's the practices that take you from the beginning of the practice up to a taste of awakening. Then there's a set of practices that help you stabilize that infrequent, unstable awakening until you have it all the time, on and off the pillow. And then there's the third map that helps you to take that continuous awakening and to develop it into full buddhahood.

And at the onset of that third map, if you set up your view correctly (which is the infinite vast expanse as the groundless ground from which everything arises in an unconditioned way as spontaneously present, and disappears back into groundless ground), if you know how to set that up, that's the view that you take. How you take that view is with what we call "leave-it-aloneness." You don't do anything to anything. And of course, you're operating out of being that unbounded wholeness. There's no ordinary you in there—you're not operating out of self. If you set up the view just right, in Dzogchen there's a technical term called *malandor*. *Langwa* means to accept something, *dorwa* means to reject something. So, *malandor*: don't accept, don't reject.

And what it means is that in our high-speed information processing system, when something comes up there's an activity, an engagement of mind that if we decide to process something further, we engage it to process it further. That's *langwa*. Or we decide to leave it alone and not process it. That's *dorwa*. Both of those are types of mental engagement where we are engaging something either with a kind of a red light/green light to process it further or not.

That activity is what causes karmic impressions to form. As soon as you engage something, you make a new karmic impression, and that's stored in the *kunzhi*, the storehouse mind. And those karmic impressions will eventually ripen over time, and they appear as spontaneously emerging states of mind. And as they get stronger, they appear in terms of behavior. And as they get really strong, they appear in terms of how the events of our life unfold.

So, you see, if you can set up the view just right at a very advanced level of practice, you are not going to form any new karmic impressions. That sometimes is called *rangdröl*, liberation in and by itself. Sometimes it's called *dharmadhātu* exhaustion. And if you set it up just right, because you're not forming any new karmic impressions, if you do this meditation 24/7, then it forces the mind to release at an accelerated rate all previous karmic impressions that would otherwise ripen more slowly.

So, you just let the whole thing go by itself. It's all automatic. And it will exhaust the bin of negative karmic impressions until there are none left. The average time, if you do this all the time, is six years. If you couple that with the secret energy channels and things like the [Six] Lamps, then you can do the whole thing in two years. And then there are no negative states left and only positive states.

Now, if you want to accelerate that process even more, in terms of the Tibetan theory of mind, karmic impressions tend to become activated and ripen primarily during dream states at night. And then they continue to influence daily behavior. So, that's why if you just wake up in the morning and the last thing you do, even in terms of Western dream lab stuff, shows us that the last thing you do is have a cycle of dreams. You have four or five cycles of dreams a night, but the longest one is the last one.

So, if you just wake up and you set up your view of groundless ground, infinite, vast, expansive, empty awareness space as groundless ground from which everything arises, and you let it all arise, leaving everything alone in its own right, then all those karmic impressions that ripen during the night will just release themselves like writing on water. It disappears as soon as you write, like snow falling on an ocean.

And then you'll feel ... because a lot of times if you wake up and you've been dreaming for a long time, there's a certain heaviness to it when you wake up. What you'll feel is the opposite of that. It would be clean. And you start the day without all those impressions from the dreams and all that heaviness influencing your state of mind or your behavior during the day. You start it clean because you've cleaned out all those karmic impressions. You see?

Student 3

You're not preoccupied.

Dan

No, you're not preoccupied, you're clean. It's gone. So, you see, skillful practice ... For some yogis, the cave yogis particularly, it was called *tun* practice. You organize sessions at different times during the day because they appreciate diurnal rhythms, and there are certain practices that are just better at certain times of the day. So, setting up the view of groundless ground and self-liberation, and everything liberating itself by itself, that would be the strongest practice when you just wake up.

So, yes, it's true that if you got up and did your *tsa-lung* practice, then the shift of the energy currents would clear off the surface layer, but not the roots of those ripening karmic impressions. So, you'd end up feeling cleaner and better, but it's not the superior practice. So, if your question is, which one do you do? You do groundless ground. And then if you do that for a while, you'll see, because at some point stuff stops coming up. And it gets nice, the field, gets very clean, and positive. And when you get *drima*, you get that cleanness. Look for the sign, it gets nice and clean. Sometimes it's translated as "stainless." I like to translate it as clean, because that's the way it's going to feel. The whole field gets nice and clean, bright and clean. And when you get that, then if you want to go back and do the *tsa-lung*, go ahead. But I think you'd find at that point it's sort of redundant. So, it's a nice practice, but this is by far the superior practice.

Student 3

But can you do some days and some the other?

Dan

Do the *tsa-lung* at other times during the day.

Student 3

When you wake up from a dream or …?

Dan

No, do it later in the day. Do it later in the morning. Just do it other times in the day. Just the first thing to do is the groundless ground.

Student 4

Great question.

Dan

Okay?

Student 5

Does it matter if you remember your dreams or not?

Dan

No. What matters is you can hold your awakened awareness during the dream process. But remembering them later means nothing—it's just all representation. There is something in sleep and dream yoga that's like what we call lucid dreaming in the West. You try and carry awakened awareness into deep sleep and dreaming. It's considered a superior practice if you can carry the awakening into deep sleep rather than dreaming. But that's the first step.

Then the second step is you have to have voluntary control over the dream content. It's not enough to keep awakened awareness while you're dreaming, like a lucid dream. You have to be able to change the dream around intentionally while you're awake during dreaming. You have to change the content. And they specifically have you do supernormal feats like jumping over mountains, flying through walls, things like that.

Then the third step is you have to go around looking at all day everyday reality until it's no different from the dream. And the fourth step is interesting. Then you have to change around everyday reality the same way you changed around this dream. You have to do supernormal feats in everyday reality.

Student 6

But we shouldn't start with that one.

Dan

It takes a couple of weeks. [Laughter]

July 17, 2013

Themes: Energy Body; Bodhidharma Tissue Regeneration; No Thing: All Liveliness

Dan

Welcome everyone. You have a question?

Student 1

An idea has sort of stuck with me in terms of how we're full of energy and how everything in the universe has a type of energy, a certain kind of density or subtlety. And so, I was just curious about your perspective of and how it ties into Mahāmudrā practice about raising vibrational energy. And even from a Western psychological perspective, what that actually means, what that actually entails?

Dan

Okay. So, the question is about energy and the relationship between energy and practice. The problem is that the answer to that question differs East and West, and it differs at each level of practice, so, in that sense, it involves more than one answer. But let's start with something that's probably more immediately understandable, and that is the Western view about energy.

The Western view of energy is a field that never quite developed, which in the West we would call energy medicine. Energy medicine was a new initiative. The Fetzer Foundation tried to put a lot of grant money into doing research on energy medicine in the late '80s. I was part of their original advisory board. And then John Fetzer died and the Foundation, as often happens, took it in a different direction and didn't plug the money into it that we thought they would.

But there's some interesting things that were done. The start of the viewing energy really started with a Nobel Prize Laureate in the West, Albert Szent-Gyorgyi. A year after he had won the Nobel Prize for the discovery of Vitamin-C, he began to study ATP—the molecule by which muscles work and use an enormous amount of energy, and the biochemical pathway for muscle exertion.

Towards the end of his life, Szent-Gyorgyi got an interesting idea. And he began to see that if you look at the physical universe in terms of the conductance of energy, then certain structures are semi-conductant and others are rather resistant to conductance. So, I mean, it's pretty clear that electromagnetic energy is better propagated by copper than lead, or rubber. You can't send electricity through rubber. That's why they use it as an insulator.

But if you take the physical properties of the body, not just things in the universe, you find something similar. Some substances in the body or physiological systems are more semi-conductant, and some are rather resistant to conductance like rubber. And what Szent-Györgyi found was that structures in the physical body that approximate crystalline structures are semi-conductant. You get patterns of essentially high conductance and semi-conductance. Just as the whole Texas Instrument revolution in the '60s and '70s was the idea that certain crystalline structures conduct electricity with very little resistance and others with semi-conductance. But you can take the same view of looking at the human body. If you look at the human body, there are certain structures that are semi-conductant, and some approximate even super conductance. And those are structures in the body where the composition of the tissue is crystalline-like. So, one structure that's semi-conductant is nerve tissue. But fluid connective tissue is semi-conductant. And bone tissue is semi-conductant. And they all generate patterns of flow.

Now if you translate that into Eastern, particularly Traditional Chinese Medicine, what you find is that we have a layered energy body. Not the solid structure of the body. There's a surface layer that's called the ordinary channel system in traditional Chinese medicine. And that surface layer has flow patterns and they're called "meridians" in traditional Chinese medicine. The twelve channels of the ordinary system are basically right under the skin. That's not an accident. And it's not the sinewy, but the fluid connective tissue under the skin that behaves like a crystalline structure and propagates flow patterns. So, the body communicates with other areas of the body that are distant to it through these flow channels.

And meridian points are not a primitive misunderstanding of the circulatory system or the lymph system. The Chinese actually mapped out electromagnetic flow patterns within the conductance of the body 1,500 years before electricity was discovered in the West. And that ordinary channel system is, the bandwidth, the frequency range is wired up so that all the immune system cells, the white blood cells in the immune system, will be activated in certain frequency ranges. So, that ordinary channel system is used for immuno-surveillance and protection and disease resistance.

Then there's another system that's deeper than that. And in that [are] semi-conductant patterns that are generated by the crystalline structure of bone tissue. So, both the hard part of the bone—the appetite we call it—part of the bone, and the spongy part of the bone are both semi-conductant. So, they generate flow channels through the bones—energy information channels through the bone system. In traditional Chinese medicine, that's known as the extraordinary channel system. There are eight channels to that.

It was discovered by Bodhidharma. Bodhidharma was the famous Indian master. In about the eighth century, the Emperor of China decided he wanted to make Buddhism an official religion of China. So, they invited the great master Bodhidharma of the day to come to China, which he did. And he said he couldn't teach them because the monks were physically unfit and out of shape and lazy and they were very sickly because of all the flu-like things that people get in the air currents in Western China. But he couldn't say to the emperor, "Well, too bad, Emperor. I'm gonna go home." You can't insult the emperor. So, he stayed and he meditated for twelve years on his own body, and he came out and he wrote two texts. One is called Bone Marrow Washing Nei Kung, and the other is called Tendon Transforming Nei Kung.

The Tendon Transforming Nei Kung he realized by studying horses; and he realized that horses move at very fast speeds and they have very little leg muscle mass. So, it's not the muscles that can make the horse move at great speed, it's the tendons. So, he figured out a series of movement meditations to strengthen the chi energy in the tendons, which resulted in the capacity for great physical strength.

Then he meditated on his own body, and figured out within the spongy part of the bone marrow there are properties that regenerate tissue. That was 1,500 years before we discovered stem cells. Stem cells regenerate tissue. But what Bodhidharma discovered that Western medicine hasn't discovered yet is that bone marrow tissue ages the same way that we know that vascular tissue ages. We have great documentation of the aging of vascular tissue. We call it arteriosclerosis. Free fatty acid deposit builds up in the vasculature and it results in stroke.

Bodhidharma figured out 1,500 years ago meditating on his own body that something similar like that happens with the bone marrow tissue, and it crowds out stem cells and they eventually die. But if you do "bone marrow washing," which is a kind of [like this: Dan demonstrates pounding his arm intensely with the hand of his other arm] activate all of the chi energy patterns in the body. You do that for thirty days, and then you do bone breathing where you're actually ... Bone marrow tissue is hollow. You breathe and you activate the chi right in all the bones of the body. So, you set up circuits. And if you do that for seventy more days—it's a hundred series, a hundred-day exercise—what it does is it reverses the free fatty acid deposits in the bone tissue. And it replenishes the stem cells. So, typically, if you have any damaged cell line, stem cells can migrate to that spot and replace it.

A modern experimental paradigm of that would be take a rat, open the skull up, take a vein and tie it off, an artery and tie it off and induce a stroke. Then take another healthy rat, take a supply of blood from the rat, spin it down in a centrifuge. Take the stem cells out. Grow them in a tissue culture, radioactively tag the stem cells, and then inject the stem cells from the healthy rat into the tail vein of the rat with the stroke and wait three weeks.

And what happens is that 80 percent of the stem cells migrate across the brain-blood barrier, which we used to think was impossible, and they repopulate the tissue. They replace the astrocytes, the glial cells, and the neurons, all the cells that were damaged by the stroke. So, what we now know about stem cells is not like raising clones of sheep. Stem cells are the way that the body replaces any damaged cell line, either by injury or by genetic damage. And typically, if you have a healthy stem cell population forever, you should live a long time. Bodhidharma practiced those on himself, and he lived to be a hundred and fifty years old.

Now of course when he presented this stuff to the emperor, the emperor was very happy with this. And he wanted Bodhidharma to teach all the royal family how to live long and to make a special elite force of guards around the royal family. But Bodhidharma wasn't interested in making the practices that restricted, so they cut a deal. And the deal was that he would do what the emperor said in exchange for which the emperor would build a place that would be protected from the general public where these practices would be perfected, practiced in secret for eternity. And that place was protected until it was discovered by the Red Guard in 1954. You know it as Shaolin. And as one of my producer friends at Sundance says, "It's easier to tell the truth in fiction." When you saw *Crouching Tiger* and the people bouncing through the air, what you were seeing is the special feats that they did by doing the tendon transforming practices. That's what you get if you do those practices.

So, that middle layer of the energy body is generated by bone tissue, and the stem cell system as Bodhidharma correctly identified is how we regenerate tissue. So, if you keep your stem cell population healthy, you should live for a long time. And a lot of people, when we see they get strokes and then it reverses itself, it's because they probably have a healthy stem cell population. We see the damage in the people who don't get a chance to repair it. But the body is built to regenerate its own tissue. We're just learning about that, and that's going to create a whole new discovery and a whole new kind of medicine twenty years from now if we don't hold it up with the politics of stem cell research.

Then there's a third layer of the energy body, and that's generated by another semi-conductant tissue, which is nerve issue. And that's a little weird one because that's the central channel system. And it's not flow patterns that run because of one tissue structure like the spinal cord, but the interaction between two tissue structures—the spinal cord at the back and the vagus nerve at the front, which are huge nerves. And right smack in-between those two, you get a kind of virtual energy channel which is a huge energy channel, generated by the semi-conductant nerve tissue. And the central channel system is designed for changing states of consciousness.

So, we have a layered energy body. The body is clear light, ultimately. And we have three different layers. The outer layer is designed for immune surveillance and disease resistance, the middle layer is for regeneration, and the deeper layer is for the transformation of consciousness. But if you have a body that basically is energy information relay then you have to have a way of storing the energy.

Jwing-Ming, Dr. Yang, who was for many years here in the Boston area in Jamaica Plain, he's an electrical engineer and martial arts master who translated Bodhidharma's original works into English. And what he says, if you look at a capacitor, a battery, look at a car battery, what do you see? How do you store energy in a car battery? By having a structure that alternates high-low resistance. So, you have cells with hydrochloric acid and lead. High conductance, low conductance. High conductance, low conductance. And any time you have a physical structure that alternates high and low conductance, you can store energy. Okay?

So, now look at your gut. What you've got in your gut is twenty-five feet of intestines, and if you strung all that out, it's all interconnected with lots and lots of connective tissue. The connective tissue is high conductance. The smooth muscle tissue of the gut is low conductance. So, what you've got here is one huge battery that's much bigger than the car battery. And the second one is all the folds in the stomach, and the interconnected tissue of that. That's your second battery. And the third one is your brain and all those folds in the outer surface of the brain and the connective tissue that links it to the dura. And that, in Traditional Chinese Medicine, is your "triple heater"—it's three batteries. So, when you do martial arts, you always store your energy back in the chi. So, that's the, if you will, from a Western point of view, that's the architecture of the energy body.

So, now in terms of Dzogchen or Great Completion meditations, it is true that everything is ultimately energy, but it needs some explanation. First, you have to take the view of everything being empty. And what that means is it ... things exist relatively, but they don't have independent self-existence. The only reason that things seem to exist in relative reality is because of interactions. The Buddhists call that dependent origination. In Western science we call it interaction effects. Nothing exists in and of itself. Why does the world appear like that? Because we all share a similar brain and all share a similar perceptual apparatus. So, it all looks similar.

But what we're seeing isn't the world out there. Ultimately the brain makes models for the world. It makes representations. And what we're seeing is our own representations. You can only see the map that you make. And when Buddhists say things are empty, it means that they exist relatively speaking, but they only exist because of complex interactions. They don't exist apart from our capacity to perceive it. And if you start looking at things as empty, two things happen. One is that things lose *dzin-pa*, they lose grab. And second is they lose *mümpa*, the capacity to obscure.

And ultimately, particularly in Great Completion practice, Dzogchen, if you start seeing the world through the view of emptiness, then what you're seeing is awareness. Awareness. *Rigpa*. Awakened awareness. And awareness has, what in Dzogchen is called *tsal*, liveliness. Awareness has the capacity to express itself. And all of this display is awareness expressing itself to itself. And you know the events through their own expressions. Awareness expressing itself to itself, knowing itself through its own expressions. What's the purpose of that? The intention of awakened awareness is, on the one hand, for the benefit of wisdom. This whole display is here and displays itself every moment until you can see it just for what it is. Until you get it. That's where the word Mahāmudrā comes from, which literally means "the great gesture." Every moment is another invitation to you until you get it right and see it correctly. And, for the benefit of compassion, this whole display is for the purpose of compassion.

Now, if you practice emptiness correctly, then the world doesn't disappear, it just isn't very solid anymore. And you start seeing everything as the dance, the play, the liveliness of awareness displaying itself to itself. Now if you stabilize your awakening, so you have it pretty much most of the time on and off the pillow, then you start to see the world in terms of *tsal*, liveliness.

All visual forms are none other than the liveliness of awakened awareness. They're not solid anymore. Everything becomes like light. All sound is the liveliness of awakened awareness. There are no sounds out there. All touch sensations, the body itself is just, we say like an empty glass bottle filled with light. It's all light and energy. All smells, tastes, anything seemingly out there from the five senses is just lively awareness.

Internally, all thoughts, all emotions are lively awareness. Now if you hold that view and you practice that all the time, after a while everything is a continuous flow of lively awareness. It's rather wondrous. And you can't perceive anything other than lively awareness all the time. And the idea that that would ever go away or cloud over would seem, at some point, perfectly ridiculous. We call that stage of practice *dengwa*, confidence. Assurance. Can't lose it. Not possible.

Now, if you have that awakened awareness and manifesting it every moment, then it's not so long after that you begin to see everything in the world in terms of lively energy, as long as you don't make that energy into a thing. It's all awareness, the dance of awareness. And if you follow that route, what was once ordinary perception gets quite transformed in the process. Perception becomes non-ordinary. Nothing is solid, we say everything is like a dream, or like a mirage. And if you really refine that pathway along perception, ultimately, all five types of perception, all changes to energy. Sight, taste, smell, changes to light. Sound is not a specific sound like a car or a bird. Sound becomes the sound of liveliness of the dance of awareness. It's cosmic sound, liveliness, the sound of liveliness, awakened awareness expressing itself, creating itself every moment.

And thought is a little different because thought has the property of directionality. We can direct our thinking. And if you transform thought, thought becomes, we say "like light rays"—specific focus, unobstructed. So, all that's left if you transform the perception is light, cosmic sound, and rays of light. And that's your experience.

The hardest thing [in] transforming that process, it takes longer, is the physical body. When the body becomes no longer solid and it's like an empty glass bottle filled with light, we call that "clear light body." But if you really refine your practice, right down to the elements that make up the body, then there are practices where you ... they're called *tendrel*, making the connection. You try and see how, that what seems to be your physical body is related to the five elements. How does earth affect the stability of your concentration and your sitting posture? Take that away and see what happens. How does water affect the fluidity of the mind's movement? And these elements seem to cause certain experiences in meditation. But when you start changing around the elements, the experiences change remarkably.

And ultimately when you see even the basic elements of the body as empty, then there isn't anything left of the body except rainbow light. And those open up the teachings of rainbow body, like the Mipham [Gompo] story I told you earlier. That takes a little longer to do. It's considered one of the hardest things to do. That's why in two hundred ninety Dzogchen practices, Great Completion practices, sometimes the achievement of rainbow body is seen as the highest attainment of a great master. They wait until he dies and see if he changes into rainbow light.

So, in the older Buddhism, they used other markers, but they're interesting. One of the big debates, maybe a hundred years after the Buddha, was the thirty-two marks. And they seem rather strange to us as Westerners who are scientifically minded. If you listen to the *dharma*, you have long earlobes. If you speak elegantly and truthfully, you have a long tongue. There are thirty-two physical characteristics of a buddha. What are they really talking about? Something quite extraordinary—that if you refine your enlightenment, it actually changes the physical structure of the body. Remarkable. Not something we've considered here in the West as possible. Body follows and conforms itself to the realizations of the mind, not the other way around, at a certain point.

So, in Buddhism, there are different points; in the tradition there were different markers that were used for what the ultimate attainments really were. Nowadays, rainbow body is popular, but the thirty-two marks were very popular way before that. And it's changed at different points in the history of Buddhism.

Now that stuff's pretty far out. But, now, always right here, every moment, is a boundless, vast ocean of awareness-love, which is your true nature. We call it buddha nature. You're never apart from that. But you don't recognize it because there are many layers of experience that get too solid and cloud it over.

Awakened awareness is like the sun that's always shining, but you can't see it if it's cloudy, until the clouds clear. Emptiness practice clears away the clouds, gives you more of a chance to see it just for what it is. And recognizing that is the heart of these teachings. Shifting your basis of operation so you're operating out of being that ocean of awareness-love is the heart of the teachings—refining that to full buddhahood. That's the completion of the path, that's why Dzogchen means literally, Great Completion. It brings the practice to full buddhahood.

Now, the trouble is, and the reason why things cloud over, is because our ordinary information processing system, every moment, breaks up this unbounded wholeness. Every time you conceptualize, you're partializing. As Mipham says, "The function of conceptualization is to delineate." So as soon as you say, "This is it," it's not that. That impulse to conceptualize blocks the unbounded wholeness that's always right here. As soon as you fix your attention on something, you're not fixing it on something else. So, every moment of paying attention blocks it. Then in Buddhism, the quickest information processing act, we don't even have a word for it in the West, it's *manasikara* in Sanskrit, or *yilajepa* in Tibetan. I like to translate it as "the tendency of the mind toward something," the outcome of [which is] something particular. The quickest act of the mind partializes—every act of your information processing system, from slowest to fast, partializes. It clouds over what's always right here. And what's always right here is a boundless field of awareness-love. On the one hand, like vast empty awareness space; and like a field of empty infinite love on the other hand. But here's the thing, as soon as the mind starts to particularize and make something into a thing, it clouds it over. This whole thing is about the nature of lively awakened awareness.

So, you've got to watch out with this energy thing. Because as soon as you start looking at it in terms of energy, you've made it into a thing. See the difference? Now if you see that energy as the dance of awakened awareness, that's different. That will keep you on the right track. But as soon as you start viewing it in terms of energy, you're going to miss it. Understand what I'm saying? Don't make it into a thing. You just get more clouds that way. It's a good question. There's a lot to it, you see, there's a whole world in there. Ultimately the body is just energy. The energy is not energy. It's lively awareness, awakened awareness.

So, if you view the body as all the energy of manifestation of lively awakened awareness, then you're going to stay on the right track. It changes every moment. It's a wondrous show. Good question.

January 29, 2014

Themes: Importance of Lineage; Heart-to-Heart; Beware of Spiritual Pride

Dan

Welcome everyone.

If you look at the most advanced practices in Dzogchen, or Great Completion practice, those are the *tögal* practices. They're using this secret energy channel of the body and working up the visions of ultimate reality. And the Nyingma's version of that, of those precious teachings, is a book called *Yeshe Lama*. And it's rarely given out, even if you have your hundred thousands.[19] They're a guarded secret. But the Bon have a version of *tögal* practices which is far more extensive, from Tapihritsa, that's been around a long time, and it's much more developed, and the commentarial tradition is far more developed around it, so it's a much larger set of teachings. But they never gave it out either.

But what happened was in 19..., I think it was '46, or something like that, roughly around that time, the great yogi of the Bon, Lopon Tenzin Namdak was in deep meditation, and he had a vision from Sherab Chamma, the mother goddess, protector in the Bon, rather like Green Tara in other parts of Buddhism. Sherab Chamma came to him and said, "Look, if you don't change how

---

19 Referring to the one hundred thousand repetitions of each of a group of specific practices that constitute the "preliminary practices" or *ngondro*.

you're conveying these teachings, then it'll all die out in this single generation. There will be none left forever for humankind."

She gave him explicit instructions to write everything down, including all the secret pith instructions. Pith instructions are like if you play a video game, you could probably figure it out, but if you have the key, it goes much faster. Pith instructions are like the key to how you put this meditation into practice so it actually works. And when Tibetans write a book, they always leave out a piece of it so you can't just go out and try and figure it out on your own without the pith instructions, because they're trying to prevent you conceptualizing too much.

They wrote down all the volumes, printed them all up on block prints, including the pith instructions, and that was thirteen years before Tibet got taken over. And a lot of the places that were active places of Bonpo practice, like Dolpo (a part of Nepal) and other areas, they were not destroyed when Tibet got taken over. Nepal was not. So, because of that vision, they were able to preserve their scriptural tradition in a way that was relatively intact.

And the second thing that Sherab Chamma said was that—and this was in 1946, mind you, before Tibet was taken over, and at that time Tibet was very isolationist—Sherab Chamma explicitly gave the instruction that Lopon Tenzin Namdak and the other Bon teachers had to teach this in the West. And as a result of that, Lopon Tenzin Namdak started to teach in Europe, largely in France, and His Holiness Menri Trizin who was, as you know, my teacher, he started teaching in London, and later in Oslo. That's why he has good English.

So, by the time Tibet was overtaken, the whole scriptural tradition had been preserved pretty much in an unbroken lineage, and these teachings, for the first time, became much more available to the West, including the guarded secrets like the Tapihritsa Lamps teachings. It's an unusual time in history that these are now made available.

The reason that they're kept secret is because if you try and figure it out conceptually, it actually hardens the mind and makes it harder to awaken, so you're actually harming yourself by trying to think your way through this stuff.

When you get teachings, there are certain things that happen. Usually, it starts with what's called a lung, where a teacher will read you a certain body of teachings that they want you to learn, and they will read it really quickly, you know, like the end of some advertisements, when they cram the legal boiler plate stuff in there, talk about a minute. It's like that in Tibet. They read the whole text that way. It's like that. [Laughter]

What they do by reading it very quickly (lung means wind, air, or breath) when they convey the lung, they're doing several things: by reading it really fast, they're giving you an overview of what this is going to cover, even if you don't understand a word of it. Second, they're reading it in the way that they're actually breathing life into it—that's what lung means. They're making this body of teachings, this ancient body of teachings, come alive for you. Third, by virtue of conveying the lung to you, they are giving you the authorization to then practice it. You can then go out and put it into practice.

Now, the other thing that happens during that is called *chingilap*, which is often translated as empowerment or initiation. But I don't like those translations at all. *Lapa* means waves, like waves on the ocean, and *chingwa* means giving. So, the term literally means gift waves.

What it means is that when you work with a lineage master, these fully realized beings, because you can't be a lineage holder unless you're a buddha, you have to realize the full embodiment of that set of teachings. Okay? So, these realized, fully realized beings, as non-ordinary beings, they can directly intervene in your unfolding mindstream. They can do three things: one is that they can remove obscurations, remove negative states; two, they can activate the positive qualities, the *yonten*; and three, they can instill the view, *dawa*, because getting the view right, how you approach a meditation, it's all about *dawa*, it's all about getting the view right. So, they install the view directly in your mindstream, which when practiced, will increase the probability of bringing this to fruition as awakening, and ultimately as buddhahood. So, they're setting the mindstream right.

But you have to put the intention into wanting that. You have to *solwadeb*, you have to throw out a request. Let them know you want this, and then you get the influence, and then you have to put it into practice. You have to do two things: you have to put the intention into wanting it as a formal request, and then you have to take the teaching and actually practice it.

But for lots of Westerners, lamas come over and they give empowerments—I don't like the translation; it really means influence. Then, what happens is they collect the empowerments, and say, "I got my empowerment for this, and for Hevajra Tantra and for Chakrasamvara," and then don't do anything with it. They just go around and collect empowerments and it's gone. If you don't put it into practice shortly thereafter, the window of opportunity of that influence is lost. It means nothing after that. But if you put it into practice—because the view, which is the precious heart essence of any one of these lineage teachers, has been planted directly in your mindstream—it will ripen like a blossoming flower. It will come to fruition as buddhahood.

So, you see, from that point of view, if you get three things, [first] the lung, which we call "oral transmission," then along with that is what's called a *menag*, where they explain to you (with the pith instructions) the key—they have to give you an oral explanation as part of the relationship about why this works this way, and how you actually set up a view, and how you do it. And the third thing is you have to then practice guru yoga on whoever is the holder of that lineage to get the view, and to reinforce the view that's ripening in your mindstream.

So, for example, if you were working with Rahob Tulku, and as we just did, we just did the book called *Lion's Gaze*—which is Garab Dorje's main teaching in Nyingma Dzogchen, and then Patrul's main commentary on that—he read the lung, he read the book to everybody, except he does it in English, sort of his version of English. You have to get used to it. His pronunciation is like "absoluty" and "relativy," and "chipmonkey," he puts "Y"s on everything. "Grassypen" instead of grasping – it's adorable. Anyhow, he does that and then we both explain the *menag*, the instructions on how you make it practice, and then you do guru yoga, and because he's the emanation of Padmasambhava, as you can see in the lineage tree, then you do guru yoga on Padmasambhava, and he implants the view that will refine itself and bring you to awakening, and then the refinement of that awakening of buddahood.

And if you were doing a different lineage, like the Bon lineage, and you were doing Shang Shung Nyengyud, then you would get, as I do, teachings directly from His Holiness Menri Trizin in terms of the oral reading, and then the explanation. Then I'll go and meditate. Then he has me translate it and so I'm both translating and putting it into practice. We're making the connection.

If you get the lung, the *menag*, and then you do the guru yoga, you have essentially, we say *rigpa tendrel*, you make a connection with the lineage. You've established a direct linkage with this lineage with your own mindstream. Or, if you want to say it more colloquially, you've made a direct connection in your heart. All of these teachings come from heart to heart. They're giving us something, a precious gift, because they lead to awakening.

As a result of getting that direct teaching as part of a lineage, not only does it come from heart to heart, but by virtue of having done that, you then become what's called *rigpu*, child of the lineage. You are now a spiritual child, a spiritual infant, and the teachings then will nurture you so you grow up, until you become an awareness-holder or lineage-holder, a full buddha.

And if you look, for example, some of you know this, but the more advanced book that Rinpoche's been teaching from is *Buddhahood Without Meditation* (it's a series of mind-to-mind transmissions), and he teaches about this third map of teachings. And if you look very carefully, a vision comes during meditation to Jigme Lingpa and then another vision and another vision—each vision is a teaching in itself. He has a question and then a vision of, say, Saraha comes and says, "That's a good question. Here's the answer, my little child." And then later it says something more like "my spiritual young adult," and later it becomes "my realized one." And the way that the visionary beings are dressed then shows a transformation as you grow up spiritually. So, all of you, by virtue of getting these teachings as lineage teachings are now "children of the lineage." Precious.

And that comes with *damchik*, or *samaya* in Sanskrit, spiritual duties. If you've been given something precious … *damchik* means if you're given teachings that are not at all obvious that will help you to realize awakening and the preciousness of that, [and will] completely transform your life, it's very precious. And if you get that, then the duties are, in Western terms, you can reduce *samaya* to one thing: "Don't fuck it up." [Laughter]

That's basically what they come down to. It means that you have a duty to put it into practice, to continue to be diligent in your practice, and bring it to fruition. Don't waste it. Use the opportunity and the connection to lineage to do it. So, you have to practice and that's your duty. You have to listen to the teachings.

And the other part of it is if you're given something precious, you have to have the level of mind that you treat the teachings respectfully. You don't go out and talk about them in a way that's going to water them down, cause them to be misunderstood, develop spiritual greed. If the teachings help you awaken, you don't go out and say, "Hey, you're going to get awakened!" What are you going to send? All the people who have spiritual greed, and they're all coming for the wrong reasons. So, your duty is to be careful with how you convey it. Better to shut up about it and to live it. Because you convey it best in terms of who you are, not what you say. And your duty is, if you're given something precious, which most people won't get, then understand the preciousness of it and don't let it deteriorate. Those are the duties that come with it.

But the value of this is that if you have lineage teachings, a couple of things happen: one is that you plant the seed for full buddhahood, and you're given the teachings that are proven, that will help you to develop that buddhahood, nothing short of that. We're not talking about a meditation technique here. We're talking about a fundamental transformation of your being as a manifestation of ultimate reality and nothing short of that.

And by virtue of practicing as part of a lineage, which you have duties to, then it sort of serves as a check and balance system, because it requires enormous responsibility, to practice as part of a lineage. Because you can't just go out and do anything you want to do. You have to be responsible for the greater social good, to not screw up the practice. And you have to be mindful of spiritual pride. That's probably the best advantage of lineage teachings. Because there's always built-in checks and balances.

I don't teach. Dan doesn't teach. All the teachings come from *dharmakāya* space. I just get out of the way. And I find it very useful to be with somebody like his holiness Menri Trizin because he's not subtle about his capacity to read minds. So, I never have to say much because he knows exactly what's going on. I remember one time going there and I didn't say a word, I never said anything, and as soon as I walk in he tells me what's going on. I'll go into retreat and then I'll come back after a couple days of working on something and he'll say, "Okay, now do this," and I don't have to say anything about ... he can see immediately. It's amazing. Sort of convenient. I remember one time going there, and he says, "You're doing a lot of teaching. Watch out for the spiritual pride," and I said, "Busted, thank you." And that was useful.

See, that's a problem in the West because ... I'm not poo-pooing people's realizations. There are a lot of people in the West who teach who've had their own self-realizations. And there's nothing wrong with that. The realizations may be very profound, but they don't come under a lineage, so there's no checks and balances. And some of those things get pretty wild and out of control. We've seen lots of bad things happen from that, because if you're not part of a lineage, you have to be especially aware of the problem of spiritual pride. Because spiritual pride becomes more, not less, of a problem the further you go. The greater your realizations, the greater the likelihood of spiritual pride.

Tapihritsa was Indian, he lived in the Kailash area, and he thought that these teachings would take a strong foothold—the Bon Dzogchen teachings—in Tibet. And there was a famous tantric Tibetan master by the name of Nangzer Lodpo. He had great capacities for visualization, generating the mandala. He had great psychic abilities, super-normal abilities. But he had a lot of pride, and Tapihritsa thought that if he could tame Nangzer Lodpo's pride, that he had the stuff to make a great teacher.

Tapirhitsa lived a couple hundred years before Nangzer Lodpo but he came back and he could take any form he wanted as a non-ordinary being, so he came back in the form of a sixteen-year-old boy and he went to Nangzer Lodpo's hermitage and said, "I want to be your assistant, I want to be your apprentice and serve you." So, Nangzer Lodpo said, "Okay," and then he prepared meals and firewood and things like that and they got to talking and they started having these deep talks about the *dharma*. And Nangzer Lodpo kept getting angrier and angrier because this sixteen-year-old kid would raise deep questions that Nangzer Lodpo couldn't quite answer and the kid was showing him up.

He got more and more angry and at some point it developed to an intolerant point that he, in a fit of rage, challenged Tapihritsa to a debate in front of the king, which you don't want to do that impulsively because whoever loses the debate gets killed. So, Tapihritsa just laughed and said, "I don't want to debate in front of the king, because it's just pure conceptual," that's the whole point, you don't get the stuff in terms of direct experience. That made Nangzer Lodpo more angry and he said, "What do you know?" At which point, Tapihritsa was standing by a table, so he walked halfway through the table and keeps talking, at which point Nangzer Lodpo understood that this was not an ordinary being. And then he humbled himself, and saw that his pride had gotten in the way to see the opportunity here, and he apologized, and then Nangzer Lodpo and the king studied with Tapihritsa, all the people in that area did, and became enlightened, and the story goes on from there.

It's an interesting story in the history of this because it's really about how a great master, actually the one that was to be the lineage holder for the whole Zhang Zhung lineage, the first Tibetan, was filled with pride because of his accomplishments. That's why in the Tibetan tradition people don't talk about their own personal meditation. The etiquette is you never talk about it. The reason for that is so it doesn't foster pride. The exception for that is the pointing out style, where you have to talk about it as a part of teaching, but that's rarely the case.

So, understand what it means to be part of a lineage. These teachings have been around a long time and they're passed down from heart to heart. And it means that you have to have some karmic connection to recognize this. There's the famous line from Padmasambhava of which … Rahob is the incarnation of

Padmasambhava, and the line goes, "when the lioness roars in the forest all the lion cubs jump for joy because they think of the precious milk they'll receive, the lion's milk. But when the lioness roars in the forest all the other animals run away in fear. Tell me, my friends, are you a lion cub?" Good passage.

You have to be able to recognize what's precious. And that's karmic in part. Part of the connection to the lineages is karmic; part of it is the kindness of the teachers. And the outcome of that is you make a connection with the lineage. When I first went to Menri he gave me nothing, even though I had worked almost forty years with the Tibetans. He tested me a lot, and he gave me some things to work on, translate from the Akhrid system, in archaic Tibetan from Zhang Zhung, which was a shock for me in terms of the language [Dan chuckles] because I wasn't used to it at all. To make sense out of what he was trying to teach me I had to work on it.

And then having worked on that, he said, "There's another text I want you to work on." It was short, and it was about the relationship between special states and awakening, and how you use special states to enhance awakening. It was a practice that I had some familiarity with. And then that text was in post-Lhasa revision language, so it was Tibetan that I understood. It wasn't archaic. So I said, "Okay, you don't have to explain it to me, I'm going to translate and explain it to you," which he thought was really hilarious. So I did! And he stopped and he said, "You know this, you know it both to translate it and you know the meditations," I said, "Yeah, that's why I came, and we're wasting time. I want to learn this. I have precious time and I want to learn it."

There was a Westerner there who had done almost four hundred thousand preliminaries, and he was really filled with himself, and that was his model for what Westerners are. And he said, "Okay, I want to see your website." So, I showed him the website. He said, "You don't try and teach this yourself; you teach this under the lamas." I said, "Yeah, I'm not that arrogant about it, and I want you to teach it, and I want you to show me how to do it with you." And he said, "Oh, well what about this other guy? He puts on his website that he's a lineage holder, that's like being a fully realized buddha, with all the teachings. It's so arrogant." And he just shook his head, he said, "What am I going to do? Keep him here for more hundred thousand preliminaries?" And I said, "Well, don't judge me by his practice. That's not what I'm here for." That's when we started.

The next day he gave me all the precious instructions, the secret instructions for opening up buddha bodies and full buddhahood, and then told me I could translate that stuff. This last time, he's basically given me all the advanced teachings. He gave me a plan here. We have a lesson plan to work on.

When I left that first month, the first one he was with me, on the last day I told him I was leaving, and he said, "Well, come back later." So I came back later, and when I said goodbye he did something that just broke my heart. And then I understood what lineage meant. And what he did is he came over to me and he gave me a headbutt. He whacked my head with his forehead, and he took my hand and he put it over his heart, and he says, "These teachings come from heart to heart, from father to spiritual son, one generation to the next. I'm giving them to you." And I just sobbed.

See, that comes with responsibility. So understand what you're getting. And you're getting several lineages, and they're precious. The Bon Dzogchen lineage goes back eighteen thousand years. That's a long time; they've been doing this a long time. He didn't get to be the Dalai Lama's senior meditation teacher for nothing. But that's where these teachings come from. In the Nyingma tradition they come from Rahob. He's the emanation of Padmasambhava. Padmasambhava was the main dude to bring this stuff to Tibet, right? So, you're getting two lineages here; the indigenous lineage and the main lineage which was transferred to Tibet. You're getting the best of what's out there.

There are a lot of self-important meditation teachers out there, all filled with spiritual pride, and they'll offer you great techniques. But this isn't the time for technicians. It's a time for manifesting the full fruition of these, as a fully and continuously awakened mind that works tirelessly for all beings, because if we don't do that we won't survive. It's that simple.

It's not about meditating. It's about becoming a buddha. This is the time that all these teachings will come to the West. If you all have some responsibility in what form you'll take it coming here, in what you choose, they're not all of the same quality. So use your best metacognitive intelligence and see what you're getting. Otherwise, you'll be part of what Rinpoche calls "the *dharma* flea market."

Are you a lion cub?

Anything you want to ask, to follow this up?

Student 1

I'd like to know, this issue of spiritual pride, and I'm sitting here thinking how to make the distinction between being excited about things that unfold and cautious not to be prideful about those things.

Dan

Oh, it's better to think that you will be [prideful] [Laughter], and to expect and to look for it, and then it will be much of a lesser problem. If you try not to be, then probably you're going to put up some sort of false persona to yourself, and that's not going to go anywhere useful. We have lots of people in the world who try and act piously but they can't live it, so it's all false self stuff. Spiritual pride means that it's self-referential, that you're referring to realizations that belong to self. And your level of knowledge belongs to self, it's self-referential.

Student 1

So that's what to watch for?

Dan

Yeah, that's what to watch for. The self doesn't awaken. Dan doesn't awaken. If you set up the view correctly, and hold the view, because the view is the meditation, then awakening will happen by itself to itself. All the advanced practices are based on setting up the view and everything the path unfolds with its own intelligence. It shows itself to itself. There's a level that goes beyond this little bubble here. All of what's available in the interconnected world, everything is here all at once, so that means that you get complete downloads of teachings, but they don't come from out there, they're all in the expanse of awakened mind. Already here.

So, none of that has anything to do with the self. Dan doesn't awaken. Dan doesn't teach. Somebody once sent me a cartoon that I like a lot, and it says, "I finally looked at the bigger picture in life ... I wasn't in it." That's a pretty clear statement. It doesn't take much. There are some people who have self-realizations and you have to see what they do. If they spend a lot of time talking about their realizations, how does that work for you? How does that help? On the other hand, if they show you methods on how you can transform your own mind, and you can see that working, that's a better practice, in my opinion. Because unless I can convey to you teachings that make you come to the realization yourself, nothing I have to say to you is worth the while to waste your time on.

Student 1

Then it's just concepts.

Dan

Yeah, but that's self-referential. I remember going someplace to teach, and there were three of us that were going to teach there that weekend. There was myself, representing these lineages, a Zen master, and a Western person who had written a popular book on spiritual realizations. I had taught there for a couple years and when I got there they told me that the faculty building that we all stay in was taken. We weren't going to stay there. I got put in a regular room like everybody else; it wasn't even clean. And I said, "Why are we staying in the dorms?" It's not like we get paid a lot to stay here, usually the... "Well that's because this teacher, her attendants are all staying there." So, I said, "Let me get this straight, you have this Western person, who's written a book, who has no lineage, who has self-made realizations, and you displaced myself and a Zen master for her attendants, without even telling us ahead of time that you did that?" I said, "How disrespectful is that?"

But from their point of view, she had asked for that because she wanted it for herself, and they said yes without even bothering to tell myself or this other teacher. I didn't even know who this person was. I thought, I have to find out more about this. We work our butts off in these retreats. We teach morning, afternoon, and evening. Her teaching was to show videotapes of herself talking about her own realizations for the whole day, then show up one hour at night, and impose silent retreats on everybody else, even though we didn't ask for that. I said, "How arrogant is this?"

And that's this Western stuff, and people go ga-ga over it because it wows them. Because she can talk about her own states, which are mostly just that, states. And that's where we get confused in the West, because we can't tell the difference between states and a realized mind. And there are a great number of teachings on how you learn to tell the difference. Maitreya, the future Buddha is attributed to five great sutras which he downloaded to Asanga. They're called the Five Great Sutras of Maitreya, and every one of them says the same thing: "Don't confuse states and experiences with the nature of ultimate reality." Why did he hammer home that point in five sutras? Because everybody does it, and they're very relevant to this time. We all want more states.

I've had a number of people come to the Level 1 courses whose background was they did a lot of ayahuasca, and they're attached to drug-induced states. Almost none of those students ever stuck, because they're just part of the *dharma* flea market and they're going out and looking for other experiences. They got a little hit from the retreat; they went out to look for some other state. They're not lion cubs. They're fearful animals in the forest who keep looking for more.

The mark of a teacher is they should be able to show you explicitly how you can look into your own mind in a way that leads to realization. If I can't show you that, I haven't helped you. Because that's all that matters, because it's the heart essence. All these teachings. Whether you do Theravada, or whether you do Mahāyāna, or whether you do any of the essence practices. There are eighty-four thousand different types of practices within Buddhism, and the confluence of all of those practices is the nature of an awakened mind. If you have that, you have the heart of all the teachings, so you don't lose the forest through the trees. All of those teachings should convey to you exactly how to do that in your direct experience, and if they're not doing that, don't waste your time.

My first Root Lama, Geshe Wangyal, was Mongolian, and he was a horse trader. He said, "Don't buy just any horse! When you buy a horse you check out the mouth and teeth, you check out the fur and the skin, you check out the hoofs, you want to make sure you get a good horse. Finding a good teacher is like finding a good horse. Check out the teacher, don't just take any teacher. Make sure you know what you're getting." But look for the signs of self-reference. Look at what it is they're teaching, because those things you can count on.

May 15, 2014

Themes: Three Categories of Meditation; Clearing Clouds Layer by Layer

Dan

Welcome everyone.

I'm inclined, since almost every one of the new people talks about a background in mindfulness that maybe we should clarify different types of meditation and what they do and don't do. I think that would be useful. So, I just think that it might bear some commentary, given that mindfulness is now extremely popular, and that's illustrated, or exemplified just in this room because most of the new people who come, what they know is mindfulness because that's what's readily accessible. The broader context of this is that not all meditations do the same things, nor are they designed to do the same things. There are two broad categories or maybe, if you will, three broad categories of meditation.

The first category is concentration. And when you're engaged in a pure concentration meditation you are focusing on one thing and tuning everything else out. And the goal is to stay on the intended concentration object for longer and longer duration without distraction, or by resisting any distraction. So, there's only two possibilities. Either you're staying on the concentration object or you're off somewhere else, distracted. And if you repeatedly practice that, you're practicing the primary skill of concentration which is staying for extended durations of time.

The word in Tibetan for concentration meditation is *shine* [sounds like shenay]. It's a compound term made up of the word *shiwa* and *neywa*. *Neywa* means to stay. And I like the literal translation of it. So when you're concentrated, you're staying for extended periods of time on whatever the intended concentration object is. And as a consequence of that, all the background noise, particularly of thought activity and other distractions, progressively gets quiet. Calms itself. So, the word for concentration in Tibetan really is *shine* which literally means staying-hyphen-calming meditation. You stay on the object and all that background noise gets increasingly calm.

Now, that's a skill that's not restricted just to meditation but basically is applicable to anything in your life. Think of a time that you are really interested in something. If something really catches your interest you can absorb yourself in whatever that is for long periods of time. Let's say you found a book that you can't put down. You would get so absorbed in that book that other things didn't matter. You could keep a single pointed focus on that book and keep reading it and reading it with sustained concentration. And if you're really completely absorbed in it, you'd certainly be less interested in other things. It might be that you're so absorbed in it that you don't even hear the telephone ring. Or you don't hear other distractions that are going on around you. And you can do that with reading a book. You can do that with absorption in cooking, in art or playing a musical instrument. There are lots of activities of daily living that naturally pull for us to be more concentrated. So, it's not like it's foreign to us.

So, when we concentrate, we get better and better at staying for longer periods of time. And what it involves is staying on one object and resisting the mind going anywhere else. So, there's an interplay here of two things: staying, *newa* on the object, or it's opposite, *yewa*, distraction. Either you're staying or you're distracted.

Now, there's a whole other type of meditation, a class of meditation. And those would be categorized as awareness meditations. In awareness meditation the goal of training the mind is completely different than concentration. The goal is continuity of awareness. Because if we look at ordinary awareness, it's discontinuous. What does that mean? It means that there are chunks missing in our awareness, our lapses, our periods of forgetfulness. I'm always putting my reading glasses down, and I can't seem to find them because of moments of mindlessness. So, in our ordinary everyday life, most of us have periods where we don't have continuous awareness of everything that comes into our field of experience—it's all chunked up with gaps in between where we are basically mindless. So, when you train with an awareness meditation, you're basically trying to approximate the goal of continuous, uninterrupted stream of awareness.

Examples of awareness meditations would be Krishnamurti's Choiceless Awareness; be aware of everything in the moment; every moment by moment by moment without a break, without gaps. *Shikantaza* in "just sitting" style of Zen. They're pure awareness meditations. Aldous Huxley's mynah bird, where the mynah bird was taught to say, [Dan speaks in a high squeaky voice.] "Here now. Here now. Quack. Here now." [Laughter] And it constantly reminded him to stay present in the moment. It was an awareness meditation.

Student 2

An irritating way to learn.

Student 3

It makes you learn faster. [More laughter]

Dan

Now you see there's no concept of distraction in awareness meditation because whatever comes into the field of experience next is the next thing to be mindful of.

Those are the two broad categories of meditation. In the East, the metaphor to understand those two broad categories of meditation is the wild elephant. The ordinary, undisciplined, dysfunctional mind is like a wild elephant. Elephants are very smart and they're very strong, but they also get very afraid, so, on the game preserves if you spook an elephant it will stampede and cause a lot of damage. Our ordinary mind, our daily experience of our mind is like a wild elephant stampeding out of control. So, the whole purpose is to train the mind to discipline it.

So, there are two ways of training an elephant. One is you can tie a chain around the elephant's neck [or leg] and put a stake in the ground and every time the elephant wanders too far it feels the tug of the chain and every time it wanders too far it's pulled back by the tug of the chain, and it tries thousands of times to wander off, and every time it feels the tug of the chain and after a while it learns, it figures out that it's not going to go anywhere, so it stops pulling away. And that's a metaphor for concentration meditation. You tie the rope of concentration on to a concentration object. And whenever the mind wanders off, where does it go? It either wanders off chasing after what, a thought, or sense experience—thought and emotion on the one hand, which includes memory and anticipation of the future, or it wanders off to sensory experiences—chases after that sound or that sight or that smell or that taste or that body sensation.

So, the wild elephant is always chasing after something other than what it's focused on. So, when you train concentration, you tie the rope of concentration on to a concentration object, so that every time it wanders off you pull it back and you keep pulling it back until it stays. If you have to pull it back thousands of times and put a certain effort into bringing it back to the concentration object, the cumulative learning effect is that it stays for longer periods of time. Then after a while it just stays. When you fully concentrate the mind will stay on whatever you intend it to stay on for as long as you want and without any distraction.

When I was in Burma many years ago, the criteria for concentration was that you could stay on the rising and falling of the breath for an hour, have no more than four distracting thoughts, catch the distracting thoughts at the head, and go right back to what you're doing. In the Tibetan system, The Nine Stages of the Elephant Path or The Nine Stages of Staying, the Semnegu, the criterion is that you ought to be able to concentrate on whatever the concentration object is for four hours with no distracting thoughts—a little bit more strict criteria.

So, that's concentration. Either you're focused, concentrated on the object of concentration or you're distracted. You keep bringing it back to the concentration object. We don't care what the concentration object is. It doesn't make any difference whether you use a visual object like an image of the Buddha, a sound like a mantra, the rising and falling of the breath. The object's not important. Staying on the object is the goal of concentration training.

So, in the Indo-Tibetan system, which is Asanga's system developed in the year 506, which is the standard of concentration in all Indo-Tibetan Mahāyāna Buddhism, everybody learns this system. It's called the Semnegu, The Nine Stages of Staying. It's no accident that the title of the concentration is in terms of degrees of staying. It doesn't talk about what you're staying on. It's an object. And the reason for that is, let's say we're focusing on the breath as an object. People will say when they're just learning to do it, "Well should I focus in the tip of my nostrils or should I focus here? Should I focus deep in my belly?

Should the breath be soft or hard?" It doesn't make any difference what the experience of the concentration object is. What makes a difference is staying on the object no matter what. If you start thinking that you have to focus on the … [The sound of someone's phone rings loudly.] See, that's when the mind goes to distraction, see. It goes right to that sound. [Light laughter]

If you think that you should be staying at the tip of the nostrils, what about all the other times the breath is doing something other than that? So, you've got to train yourself out of looking for certain kinds of experiences because no matter what it's doing, it's about staying on that experience of the breath through all the changes, so you've got to track it. And that's why they call it The Nine Stages of Staying. [Someone's phone rings again.] The Nine Stages of Staying, not Nine Stages of What You're Staying On, because you measure progress in terms of degrees of staying. When you're training concentration meditation, a good criterion for making progress is the percentage of the meditation session when you're actually staying on the object. So, most beginners, let's say you meditate for fifteen minutes. You'll be staying less on the object more than on the object in under 50 percent of the session. What it means is you'll be distracted more than you were concentrated on whatever the concentration object is, say the rising and falling of breath.

But when you get pretty good at it, you stay over 50 percent of the time. And when your concentration gets very good, you're up into the 80 to 90 percent range. So, 80 to 90 percent of that session you're staying on the concentration object and your mind's not doing anything else other than staying on the concentration object. When you get up to the range where you're staying 90 to 100 percent of the time, you'll probably notice that there's a substantial reduction in all that background noise of thought. It just stops. Gets kind of quiet in there, and sort of pleasant. So that's pure concentration meditation.

Now awareness meditation is different. And the metaphor for the elephant path would be that instead of tying a chain around the elephant's neck [or leg] and tying a stake into the ground, you don't tie the elephant up at all. You simply watch the elephant and let the elephant wander anywhere it's going, but no matter where the elephant wanders you never take your eyes off that elephant. Whatever the elephant's doing, you stay on it. Because what you're training there is a continuity of awareness without interruption. So, there's no concept of distraction in pure awareness meditation. You're staying present every moment by moment by moment by moment with no gaps or lapses in your awareness. It's hard to be aware of everything in every moment, but you can train yourself to have that kind of awareness present in the world.

Now in this generation of modern neurobiology, we now know that not only does concentration and awareness meditation require a different skill, but it involves different neural circuits of the brain, because we can take a live action shot of what the brain's doing with functional MRI. We can see what areas of the brain get activated by virtue of watching the cerebral blood flow patterns. So, that when people are training concentration, they're using a part of the brain called the ACC or the anterior cingulate cortex. The ACC is activated in divided attention tasks. The way it's traditionally studied in psychology is I would hold up an index card, and on the index card there'd be the text that's written out "green," only the color of the text would be red. And most people do a double take with that. "Do I respond to the color or the text?" So, there's a competing attentional demand, and in order to focus on either the text or the color it requires more effortful concentration to focus on just the text and tune out the color or vice versa. You follow me?

And when you present ordinary people in their daily life with competing attentional tasks like that, the ACC lights up. It gets more activated. The ACC is that area of the brain that's underactive in children and adults who have attention deficit disorder. It's sort of offline. Drugs like Ritalin and Adderall selectively activate the ACC. That's how they work on the brain which is why they're useful in treating ADHD. When people get hypnotized and they go into a hypnotic trance state, the hypnotic induction ceremony activates the ACC. When people do concentration meditation, they activate the ACC. When athletes or other people get into the flow and they get into a peak performance state, when they're really in the flow, they activate the ACC. The brain's sort of an equal opportunity employer. It doesn't seem to care whether you use drugs or mind-body techniques. They all do the same thing. They activate the ACC.

But, that's not the case in terms of ordinary absorbed attention. If you're reading a book in your daily life or being absorbed in watching a play, that doesn't necessarily activate the ACC. It's really heightened state of focused attention, it has a certain intensity to it, and that requires effort.

Now, in this generation of neuroplasticity we know the brain isn't the constant organ. It changes volume and structure depending on use. If we use certain areas of the brain they grow in size and they grow in structure. They put down more white and gray matter. And if you stop using those areas of the brain, they shrink in size and they lose part of their structure. That's why it's so important with elderly people, a lot of the loss of brain structure with what we call normal age-related cognitive decline is because they stop using their brain. But, if they stay active because they're still learning new things and so forth rather than vegging out and watching TV, if they're always learning new things, they keep the brain going. It doesn't lose structure. For example, there are neuroimaging studies that show that people who train concentration meditation have an increased volume of the ACC over time, and there's an increase in white matter with the networks and circuitry that goes into the ACC, and an increase of gray matter within the ACC.

So, what that means in common sense terms is, it's hard work to train concentration. But if you learn it, it sticks after a while because you change the brain structure, so it gets easier to do it. You can generalize it to other things in your life beyond being on the meditation pillow. In my daily life I'm a psychologist and I'm a trauma and abuse expert. So, I'm always testifying in court in trauma and abuse cases on behalf of victims. And that requires memorizing crates of records sometimes. The concentration meditation on the pillow helps with that off the pillow. It just makes you much more efficient in focusing without getting caught up in lots of distractions.

Now awareness meditation is where you're trying to be aware of everything without gaps. It's a different skill. Training for continuity of awareness or what we might call mindfulness is a whole different kind of brain skill. In terms of neurocircuitry, it involves kind of a frontal-parietal loop in certain areas of the parietal system. The right parietal system mainly that has to do with a kind of more broad awareness. It's because it involves a completely different neurocircuitry; it's like training a different skill. So, it's not the case that all meditations are the same. They're very different.

Now, I think what makes that confusing is that the style of meditation that got very popular in the West is Burmese mindfulness, and that's a hybrid system because it combines elements of concentration and elements of mindfulness, but it's neither a pure type of either. And that's because Burmese mindfulness, the one that got popular in the US, was developed by Mahāsī Sayādaw. I learned it from him, in Burma, in the 1970s, directly.

In South Asia, Burmese mindfulness, anthropologists would call "a revitalization movement"—it's not traditional. And what that meant is in South Asia most of the actual meditation practices in Theravāda Buddhism had deteriorated to folk practices —local prayers and chants and things like that. And there was a great vacuum. People wanted to learn traditional meditations. And the traditional model for meditation in Theravāda Buddhism was called the *Visuddhimagga*, or "The Path of Purification." There are two translations of that in English. The best one by Nyanaponika Thera, T-H-E-R-A, is called *The Path of Purification* published by Shambhala.[20]

That's the standard stage model for early Buddhism, step by step, all the meditations. But it's a huge compendium. And not all the meditations are relevant. So, what Mahāsī Sayādaw did is he went through and stripped it down to something much simpler, and made it easy to understand as a direct practice, but he didn't foresee the enormous popularity of that. So, in the first half of the last century, Burmese mindfulness spread throughout Burma. Now there are over two hundred meditation centers in Burma, spread throughout Thailand, Sri Lanka and parts of India. But as a revitalization movement that became very popular, it was a stripped-down version of a much larger system and that means he made some decisions about how to put together this model which is not exactly traditional.

For example, he made two major changes in the traditional way of teaching this. One is that he thought that if you just tell people to be aware of everything, that's impossible because you get so distracted. So, you start by concentrating, so you get modestly concentrated, by using the rising and falling of the breath. And then once you get reasonably concentrated, so it's not all full of distraction or what William James once called, "the buzzing bloom and confusion of the ordinary mind"; once you do that then you then open up your field of awareness and practice trying to be aware of everything in every moment. Tracking whatever comes into your consciousness next, with no concept of distraction. Whatever comes in next is the next object.

But, since he felt that was difficult to tell people, "Just be aware of everything," he made another change. He started using labels. So, when a thought comes into your field of awareness you use the label, "thought." You don't care about the content of the thought, just at that moment thinking is happening. If you have a body sensation, you use the label, "sensation." We don't care about whether it's an itch or a pain just that at that moment you're sensing. If you look at something, in that moment, "seeing." If a sound comes in, in that moment, "hearing." We don't care about the source of the sound or what sound it is, just this, it's "hearing." So, every moment by moment: "Thinking. Thinking.

---

20 We've not been able to find this book listed online.

Hearing. Seeing. Sensing. Thinking." And by the use of those labels, you're approximating the goal of continuous uninterrupted awareness. You follow me?

So, those were the changes. Now the trouble with that, since that became the system that became also very popular not just in South Asia but now in the West is that it is neither a pure type of concentration nor awareness meditation. It's a bit of both, and in the best sense, we could say that it gives you an introduction to a little bit of both concentration meditation and a little bit of awareness meditation. But the criticism that one could then say is that it does neither one of those thoroughly, because it doesn't have some of the basic tools of deep concentration as part of how it's taught, on the one hand, and it's not a pure awareness meditation because of the use of the labels on the other hand.

And if you look at brain functioning, there is an activation both of the ACC, which is the concentration center, and the activation of some of the parietal system, frontal parietal loop, which is part of the mindfulness system. So, it does a lot of things, and it activates other brain areas depending on what your mindful of. So, since a lot of it is being mindful on body sensations, you activate the insula, which is the part of the brain, of the basal ganglia system, that has to do with awareness and representation of body sensations.

So, depending on what you're mindful of, it gets rather complex in there. Not that there's anything wrong with using this system. It just doesn't go far enough with either deep concentration or pure awareness meditation. But as an introduction, it's good. The trouble is, now it's so popular people think it's an end in itself. So, they can't go beyond it to the more traditional meditations. The reason why the more traditional meditations have been around for a long time is because they basically work. But now that mindfulness is popular in the West, where everybody says, "Oh yeah, I know how to meditate," and they never look further into it. But, there's a lot more to this whole world than just trying to approximate mindfulness.

Now in both of these systems—pure awareness meditations and concentration meditations—there's something else that you're using. And that is your own metacognitive intelligence. And metacognition is the ability to reflect on your state of mind and see it for what it is, and to make changes. If you're learning a new skill, like for the first time and it's complicated, like driving a car, some people keep making the same old mistakes over and over again because they're not looking at it metacognitively. But if they're looking at it metacognitively, some people know what mistakes they're making. They self-correct. They're aware of their own strategies to solve the task. So, they keep correcting it and self-correcting and they learn much quicker. Now metacognition has caught on in teaching math education. Kids are taught to think through and to be aware of strategies they use to solve their problems. And you can technically get the answer wrong and a good grade if you can illustrate the metacognitive steps in it, because people learn quicker when they have metacognitive capacity. And that's not just true for learning math; it's true for learning meditation.

It's not enough to just sit quietly. You have to use your best metacognitive intelligence to evaluate the quality of the sitting so you're always improving it. There's a Sufi tale that says, "A log sits very quietly on a wood pile for years, but logs never realize God. So don't sit like a log. Sit intelligently." You have to reflect on the quality of the meditation.

Now in terms of modern functional neuroimaging studies, part of the executive control system, what we call the right dorsolateral prefrontal cortex, which is up here [Dan gestures to the left side of his forehead], whoops wrong side, here [changes hands to show the location on the right side of his forehead]. [Laughter] So right here, that part of the brain is part of the executive system that is activated when we're involving our metacognition in our tasks.

And there are studies … there's one study that shows the difference between people learning concentration meditation who are more beginning and more advanced. And from a neuroimaging point of view, both the beginning and the advanced concentrators activated the ACC, as we would expect. And the fundamental difference between the advanced practitioners and the beginning practitioners was the activation of the right dorsolateral prefrontal cortex. In other words, the advanced practitioners were advanced because they figured out that they had to use their metacognition to constantly evaluate the quality of it. That's not thinking about it. Just seeing it the way it is. Seeing it the way it is at very high speeds with awareness, and then making the adjustment. So, they're constantly making adjustments at very high speed with the lightning speed of awareness. And they learn much quicker. So, using metacognition or what the Tibetans call *shezhi*, which the Dalai Lama translates as "metacognitive awareness" these days, is necessary if you want to advance with meditation practice.

So, those are the basic skills to mind training. They're not just useful in meditation. They're useful in everything that we do. Training yourself to concentrate and tune out all the distraction; being continuously present to whatever comes in our field of awareness without being out of it; these are not just things to do on the pillow. They're necessary skills for everyday living.

But being more concentrated and/or being more continuously aware are not ends in themselves. They're just the very beginning of a rather long path of mind training. There's nothing useful about just training the mind to be more concentrated or more mindful or more aware without thinking of the larger picture of where these pathways take you to. And, essentially where they take you to depends on the level of the Buddhist tradition we're talking about.

You wouldn't say as Westerners that all Christianity is the same. I mean, there's a common factor, that you have to believe in Jesus in Christianity, but there are fundamental distinctions we could make between different denominations. Not the least of which is the difference between Catholicism or Protestantism. Or the huge difference between Roman and Greek Orthodox Catholicism. Huge differences. So, why would we think it would be any less complicated when we get to something like Buddhism.

Not all Buddhism is the same. And within Buddhism there are three fundamental layers of the Buddhist tradition. They're called The Three Turnings of the Wheel of the Dharma. And I like to think about them very much like how we think of scientific revolutions in the West. We think that the world is flat, and then at some point we collect enough anomalous evidence that somebody puts it together in a whole new way and we get a different world. Then we see the world as round, and some see a number of exceptions to Newtonian physics and then we get a whole new paradigm shift to quantum mechanics. So, it's like that within Buddhism. There's The First Turning of the Wheel, and then there's a whole new shift to something completely different.

The First Turning of the Wheel is the teachings of Shakyamuni Buddha. The Truth of Suffering; The Four Noble Truths and The Pathway Out of Suffering. That's pretty much early Buddhism—The First Turning of the Wheel. The main pathway is the *Visuddhimagga*, The Path of Purification, the step-by-step meditation. There's a way out of suffering.

The Second Turning of the Wheel is Mahāyāna Buddhism. And there, there was the notion of emptiness and the *bodhisattva* activity. Those are the main necessary ingredients. And what changed that was really it came out of a debate about meditation, because in the earlier turning of the wheel, you get to a point where you get deeply concentrated and there's no more thoughts coming up and you shift over to what's called the subtle level of mind where everything is reduced to quick bursts of movement and energy. And you watch everything just like a quick burst of movement and energy arise and disappear, arise and disappear. And if you keep watching that over time at some point the whole thing begins to break up. It's called, *bunganyana*, or dissolution experience. It's not very pleasant. But, if those basic, observable elements in your mind break up, you can see that there's kind of large, mirror-like awareness that's no longer distracted by all that activity of the mind. If you look into the nature of that awareness, it opens up a possibility for awakening, what's called First Path in that system.

However, some years later Nagarjuna came along, and he said, "When things come and go, come and go, come and go, after a while naturally you focus on the going and everything starts to break up. That's all true. But the whole idea of things coming and going is its own illusion. What if time is not real, but it's just another construction of mind?" So he developed this funny thing called "The Nagarjuna Dialectic," and if you look at it in a certain way, if whenever something comes in time you look at it as if it doesn't really come up in time because it's already here, then whenever it goes away, you look at it as if it doesn't go anywhere but it stays here, that's going to screw around with your direct experience of time.

And if you do that meditation just right the whole thing busts open, and you end up with an experience of the mind where everything is here simultaneously and interconnected. That's a very different experience. And there are certain meditations that will open this up. And if you do, you'll have the direct experience of everything being interconnected and everyone being interconnected. Out of that comes a different way of viewing activity in the world, like the *bodhisattva* path, that what you do actually affects everybody else. So, how you act towards other people matters.

So, that began what we call The Second Turning of the Wheel. And the other thing that was different is, rather than trying to make certain states go away, like you're trying to make suffering go away, the other big, huge part of The Second Turning of the Wheel was the idea that everything is just a construction. Our sense of self is a construction. Our sense of time is a construction, and the one thing that we do, the way the mind works, is to construct things. I wasn't born with a psychological sense of self. I wasn't born with Dan-ness. Western psychologists tell us the psychological sense of self develops at about eighteen months, roughly corresponding to when children have the capacity for representational thinking.

This convention of time takes about eight years before we develop it in childhood. But once we develop these structures of mind, they're useful in everyday life. The sense of self becomes a central organizing principle. Everything gets organized in my life about Dan-ness. So, sense of self or personal identity becomes a central organizing principle. Later, time becomes a central organizing principle. It's how we can get by and make deadlines and live in a social world. And in relative reality it's useful to develop these constructions of mind, but what Buddhists tell us is that the mistake that we make is once we develop these constructions, because that's what the mind does, we forget that they're constructions. That's called *nozhin* in Tibetan, taking it too real; it's close to the English word reify. I actually think that Dan exists. As a result of that I take Dan way too seriously. I actually think that time exists. I think there's an independently existing external cosmic time clock. I locate it in Greenwich. And what Buddhists say is, "No, they're just constructions."

What Buddhists say is that emptiness is a constructivist theory. Emptiness means just a construction of mind. It doesn't mean that things don't exist. It means that they exist as constructions, and in relative reality they're useful constructions. But here's the problem: ultimately, they're just constructions and when we forget that they're just constructions, there are two consequences. One is *dzin-pa*, things have grab. Dan has a lot of grab. If you don't like what I'm saying, you criticize me—grab. If you like it, praise me—grab. If we have a dispute about something—grab. Grab is perceivable. And we organize most of our life around experiences of self-grab.

The other consequence is *mümpa*, the capacity to obscure. It clouds over seeing into the real nature of the mind. So, the big turning of the wheel in Mahāyāna Buddhism was then if you do emptiness practice, you're not getting rid of anything, you're getting rid of its capacity to obscure. You see its true nature as just a construction in a way that it doesn't get in the way.

And then in The Third Turning of the Wheel are what are called the Essence traditions. The huge change was two things. One: a view of the mind that we all have buddha nature. Every one of us is awake all the time, but that awakening is clouded over so we don't realize it. And the other thing that goes with that is that when the mind gets clouded over, we can't see the original purity of the mind and all of the positive qualities. So, there's much more in the Essence traditions like Mahāmudrā—the Great Seal meditation, and Dzogchen—the Great Completion meditation, and the *tantras.* Those are all Essence traditions. There's much more emphasis on the positive qualities of our original nature. So, not all Buddhism is the same.

The Essence tradition means that what we do is we use emptiness practice to remove the clouds layer by layer. So, the first cloud is thought. We get so caught up in thought we think our whole world is thought. In the Essence traditions, the whole key is understanding in our direct experience the nature of awakened awareness. It's always here, you're awake all the time, you just don't recognize it. If it's dark clouds and rainy out, we can't see the sun. But after the clouds clear and the sun comes out, what do we say? "The sun just came out." Is that true? The sun's always shining, but we couldn't see it, so it appears like it comes out only after the clouds are removed. And it's like that with essence meditation practice. If you remove the clouds enough, the radiant awake mind shines forth enough. You can say, "See, it's here. Always right here." So, the practice in the Essence tradition is to remove the clouds layer by layer until there are no clouds left. And then your radiant and awakened nature just shines forth all the time … until you crud it up and cloud it over again, which is probably immediately. Then you have to practice developing it.

So, what do we do? It's all about the nature of awakened awareness. The key to understanding the Essence traditions is about awareness. So, we confuse awareness with thought. We think that thought and awareness are the same thing. But if you concentrate enough all that thought activity winds down and stops so you get big periods of stillness. During the periods of stillness there's a window of opportunity to look purely into the nature of awareness as something different from thought.

Once you can see that awareness and operate out of that awareness rather than operating out of being lost in thought mode, you've made a shift. You're directly operating out of a pure field of awareness (we call that *rigpa*) rather than thought. But then that awareness is all clouded up and mixed up with our personal identity. I'm operating out of Dan-ness, but if I do emptiness of self meditation, I don't have to get rid of Dan, I just have to get rid of Dan's capacity as a construction of mind to obscure. I'll go beyond it. Then I can, with emptiness of self meditations, I can open up a level of awareness that's gone beyond personal identity. We call that awareness itself.

Now if I go back to meditating and my basis of operation is that of pure awareness itself, it's not Dan doing the meditation, it's the awareness doing the meditation. It's going to do a better job. But that awareness will still fluctuate in the convention of time. And if I do the emptiness of time meditation, I see that time is just an empty construction of mind. I'll go beyond time and then I'll open up a level of awareness that's absolutely beyond time—can't ever change. That's sort of convenient because if I open up that level of awareness I can't lose it, because losing it means it goes away in time. And since time and space are related, if I do that meditation correctly, it's going to open up this awareness that's absolutely huge. We call that ocean-like, changeless, boundless awareness. That's a big shift. Changeless, boundless awareness, going way beyond the convention of time.

But I'm still operating within the constraints of my individual consciousness and my information processing system. You see, the trouble here now is that always right here is this infinite, boundless ocean of awakened awareness-love, but we don't realize it. In every moment, my information processing system partializes things that obscure that unbounded wholeness. Every time I think about something or engage in thought, thought by definition conceptualizes, partializes. If it's this, it's not that, so it can't be the whole. So, every instance of conceptualizing clouds over my true nature. Every instance of paying attention clouds over my true nature. If I'm focusing on this, I'm not focused on that. And the quickest operation of our information processing system the Tibetans call particularizing—the tendency of the mind towards something that makes it something particular. It's like an action potential. It's before stimulus perception.

If I say, "Look at the entire room and take in everything all at once and nothing in particular, try and get the whole show at once"; do it now—take everything in. What happens as soon as you try and hold the panoramic view? You can see the mind going to pick out certain things. Every one of those high-speed movements, in that moment I'm partializing.

So, in the advanced meditations you're given certain instructions that would help you to cut through, to see beyond that, all those tendencies to partialize, so you're operating out of being that unbounded wholeness—that vast ocean of awakened awareness-love. We call those "crossing-over" instructions. Once you're operating out of that, so you're operating out of that ocean of awakened awareness-love at all times and stabilize that, it will fundamentally change your nature.

That whole path in the Essence traditions is described in the mantra of the heart sutra, which is why it's very popular. [*Gate* is pronounced gah-tay] *Gate gate pāragate pārasamgate bodhi svāhā.* There's your whole path. Literally it means, "Gone, gone, gone way beyond, gone way way beyond, ooooh what a realization."

So, to translate: First you're lost in thought, you practice concentration, and you open up that stillness, and you can finally see directly into the nature of awareness, which is different than thought. That's the first *gate.* Awareness, *rigpa*, gone beyond thought. But you're still caught up in your sense of self, your personal identity. You practice emptiness of self meditation, you move beyond personal identity. That's the second *gate*. Awareness itself gone beyond personal identity. But that awareness is fluctuating in time. If you do the emptiness of time meditations, that's a huge shift to changeless boundless, ocean-like awareness; that's *pāragate*. Changeless, boundless awareness gone way beyond the convention of time. But you're still caught up in the moment of instant-by-instant information processing system. And with the crossing-over instructions, you go way beyond that, and you are that unbounded wholeness of awakened awareness-love. That's a big shift. *Pārasamgate*, gone way, way beyond the constraints of your information processing system to awakened awareness. Ooooh, what a realization, *bodhi svāhā*. It's your whole path. Why is the mantra popular? Because it defines the whole path. It's not even hard to do.

So, here's the problem. There are three maps in Buddhism. The whole basic idea here is if you follow this path, there are three maps. There's the map that takes you from the very beginning of this to a taste of awakening, to getting a taste of being that great ocean. That will change everything. In some ways it's the end of the path because there's no more longing. You've done that one. You've found your way home. Changes everything. But you've got to stabilize it, and that's the beginning of the path. Then there's a whole other set of teachings, particularly in Dzogchen, that help you stabilize that awakening so you have it all the time and it never can possibly go away. And when you have it all the time you've finished the second map. And then when you have it all the time, so it stays automatically, then you develop that to full buddhahood. We reserve the word enlightenment for full buddhahood.

Along the way, you stop the formation of all new karmic memory traces and their ripening. And there are certain meditations that will open it up, so that you'll automatically release the entire storehouse of all previous karmic impressions. It's called the path of *dharmadhātu* exhaustion. And the endpoint of that is there are no negative states left. Then what will flourish are all the positive states of your original buddha nature. There are eighty positive states of mind that just cascade, flourish. That's what the Tibetan word for buddha means. *Sangye*. It's a compound term. *Sangwa* means the purification of all negative states. *Gyewa* means the flourishing of all positive states, one of the properties of buddha mind.

Nothing is solid at that point in terms of the perceptual world. You live in a world of light and energy. Everything is illusory, not solid. Including the body.

The body becomes clear light body. And then the big change is you open up all-at-onceness. This bubble that we all think we live within, what if that's just one little bubble? At some point you "crack the eggshell," as we say in Dzogchen, and there are millions of worlds that are here all at once, simultaneously, and your mind pervades all those worlds, past, present and future. It lives in all those simultaneously with inexhaustible energy that helps beings across all those realms. That opening up all-at-onceness is truly stunning. You're locking into the structure of reality. If you open that up … when you die you lose your form body, but you never die. You don't even recycle yourself at that point. You can come back and work on any plane of reality in any way you want for as long as you want, or many planes simultaneously, for the sake of helping beings in this mess that we've made.

So, that's the whole path. And my concern is that as meditations get popular in the West, they become an end in themselves. It's not about a meditation technique. I'm concerned about how many people in the West teach meditation and they never talk about awakening. Why are we doing this? It's not about sitting on the pillow. It's not about even concentrating or training to be mindful.

Rechung, a contemporary of Milarepa, says there are different levels of awareness. In the heart sutra mantra, we keep opening up each level of awareness until there's no clouds left, and then our real awakened nature is obviously always right here. It's closer than you think. But if we don't talk about that as the goal, what are we doing?

Mindfulness is good to train the first step. Burmese mindfulness is very good to get a sense of continuous non-reactive awareness, but there's nothing in that particular style of mindfulness teaching that comes from Mahāsī Sayādaw that deals with emptiness of self or anything like that. Why? Because what he did is—this is a revitalization tradition in the *Visuddhimagga*, which was the original source—he stripped out the aggregate practice, which is the meditation on self. I find that very interesting that that's the meditation that got very popular in the West. [Laughter]

Now we have thousands of people teaching mindfulness, and they're very mindful and very filled with themselves. We forget this basic lesson. If you learn anything in spiritual practice, it's this: Self-importance is not important. One of my students sent me this wonderful cartoon that says, "I looked into the bigger picture in life. I wasn't in it." [Laughter]

So, it becomes a new form of self-importance. "I'm a mindfulness teacher. I'm a mindfulness practitioner." What good is it? Because it lacks the techniques to go beyond self and see into the deeper picture. And it lacks any articulation explicitly that the goal is not to be mindful. You can be a mindful asshole. The goal is to fundamentally change, and you look into the real nature of the mind and the outcome of that is always conduct —how you manifest spontaneous conduct that's helpful to other people. And if you really train in these practices, you'll move beyond awakening to open up all the positive qualities of the mind.

There are eighty positive qualities of a buddha mind. It's not good enough to use the first level of Buddhism and say, "Everything is suffering." There are mindfulness people in this country that have been, have worked on mindfulness for forty years and they're still talking about everything is suffering. Well, what happened to the rest of Buddhism? Buddhism went beyond that a long time ago. And none of these individuals talk about the positive qualities of the mind.

In Mahāyāna Buddhism, the positive qualities of the mind are explicit as things that we train. Matthieu Ricard was a French molecular biologist, a scientist, who, at the age of twenty, dropped out of molecular biology and became a Tibetan monk. He's practiced for thirty years, mostly in the Gelugpa tradition, particularly Rime. And what does he practice? He practices largely compassion meditations. That's his main practice. Richy Davidson, a meditator who's also probably one of the best neurobiologists in this country brought him into his lab and looked at the neuroimaging and compared it to norms that we have for regions of interest in the brain. And what did he find for somebody who spent thirty years practicing compassion meditations? That the medial orbital prefrontal cortex, which is the positive emotions part of the brain and the social center of the brain, was very well developed and activated through these practices. He trained himself to be a better person, as illustrated by the areas of the brain that developed.

A person who is consistently concerned about other people is not selfish, and he's happy most of the time. It's not about the end of suffering. The absence of suffering is not a positive thing. You have to cultivate the positive states. Mindfulness as we teach it in this country doesn't address that explicitly enough, except through the Four Immeasurables. And there's a whole world of practices that go beyond the foundation of the Four Immeasurables that handle that in much more depth. So, we need to step back and say, "What are we doing here? Where do we want these paths to go?" Not all paths take us to the same place. It matters that you know about that and think about where you're being taken.

If the path leads to awakening, you're on the right track. If you practice them for years and it hasn't led to awakening, then something isn't right, either with the method or how you're going about it, or how it's being taught. If the path leads to buddhahood, you're on the right track. Anything less than that ... maybe you ought to look at that.

Buddhahood is achievable in a single lifetime with the right methods and the right teachings. Life is very short and precious. Don't waste it on something that's not going to bring you there, because if we want to get out of this mess, we all have to do it by evolving ourselves. And choosing the right methods that are going to evolve you matters. It's not all the same. So maybe this is, with the popularity of all this, maybe it's worth some stepping back and taking a larger look at the bigger picture here.

May 21, 2014

Themes: Dealing with Aging and Dying; The Four Attitudes

Dan

Welcome everyone. You have a question?

Student 1

Well, this has to do with things that I've been noticing about work, and things that are coming up around work, and that is that when new patients come into the facility, and I go to meet them, often times they have a lot of worries and concerns, and their family members have a lot of worries and concerns and I'm recognizing that, that we all bring issues and things and concerns to these kinds of new situations. And so, I'm wondering: how can I be of most benefit, be most helpful in these kinds of situations.

Dan

So, it's really about people who come into the nursing home for the first time, and they deal with all the concerns of their adjustment to that phase of life, and all their family's concerns. Is that specifically what you're asking?

Student 1

Yes, and we have staff members also bring our own worries and concerns and stuff to the situation as well.

Dan

Well, the larger issue in that question is how as a culture we deal or don't deal with the issue of an aging population. It was striking when we went with Rinpoche this last visit to Kham, Eastern Tibet, because Kham is a nomad country, Tibetan cowboy country. And the nomads live mostly in tents off the land, raising cows and yak. And I mean the yak is their life, the same way that Native Americans of the Plains, the buffalo was their life. But what was really most interesting was to see not just the single nomad family tents, but what a nomad village looked like, because what they had is all the tents were arranged as spokes around a wheel. And in the hub of the wheel was one large tent, and that's where all the elderly people lived. And the entire village, as a village, takes care of the elderly every day—everybody participates in it. It's very touching. Aging isn't old there, most people die around fifty, maybe sixty. I remember this old woman, who was eighty-four—which is unusually elderly, nobody lives that long. But she couldn't walk, and she was mostly blind. Rinpoche is eighty-two now. And she knew him way back when, because they're the same age. So, she was very heavy, the villagers carried her all the way to the tent where we were having a Padmasambhava festival, and carried her in by hand so that she could meet her old friend again and pay her respects and get his blessing. It was so moving. And the idea was everybody just did it because that's their duty.

So, the entire village participates in the process of aging, and what we would call hospice care, right to the point of death. Here, aging and death is messy. We just don't deal with it. As a psychologist for twenty-five years teaching continuing education classes, one year I reviewed all the psychology of aging work and decided to do a course on the psychology of aging. My total enrollment was six mental health professionals. It's the lowest enrolled course I've ever had, ever. And that tells you something. So, the attitude in this culture is we don't want to deal with aging. We don't want to deal with death until it happens, and it sort of ambushes us. And the best is that you'll assign it to professionals to deal with it, so you [the professionals] get to deal with it. So, the families don't have to deal with it.

So, when somebody comes in to any one of your facilities, the family is totally unprepared. So, there's a lot of stuff to deal with. And they don't want the burden of it, but they feel guilty for not wanting the burden of it. And of course, much more than one sees in the arena of weddings and funerals, all the family dynamics get played out. [Dan laughs.] You know exactly what I'm talking about. So, whatever the conflicts, the unfinished business of the family may be, you know it gets played out in the facility. Whether it be nursing home or palliative care, or hospice, it gets played out, all the way to the end.

So, I mean the best way of dealing with that … a simple Buddhist answer is compassion, but I don't think that's good enough. You have to know something about it. It's more in the wisdom aspect than the compassion aspect. I mean they're both necessary. But it means you need to know something about the aging process. You need to know something about the dying process and the stages of that, and how the individual deals with it internally. And you need to know something about how families deal with it or don't deal with it, because there are many, many complex levels of this. And with an aging population, it's not going to go away.

And for families, there's a remarkable opportunity there, I think. You get a chance to work it out differently. You know, as a psychologist, I spent about four years, twice a week in therapy, and then nine years, four times a week on the couch in analysis. That's a lot of therapy. But I have to say that the thing that settled my own attachment issues with my parents was caring for them when they were elderly and being a good attachment figure towards them the way that they couldn't towards me. And I walked away free. I didn't foresee that result. I was just trying to do the right thing. But it had a profound effect on me personally. Because in caring for elderly parents, you get to be different, and the roles switch—you get to be the parent, and they get to be the child. And based on their limitations, which you know better than anybody else, you actually have a remarkable opportunity to do it differently and get it right for both of you.

And I think to lose sight of that opportunity is really to miss something important. When families dump their parents in the nursing home, or palliative care center and then let them deal with us professionals, they're missing out on something terribly important. But that's where your own practice comes in.

In the early 1990s, which was the height of all the research on psychoneuroimmunology—which is now the biggest word in the dictionary—a husband-and-wife team, Ronnie Glazer and Janice Kiko Glazer, did work on the effects of various stressors on different immune measures—what causes the kind of chronic suppression of the efficiency of immune functioning. And what their research showed was, in terms of the immune functioning in the body, the winner, hands up, nothing else came close to it in terms of stressors and their effect on the body and the immune system, was caring for an elderly parent. It was number one on the list.

It's very stressful to do, because as an adult, it encroaches on everything you put together in your own life, having separated from those parents, and forces you to leave all of that and the busyness of all that, and to provide a level of caring in ways that you never quite got, and to do it anyway. Of course, it's much easier if you can do that with a practice, because it gives you the presence of mind and maybe even the larger vision in terms of why that might be important. But if you can frame it that way, it's a rich thing to do. And you can do it without undue stress on the body.

My mother had lived with me recovering from four heart surgeries before she died. Every time she had another one, she'd come up to Boston and do it and I'd take care of her. So, when she died, I felt complete. There was no unfinished business between us. Whatever complaints I might have had over the years, which I might have given voice to in therapy, because that's where we blame mothers for everything, I didn't have any complaints anymore. I was just done, in a good way. And there was a kind of contentment in my life.

In this culture, you don't get the support to see that what you're doing is so valuable. Maybe as the culture is aging even more, there'll be some appreciation for the kind of work we're trying to do. It's a bizarre culture in that way, because so much of it is about accumulating more stuff, more wealth. And the two things which are most important, we don't value. We don't value the caretaking of our elderly. Like in other cultures the elderly are seen as wise, and they're given a certain respect. Here, we basically die alone. At a certain level, you die alone, no matter what. You can get support for dying alone.

And, we don't value our teachers. So, the things that are most important to us, our children and the education development of our children, we're entrusting children to teachers, entrusting our own parents to nursing home and palliative care workers; hospice workers. The very people that were most involved and we love the most, we don't value what happens to them. What a bizarre culture. That's how selfish it's become.

Maybe … I mean I think the best way of handling that so you don't distance yourself, which is what we do, is impermanence practice. And when you do that as a meditation, the best practice is to visualize all the steps in your own aging process, do your own dress rehearsal, your own aging process, and dying process. Go through all the steps of it, right through dying. And keep doing that. Put your face right in it, until there's no fear left and no avoidance.

In Western psychotherapy, in all the schools of therapy, one of the ones that is the most effective is exposure-based cognitive behavioral therapy. What did we learn in fifty years of exposure-based therapy? The greater the avoidance, the more likely exposure-based treatments work. If it's something you want to put out of your mind, the more you go running to it, it's no longer a problem. And that's true for generalized anxiety and pain and panic and phobias and lots of other things—trauma. And it's like that here, too. Impermanence meditation is viewed in Western terms as very strong exposure therapy. And they work by the same rules. Our own aging and dying process is the thing that we most avoid. So, put your face right into it. Stop avoiding it.

The best thing that happens out of that is there's not a fear of dying. The best thing that happens from that is life gets very precious, and you stop wasting it on stupid stuff. All of this is contained in Tibetan Buddhism as part of preliminary practice. And there's a whole world of preliminary practices, but there are four broad areas of things that you need to accomplish to "build the vessel" of the mind before you can do meditations like concentration, and then emptiness, and insight practice.

And the first of those is motivational practices. Why do we need them? They're no different from Western research on stage of change practices, what makes people motivated to be in therapy and stick. What makes people motivated to do a spiritual practice and set that as a priority in their life? And the answer to that in Indo-Tibetan Buddhism is what's called *lözhi* practice, the Four Attitudes. And they're designed to be done in the context of everyday life.

In other words, you don't sort of suddenly go off and start doing spiritual practice. Suddenly, you get bitten by the bug. You come here and you get excited by the meditation and you drop everything in your life and you want to go and meditate all the time. Tibetans call that *charinyenju*, "hairy renunciation"—it's an idiom. And hairy renunciation can't stick. You get really excited, you go off and do something, it's over idealized, it's unrealistic, and the higher the expectations, the greater the disappointment, the disillusionment. And then you drop it and you never go back to it. And that kind of motivation they say is harmful.

So, the better motivation is to stay in the context of everyday life, do exactly what you're doing, and do these little visualizations each day and slowly it begins to change your attitude. The first you know, when you go on the retreats, *daljor*, precious opportunity.

You imagine all sorts of difficult life circumstances of different people other than yourself, and having visualized the difficulties that would have made it difficult to actually get the precious teachings, you then put yourself in that situation as if that were you. And then you contrast that to what you now have. And each time you do a visualization, dissolve it, contrast that to what you've now got, it hammers home the point of the preciousness of this. The fact that you have reasonable health, you have all your mental faculties, the way many people don't. The fact that you live in a time and geographic area which is relatively stable and not war torn. The fact that you live in a time where there are many teachings available, that so many other people will never live at those times. The fact that you have the life circumstances to actually practice. When you go through a systematic series of visualizations, each time it intensifies the preciousness of what you've got. That's the first *lözhi*.

The second is *girdundrebu*, cause and effect. Every action has karmic consequences. Everything that you do, both in mind and behavior, form *bakchaks*, karmic traces, and those get put in *kunzhi namshe*, the store house consciousness; and they eventually ripen. And when they ripen, they influence first the spontaneously emerging states of mind. All of the spontaneously emerging ripening states of mind come from ripening karmic impressions. Then as they get more strength, they influence our behavior, not in ways that are obvious. And last, they influence the unfolding of events in our life, the fortunate and unfortunate things that happen to us. All the ripening of karmic impressions.

If you want to see the fast-track ripening of karmic impressions, you do dream yoga, because that's when they ripen the most, in dream states. So, what you do is a kind of cost-benefit analysis, in Western terms. You reflect on various actions you engage in, and then you imagine or anticipate the likely outcomes of that over time. And by doing that with all of your actions that you spend some time in, you suddenly see that a lot of things you engage in aren't terribly important, and they're not going to have fruitful consequences. And you slowly start disengaging from all the extraneous stuff that we do in our life, because it doesn't matter.

And then the third of the *lözhi*, the third of the four notions or four attitudes, is the sufferings of *samsāra* you go through, the visualization of the suffering of all the realms of different beings. So, you can grasp the full extent of the suffering. It's like your own individualized Dante's *Inferno* journey.

And then the fourth and the last is impermanence. You visualize that everything in your life changes and doesn't last. All the material possessions that you've had don't last. Think of how many relationships that were important to you that you don't have anymore. Then you think about your own aging process and you visualize in detail all the steps of that and your own dying process, culminating in visualizing your own dying.

If you repeat that visualization, the consequence or the cumulative effect of doing these *lözhi* practices is that you find that you sort of naturally disengage from all the stuff in everyday life that doesn't matter. And your own spiritual development begins to matter more. How you treat people begins to matter more. You change your attitudes. (Alan Wallace put out a book on the *lojong*.[21] I like the title of the book. It's called *Buddhism with an Attitude*. So, that's *lojong* practice.) And if you do the [*lözhi*] practice, it will clean up all your extraneous involvements in life.

It's a good preliminary practice. In fact, in the Bon system, the Akhrid system of Dzogchen, which is the fourteen sessions from the very beginning of the practice to buddha, stripped down to fourteen lessons, each takes a week long. Some of you did that course. It's interesting; there's no emptiness of self practice in that system. It's implied in the impermanence meditation. If you go through your own aging and dying process, emptiness of self is sort of accomplished through that process because visualizing your own dying process will level any self-importance. Somebody once sent me this wonderful cartoon. It said, "I looked at the big picture in life. I wasn't in it." If you learn anything from spiritual practice, it's that self-importance isn't terribly important. And impermanence practice is the gateway to emptiness of self, or another way of saying that is impermanence practice is the remedy for self-importance.

I once asked my Root Lama [Geshe Wangyal] years ago, what was the best remedy for spiritual pride. And he said, "Enumerate all the immeasurable beings in this universe that are suffering, countless numbers, and somewhere along the line you lose your self-importance." It's a powerful practice.

---

21 *Lojong* usually refers to Atisha's "Seven Point Mind Training," whereas *lözhi* is called "The Four Attitudes" or "The Four Thoughts that Turn the Mind," and is generally considered a related but more basic training.

So, you see if you do these, then you're going to be a strange being, because you're going to be a being that's not afraid of dying. And as you know, if you do the practices enough, there is no dying. If you develop your awakening, it's not possible to die. The body dissolves, that's just the body. In Tibetan terms, we all have what sometimes translates as an "indestructible essence." It's like a little computer chip of awareness. And that indestructible essence is uniquely a signature to you. And that indestructible essence is lodged within the center of the heart at conception and held there by energy knots. And during the dying process, the energy knots loosen, and the indestructible essence is released from its lodging in the heart, and settles into the central channel, and stays in the central channel for up to three days—not three days, but up to three days. It could leave immediately. And at some point, it leaves the dying physical body through some orifice. And how it leaves in the circumstances determines how it will recycle itself. But it survives the physical death.

So, after dying, in the *bardo* states, you have a mental body not a physical body. But the mental body still has certain faculties. It can see things. It can hear things. It can touch things. And it has supernormal abilities, so a thought, it can go anywhere it wants just by intending where to go. But it doesn't have a physical body. Rinpoche says, "When you die, indestructible essence sort of like a homeless person looking for a body." And depending on the circumstances of dying, it recycles itself.

Now that seems very strange to us. But if you practice and you have a taste of awakening and stabilize that, you see that the nature of awakened awareness is never localized in the body, it only seems to be localized in the body. It is not limited to what happens to the body. So, you can't die from that perspective. The body dies, but the awakened awareness just continues.

And if you do certain practices like *phowa*, which means consciousness transference, you can actually get voluntary control over how you want to recycle that essence. You can recycle yourself to come back to help beings, in any plane of reality that you want, or simultaneous planes of reality, because you have control over that process.

It's possible to have voluntary control over the dying process. So those teachings are helpful because then you can come back and help out some more with the mess we've made here. And great beings who have profound realizations have complete control over how they want to come back. You know that process in the word *tulku*, which means "an emanating being." They can intend to come back in any form that they want, in any plane of realty, in any geographic location, in any time span in history for the sake of helping or teaching. And they emanate for a certain period of time, and then they disappear.

Like Rinpoche, he's a *tulku*—starting in the thirteenth century in his area of Kham—and he recycles himself in the same geographic area every time, except he's told his monastery that that's the end of the line. He's not going to come back there. So, he's giving them his final teachings, which is writing a Tibetan commentary on the *Bochicharyavatara*, which he's writing right now and leaving behind. That will be his last testament to his people.

There's an interesting Western equivalent to this idea of indestructible essence. You know, in science we don't deal with this kind of stuff, but not entirely. There are exceptions. The great American psychologist William James, 150 years ago, was terribly interested in the survival of the human personality beyond bodily death. And his best friend was a Brit by the name of F.W.H. Myers who wrote a rather extensive book on his own studies. I think the book is called *Survival of the Human Personality and its Survival of Bodily Death.*[22] So, it was actually a topic that was discussed among respectable scientists in the Victorian era, quite openly until the rise of behaviorism and then it disappeared.

I remember once when His Holiness the Dalai Lama wanted to study miraculous abilities like flying through the air and making elements and becoming invisible. So, he asked me whether scientists would study this; so I talked with many scientists about that. Most of them wouldn't touch it. I found one scientist who was studying psychic abilities, head of the engineering school at Princeton, who was open to the idea. So, I set up a private meeting with him and the Dalai Lama with the understanding there'd be no press.

He [H.H. the Dalai Lama] didn't come; he sent his assistant because he didn't trust there was going to be no press. He was only two hours from where the meeting was, [so] his assistant came and saw there was just the Dalai Lama and herself and me, and then she called her boss and said, "Look, there's no press here. You really have to come right away." So, he raced his car, and he and the Dalai Lama spent a whole day together talking about this stuff. It was a wonderful private Dalai Lama. I got to hear it all. But most scientists won't do that if it's controversial. I suppose that means scientists should practice emptiness of self.

---

22 *Human Personality and Its Survival of Bodily Death*—essays collected and published posthumously in two large volumes in 1903.

But you see, if you do these practices, you're preparing for your own journey. If you awaken and you use the Dzogchen practices to open up the view so that every time you set up the view you shift your basis of operation to awakening, and then you have that awakening more frequently and for longer duration, and open up more easily, it's like a learned pathway. And as you know, the goal of that is that you have the awakening all the time and at all times and all situations, as Patrul's commentary to Garab Dorje's teaching says, "Continuous flow of awakened awareness with the ups and downs of the *dharmakāya* at all times in all situations," after a while, it's not possible for that awakening to ever leave.

When things cloud over, it's like a very thin veil. The intention to look is always here. If you have that, how do you think that's going to affect the dying process? You're well prepared, and all that stuff that comes up isn't going to affect the awakening. It just won't. The greatest test of your practice is how you die. If your realization is conceptual, it will fall apart. You're going to have trouble with the dying. You'll say, "Oh shit, I'm not prepared for this." But if your practice is strong, you welcome the dying process. It's your friend. Just a change in the state. It's a good test; practice.

They say a teacher's greatest testament is how they die. My first Root Lama Geshe Wangyal, we had the privilege of being there when he was dying. And he gave us a live commentary on his dying process up until the point that he couldn't talk anymore. It was amazing to watch. He had advanced liver cancer. I remember at one point, him throwing up lots of blood and we just sat there in horror. And he very kindly said, "The way it looks to you isn't what's happening for me. Don't worry. It's perfectly fine for me." And he was reassuring us. And when he gave his last breath, his eyes rolled up and his last move was his finger pointing to the image of the Buddha right behind his head. That was his last gesture. Sort of like in the psychedelic generation, when Aldous Huxley died. Laura said, "He took psychedelics on the way out. And his last words were, 'I thought so.'" [Laughter]

It's a big trip. You want to be well prepared for it. But you see the teachings on dying, like what you know as *The Tibetan Book of the Dead*, it's like the GPS for the dying process, that's what it is, a GPS for dying. And the words translated as *Tibetan Book of the Dead* are actually, in Tibetan, *Bardo Thodol*, where *thodol* means to hear. And the exact title translation is "that which can be heard through the dying process." Because once you lose your body, the mental body that survives can still hear people. So, you read this as a guidebook to the person that's already died—they can still hear it. And they say, "Okay, turn here," so you're giving them the GPS signals. So, if they didn't get the GPS hooked up before they died, if you read them the manual out loud with the intention of connecting to them, it will connect with them and they can hear it. So, you're the GPS. That's how *The Tibetan Book of the Dead* is read.

Good question.

So, the best thing, you see, is if you're comfortable with this terrain, then you're going to be strange, because you're surrounded by people who are aging and dying, you watch people die every day, and you are fearless. People are going to see that and they're going to say there's something weird about you, in a good way. And they might look into it a little bit more. They might be a little bit more curious into what you know about all this and why, in the face of something that we're most terrified about, you have complete calm, and you're going to model something for them.

Someone is going to be curious about what's going on for you, what got you to this fearless calm in the face of the things that we're most afraid of, aging and dying. Then you see, you shine forth like a beacon by your very being.

That's my answer to your question.

July 16, 2014

Themes: H.H. Menri Trizin and Rahob Tulku; Clear Light Body; Marks of Realization

Dan

Welcome everyone. You have a question?

Student 1

So, if you had to place his Holiness Menri Trizin and Rinpoche in a hierarchical [order], who would go first? Who would be more senior?

Dan

Well, first of all there's a conventional and an ultimate level of reality answer to that question. So, Rinpoche is the emanation of Padmasambhava. So I should say something about what that means. Full enlightenment manifests as what we call buddha bodies. The vast expanse of groundless ground, the matrix of being, is called *dharmakāya*, the embodiment of all the teachings, *dzoku* in Tibetan. The lively manifestation of, or the energy of manifestation of the world is *dzoku*, or the completion body; and all of the seeming forms of reality that appear in a certain way for the sake of helping beings to develop their wisdom and compassion, all those forms are intentional emanations from the body of enlightenment, and those are called *tulku*. *Ku* is the honorific for body, the embodiment of, and *trul* means emanation. So, a buddha, a fully enlightened buddha, has opened up the issue of all-at-once-ness.

So what that means is that this little bubble that you see is only one little bubble of reality. You think this is the whole show, but in Nyingma Dzogchen, they talk about cracking the eggshell. In Bon Dzogchen, they talk about tearing down the nets of consciousness. So, beyond what this seemingly bubble is are infinite realms, all realms and times exist all at once, and you open up all that, all at once. And the fully enlightened mind of a buddha embodies all of that in, we say, *thigle chenpo*, the one great ultimate sphere of ultimate reality within which all beings are interconnected by loving filaments of compassion and love. So, since a buddha's enlightened mind operates on many planes of reality simultaneously and engages in spontaneous enlightened activity for the sake of all beings, buddhas can decide to emanate into certain planes of reality at certain times in history any way they want, and that's called a *tulku*. So, a *tulku* decides that he's going to emanate in a certain time in history in a certain plane of reality for a certain number of generations in order to teach.

So, Rahob Tulku, your precious Rinpoche, is a *tulku*, which means that out of the intention of enlightened *dharmakāya* space, he decided to appear in a series of successive generations starting in what, maybe the fourteenth, fifteenth century in a certain area of Kham, eastern Tibet, for a certain tribe of people, in order to be their senior teacher. And he can take any form he wants. And what's unusual about Rinpoche is that the form he decided to take was an emanation of Padmasambhava. So he is Padmasambhava—because Padmasambhava never dies—and he can take any form he wants in any plane of reality he wants simultaneously.

So, the historic Padmasambhava was the one who walked to Tibet and, at the invitation of the king, brought twenty-five disciples; and they translated thousands and thousands of volumes of Sanskrit Indian Mahāyāna Buddhism into Tibetan for the first time. And it was the first of just about, not completely the first, but just about the, it was the first systematic introduction of Mahāyāna Buddhism into Tibet. So, there are many *tulkus*, but this *tulku* is an emanation of a great historic figure in Buddhism, which is Padmasambhava. He is Padmasambhava for this generation, just like the Dalai Lama is the emanation of Avalokiteshvara, the buddha of compassion for this generation. He is Avalokiteshvara.

Now, His Holiness Menri Trizin represents a completely different lineage. There are what we call the five great chariots or the five great schools, and the oldest is the Bon. The Bonpo are the original indigenous religion of Tibet. They go back to a buddha that predates Shakyamuni—probably historically we can date it to about six thousand eight hundred years ago—in the Zhanzhung Empire, which was a huge empire that covered most of Pakistan, Western Tibet and the Eastern two-thirds of Afghanistan, and most of Tajikistan. And that original buddha, Tonpa Sherab, was actually from an Iranian or Parsi-speaking group, which is part of the Zhanzhung Empire, and they actually lived in Tajikistan. So that was the buddha before Shakyamuni Buddha. The next buddha, which was twenty-five hundred years ago, was Shakyamuni who lived in, well, was born in an area of what's now Nepal, but practiced and got enlightened in India, in Bodhgaya under the *bodhi* tree, and taught mainly in India and Nepal. So, the Bon represents the oldest lineage of mostly Dzogchen or Great Completion practices.

Then the other great chariots were … the next were all starting around the same time. There's the Sakya, which is the original Kadampa practice, which arose from the teachings of Atisha who came to Tibet in about the year ten-fifty, around the same time that the Kagyu sect started; and the Kagyu practiced mostly Mahāmudrā. And then maybe prior to that, maybe about the eighth century is when the Nyingma, or the old school started, which is a different version of Dzogchen. And then some years later was the Gelugpa, the Yellow Hat sect, which is the Dalai Lama's tradition. So those are the five great schools, and each school has a head. The Dalai Lama is the head of the Gelugpa, or now he stepped down from that. And now it's Denma Locho Rinpoche. He's the head of the Gelugpa. Sakya Trizin is the head of the Sakya. The Karmapa is the head of the Kagyu. And the incarnation of Dudjom is the head of the Nyingma. And his Holiness Menri Trizin is head of the Bon. So, he's the spiritual leader and lineage holder for all the Bon lineages.

In terms of classification, they're both buddhas. So, from the perspective of ultimate reality, there's no difference. They're buddhas that represent different configurations and teaching, both within the domain of Dzogchen or Great Completion teaching. In terms of relative reality, there are many *tulkus*, but Rahob would be considered a special *tulku* because he's the emanation of Padmasambhava, which means a lot in the Nyingma tradition. But he's not the head of a chariot. So, his Holiness Menri Trizin, in relative reality, carries more stature by virtue of being a lineage holder and head for the entire Bon tradition.

In ultimate reality, in terms of the realization, there's no distinction. In terms of the stature given to status in one's spiritual life for what they do, His Holiness would be considered a level above because he's the head of one of the five great schools and the leader of the whole Bon tradition. I hope that answers your question.

Student 1

[Inaudible]

Dan

Is that what you thought the answer would be? Pretty much? So, if you have an accomplished teacher who's known and valued for his teachings, then all of those, such teachers are given the title "Precious One," Rinpoche. That's what it means, except that term got corrupted in the *Lord of the Rings.* The ring became the precious one. [Laughter] But, the nature of His Holiness is usually given to chariot leaders. So, the Dalai Lama, Menri, Sakya Trizin, Karmapa, [inaudible], the title would be reserved for heads of a chariot or great school. And if you saw the film of Asonam's life, *Bon from Mustang to Menri,* then you can see the complicated procedure that goes on to select the head of a chariot. It takes a couple of years. It's sort of like the NBA draft. The nomination for who gets to be in the NBA draft, that's a whole other story, but ultimately it comes down to choosing balls in a container the same way they do in the draft. One would argue that what balls come up [are] as a matter of influence from the side of awakened *dharmakāya* space. So, it's not just random.

One thing I should say in terms of our Rinpoche is, you know, he's old (he's eighty-two) as is Menri, who's eighty-seven. But Rinpoche's been giving a clear message that he's not going to be in his form body that much longer, and he's saying the most is this year or next year. So, for those of you who are his direct students, you need to be aware of that. So, a couple of weeks ago I drafted a letter to the Foundation about how this is the time to build a *stupa* to honor him. It's the duty of the students to honor their teacher. In traditional Buddhist culture, as one ages you build a *stupa*, while they're still alive, to honor them.

So, I talked with Loretta [Rahob Rinpoche's wife] about the updated price and that we could build a *stupa* at his site for $27,000, and based on a variety of phone calls and emails, in just the last week alone before we sent out the letter to any of his students, we've generated—what is it—$16,000 of the twenty-seven. So, we're over halfway before we send anything out to any of his students or to the larger network of students. So, I'm fairly confident that we're going to do that. So, I called Loretta today based on our projections to say we're over halfway; we can put down half ahead of time. So I told her to get the construction schedule on docket. We start building it as soon as we can get the lama who builds these things to free up his schedule to do it. It would be nice to honor him while he's alive, to be honored at least in this form body. But as he's been preparing you for what's called mind-to-mind transmission, if he leaves his form body, he's saying no big deal, he'll still teach you. And he means that.

So, the teachings might be clearer because they're not [given] by the trappings of this level of reality. He'll just download directly into your mind. That's how mind-to-mind transmission works. But it doesn't come from out there, because there isn't any out there. So, there's lots of changes coming up; be prepared. That's why we're moving the project along. For those of you who've been part of that, I appreciate all your generosity and response. Everybody's responded swiftly and quickly and we're already halfway there within less than a week. It's remarkable.

Okay. Anybody else?

Student 2

Thank you. I'm trying to get past the conceptual thought of dreaming and wishing to obtain my light body.

Dan

To what?

Student 2

To obtain my light body, because in one aspect that's a conventional thought because I'm beginning to understand that I already have a light body, I'm just in a human form, but I'm having a hard time making the connection of not thinking about it and wishing for it and being able to be it.

Dan

What's the distinction you're making between ordinary body and light body?

Student 2

Well, ordinary body would be this dense, physical, three-dimensional body that carries pain and suffering and joy, versus an illusory body that is free from these things.

Dan

Pretty much. Okay, that's a good distinction, an accurate distinction.

Student 2

But I just find myself either in meditation, or I'm just lying in my bed and wishing and dreaming about what would it be like and what is that process, which I know is a conventional way, and my human mind probably can't even conceive what that even is. And I just want to shift from thinking the process out and trying to understand with a conceptual mind the process of what it would be like or what is it like to abandon this, not so much abandon this body, but move the transition from this physical body and get more in touch with what already exists—my light body—especially now where energy is changing with the rising out of the third dimension and getting into higher dimensions and the energy and the vibration rate is here to be able to do these kinds of things, and I just want to help my mind along or even make the connection of emptiness. Do I use emptiness to abandon these conceptual thoughts and trying to feel and wish and long for this? I'm unclear about that.

Dan

Okay. That's a good question. There's a lot to it. The trouble is that there are a number of answers to that question depending on level of practice, so we'll have to take them one at a time. And then maybe after the break we'll do a practice on clear light body so you can see for yourself.

So, when you're concentrating, at the initial stages of concentration at what we call the coarse level of mind, the coarse level of mind is the level of mind of content. You have specific thought content, specific emotions, sights, sounds, tastes, smells, sensations. And at the coarse level of mind, the body seems pretty solid. Although if you observe the body at the coarse level of mind, even though it will seem, as you say, dense and relatively solid, at that level of mind, the easiest insight that you'll get into the nature of the body is impermanence.

Although the body seems relatively solid, the processes within the body, if you observe them, are always changing. And sometimes we say that the pathway to emptiness is through impermanence; so, you know, every cell in your body is replaced by two or three days. Some cells were replaced much quicker than that, like the cells in the eyes, but there's nothing about your body that's constant. And if you did a meditation of the body at the coarse level of mind, you would come to see that it's a constantly ever-changing process. Still, it would seem to have solidity to it and density.

If you got deeply concentrated at the subtle level of mind where everything is, it remains in what we call an unelaborated state, [inaudible Tibetan word]. Then, everything is, all the content of the mind and the body is reduced to very quick momentary bursts of energy and movement, and light.

So, thought is just all bursts of energy and movement. Emotions are just bursts of energy and movement; sight, sounds, the body sensations are all bursts of momentary energy, what are called mind moments. So as a function of depth of concentration, the seeming density of the body will naturally drop away with no more than concentration practice. And at that point the body is just a field of energy and space, with this density and solidity seeming to come and go. It's not very solid, and that energy is very alive and vibrant. And that's what we call the subtle level of mind, the level of mind moments.

If you practice emptiness, emptiness doesn't mean the body goes away. It means that you see it for what it is. It's something that we've reified, we've made it a solid structure. But a synonym for emptiness is it's just a construction of mind. The idea that we have a solid body is just that, it's an idea. So, if you practice emptiness, all emptiness practice is looking into the nature of things to see beyond its seeming solidity. There's no independently existing thing that we call the body. It's an elaborate idea that we've thought of to label it. And if you practice emptiness of the body, then the body is reduced to lively awareness, manifesting as sensation. It's all lively awareness manifesting as sensation. So, I don't much like it, but the most widely used meditation on the body for basic standard of emptiness of the body practices is from Shantideva, and from his *Bodhicaryāvatāra*. But it does allow you to see beyond the seeming solidity of the construction in your mind of a body to seeing it as just all the manifestation of lively awareness.

So, at the level of emptiness practice, that's what the realization would be, emptiness of the body. It's another way of saying it all is the lively manifestation of the dance of the play of awareness, manifesting as what seems to be your body as you know it. And if you practice emptiness carefully, the grab of the body gets lost and the seeming solidity of it as an independently existing thing gets lost, yet there's still sensation. That's not going to go away. But the sensation becomes the manifestation of lively awareness. So, you start seeing the body, in any kind of emptiness practice, as none other than lively awareness. If you practice emptiness of thoughts, you would come to see all thoughts as the radiance of none other than lively awareness. If you practice emptiness of emotions, you see the pure energy of manifestation of this lively awareness. You don't get rid of something through emptiness; you see it for what it is. You get rid of its capacity to obscure; you get rid of its solidity. So that would be an example of practicing emptiness of the body.

Now, if you open up the next level of mind, which is called the very subtle level of mind, the awareness that you open up at that level is changeless and boundless. We call it ocean-like, changeless, boundless awareness because you've gone beyond the convention of ordinary time. And since time and space are related, if you see beyond the convention of time, and stop making time into a reified thing—like there's an external cosmic time clock somewhere—and you see beyond it into the emptiness of the convention of time, and since time and space are related, you open up a level of awareness that's absolutely changeless because it's beyond time, so it can't come and go anymore, so it's always here. So, you can't lose the realization, and that level of awareness is, because time and space are related, is huge, it's boundless.

So, if you set up the ocean-like, changeless, boundless awareness as your view, and then you ease up so you let all the ordinary content of the coarse level of mind occur within that view, that's a practice that Milarepa calls "Ocean and Waves"—like an ocean of changeless, boundless awareness, viewing its own waves—and everything that comes up is another lively expression of emptiness. And the body is just another wave in this vast ocean of ever-present changeless, boundless awareness. If you put the intention of looking at the body, it's just like another thing that arises within the ocean-like awareness, like anything else—it doesn't have any solidity, it has no grab—and the body will sort of arise as suspended in that space, that vast expanse of space in a way that has no substance to it. But at that level of practice, it will still seem to have boundary and shape.

Now, if you open up the next level of mind, which is the awakened level of mind, and are operating out of awakened awareness, then from the perspective of that vast expanse of lucid, awakened awareness, if you put the intention of looking at the body, the body will sort of hang in that vast expanse of empty space, awareness space, and it will have absolutely no substance at all. We say, like an empty glass bottle filled with light. There's your illusory body. And if you put the intention into looking at processes within the body, operating out of that vast domain of awakened awareness, just by looking, just with the intention to look, the coarse level breath will naturally arise with absolutely no impediment or interference. And if you look more carefully with that intention of awakened awareness, all the energy currents in the body, particularly the main channels, will spontaneously manifest themselves. So, at that level of what we call illusory body practice, it's not like you have to visualize the channels; that's stupid. They spontaneously manifest themselves. The display shows itself to itself by itself. Okay.

And then you understand clear light body. Clear light body is, if you're an old man like me, it's very convenient, particularly if you have a lot of arthritis [laughter], because it allows me to keep going with the illusion that I don't feel any discomfort, because I don't anymore. So, it's the mind that keeps the body going at this point, not the other way around. Now if you continue to hold that realization of clear light body and refine it, nothing about the body will have any grab to it anymore. There are no states of discomfort, and the body returns to its original purity, and ultimately it just becomes an energy body.

Now, the channels become part of the spontaneously emerging display at that level when you are operating out of awakened awareness. Now if you have continuously stable awakened awareness, then another funny thing happens. If you have awakened awareness more of the time than not, if there's a continuous flow of liveliness, everything is none other than the liveliness of awakened awareness. Then we talk with a little bit different language.

We start to talk about not everything being the liveliness of awakened awareness, but the liveliness of primordial wisdom energy, *yeshe*, because what begins is, if awakened awareness is stable and it doesn't go away, it doesn't cloud over, and you got that down, you don't have to keep opening up the view for what we call the ground aspect of awakening—you know that one now—so the mind naturally turns to what we call the appearance aspect of awakening. So then the view becomes everything is none other, every moment of the lively play of awakened awareness; it's its own dance. Or at that point, since it's all liveliness, we usually talk about it in terms of the liveliness of awakened wisdom energy, primordial wisdom energy. Because what you're going to see is the energetic manifestation; every moment of awakened awareness, it's lively; it's always creating itself, showing itself to itself and knowing itself through its own display. It's a remarkable display.

So, at that point there's a natural tendency to look at how everything comes into being. Out of the vast expanse of groundless ground, out of that empty space, energy drops manifest; and the energy drops immediately turn into elemental energy; and the elemental energy immediately turns into the elements, and that confines the body. So, if you're looking at the body at the coarse level of mind, it's solid. Now you're looking at the energy of the body prior to the elements of the body, which is why we call it the dance of wisdom energy. Then, you see, if you can hold that practice continuously, there's no solidity to the body.

Operating out of that vast, infinite, boundless, awakened awareness space, you can put the intention with an awakened mind of having pinpointed focus on anything, and with no more than the intention, the lightning speed of what the mind's awakened awareness intends, it goes just to that. We call that King of Samādhi. It's like a great bird of prey who has a vast scope of the horizon when it flies, but pinpointed focus on its prey. There's no contradiction between holding the vast expanse of awakened awareness with pinpointed focus simultaneously. If you can do that, we call that the King of Samādhi. So, operating out of King of Samādhi, what you do is you put the pinpointed focus on looking at clear light body. And you look particularly at locating the seat of your concentration within the central channel, because that's the location of what's left of the body. We call that the seat of *bodhicitta*.

So, out of King of Samādhi, if you put the intention into looking like that, then what will spontaneously display itself is the lively dance of primordial wisdom energy, creating itself to itself, and knowing itself with an awakened mind every moment. And that's the best seat or location to observe the activity of how everything comes into creation from *thigles*, from energy drops to elemental energy to the elements of the body. What do you think is going to happen if you do that practice and play it out over time? You're looking at the body prior to the solidness of the elements that make up the body. And there are several things that arise from that.

One of those practices [is] that if you can hold the mind at the level of *dungpa*, or elemental energy, which is prior to the elements of the body, then you transcend the physical limitations of the body. We just came back from Nepal and the old Bon lama that was there offered us a teaching, and he gave us the very guarded teachings on how you live off of the elemental energy of the universe rather than eating or drinking for months or years as a cave yogi. So, if you go into a cave, your practice isn't limited by having to eat or drink. And it's actually a fairly straightforward practice. But the key is you have to be able to open up that level of elemental energy and extract the energy directly from *dharmakāya*, *sambhogakāya* and *nirmāṇakāya*, directly from enlightened structure of reality. And then you transcend the physical limitations of the body.

Now the other practice that comes from that level is that if you understand the nature of elemental energy, *dungpa*—the *thigles*, energy drops—and that all elements of the body are made up of elemental energy, which is kind of a precursor to that; and then all of the organs of the body and structures of the body are made up of those elements; and then by gaining the mastery at that level of mind, essentially the body transforms itself into light. So, at the point of one of the culminations of the practice is rainbow body, *jalu*. So, at the point of death, you manifest as rainbow light. The body disappears and pops into rainbow light and disappears, and all that's left is the nails and the hair.

Now this is part of a long debate within Buddhist practices, in terms of how do you find the ultimate state of a buddha? And the earliest answers to that, if you look at the sutras for the first 500 years after Buddha Shakyamuni, there were two answers to that.

One is, you define it in terms of the number of multiple realities you open up at once. So, if you open up hundreds and hundreds of thousands and billions and billions of realities, the scope of how many realities you open up at once, that defines the nature of how deep your enlightenment is. So, there are differences in terms of that scope.

But the other answer is interesting. The first answer that was given, which is in the *Lalita Vishastra Sutra,* was the notion of the thirty-two major marks and eighty minor marks. And it's a strange system. And the system is that the thirty-two major marks are changes in the physical structure of the body resulting from enlightenment. So, the ultimate answer is the way you test your realization is by whether the nature of that realization fundamentally transforms the actual physical structure of the body. So, if you speak the elegant truth of the *dharma*, you develop a longer tongue. If you hear the elegant speech of the *dharma*, you develop bigger earlobes. If you walk the true path of the dharma, you develop bigger feet. And they meant this!

I mean from a scientific point of view we probably have a hard time with this. It's sort of like a Buddhist *Zelig*. Remember Woody Allen's movie *Zelig*? It's sort of like that. They really meant it, that they were looking for markers of authenticity, that the ultimate change in the physical structure of the body was one of those, and that was one of the first systems that came out.

Then the second system that I found in some of the early Akhrid Bon Dzogchen texts when I was translating the Akhrid system, the commentary, with a Bon monk, we came across this later section of the commentary about the nature of a buddha. And there was this thing about *zagme*. And *zagme* usually means no karmic outflows, which means you've stopped, you've exhausted all the ripening of karmic impressions. So that's how I translated. And he said, no, that's wrong. I said, why? Because, he says, it's a different context. And I said, what does *zagme* mean? He said, they're talking about the physical structure of the body of a buddha. I said, so what does it mean? He said, well, buddhas don't go to the bathroom. They don't have snot, they don't poop, they don't piss, they don't have saliva, but they can make tears intentionally for the sake of compassion. So, the only outflow that's left of a buddha is tears.

So that's another model that you see. You transcend the limitations of the physical body. But in both Bonpo and Nyingma Dzogchen, the ultimate test was rainbow body, that you transform the body right down to the pre-elemental existence of the body. So the body basically turns into light. So, at the point of dying, a great lama who wants to show his students that he meant business will tell people in advance when he's going to die and pop into rainbow light. And all that's left is the inanimate substance of the body, which are hair and nails. And there are many recorded histories of Shardza Tashi Gyaltsen Rinpoche, who was the great yogi in the Bon tradition for the last thousand years. He died in 1935. And he announced ahead of time when he was going to die, and he demonstrated rainbow body in front of three hundred people.

The guy who taught me the pointing out style of meditation, he changed into rainbow light after he taught me this style of teaching. He changed into rainbow light while he was still alive. That made a deep impression on me. And then he changed back into his form body. He died three weeks later. So, he was close to that point anyway, but he wanted to make a point and he got my attention.

So, great lamas actually have complete mastery over the physical body. Ultimately, the way the tradition went, the ultimate mastery is not whether you can change your body. That just shows you've got a depth of realization. The ultimate realization is *trinlé*, enlightened activity. If you have the vast scope of a buddha mind that operates on many planes of reality, you inexhaustibly work with spontaneous conduct for the sake of helping all beings. So nowadays, the consensus is [that] the best mark of realization is conduct. It's how you live your life. But there is a specific tradition that's changed over the years about the nature of the body. So, for every level of mind, we can develop a practice for the body.

And clear light body is a very profound practice. It's not even hard to do. But without the instruction you wouldn't think of it. But if you want to see it, I'll show you. It's not hard to do. It's not one of the guarded secrets. It's just considered hard because most people have such an attachment to the solidness of the body. And I think that partly if you look, and step back and look at the history of this, most conventional Buddhist practice, not the *tantras* or Dzogchen, but most conventional Buddhist practice uses Shantideva. And I don't think that's a good source myself. My personal opinion is that, I mean, Shantideva weighed three hundred pounds and he had an eating disorder, he had a binge eating disorder, and the *Bodhicaryāvatāra* may be the most popular book in Indian Mahāyāna Buddhism, but it's a complicated book because, even though there's wonderful stuff in that book, he does not have a good attitude to the body.

There's a lot of hatred towards the body, and as a monk he doesn't have good attitude towards women. So it represents some of the worst of the monastic tradition in that sense. And in that sense is not so different from other monastic traditions. I'm reminded of *Monty Python and the Holy Grail*. And there's that wonderful scene with the Catholic monks in the Middle Ages; and they have wooden bibles and they chant, take two steps, and they whack themselves over the head with the Bible, and they chant and take two more steps and whack themselves over the head again. And it's like that. It's that kind of negativity that has no place in this tradition.

See, in Buddhism there are three Turnings of the Wheel. The first is the teachings of Shakyamuni Buddha and the Noble Truth: everything is suffering. Well, Buddhism goes beyond that. In the Mahāyāna, it's not all about suffering. It's about the way of the *bodhisattva* and emptiness practice. But in the Essence traditions of the Third Turning of the Wheel, it's more about positivity. The eighty minor marks. There are eighty positive qualities or *yonten* of a buddha mind when you clear up all the negativity. So, there's none of that left. What flourishes is all the positive qualities. In fact, the word *budh*, in Sanskrit, means "realized one." But when the Tibetans translated buddha, they didn't translate it like that. The Tibetan word for buddha is *sangyé*. It's a compound term. *Sangwa* means purify. *Gyewa* means flourishing. So, the word in Tibetan literally means the purified flourishing mind. And what it literally means is that you purified your mind of all negative states. There are no negative states left. We call that *dharmadhātu* exhausted. You've exhausted all negative states. And then, as a consequence of that, those negative states don't mask or obscure the real nature of the mind, so what flourishes are all the eighty positive qualities of a buddha mind. So, in the Essence traditions, it's much more of, it's not all suffering, that's old Buddhism. It's much more the nature of all the positive qualities of mind and the flourishing of those and manifestation of those positive qualities, what are called *yonten*, and also the positive conduct inexhaustibly for the sake of helping other beings.

But as part of that larger tradition, there's a lot of practices on clear light body and beyond, like the practices of the manifestation of *bodhicitta* in the central channel from King of Samādhi, and the practices of clear light body and ultimately of elemental energies, and extracting elemental energy, and rainbow body, and there's a whole domain of advanced practices there. So you see, it's a great question because there's a different answer for every level of practice. I'm happy after the break if you want to open some of that up. We'll give it a try; see how far you can go with it. Some of you will be able to follow it more than others, but take it as far as you can take it.

Student 1

Thank you.

Dan

It's a good question. It's got some depth to it.

Student 1

It's all I think about.

Dan

But watch out for the nihilism. This is middle path. You're not getting rid of the body. You're getting rid of its capacity to obscure. But as long as you're alive, you're still going to have a body. Even if it turns to rainbow light, it's still going to have something that's residual. You understand me?

Student 1

Yes.

Dan

You're not getting rid of it.

Student 1

I think that's what I'm finding.

Dan

Rinpoche says, "Body like a hotel; you like guests." He says, "Better that it be a good hotel; take care of body." He says, "Because after you leave body," he said, "you're sort of like, kind of like homeless." [Laughter] "Mind is homeless." It wanders for a while until it finds a new body. So, it's important, it's the foundation. If you don't keep the body healthy it's a problem. The old Bon lama who taught us the *chülen* practices for extracting energy from the universe wasn't subtle about why he wanted to do that. Basically, he thought that, look, if we want to stay around and do these practices and teach these practices, and the single most contributing cause to shorter life is eating the wrong foods and eating too much, he wanted us to clean up our diets as Westerners so we could stay around and do this stuff.

And that's consistent with about ten years ago when, in Colombia, we did a week-long conference with the Dalai Lama through Menla, Bob Thurman's place. And it was on longevity and regeneration of tissue. So, it was one of these dialogues with stem cell scientists and the Dalai Lama. It was fun. And one of the themes of the Western research was to do, not extreme, but mild, but continuous starvation of laboratory animals, and controlling for all of the variables. If you systematically starve laboratory rats, but not severely, they live much longer. And the study seems to suggest that eating too much is one of the reasons that we don't live long. So, cutting down the amount that we eat, and what we eat, and then living in a state of mind where we're extracting elemental energy from the universe—that is the key to longevity.

So, there's a lot of work to get done; so we've got to stay around to do this. So that's what he wanted us to know. It was amazing because they allowed us to videotape the whole thing. I got a copy of the text and I've translated it, and now I've got to go into retreat and figure it out. And it doesn't look that hard. And at some point we'll show you this stuff, but not yet. It's not ready yet, but we're working on it.

Good question.

A meditation session was guided by Dan, and then he offered the following review:

Dan

So, just to review, there's the level of practice at the coarse level of mind where the body is sort of dense and solid. There's the level of practice at the subtle level of mind where it's all mind moments, infinite bursts of movement and energy, space, where it loses its density and solidness. With ordinary emptiness you free the body of its constructions, its solidity, its labels, all the stories that go with it, the grab. And the affirming part of the negation is that the body becomes lively awareness. The body is awareness manifesting itself. At the very subtle level of the mind, the body hangs within the ocean-like domain as lively emptiness. At the awakening level of the mind, with King of Samādhi practice, then the body becomes clear light body, like an empty glass bottle filled with light. If you stabilize that awakening, then the view that you have is the body is liveliness. At that point you look at it in terms of, or from King of Samādhi against the backdrop of the vast expanse, pinpointed focus on the upper part of the central channel, which is the seat where you can most transparently view how energy comes into existence from the empty domain of [inaudible], and how that energy manifests as elemental energy and then as the elements and then as all these solid forms of the world. You watch the whole, all of creation coming into existence every millisecond. And there, rather than clear light body, it becomes the seat of what we call *bodhicitta* body, or bliss body. Empty bliss body. Then if you can hold your awareness at the level of elemental energy, that's when you start transforming the body, the elemental structure of the body into light and energy, of the elemental energy. So, that pretty much gives you 80 percent of the whole path of the body except for the most advanced teachings, which I can't give you at this point. Clear enough?

Each level of mind has a different practice for it.

It's better if you can do it with a certain level of awareness, like either ocean-like, changeless, boundless awareness, or better, awakened awareness, and then you're not visualizing, you don't have to visualize the body or the currents in the body. It all spontaneously defines its own pathway to itself by itself. That would be a superior practice than trying to sit there and tediously visualize the body this way with the channels set up here. Nobody does that. It's too much work.

August 27, 2014

Themes: West and East Views of Emotion; Clearing the Storehouse of all Negative States

Dan

Welcome everyone. You have a question?

Student 1

I've been preoccupied lately with the question of emotionality and attachment, and all emotionality is based on attachment and something to be solved or just experienced and let go, and I'm just preoccupied with that. The question has formulated over the summer when I've had lots of guests, and I find myself pained when they get on a plane and go away. My heart is yanked, I miss them before they've even boarded. And then it just broadened to a bigger question about how any time I'm having an experience of emotionality, whether or not that's just a matter of attachment, as though that's diminishing it in some way, but there you go. That's the question.

Dan

It's a good question. There's a whole world in that question. That's a great question. So, there's a different answer to that question, East and West. And let's start with the Western perspective. The question is, what about the issue of attachment that comes with certain emotions? Is that a fair way of saying it?

Student 1

Mm-hmm (affirmative).

Dan

The grab of the emotion.

Student 1

Well, and the other thing that's occurred to me is what's the distinction between attachment and loving somebody, and it seems like there's a single answer, but it doesn't come in a way that resolves it for me.

Dan

Well, first from a Western perspective, there are two dimensions to emotions. There's a pre-dispositional hardwired part of the emotion. That's the expressive aspect of the emotion. And then there's the internal state of what we feel. And in the best sense, they are coordinated. Work on this was pioneered by Silvan Tomkins in the West, and what he said was that infants come into the world with about eight to ten totally independent muscle groups within the face. We call that the facial display system. They're all hardwired. They're universally recognizable in all cultures. And those facial display muscles reflexively react to whatever is going on in the immediate caregiving environment. And without thought, in milliseconds, they immediately display what our feeling is.

Why do we have them and what's the adaptive or evolutionary function of a facial display system? Tomkins calls them "amplifiers." They amplify to the caregiving environment what the internal state of the infant is so it makes it more salient, more obvious to the caregiver how to change the environment to get it right. So, if the caregiving environment for the child is just right, the automatic reflex of facial display system is interest, sustained interest. If there's a sudden change in that caregiving environment, so that the child can't process it because for one, two, or three months, they don't have much processing ability, then the automatic reflex of the display is surprise. If the change continues to be in a direction that the child can't handle, the automatic reflex display is frustration and anger. If the caregiving environment supplies the optimal stimuli in a sustained way, the automatic facial display pattern is joy.

So, what does that tell you? It tells us that the reason why kids are equipped genetically with a facial display alphabet is so they can automatically, reflexively cue the caregiving environment to get the conditions just right moment by moment, to prime the perceptual system to its own maturation. The child is constantly cuing the caregiver how to get it right, and a good enough caregiver responds they're attuned enough and they get it right, and not only will they change it in the way that's optimal, but they might just add something to it to get the child more interested in the development, so it becomes a mutually regulated system.

More recently, people like Beatrice Beebe have done a microanalysis of moment-by-moment frames of mothers and infants in interaction, and you can see the facial display patterns in a fraction of a second. You have to look at it that quickly. You break it down frame by frame. Most of the reactions are about a quarter of a second. Remarkable. So, if you slow it down, you see a lot going on that we would normally miss.

And even adults have that lightning speed expressivity in their face. When somebody picks up on another person's feeling, when they read that, we call it intuition. What they're really doing is they're seeing that at micro-speed. A person might be talking in a kind of gentle way about something that's very bland, and if you slow down the films, there's a split second of rage there. The intuitive person would pick up on that anger, but most of us let it go by because we're not trained to see that expressive display so quickly. We suppress our ability to do that.

So, as Tomkins says, the purpose of that facial display system is to amplify the immediate need to cue the caregiver to get it just right, and a carefully attuned caregiver is always adjusting to what the child needs. In that sense, you see, the infant is training us to respond in the right way, repeatedly so. Some people call that "contingent communication." It means the child actually sees that they have an impact, and they repeatedly see they have an impact on an attuned parent, so they develop a sense of "effectance." They know that they can have an effect on the other, and that's healthy. From that will develop social confidence. All that's present from birth.

Then the second part from a Western point of view is the internal state. William James once said you need two things to have an internal emotional state. You have to have some visceral change in the body, and you have to have awareness of that visceral change. So, the internal emotional states don't appear until later. They're a nurture issue, not a nature issue.

So, if you take autonomic measures of an infant, it's all over the map, but it starts to stabilize at about four months. At about six months, that's when the child develops what we call "the capacity for reflective self-awareness," the famous rouge spot experiment. If you take a red lipstick and you put it right here, and you look at a child every month, one month, two months, three months, four months, five months, looking in a mirror, a funny thing happens at about six months. They start going like this [Dan moves his head and hands back and forth], and they start going like this [a little more hand waving]. You can see that they're figuring out that that's their reflection in the mirror. With the highlighting on their head, they move the head around a lot, and the rouge spot, and you can see that they're figuring out that that's really them in the mirror. And that's why we usually mark six months as being when self-reflective capacity develops.

So, if the autonomic nervous system stabilizes at four months and self-reflective capacity stabilizes at six months, what does that mean? Now the child has the capacity to become self-aware of broad changes in their internal state, which we call moods. But they're not very specific.

Then a funny thing happens from nine to twelve months, cognitive maturation. The child develops the capacity for perceptual categorizing. And with those categories, they can now differentiate a finite number of visceral changes into specific, what we call "categorical emotions." We only have maybe a dozen or so internal state changes, visceral changes, but a nine-year-old can experience about a 160 different emotions, about the same as an adult. What makes the difference? Cognitive maturation. The more sophisticated cognition becomes, the more you differentiate the subtlety and richness and texture of internal emotional states.

So, between nine to twelve months of age, that's the beginning of categorical thinking: happy, sad, mad, glad, afraid. And by eight or nine years old with concrete operational thinking, you end up with lots of nuanced and textured emotional states. Without the cognition to differentiate, emotions remain rather undifferentiated.

There's a famous experiment that was done by Schachter and Singer years ago showing that you need cognition in order to differentiate what the emotion is. What they did is they had college volunteers come in to test a "new vitamin." They were only told it was a vitamin. Of course, those were the days when we did deception in social psychology research, and they weren't given a vitamin. What they were given was rather large doses of epinephrine. And when they were told it was a vitamin, what do you think they did? They suppressed the effects of the epinephrine as if nothing happened.

Then what they had is they had the person wait in the waiting room for a follow up test. And they had other people, another person, waiting in the waiting room who was a confederate to the research who said that they were waiting too. And the confederate was told to act out certain emotional states. One person got giddy and sort of a little bit excitable. Another person was depressed and sad. And no matter what the person saw in the confederate, that's what they described the vitamin did to them. And what Schacter and Singer were saying is, look, if you're told it doesn't do anything then you rely on the immediate social environment to get what the effects are. In other words, we learn to differentiate our internal state based on what we're told.

You can all see that in terms of developing categories to understand an internal experience. Think about the first time most people get stoned. They're puffing weed over and over again, their eyes are bugging out of their head, and they say, [Dan using a slightly goofy voice …] "I don't feel anything." [Laughter] Why? Everybody knows what I'm talking about, right? Why? Because they don't have the cognition. So, they actually suppress the effect of the drug, the same way that the Schacter and Singer subjects suppressed the effect of the strong stimulant without having the cognition to explain it. So, the more we develop different subtle cognitive categories, the more we can differentiate those visceral states into a whole range of emotions.

And somewhere between nine to twelve months of age, the facial display system and the internal state system—which are two separate systems—become integrated. How do we know that? Visual cliff experiment. You take a kid on a four-foot piece of rug, here's a piece of plexiglass [Dan raises his hands to indicate two places on an elevated platform, one on the left and one on the right]; you put the kid here, you put the mommy here, and the kid paddles over across the depth; it's about a four-foot drop, to the mommy. And when the kid looks down, you see a fear response. Or, you see spiking of heart rate or skin conductance. The trouble is if you test the same kid when you see the facial display of fear at six months, you don't get the physiological spiking. You get it at a separate point in time.

But with the same child from nine to twelve months, the physiological spiking occurs at the same time as the facial display of fear. So, what does that tell you? During that period, the facial display system gets linked up with the internal state system which were two separate systems. There are psychiatric patients who fail to make that linkage. We call it inappropriate affect, which means they're talking about something and their facial display system is completely out of sync with what they're talking about and what they're feeling internally. But most people make that linkage, so what they express in their face to others conveys to others what their internal state is. Now we have a complex emotion, which is the awareness of our internal state and spontaneously expressed. So, most of that system is in place by one year of age.

What good is it? What's the adaptive purpose of having emotions? And the answer to that question is somewhat different for negative and positive emotions in the West. What negative emotions do, the purpose, is to cue the interpersonal environment what we need. All negative emotions are trying to get the caregiving system to do it right. So, for young children, the reason why they're expressing a negative emotion is that something isn't quite right in their world, and they're trying to give a clear cue to the caregiver to change things, to be responsive in the way that they need. It's all about getting the person to be responsive.

Why do we persist with negative emotions? Because the person in our caregiving environment that we want to be responsive still isn't responsive in the way that we need, so we keep at it. We're persistent little creatures, us humans. That's really what negative emotion is about. It's trying to put out cues to the caregiving environment, and later that doesn't mean mommies and daddies, it means our intimates and our friends and peers or our work colleagues to try and cue people how to get it right. That's what it's about.

Student 1

For ourselves?

Dan

It's about what we need for the self. It's about the self.

Now, positive emotions have a slightly different purpose. That was work done by Barbara Fredrickson called the "broaden and build model." She got the Templeton Award for that, which is sort of like the Nobel Prize for positive psychology. And what she says is positive emotions build our coping resources. They strengthen us and broaden our attentional span and our cognitive capacity. So, there are many laboratory studies that show that if you induce positive moods with music, for example, and you give people tests of creativity after positive mood induction, they're much more creative. They make much more cognitive connections and more and more sophisticated and elaborated cognitive networks.

If you induce positive emotions, people pay attention more carefully. People pay attention to positive things more than negative things. And positive emotions built up through play, for example, builds our coping resources. Most higher order animals play. Higher order animals have positive emotions. Why? Because it builds coping resources. You can see the caribou in the off-season locking horns and playing at fighting, but why do they play at fighting when it's summertime and there are little predators around and they have plenty of food? Because during the off season, those positive emotions and the playful fighting is a way of building coping resources, so they'll be better fighters in the middle of the winter when food is scarce and they're going to be vulnerable to a pack of wolves. They're going to fight better.

Humans are like caribou. Our positive emotions build our coping resources so that under times of stress, we're better prepared. So, both negative and positive emotions are adaptive. They signal what the self needs and they build the resources of the self. In relative reality, that's useful. That's the Western answer to your question.

The Buddhist answer to your question is, the trouble with emotions, like the trouble of self and the trouble with thought and perception, is we reify it. It becomes too real, too solid. We forget that emotions, like self, are all constructions. Emotions in Western terms become the vehicle of self-expression. But what if the self is just an empty construction that we take way too seriously? And what the Buddhists say is that any construction of mind, if we reify it and make it too solid, and make it independently self-existent, there are two consequences.

One consequence is the self and the experience of the emotion as felt by the self has grab. *Dzin-pa* means grab. So, emotions have a lot of grab to them. That's what you're calling attachment.

So, the grab becomes a source of suffering. So, if we continue to try and signal our interpersonal world about what we need and they don't get it right, rather than getting it right, what happens instead? We get more miserable because they're not responding. And if we grew up in an environment where there were repeated failures in responsiveness, then we tend to select people in our lives who will repeat that problem. They're not responsive. So, we continue to not get what we need, and we continue the same old, same old, playing out repeatedly the same old negative feeling states, trying to get them to respond; but rather than getting them to respond, we get them to repeat the unresponsiveness, over and over again.

As one famous Boston analyst, Felix Deutsch, once said, every new relationship is an attempted solution for the previous one. Unfortunately, it's true. [Laughter] So, we keep playing out the same old, same old with more and more grab, which means suffering.

And the second thing from a Buddhist perspective, which is more important, is the more we reify self and the emotions associated with self, the more it has the capacity for *mümpa*, to cloud over, to obscure. *Mümpa* means to darken. And it takes our true nature, our awakened awareness, and it becomes like a huge cloud that darkens the shining of the sun. The sun always shines, but when the gray clouds are out, it gets dark and we can't see the fact that the sun is still shining, so that we don't see the fact that our awakened nature is always radiantly shining all the time because it's covered over by clouds. And the thickest and darkest clouds are usually the emotions of self. That's what you're calling attachment.

So, how do you work with this stuff? Again, the answers are different from a Western point of view and from a Buddhist point of view. From a Western point of view, the consistent theme in Western therapy is about finishing unfinished emotional business. Look at where you're most hooked, what you're calling attachment, or what I'm calling the grab. The best work on that is the so-called Confessions Studies of Jim Pennebaker. If you give people the assignment to review in their mind or talk out on a tape recorder or write in a journal or talk to another person, it doesn't make any difference what the format is. You give them the assignment to bring to mind whatever feels most emotionally unfinished and to keep reviewing it in their mind and processing it with all the thoughts and feelings about it, and keep going over it until they feel settled.

After about four twenty-minute sessions, they feel settled. It doesn't take long, particularly if you word it in terms of "what's most emotionally unfinished."

And that can be lots of things for different people. For most people in the Pennebaker studies, it was relationships that ended and never felt finished. It might be losses; it might be a traumatic experience of some sort. It might be something that a person did that they feel guilty or ashamed about. Whatever it is, it doesn't make any difference. The idea is to set up the context to process what isn't finished until they get more processed and therefore settled. At some point you let go of it.

If we learned anything from fifty years of cognitive behavioral exposure-based therapy, the greater the avoidance, the greater the exposure works. The more a person is avoiding it, the more you get them to deal with it and to keep focusing and keep focusing, it settles out and stops. So, finishing unfinished emotional business seems to cause people to feel more emotionally settled, so they're less conflicted. They have higher well-being after doing their confession studies and they also have higher wellness. Pennebaker found that after four twenty-minute sessions, they had enhanced immune response, and for the next year they were less vulnerable to basic illnesses that were going around like colds and flus and things like that.

So, traditional Western spirituality tells us that confession is good for the soul, and the modern psychologists tell us it's good for the body, and it's also good for the psyche, not just the soul. It's a simple procedure. But if you target the focus on what's emotionally most unfinished, it works better.

Now for positive emotions, it's quite different. If positive emotions broaden our attention span and our cognitive capacities and build our coping resources, then positive emotions, we want to experience them more. In Barbara Fredrickson's work, she found something quite amazing. She gave people a little instrument that measured negative and positive emotions that they experience in a typical day, and then they can self-score it and work out a ratio of negative to positive emotions. What do you think she found? Most people experience more negative than positive emotions.

But then she did mood induction. She had people listen to music or use their imagination to induce positive emotional states, and she kept doing that repeatedly over time. And a funny thing happened. She actually mathematically calculated that when most people got to the point where the ratio of positive emotions during their day was 3.2:1 of negative emotions or higher, then they started to experience spontaneous positive changes in many areas of their life without doing anything else. She called it a "tipping point." And people would have more positivity because positivity feeds on positivity.

And she observed those people over time, and she found out something else happened. A couple of years later, when those same people got to the point that their ratio of positive emotions to negative emotions was 11:1 or higher, then without any further interventions, their life worked on all pistons, all cylinders. They started to get their relationships to work. They started to get their sense of self to develop to the best self. Their work started working better. They got more satisfaction out of their leisure activities. On all levels of their life, it worked. And what initiated this positivity and eventually the life working on all areas at once positively, which she calls flourishing, what led to flourishing was this cascading of positive emotions. A strong test of her model.

The more positive you are, the more you leave all that negativity behind. So, from a Western point of view, finishing the negative unfinished emotion business and then putting a stronger emphasis on cultivating the positive, which, of course is rarely done in psychotherapy. That's one of the blind spots in the West. It's all about the negative. But we now know that focusing on the positive is a really important aspect in mental health. It needs to be done.

Now, from an Eastern point of view, there are two things you want to do here, from a Buddhist point of view. But the answer in Buddhism to what you do with emotions has to do with the level of Buddhism because there are three major levels of Buddhist development in what we call the Three Turnings of the Wheel. And the answer is very different in each of those.

The First Turning of the Wheel was the teachings of Buddha Shakyamuni—the Four Noble Truths. The first is the truth of *dukkha*, which is often translated—or mistranslated—as the truth of suffering, but it's really not. *Dukkha* means reactivity. It means that the mind, moment by moment, is reactive to what you do.

The practices that represent the First Turning of the Wheel in this country are very popular: Burmese mindfulness. If you cultivate a continuous nonreactive, nonjudgmental mindfulness and just allow everything to rise in that field of continuous awareness without the reactivity, you train yourself out of that reactivity. And if you train yourself out of that reactivity, you diminish suffering. You let everything be there just the way it is. Those First Turning of the Wheel practices are very popular now in the West. But the trouble is that that model of Buddhism never went beyond suffering. It just diminishes the reactivity to suffering. And it never went beyond the model of "no self."

The Second Turning of the Wheel is Mahāyāna Buddhism. There you get 500 years of revising the notion of "no self" into something quite different:

emptiness, which means everything is just a construction, and we have to watch out to not reify constructions of mind. So, in that sense, the self that experiences the emotion and the self that has the grab to the emotion, the self itself is just a construction of mind. There's no Dan that's feeling happy or angry. So, if I do emptiness practice, I see beyond that structure of mind into a level of awareness that's beyond self. See, the trouble with Burmese mindfulness is it doesn't clean up the issue of self. You can be very mindful. You can be so mindful that you just allow all the feelings to come up and not be reactive and still very filled with yourself.

But emptiness of self practice cleans up that issue of self. And emptiness of emotions cleans up the reification of the emotion. So, it's just a construction of mind. Anger is a label. Happiness is a label. And if you clean up all that, what you're left with is what we call "the pure energy of manifestation." There's still something left—it's just pure energy. Anger isn't anger anymore—it's the pure energy of determination. Fear isn't fear—it's a wonderful state of alertness. And the pure energy is always positive, you see, when you clean up the story and the label and all the reification that goes with that.

So, you see, if you practice emptiness of self and emptiness of emotions, you get a level of freedom that goes beyond just diminishing the reactivity. It brings it to a whole other level. Now you're operating out of a field of awareness that's cleaned up of self, it's cleaned up of emotions, and all that stuff just becomes liveliness of awareness.

But the Third Turning of the Wheel is far more interesting, and that's the Essence traditions like Mahāmudrā, Dzogchen, and the *tantras*. Because in the Essence traditions, or that third development in Buddhism, they move far away from the notion that everything is suffering, and much more into the field of positivity.

You see, if you continue along this path, each practice of emptiness, you learn something about the nature of awareness. When we start the practice, we think that awareness is the same as thought, so we have to concentrate the mind down so that thought stops enough that we can see awareness is different from thought—awareness gone beyond thought. But still that awareness is very much tied up with self, so I still think that Dan is doing the meditation. But if I do emptiness of self, I'll see beyond that and operate out of a level of awareness that's cleaned up of Dan-ness. Still, that awareness will fluctuate with the convention of time, but if I see the convention of time as just a construction, I can open up a level of awareness that's changeless and boundless, ocean-like, changeless, boundless awareness gone way beyond time by practicing emptiness of time.

But still that awareness seems to be packaged in individual consciousness and all the things that it does like pay attention—think. And if I see beyond all that, I can open up a field of awareness that's boundless and very awake and no longer packaged within the constraints of my information processing system or my seeming individual consciousness that's non-locatable and has no reference point. And it has a lucidity that's beyond any ordinary awareness.

So, then I've found my way to awakened awareness. And those steps are illustrated in the Heart Sutra mantra: *Gate gate pāragate pārasamgate bodhi svāhā*. Awareness gone beyond thought, awareness itself gone beyond self-representation, ocean-like, changeless, boundless awareness gone way beyond time, awakened awareness gone way, way beyond our information processing system and our seeming individual consciousness. *Bodhi svāhā*—oooh, what a realization.

Now, if I opened up awakened awareness as my basis, and I do the practices in Dzogchen to stabilize that so it's not a little flame that I have once, but I can do it all the time and now I have awakened awareness all the time 24/7—I'm awake during the day, I'm awake during deep sleep, I'm awake during dreaming, I'm always awake in all my activities all the time, on or off the pillow. Then a funny thing happens.

If I take that vast domain of awakened awareness and I look at how things arise, and let everything arise in that vast ocean-like field of awakened awareness, without doing anything to it except just let it arise spontaneously and disappear spontaneously, and I bring to the setting up [of] that view what we call "leave-it-alone-ness," because I'm not engaging anything and it's all an automatic process at that point, it's that subtlest mental engagement that causes karmic impressions. If I set up that view just right with the right instructions, I won't make any new karmic impressions anymore. And if I do that practice 24/7 and get it just right—because the view is the meditation—there's an automatic process where because you're not forming any new karmic impressions, whatever arises immediately disappears; we say, "like writing on water," it immediately disappears and it forces the mind to dip into its storehouse and release all the previous storehouse of karmic impressions at a rapidly accelerated rate.

So, if I do that practice all the time on the average of six years, there are no negative impressions left in the storehouse. I clean it out. We call that process "*dharmadhātu* exhaustion." You exhaust the bin, the storehouse of negative ripening impressions. And since those negative impressions eclipse the positive, after a while, the field starts getting cleaner and cleaner, and then after a while, you start to see more positivity.

There are eighty positive emotional states in a buddha mind, and all those flourish like that positivity. They just emerge. And there are no negative states left. So, if you practice *dharmadhātu* exhaustion, after a while, there just aren't any negative states left—gone. And you live in a world where all those positive states flourish and become your way of being.

We once gave, many years ago, Rorschach ink blots [tests] to people in various stages of practice, and people who had achieved the First Path in the Theravādin system, which is where the reactivity goes down. The Rorschachs looked like ordinary Rorschachs. They had a lot of range of conflicts on them. But when we scored them with the old Holt system for defense demand and defense effectiveness, they had no reactivity. The conflict was just out there, consistent with the fact that what went away was the reactivity to what came up. The First Noble Truth, *dukkha*, no reactivity.

But they had a full range of conflict. Some of those Rorschachs were very disturbing. In Western terms we were saying [some] met the criteria for personality disorders. So, at that level, with a taste of awakening, it didn't make a dent in personality structure, which helped us understand the guru game—that there might be people out there with legitimate spiritual realizations, but they really screw it up for lots of other people because they really aren't emotionally mature, because the awakening didn't make a dent in that.

But then we found people at the penultimate and ultimate stages, the final stages of awakening. And those Rorschachs didn't look like anything we'd ever seen before. They were clean. They had no negative states whatsoever. And they were completely absent of aggression. They had fundamentally changed the substrate of their mind. What we were seeing on the Rorschachs, though it didn't have a language for it in those years because it was a long time ago [since] we did that study—now I would say we were seeing "*dharmadhātu* exhaustion:" no negative states and the emergence of all the positive states.

There's Padmasambhava over there, our big statue. He has a staff and there are three skeletons. The skeletons symbolize the extinguishing of the three poisons, the three biggest negative states: desire, aggression, ignorance or non-awareness. Sometimes five skeletons, the other two are jealousy and pride. So, if you have *dharmadhātu* exhaustion, you wear the staff to signify your gain in practice. Sometimes what you see instead is three or five. They look like little jewels or Christmas balls, and those signify the positive opposite of those. So, if you see the staff or the crown with the jewels or the Christmas balls, what's being signified there is the flourishing of the eighty positive states of mind. This is all well laid out in the tradition.

Barbara Fredrickson in the West, when she talks about the tipping points and leading to more and more positivity, it's just a little bit of a taste of what it means to have a mind where [there is] a flourishing of all eighty positive states and no negative states left. It's a good state to be in. It's a good state to be in to live your life in for the rest of this lifetime. It's quite attainable. You just have to follow the path.

At that point, you see, what you've done by the practice of emptiness—because the emptiness is the path—is you move beyond the reactivity of the self, and you move beyond the reactivity of the emotions of the self. It's no longer about you. You live in a larger universe that's vast and where everyone and everything is interconnected. In other words, it supersedes the Western model to a spiritual model that has a much more vast scope. And if you live in that scope, most of your concern isn't about what you need for the self; so, you're not always working out of that reactivity to try and get other people to be responsive and to get it right for what you need because it's not about the self anymore. It's irrelevant. What becomes of the concern is what matters for the greatest social good. Your emotions are superseded by compassion, by loving-kindness, about protectiveness of this planet that we're about to destroy.

In that sense, the Buddhist model outstrips and supersedes the Western model. There is nothing in the Western model that comes close to that except for maybe the positivity stuff, Barbara Fredrickson, but it's dwarfed in comparison. Good question.

September 3, 2014

Themes: Stages of Knowledge; Effects of Cultural Trauma; Spiritual Duties

Dan

Welcome everyone. You have a question?

Student 1

Hi. On the lower level of truth is …

Dan

What's that? [Laughter]

Student 1

Is it always conceptualizable?

Dan

Is that the question?

Student 1

Yes.

Dan

[Smiling broadly] Or is that the primer to the question?

Student 1

Is relative truth always conceptualizable?

Dan

You can try it. See how that works. [Dan and the group laugh]

The Buddhist logicians, Chandrakirti, Dignaga, in their major treatises on Buddhist logic lay a rather careful foundation for an infrastructure about two fundamentally different ways of knowing the world. One way is conceptual knowing. And the problem with conceptual knowing is it's always based on an ordinary mind; and by definition it delineates and therefore partializes in a way that has a strong potential to cloud over the truth of ultimate reality. And the other level of knowing is knowing through direct experience. Experiential knowing is necessarily about looking into things in meditation, and seeing them directly for what they are, without conceptual knowing. In that sense knowing through meditation experience is always direct and by definition never conceptual. You just know it.

But, the two ways of knowing can support each other. Despite the great capacity for conceptual knowing to obscure, to cloud over, nevertheless conceptual knowing has a certain usefulness in that it can have an orienting function. It can point you in the right direction insofar as that pointing initiates you look directly into it in meditation, and insofar as you don't confuse the conceptual knowing with ultimate truth. So sometimes in Mahāmudrā what's used is the metaphor of pointing the finger at the moon. If you point a finger at the moon, it helps orient you to seeing the moon, looking into where the moon is. You then have to see it. And the danger is that you confuse the pointing with the moon.

Likewise, conceptual thought is like finger-pointing. It can orient you to words to look into things, and so you can see them in the direct experience of meditation, insofar as you don't confuse the finger of conceptuality with the actual moon of ultimate truth. So, in that sense, you see, conceptualization has a place as an orienting point for your direct inquiry.

Usually, we talk about this in stages of knowledge. So, the first stage is *tilwa*, you have to hear the teachings directly. Then you have to process what you hear so it's not just words. So that becomes listening. Then, from that you have *tsompa*, you have to reflect on the nature of what you listened to. And once you reflect on the nature of what you listened to, it leads to *gowa*, an intellectual understanding, a kind of general intellectual or conceptual understanding of what that teaching is about. There's your orientation.

Then after you develop that intellectual understanding, you have to *nonsurinpa*, you have to take up what you've learned as a direct meditation experience; you have to look into it so you translate that into *nyampa*, into direct meditation experience.

Once you translate it into meditation experience, which always changes, it's always direct knowledge; then you have to have that meditation experience lead to *tokpa*, direct understanding—it's not conceptual. *Tokpa* is always necessarily the outcome of looking into things with meditation. It's the shift in your experience, so that you see the truth of what is.

But *tokpa*, when you first experience it, direct realization is not typically stable. You have to look into it, and have more meditation experiences, which feed back on developing, deepening direct understanding, and then the understanding feeds back on having more experience, and each goes back and forth. And ultimately that leads to the direct integration of that understanding into the mindstream. You carry it with you as part of your mindstream. Now it's just with you all the time. Then, once that direct realization is with you all the time, it begins, as a constant organizing principle for your view, it begins more and more to inform conduct.

So, the view becomes conduct, *choepa*. So ultimately all direct understanding is conduct. It's how you act in the world.

So, in the commentary to the Akhrid text that we translated, the Bonpo Dzogchen text, there's a wonderful passage that says, "First you must hear the teachings. It's not enough to hear the teachings; then you must listen to them. Once you listen to them, it's not enough to listen to them; then you must reflect on them. Once you reflect on them, it's not enough to reflect on them;

you must develop intellectual understanding. Once you develop intellectual understanding, that's not enough. Then you have to translate that into taking up the meditation and translate it into direct meditation experience. Once you develop direct meditation experience, that's not enough; you have to translate that into direct understanding, or direct realization. Once you have the direct realization, it will fuel further meditation experiences, which will feed further direct realization. Once you've really developed, in a strong way, the direct realization, that's not enough. Then you have to translate that direct realization into integrating that realization into the nature of your mindstream so it becomes an ongoing view. Once you've developed that view, that's not enough; you have to develop that view into a spontaneous expression as conduct for the purpose of all beings. Then you have a direct realization."[23] Nice passage.

Student 1

Thank you.

Dan

So, don't confuse the finger for the moon.

Student 1

Yeah.

Dan

But without the finger, you may never orient yourself to looking at the moon. So, in that sense, thought can be useful. It's the overuse of thought in a way that clouds over direct realization that's a problem.

I always find that if I'm learning some new cycle of teachings, I like to translate the text accurately, reflect on it, understand the essence of what it means, and having gotten that orientation then do the retreat. But if I just sort of sit,

---

23 Daniel P. Brown and Geshe Sonam Gurung, *Pith Instructions for A-Tri (A Khrid) Dzogchen* (Boston: Bright Alliance, 2017), 41.

without first translating it and reflecting on it and developing some intellectual understanding of its essence, then I'm just sitting, and my sitting is aimless and directionless. But if I translate it, understand its essence, *gowa*, intellectual understanding, that orients me to how I'm going to view that practice so that it becomes a central organizing principle for everything I do once I'm in a meditation retreat. Then, you see, I don't waste time. Everything about the meditation is always about deepening what I've already oriented myself to with the finger-pointing. Does that make sense?

Student 1

Yes.

Dan

So, both are necessary. Sometimes it says that you have to find the middle path between the path of the *kusāli* and the *paṇḍita*. The *kusālis* are the ones who—all they do is sit, they're somewhat anti-intellectual. They never think about their practice. They never look into the nature of how they're practicing with their metacognitive skills. They just sit. And they think that you shouldn't ever think or even metacognitively reflect on the quality of that meditation.

It's like the old Sufi tale. A log sits quietly on the wood pile for years. But logs never realize God. So don't sit like a log. Sit smartly. You have to have some metacognitive intelligence to evaluate the quality of your practice. Otherwise, you keep making the same old, same old mistakes.

The word *kusha* comes from the grass that they used to stuff their pillows. They sit so long that they develop calluses on their butts. But they never reflect on the sitting, so they never get anywhere with it because they've made a whole bunch of bad habits they don't even know they've made.

On the other extreme, we have the pandits. And the pandits are the ones who conceptualize about all states of meditation and ultimate reality. I mean we have hundreds of Western scholarship books on the nature of emptiness from people who've never done an emptiness meditation in their entire career. It's arrogant. The pandits don't ever put it into meditation practice. So, they don't know anything. But, having a balance between intellectual understanding [and meditation experience], the interplay between intellectual understanding on the one hand and direct meditation experience, that's superior practice. You orient yourself with the intellectual understanding, you take that orientation to direct meditation experience, and you keep looking into it in that experience until you generate experiences. And once you generate the experience there's certain *tak*, signs that you look for. And those signs eventually come to fruition as direct realization. So, you need both. And find that middle ground between the extremes of those who only represent meditation experience with no conceptualizing—the *kusālis*—or those who only represent meditation experience with no metacognitive capacity, and reflect on it. When there's the *kusālis*, you have the *paṇḍitas*. You've got to find the balance between those two extremes.

That's why it's good to often read some of the authoritative texts. Because it gives you a foundation for what these practices are about so you're not just sitting. That's why we have the classes. So that you can learn the basic domain of what each of these practices are about.

For each of the three maps—the prep maps that lead to awakening, the maps that stabilize awakening, and the maps that take stable awakening and lead it to full buddhahood—there's an orientation to each of those maps. And not all Tibetan texts are created equal. Some are better than others in terms of orienting you to the domain of each of those three maps. That's useful to know.

I was talking today with a very good practitioner that I've known for almost forty years now. He spends two or three hours of sitting a day. Has for decades. But he also spends at least half an hour a day reading texts. So, it's a nice balance. So, he has a good intellectual foundation for what he's doing. But he mostly practices.

The trouble with this is that as Westerners I think what's needed is guidance on how to practice it. Tibetan lamas will give you an overview of a certain cycle of practices, intellectually. And then they'll just say, "Okay, now go and meditate on that." But they never tell you how to meditate on it.

That's a common problem with the way Tibetan lamas teach this. They never explicitly say, "This is how you do the meditation," because the structure usually is you get that guidance in a three-year retreat. But the idea that they'll come and teach for a day or two or a week or something like that and then other than transmitting the oral transmission into a *lung* so that you can practice the text, and then give you the special key instructions that show you how to practice, they don't really unpack it for you. They don't say, "Now do this." And that's a common, I think, limitation in the way traditional lamas teach this. They never unpack the instructions for you. They don't unpack the instructions. Or it comes across often as just an afterthought. You understand what I'm saying?

Student 1

Yes, I do. Thank you.

Dan

And we can go over very advanced texts like the *Lamps*. But that's after getting the orientation, the transmission of that. Then you do basic preliminary energy meditation practices. That's not Lamps teachings. You need to unpack the instructions for each Lamp. You understand what I'm saying?

Student 1

Yes.

Dan

Or, talking about the Nyingma, talking about the teachings of Garab Dorje, and then never showing you how they actually do the meditation—it's enough to get an introduction to what awakened mind means—but if you don't get the step-by-step instructions on how you open up the awakening, what good is it? And that's the piece that's often lost in translation, because most Tibetan lamas aren't used to teaching that way. You do all this foundation work and then you go into a three-year retreat, and you sort of figure it out. I mean I have talked to Westerners who have been on three-year retreats, traditional Tibetan structure, and never gotten a single instruction. So even there, the instructions vary in detail.

And you know, there's a laziness about it, I think. That's why with the four volumes of the Rimé Master, Karma Chakme, there was a controversy about whether it should be published. But Karma Chakme was considered in the history of Tibetan Buddhism as the best of the three-year retreat masters ever. And the reason why he was considered that is that he has four volumes of extraordinarily detailed instructions for what you do in that three-year retreat. You don't just sit there silently. He's got a schedule that will make you work every moment, in remarkable detail. And that's all translated into the West now. You can get that in English. And the reason why it was coveted over the years is because nobody ever gave out that kind of detail before.

Student 3

What's it called again, Dan?

Dan

It's called [*Karma Chakme's Mountain Dharma*] and is from the oral tradition. I don't know what the translation is. But you can find it. It's a four-volume set that was originally published by Snow Lion, so that means it's now published by Shambhala because Shambhala bought out Snow Lion. But you can get it.[24]

It's very … it's not subtle, it's very detailed and rich. And there were contemporary three-year retreat masters who had a style not as detailed as that, but were pretty detailed as with Bokar Rinpoche, who died a few years ago. Bokar had that reputation amongst the traditional teachings like that. But most people don't.

Within the Bon, the Bonpo tradition, Lopon Tenzin Namdak, who teaches a lot in the West, particularly in France, teaches like that. He gives a remarkably detailed, explicit instruction about all this stuff.

But you know, I'm talking about a handful of people. So even though we know that this is an interplay between intellectual understanding and direct meditation experience, even within the Tibetan tradition itself, the balance is rarely struck. We tend to take foreign cultures and idealize them, but there's a lot of limitations within the cultures in how it's taught in and of itself.

Hopefully, in standing outside that culture, as Westerners, we can see those limitations and move beyond them. That's the value of bringing the *dharma* to the West. I'm not Tibetan. I don't have to teach that way. That's an advantage. The heart of this, the essence, the art of this is to do it right, to teach in a way that has the details that Westerners need, and that doesn't distort the heart essence of the tradition. That's the art of it.

That's not so easy, from a certain perspective. Maybe I'll take that back. It's not so easy from relative mind. [Light laughter] It depends on the level of mind

---

24 Efforts to locate this text through Shambhala were not fruitful. The closest we could find is a four-volume text entitled *Karma Chakme's Mountain Dharma, As Taught by Khenpo Karthar Rinpoche*, published by Dharma eBooks.

you're operating out of. And it all comes down to the intention of teaching. If the intention is to be a benefit to your students, then the instructions come forth in the necessary detail in a way that the Western mind can grasp. It's as simple as that.

See, I think, if we step back, like myself as a Westerner and as a trauma expert, then what do we know about refugee cultures? Throughout history we have this unfortunate practice of systematically trying to wipe out an ethnic group or a culture. And in the holocausts throughout history, the intention has always been to wipe out an ethnic group or a cultural group. It's not about killing masses of people. It's the destruction, the intentional destruction, of culture. That's what the Nazi Holocaust was about. That's what the "final solution" was about. And that's what the Killing Fields were about. That's what the decimation of the indigenous populations in Central and South America were about. It's all the same.

So, what happens in that kind of situation is that the surviving members of a culture get scattered around the world. And once they get scattered around the world, what's the natural inclination? To find some way of coming back together to rebuild the culture. So, if you look at the trauma literature on refugee trauma, it's not the magnitude of the trauma that's so traumatizing. It's the destruction of the culture itself that otherwise serves as a buffering effect to the other effects of the trauma. Culture protects us from the pure effect of the trauma. We learned that in the West with the famous Buffalo Creek disaster. In the '70s there was a series of slide dams that were being built in West Virginia. And of course, the construction company trying to cut costs used cheap cement that didn't last. In the middle of building these slide dams, the cement broke way and the local community got flooded with mudslides. And a number of people died.

And we did what we usually do. We brought in a disaster team with quick mobilization, and dealt with the surviving family members, and did all the right things. And a funny thing happened—they didn't get better, in the way that we reasonably expect to see. So, ten years later people began to try and say, "Why was Buffalo Creek the exception to what we usually see with disasters?" And the reason why it was an exception is because the way the floods happened was not simply that a hundred people got killed in this rural area of West Virginia. But the mudslides wiped out the local institutions. A lot of people survived, but there were no post offices, and no schools, and no hospitals, and no cultural institutions. It's just a bunch of people. Stripped of all the cultural structure, the effects of the trauma were much more serious, and raw.

So, we learned from that that culture has a kind of buffering effect on the otherwise strong effects of traumatization. And the culturalist approach to treatment of trauma, when we have refugee trauma, we don't just treat the trauma. You build the culture. That's the first intervention. We saw that in the survivors of the Killing Fields. We had a lot of Cambodians locally, mostly in Brighton. The average number of severe traumatizations per survivor was twelve. That means that the victims from the Killing Fields that we had treated locally watched other family members get eviscerated, or got raped, a minimum of twelve times each. That's a staggering magnitude of traumatization per individual. But you can't make a dent in the treatment of that unless you first build a culture. So, what you do with that is you let them get together in local groups. And then what do they do? They speak their own language. They reconstitute their folk traditions—their folk medical traditions, their folk religious practices. They eat the same food. And when you put them in together in enclaves, they rebuild the culture together.

When we saw survivors from [Cambodia] during the Killing Fields, we didn't treat the survivors for trauma. We did culturalist interventions; we helped them rebuild a culture, because that's the natural tendency. You have to rebuild the culture first. And, of course, our immigration policies do exactly the opposite of that. We take refugees and we spread them all over the country, and just separate them out, to mix them, to melt them into the society. And what do they do? They just sort of migrate from this city to that city, leave their groups, and they resist that, and they get back together again, because they need that.

But what are some of the symptoms of cultural destruction? The resistance to acculturation. So, if you have a refugee group, like from, say, Nazi Germany, or from the Killing Fields, they'll resist learning the American language. They're very bad at learning languages. They resist intermarriage. They don't get assimilated easily into Western cultural institutions. They use their own healing practices, their own religious practices. Why? Because it's necessary to rebuild that.

Now from that perspective, we can have a better understanding, I think, of the limitations of Tibetan teaching. The Tibetans don't have a country anymore. In fact, they'll probably never have a country again. Of the people now living in Tibet, only 13 percent of them are indigenous Tibetans. 87 percent are mostly Han Chinese. There is no going back to old Tibet. So, [they are] like all refugee groups where the culture has been systematically devastated.

And of course, when the Red Guard moved in, they spent a week, day and night, burning all the texts, destroyed over a hundred thousand texts in a single week—that's Tibetan Kristallnacht. But as you know, one man, Gene Smith, has reconstructed most of that library because Gene had the foresight into understanding how necessary it is to rebuild a culture. And it's the cultural legacy. That's all available within hyperspace now.

But if we look at it from that perspective, you see, what the Tibetans are struggling with is no different from what the survivors of Nazi Germany, Jewish Central European culture, dealt with, or what the refugees of the Killing Fields in Cambodia dealt with, or what the survivors of the Indian Wars in Central America and South America dealt with. They have to preserve the culture.

So, the Tibetans are ultimately, remarkably conservative. They don't change these practices at all. They teach the practice in the same old, same old way in the West. And the Westerners can't connect with it. And that inflexibility is what you see in terms of refugee behavior. If you think about it in those terms, they have to do it that way, because as any refugee group [whose] culture has been decimated, if they change it, they lose it. The same way that there are many old Jewish families where they resist intermarriage, because if they allow that, they lose the passing on of the traditions in the original way. Or at least that's the fear. It's no different.

So, in that sense, if you have some Tibetans who have allowed themselves to become assimilated into Western culture who really understand it, like Tenzin Wangyal or Dzogchen Ponlop, who really understand the Western mind, they will adapt these traditions without at all losing the essence of them. But that's really a very rare exception. Most Tibetan lamas teach the same old, same old way, and most Westerners can't relate to it at all. That's a limitation. It's a limitation based on their experience. And Tibetans and Western teachers have to move beyond that limitation and find a way of making these teachings alive in the West, in a way that preserves the heart of them.

I'll never teach them alone.

Student 1

I'm sorry?

Dan

I'll never teach them alone. I always teach with or under a lama, and that way it builds in checks and balances. So, I don't get all too far into Western stuff in a way that you lose the essence of this, because how I teach them is always going to be necessarily under scrutiny, to make sure I'm doing it right. But as a Westerner, it allows us a certain flexibility there in a way that works for you. That's my duty to you. You see, in that sense there's a certain advantage to not being Tibetan.

So, we have to have compassion for our Western lamas in their limitations. Given what they went through in the remarkable decimation of a culture in a nation that will never exist again in that form. The fact that they're willing to open this up at all is remarkably generous. That, we have to celebrate.

But even if it's even in Western form, it comes with the same duties. Maybe we should talk about that a little bit.

Damchik, or *samaya*, in Sanskrit, is something quite misunderstood in the West. We've talked about this a little bit before, but it's worth a review. The Western stereotypical misunderstanding of *samaya* is that in the essence and *tantra* traditions you owe a total obedience to your *tantra* master; and they can do whatever they want, and you have to accept whatever they do, whatever their form of teaching is, with uncritical acceptance, because they're taking on your karma for you. That is a total misunderstanding, a kind of Western projection of *samaya*, *damchik*. It's not like that. It's not so hard to understand what *samaya* or *damchik* is. I like to think about it in terms that we well understand in the West, mostly drawing from legal ethics. Because in legal ethics, we talk about duties owed.

In a fiduciary relationship—a fiduciary relationship is characterized as one where the senior party owes a duty to the junior party to put aside their own personal needs and single-mindedly work for the welfare of the junior party. Parent-child relationships are fiduciary relationships. Teacher-student or mentor-student relationships are fiduciary relationships. Priest-minister relationships are fiduciary relationships. And supposedly relationships between bankers and security advisors and their clients are supposed to be fiduciary relationships, [Laughter] but somehow that got lost.

You can't explain fiduciary relationships. But each party owes duties. So, we can think about, in terms of Western legal ethics, we can think about certain relationships in terms of duties owed. And I like to think about *samaya* or the Tibetan word *damchik* as spiritual duties, spiritual duties owed.

Now, in ordinary Buddhism you don't owe anything. You know, you learn meditation practices, and you can do them or not do them, and that's okay. But in the Essence traditions, which means Great Gesture, Mahāmudrā, or Great Completion, Dzogchen, or the *tantras*, those carry a certain *samaya* vow. And the reason why those are the exception is because what's common to the Essence traditions is the otherwise precious guarded secret teachings, which directly open up the direct experience of awakening in your mindstream, and, hopefully, the precious teachings that will bring that awakening to fruition as buddhahood. Those are not ordinary teachings. And if you are given the gift of those teachings, then there are certain duties owed. You don't get them for free. You don't have to pay for them in a monetary sense, but there are certain duties owed, or responsibilities that come with that. And the simple Western term for that is, well, every time a secret teaching is given out, say by Padmasambhava, he'll always end the teaching by saying, "*Gya, gya, gya*"—"Seal, seal, seal."

And in Western terms, "seal, seal, seal" basically means, "Don't fuck it up." [Light laughter] It's the closest meaning that we can give it in Western terms. Which means if you're given something very precious that will open up the direct experience of awakening, which is a jewel, and then you are given the teachings that will help that awakening transform your mindstream into full buddhahood, you have to appreciate the preciousness of that. That's your duty. You can't take it casually. It's that precious.

So, appreciating, grasping the preciousness, is a duty. And second, you have a duty of respect. And that translates behaviorally. The duty of respect means that you will not talk about these, or disseminate them in a way that will weaken them, in a way that will water down their effectiveness. So, you don't just go out and talk with anybody about this stuff. [That's] disrespectful. So, the idea is to not let them be disseminated in a way that causes them to weaken their influence, their potency. And not to, in your own practice, develop the disrespect of not bringing these precious teachings to fruition. Those are really the duties.

So, respect means, you have the duty to seal this in your mind, to seal it preciously in your heart, and to keep it close to your heart, so that it informs everything about your practice. And then that practice brings us to fruition. So, the ultimate respect is to awaken, and ultimately to become a buddha. That's how you show your respect, by being what's being shown to you. And you show your respect by living them in a way that sets an example for others, rather than letting them deteriorate in the way that they get trivialized. That's the respect. That's what *samaya*, or *damchik* means.

So, you seal it in your heart, and you practice it, and single-mindedly bring it to fruition. And you seal your lips in a way that you don't trivialize it in a way that leads to misunderstandings for others. That's the best definition I can give you of what having a spiritual duty means. It's important. Particularly, it might be more important at this time in this culture than at other times in history with these teachings, because we make spirituality into spiritual materialism. We make it into commodities.

You know, some people come and they want to write down and take notes and start going out and teaching it. These are transmission teachings. And we see that kind of thing all the time. So, we tell people they can't tape it, so they secretly tape it. What do you do with that? They just don't get it. Or, I bust my gut all week in a retreat trying to get people to move along with the practices so they can get a taste of direct realization of awakening. And then somebody walks out just in the middle of the crossing over instructions. What kind of disrespect is that? It happens.

And we have people who are awakened and it profoundly changes their life, and they never practice after that because they've gone with the dollar flea market, and they found some other practice. Breaks my heart. And it happens all the time—because we don't know how to seal with respect. And I'm not saying that in a blaming way. As a teacher I see it as my duty to teach people how to respect it. Because we just don't know any better.

Student 1

Ignorance.

Dan

Yes, so maybe we need a course in spiritual etiquette. [Light laughter] But, you see, if you grasp the highest sense of this, it's not possible to disrespect it. Not possible. Not to be arrogant about that, it's just not possible. If you grasp the highest sense of this, you live it. It's not conceptual. And you become an example of that. And your being becomes like the finger pointing at the moon. It fosters a genuine curiosity in others about what all this stuff is about. That's a good thing.

What I'm saying you can test yourself, in your own common sense experience. It makes sense. You can see it.

So, I think, you see, there's a way of bringing the heart essence of these teachings to the West in a way that commands respect despite all of the negative forces in this culture that are potentially erosive to that respect. If you've learned anything from me, the *dharma*'s not for sale. It's not about self-importance. And that I try to live by, at least. Not just in terms of *dharma* teaching but in my life in general. When I work in the court, my opinions aren't for sale. And it's that single-minded determination about what's true that establishes a certain credibility I think. In any aspect of life it's true.

So, good question.

October 29, 2014

Themes: Mindfulness vs. Emptiness of "Grab"; Mixing Practice; Awake in Deep Sleep

Dan

Welcome everyone. You have a question?

Student 1

I have a question just about off the pillow. I think part of the challenge is thinking about spiritual practice outside of a setting like this. I'd just be interested in exploration of that idea, but maybe other people have other …

Dan

Okay. That's a great question. If you didn't hear the question, the question is, what about practice off the pillow? And of course, the answer to that is that what you do as practice off the pillow pretty much depends on the level of where you're practicing.

Usually, we divide the day into formal sitting practice—concentration, for example, Tibetan *nyamjak*, and then the post-meditation practice, called *jepto*, which is what you do the rest of the day. Some people have the view that meditation is sitting on a pillow, that that's the only practice. But, that's a Western view. And it comes from this idea that meditation is like relaxation therapy.

But, in the Indo-Tibetan tradition, there is a very strong emphasis on practicing all the time, on and off the pillow, both. So, there's *nyamjak*, the practice that you do on the pillow, and then there's *jepto*, there is the practice you do the rest of the day. So, it depends on what level of practice you're doing. If you are practicing, say, Burmese mindfulness, which is very popular, on the pillow you would concentrate, stabilize the mind, and then you would open up the field of awareness, and be mindful of everything that comes into the field of awareness in a non-reactive way, every moment. And then, you'd do the same thing off the pillow. You would try and be mindful of every movement, everything you're saying, every body sensation, every thought, every act of seeing, every act of hearing, every act of smelling and tasting, every body sensation that you feel.

The practice off the pillow would be approximating continuous mindfulness. So, you get rid of the gaps, the discontinuities in our awareness. So, the purpose of that is for more continuous awareness. In traditional practice, that's called *trepa*, which is mindfulness you would cultivate during meditation, and then *shezhin*, which is the way you would continue the mindfulness off the pillow in whatever activities you're doing. So, the approximation would be to be more mindful. That would be a First Turning of the Wheel example of off the pillow practice—very popular.

And in the First Turning of the Wheel, the First Noble Truth is the Truth of Reactivity. You can observe the ordinary mind going towards things it likes to make more of it, and you can directly observe the mind going away from things it doesn't like to make less of it. So, it's always going towards to make more, going away to make less of what it doesn't like, and it's that obsessive reactivity that's explained as the cause of suffering in the earliest Theravāda Buddhism. You find that in Buddha's lectures on the Four Noble Truths.

The second would be mindfulness, or off the pillow practice with respect to the Mahāyāna. In the Second Turning of the Wheel, in Mahāyāna Buddhism, they give a slightly different explanation for suffering. They say it's all well and good that the mind moves toward what it likes to make more of it and moves away from what it dislikes to make less of it, but all of that activity is centrally organized around self, so, it's really the grab of self. What causes the mind to move towards something it likes is the preferences that the self has learned. What causes the mind to move away from what it dislikes is the self that's learned to dislike the reverse of the thing. So, you see, it's a slightly different explanation.

So, in Mahāyāna Buddhism, the Tibetan word for that kind of reactivity is *dzin-pa*, which I like to translate as grab. And grab is perceivable. If you don't like what I'm saying and you tell me that, grab. You feel it right away. If you like what I'm saying, grab. If I get attached to an idea, grab. If I'm running late to get here, grab.

So, you see, if you take, as many of you have, the Level 1 retreat, and then you develop a meditation practice on the pillow, what we ask you to do at that level of practice off the pillow is look for the grab in everyday life. Grab is directly perceivable. Look and find out when you have the most grab during the day, and you'll see if you start looking into it, that grab is not only something you can perceive, but there are degrees of grab. Sometimes the grab of experiences is stronger than others, and sometimes they're there, but they're weaker. So, look in terms of where the strong grab is, or the weaker grab is.

And then whenever you find grab, at that point in time, that's when you practice emptiness, which means, you take your awareness and you roll around, right in the midst of the grab, and you stick your nose in it, and see if you can find anything substantial about that grab. And of course, if the Dalai Lama's in town, whenever he talks about emptiness practice, he summarizes, and makes a rather simple point. The essential nature of emptiness practice is *nyedme*, un-findability. If you look for something substantial or solid about whatever that grab is about, the more you roam around in that in your awareness, you can't find it. So, we recommend, for people in their daily practice off the pillow, when they're practicing Mahāmudrā, frequently during the day to look at the issue of grab, and to find what grabs you the most, and to roam around and look into that.

The second part of that practice is to look at the patterns. What is it that you get lost in? What grabs you the most? Is it that you get grabbed by attachment to thought and your own ideas? Maybe it's a particular emotion that grabs you, and you frequently get grabbed by that same emotion. Maybe it's emotionality in general that grabs you, rather than a specific emotion. Maybe it's out-thereness, attached to the seeming solidity of this seeming outside world. Maybe you get caught in the grab of time as you try to rush and meet deadlines, or multi-task and do too much.

This kind of practice means you use your metacognitive intelligence to look at the patterns in your own experience, because not all grab is created equal.

Some things consistently grab you more than other things, what one of my students called, "my favorite clouds." With your best metacognitive awareness, come to see what your favorite clouds are. And then do a specific emptiness practice around that, the way we would do in the Level 1 course. So, if you get caught up in thought a lot, then you do some care[25], practicing on the pillow, emptiness of thought. If you get caught up in emotions, you do some care, emptiness of emotions. If you get caught up in self, do some care of emptiness of personal identity. If it's time, emptiness of time. You do the application of emptiness practice according to what you noticed may have the biggest grabbing. That's pretty much the level of what we tell people to do off the pillow, in following the retreat.

Now, the answer to that question changes depending on the level of proficiency. So, if you have a taste of awakening, then what you need to do is set up the view that shifts your basis of operation to awakened awareness. And on the pillow, keep setting the foundation—the foundational state is always the natural state of the mind, or what we call automatic emptiness—and from that foundational state, use the view that will open up awakening. So, it becomes a learned pathway, so that every time you set it up, the conditions to view it a certain way, your basis shifts to awakening. So, you're operating out of awakened awareness.

So, your task then is to shift your basis to awakening frequently, on the pillow, and for longer and longer duration, until just putting the intention into setting up the view, just like that, you shift your basis to awakening and stabilize it.

Now, then the practice off the pillow will become what we call *drewa*, mixing practice. You set up your view, shift your basis to awakening on the pillow, then get off the pillow while you're still in awakening, and then do so some activity and see how long you can sustain the awakening in that activity before it clouds over. And in mixing practice, you make a hierarchy. It's easy for people if they have some familiarity with shifting the basis to awakened awareness. It's easy to hold that awakening out in nature, at least for some period of time before it clouds over. But it would be a much harder task to hold that awakening when

---

25 This use of the word "care" is unusual in Dan's teachings, but refers simply to making an intentional, "caring" effort to look at one's experience and improve understanding.

you're conversing with somebody, or doing some cognitive activity, or you're thinking.

When I first went to work with Menri, I spent an entire month in retreat, and the entire practice, except when I was doing inner fire practice which was several times a day for short periods, the whole rest of the day, which means all of the time mostly, was off the pillow. And all of the practice was trying to maintain awakened awareness while talking with people. He would have me sit outside of his room, and he had a steady stream of appointments, people would come to visit him, and I'd have to converse with them. And the task was to converse with them while maintaining awakening, and mix the awakening into the conversation.

Then, the harder task for me, was going back and translating, and working on my computer. And I had to mix awakening into working with that cognitive activity, until I could mix awakening into all daily activities, so you never lose it. It's always here. So, at that level of practice, you see, the answer to your question changes. It becomes, off the pillow means maintaining awakening off the pillow all the time.

Now, as you go further up the path … see, there are three maps here. There's the [first] map that takes you from the beginning up to a taste of awakened awareness. The second map is all the teachings that help you stabilize that awakening so you have it all the time, on and off the pillow, all the time. And, during daytime reality, sleeping and dreaming, all the time. You have it all the time. It never goes away. You're always awake.

And then the third [map] practice is, once you have continuous awakening, how you bring that up to full buddhahood and the enlightened buddha bodies—full enlightenment. Then you're a buddha, and that's the end of the path. So, in that third set of practices, when you have awakening all the time, the nature of the awakening spontaneously manifests more and more as *choepa*, conduct. And how you act during the day, becomes very central.

There are, I'm just actually working on that right now, I'm translating a trilogy of texts on conduct, from Shardza Tashi Gyaltsen Rinpoche, a Bon yogi. The first of the three is called *Skillful Conduct of an Advanced Practitioner*. Skillful conduct means during the day what you do with your practice. It's no longer sitting practice. You do it all the time, off the pillow. And, skillful conduct means you learn to continuously see all perceptions as lively emptiness.

So, everything, all the visual forms that you see, are essentially just light. All the smells, all the tastes, all the body sensations are essentially light. The sound that you perceive is not the sound of the car or the bird. What you hear is the sound behind the sound, which is the sound of the liveliness of awakened awareness expressing itself. So, you live in a world of ultimate sound and light. And thoughts that come up are no longer solid, they're radiant. So, they're like rays of light, because thoughts are different from perceptions, because they have directionality. So, you live in a world of light, light rays, and ultimate sound. And how you conduct yourself is how you look into the nature of perception. Sometimes, that's described in terms of everything turning to light and ultimate sound.

Another way of describing that pathway is everything becomes illusory light. And that's called becoming the yogi of illusion. You find that in the great woman master, Niguma, called "The Lady of Illusion." You find that in, for those of you who have taken the Level 3B course on *namjang*, the refining of perception, because everything you do there is to see everything as a variety of dreams and illusions. Everything becomes illusory, nothing solid.

And then you look at thought, all thought, as insubstantial, like rays of light. If you refine perception, and thought, and emotions over time, at that level of practice, conduct becomes what we call "blazing splendor." The whole world is reduced to brilliant energy, and the world is alive and on fire with energy. Absolutely nothing has any solidity to it. Sometimes that's referred to as *hedawa*, a state of chronic wonder. It's remarkable, fantastic. But you can't see anything as out there, it's all nondual perception, and as soon as you see it out there, you screw it up. And the visions are so remarkable that it's hard not to see them as out there, which is why this stuff isn't given out so easily—so you don't screw it up.

Now, what you do, the second part of the conduct trilogy, is sleep and dream yoga. You have to conduct yourself at all times. You conduct yourself all day by looking at thought and perception, and you conduct yourself all night. The practice never stops. So, in the dream, the first thing you have to do is set it up so that you can have awakened awareness during each dream cycle. We have on the average, four or five dream cycles a night. You have to be awake, have awakened awareness during every dream cycle.

Now, somebody once asked me, "What's the difference between lucid dreaming in the West, and dream yoga?" And the difference is the level of awareness you bring into it. In the West, lucid dreaming means you learn to be aware, but it's ordinary awareness during the dream, whereas it's very specific when you're doing dream yoga; it's not ordinary awareness, it's awakened awareness. You have awakened awareness throughout the dream cycle.

It's hard to train yourself to do that. What was explained to me is a little trick, and it's like having a *rigpa* body, your awakened awareness body. And what you do, is ... what the lamas do with each other when they're training themselves to dream is they'll have a buddy who will wake them up every hour. You wake them up suddenly and say, "What's your basis of operation right now?" [Light laughter] And they have to train their metacognitive intelligence to see that they are, indeed, at times, awake during the dream. And you keep waking the person up until they start doing it themselves, and they train to carry that metacognitive awareness into the dream state, and they know that they're awake during the dream.

So, we taught the Level 1 course in Davos, in Switzerland, and then we had four days off. And then we had some visits, and I taught the Level 3B course. So, in those four days off, Andy, many of you know, who organizes the course, he said, "Well, let's get four days off, come to my place in Milan, and we'll just rest for four days." So we were in the plane, and he was reading the dream yoga book that I translated, so he was falling asleep. So, every time he ... He sat in the seat next to me, and I'd poke him every few minutes and say, "What's your basis of operation right now?" And by the end of the flight, he was saying, "You know, this works." [Laughter] He was doing it. He tried to do that with his iPhone, but it doesn't work quite as well. But you can do it that way.

So, the first step is you have to be awakened-aware, during the dream. The second step is you have to—and this is not something you find in Western lucid dreaming—you have to get voluntary control over the dream content. And they explicitly have you do magical feats. So, you, in a single leap, you jump over a mountain in the dream. You fly through a wall. You do any kind of magical feats that are impossible. And, you think of the mystical bird, a *garuda*, and then you fly on the *garuda* to whatever land you want to fly to, immediately. And you do all these magical things.

And the purpose of doing that is to show you two things. Number one, that you can have voluntary control over the content of the dream, and change it at will, by intention, the intention of awareness. And, number two, the reason why we can't do all these magical abilities, like the *gunshes*, the supernormal abilities, is because we have these limiting beliefs about reality.

And what they'll tell you is that it's easier to change around those beliefs in dreams than it is in everyday reality. So, as you use the dreams to sort of flexibly change around the dreams, you're flexibly changing around all of your beliefs about how reality works. But it doesn't challenge it because you say, "That's just a dream, so I can do all that stuff." But once you try and do all that stuff, then the next step is you view everyday reality as a dream, until there's no difference between the waking reality dream and the night dream. Then once it's flattened out, the difference, so it's all one big dream, day and night, then it's not so much of a leap to think that you can change around everyday reality in the same way. So, that's the second step.

The third step is what's called *pelwa*. When I was translating that part of the dream yoga with Asonam, I mistranslated it. I said *pelwa* means to increase, so I thought it meant to increase your skill in working with the dreams. He said, "No, that's not what it means. It means multiplying." I said, "What does that mean?" He says, "You emanate multiple copies of yourself."

So, now, you have to dream thousands of copies of yourself, each doing different things in different realities. And the third level of conduct with dreams is to emanate multiple realities and multiple copies of yourself, acting in different realities, because that's the beginning of buddha training. Because enlightened activity means you can act on many planes of reality simultaneously, helping beings. So, unless you can multiply many copies of yourself, you can't get enlightened activity. So, this is part of the precursor to that. In Western terms, it's the epitome of multitasking. [Laughter]

So, that's dream yoga, and the other part is that your task is then to do sleep yoga. Sleep yoga is that you need to recognize the clear light of awakening in deep sleep. So, it means what? That you have to be aware during deep sleep, and deep sleep has no content. So, if you're aware during deep sleep, at the beginning it's like being aware of this vast, blank field, but you're aware during that.

But, if you recognize the clear light, then what you have is a brilliantly lucid luminous field during deep sleep, with actually no activity in it. And you train yourself to recognize the lucidity of awakened awareness during deep sleep, when there's no activity. It's like … it would be comparable to you trying to develop awakening as your basis of operation during non-conceptual stillness—a deep *samādhi* where there's no thought, which is hard. It's about the same level of difficulty. And it's considered superior practice to develop the recognition of clear light of deep sleep than it is to do the dream stuff because that's more interesting, but it doesn't have the same central focus of refining awakening.

So, then of course, the result of this is you do have awakening throughout dreaming, and throughout deep sleep, and throughout the day, and now your conduct is such that you're practicing all the time. There's no pillow anymore. There's no formal sitting meditation practice. Everything of the day activity is the conduct of practice, and everything at night, sleep and dreaming are both, are the conduct of lucid dreaming.

Now, as you get more advanced, there is another level of conduct for more advanced practitioners, beyond the daytime activity that I mentioned, where you use thought and perception, and the practicing of refinement of illusion. The content beyond that, of more advanced practitioners, is what's called "heroic conduct." Heroic conduct means you take, you purposely put yourself in the most difficult of life circumstances as a way of deepening your realizations. That's called "the practice of heroes." So, whatever your most difficult things for you are, you go right into the midst of that. Or, you put yourself in difficult role situations that involve enormous difficulty, and that's heroic. So, if you went to work in West Africa, with the Ebola situation, or somewhere where there's a war breaking out, and you went to help out, that would be heroic conduct.

Then, the last level of conduct in the daytime series is called "Immeasurably Courageous Conduct." And what you practice is, every instant is the conduct of being fully awake, no matter what comes up. Everything is path, and you can't depart from anything other than it being the path to buddhahood. And, the difference is, you're operating … your mind has opened up all-at-once-ness, so your conduct is operating on many levels of reality simultaneously, number one, that's one of the parts of Immeasurably Courageous Conduct; and number two, it's fully automatic. You're not doing anything anymore. It's doing itself, to itself, by itself.

And then the last of the three books on the trilogy of conduct is the conduct for the dying process. Your task is that in the process of losing this form body, you have to recognize the clear light of awakening as all the organ systems, one by one, systematically shut down, and you go through a series of states of consciousness, and then you have to see all that as just empty, magical display, and not get caught up in it at all. And ultimately, you have to see the clear light of awakening through all that stuff that's happening—all the shifts in state of both body and mind—and recognize the clear light of dying. So, that pretty much concludes conduct at the level of that third map, the buddha training map.

Then the fourth level of conduct is the conduct of a buddha. How do buddhas act? And there, the conduct is described in terms of *trinlé*, or often translated as enlightened activity. Buddhas act inexhaustibly on many levels of reality simultaneously to help beings, and they have the vast scope of omniscient knowledge so that each being they help they do it a different way, according to the capacity of that person, and what they need.

So, if you look at another trilogy—*Lion's Gaze* is the first book; the second is *Discovering Infinite Freedom*; and the third is *The Twenty-One Taras*, the third in that trilogy—*The Twenty-One Taras*, is a metaphor for enlightened activity. Each Tara is a metaphor. There aren't twenty-one Taras. There's one Tara. Each Tara has different ornaments and things like that, but it's really a metaphor for a particular type of enlightened activity. So, if you read that book carefully, what you'll see it is, it's a description of … it's a buddha behavioral manual. It's how buddhas behave. And each Tara is another way that buddhas engage in a specific type of enlightened activity. There are twenty-one types of enlightened activity.

If you follow the implication of what I'm saying then, the more you deepen your realization, the strength of that realization is always and necessarily best measured by conduct. Or as we say, the full measure of realization is always necessarily expressed as conduct. It's how you live your life that expresses the authenticity of that realization. If you don't live it, then realization is not authentic. It has to be expressed in conduct.

And that was something that the great American psychologist William James said over a hundred years ago in his classic book *The Varieties of Religious Experience*, which is a description of mystical experiences in mostly Western, Judaeo-Christian culture. They asked him at one point, how you judge the authenticity of a mystical experience, and his answer was "By their fruits, ye shall know them."[26] In other words, the answer is about conduct. How they lived their life. Realized beings leave behind a wake of positivity, and that's the only imprint that they leave. Sometimes, we call that wake of positivity "the footprints of a buddha." The tracks of a buddha, that's all that's left. Like going to the forest and seeing paw prints. All that positivity is the paw prints of a buddha. It's all that's left, when a buddha disappears.

So, that's a good question. There's a lot to it, but for every level of practice there is a different answer to it. Given that, we'll try and translate that into practice off the pillow, after the break.

Any follow-up questions about what I've said so far? Anything you want me to address further about this?

Yeah?

---

26 Quoting the Christian Bible, Matthew 7:15-20.

Student 2

I guess I'm relatively new to the whole practice.

Dan

Sure.

Student 2

Where should I begin? Because if you take all those steps, on the pillow, off the pillow—but where should I begin?

Dan

Okay, that's a great question.

Student 2

[What's] the right practice for me, to start this thing?

Dan

Well, in the Indo-Tibetan Buddhist tradition, and in Western psychotherapy, surprisingly, the answer would be the same. And the answer is, you always begin with motivation. In Western terms, we call that "stage of change." It was work that was discovered by first looking at smokers. And the four stages of change are pre-contemplation, contemplation, action, and maintenance.

Most people, when they get motivated to the point that they want to stop smoking, they start thinking about how they're going to go about it, and they come up with a plan of action. That's when they enter treatment, or they take a patch, or whatever else. We call that the contemplative stage. They've thought about the fact that they have a problem with smoking, and then they've decided to … they thought about how to go about getting some help with it. Most people enter psychotherapy when they're in the contemplative stage.

If they worked on something for a while in therapy, and they start changing, then there's a whole other set of interventions that they need to stabilize that change. If they have relatively stable change, and they stop treatment, then they need another set of interventions to not relapse, to maintain the change.

But in that literature, it was discovered there were a number of people out there who really aren't motivated enough. We call them "precontemplative." So, if they go into therapy, or they try to work on something, they just go through the motions of it, because they're not really taking themselves seriously that they're going to change, or they don't think that they can change. Or the reason why they go into the treatment is because someone is pressuring them to, and they don't really want to.

"Why do you want to stop smoking?" "Because my doctor tells me I have to." That's not good motivation. They're precontemplative. And precontemplatives either can't acknowledge that they have a problem—in that sense we say they're in denial—or they can acknowledge they have a problem, but that they're not ready to really deal with it yet.

So now, in the psychotherapy field, in the addictions field, there's a whole set of interventions to move people from being precontemplative to contemplative, so they take themselves seriously and they start working on it with good motivation. What was discovered is that a lot of people go into therapy or work on their addictions when they're precontemplative, and it nearly always fails, because they're not really taking themselves seriously. They're just wasting their time going through it.

Now, similarly, in Buddhism, the idea is that most people out there aren't really motivated to put the work into what it takes to do a spiritual practice. So, you start with what I call *lözhi*, with the Four Attitudes. And the Attitudes are designed to get you to slowly change your motivation, so, you change around the priorities of your life and make a place for a spiritual practice. It's a lot of work. How do we get beyond our normal busyness?

I was once teaching with Denma Locho Rinpoche, who was the head of the Gelugpa under the Dalai Lama. We taught together for twenty years. He died last week. It is a loss for … [Dan's voice softens to inaudible]. But one time I was teaching with him, and a Western student says, "What do I do when I'm lazy?" And he shot back at the student, and said, "No. Laziness is for the monks in the monastery. You Westerners aren't lazy. Your laziness is busyness."

Busyness is what our laziness is. We get so caught up in what we're doing that we don't take time to put in … we don't make spiritual practice a priority. So, the first thing is how to make it a priority. Then there is a whole world of interventions in Buddhism the same way there's a world of stage-of-change interventions in Western psychology, and the *lözhi*, or the Four Attitudes, are the usual way to do that.

What they say, is avoid *charinyenju*, or hairy renunciation, hairy. And hairy renunciation is a colloquial term that means somebody gets, "Oh, wow." They go to a lecture, or they go to a meditation thing, and they say, "I'm going to change my whole life around." And they give up everything in their life, and they go out and do this thing, and it's not natural to give up everything and try to do this. So, six months later they get sick of it, and they never go back to it again, and that's damaging. The better way to do it is to stay in your everyday life and slowly change your attitude.

So, the first of the four attitudes is *daljor*, precious opportunity. You do a serious of visualizations about all the unfortunate circumstances in people's lives, and you imagine that that was happening to you. And then you come back and contrast that to what you've got that they don't have. And each time it hammers home the preciousness of the opportunity that you're not taking.

Then you do … the second is called the cause and effect of karma. It's like what in behaviorism is called cost/benefit analysis. You think of some action that you're engaging in, and then you predict the likely consequences of engaging that over time, good and bad. So, you can see where this is going to take you if you keep going down this road. And if you keep doing that kind of cost/benefit analysis some of the things that you do in your life that are just useless or destructive, you just don't go there anymore, because you can't avoid thinking about where you're going to end up if you keep going this way.

Then the third is the sufferings of *samsāra*. You take all realms of existence, and you do vividly detailed visualizations about all the suffering on every plane of the six grounds of existence. It's sort of like your own personalized Dante's *Inferno* trip.

And then the fourth is you imagine the change and impermanence of everything, culminating until you actually imagine your own … you predict that, you actually go through the vivid, imaginative details of your own aging and dying process.

By the time you finish these four visualizations, you find that naturally you're cutting off the things in life that seem less important, and you make a place for it—naturally, without *charinyenju*, without hairy renunciation. Then, it's likely to stick.

So, that's the first thing. It starts with motivation. Then, at that point, you want to start with the meditation practice. The foundation is to train your mind. So, that means starting with concentration. You have to train the wild elephant of your mind that jumps around all the time and is distracted by everything. And standard concentration practice is what you want to do with that. That's the starting point. So, that's where you start.

And then the last of the three books on the trilogy of conduct is the conduct for the dying process. Your task is that in the process of losing this form body, you have to recognize the clear light of awakening as all the organ systems, one by one, systematically shut down, and you go through a series of states of consciousness, and then you have to see all that as just empty, magical display, and not get caught up in it at all. And ultimately, you have to see the clear light of awakening through all that stuff that's happening—all the shifts in state of both body and mind—and recognize the clear light of dying. So, that pretty much concludes conduct at the level of that third map, the buddha training map.

November 19, 2014

Themes: Signs of *Tulku* Emanations: Rahob Rinpoche, HH the Dalai Lama, Panchen Lama

Dan

Welcome everyone. You have a question?

Student 1

I don't think this will be a long question, but you've mentioned that Rinpoche said that he's not going to be reincarnating in the lineage, but certainly intends to come back.

Dan

He says that. I didn't say it that way.

Student 1

Or that, as I understood it, there won't be another Rahob holder of the lineage. That's how I understood it, so maybe I misunderstood, but the reason I'm asking is if that's true, then His Holiness the Dalai Lama has also been talking about him being the last Dalai Lama. I'm just curious about this; now it seems like a pattern. Maybe you could talk about that?

Dan

Well, I don't know how much I know about this; but I'll tell you what I do know, maybe very little. But the two situations are very different. Enlightened beings, non-ordinary beings, through *gongpa*, their own intention, can emanate in any plane of reality or simultaneous planes of reality that they want for the sake of conveying teachings or helping beings in a certain plane of reality, in a certain geographic area for a certain length of time. That's what we call a *tulku*. *Tulku* is an emanation. *Tulku* is the same word in Sanskrit as *nirmāṇakāya*—the enlightened body of emanation. But really, it's plural: there's not one *tulku*, there are many emanation bodies on simultaneous planes of reality.

But it's such that these beings have the intention of appearing in any world for the purpose of conveying teachings. So, what that has meant traditionally in Tibet, and in the whole Himalayan plateau of cultures, is that *tulkus* generally hang around in a certain geographic area for many generations. So, when they still have a form body, they can emanate a form body. They can grow up, rediscover their old identity as a great teacher or a buddha, and then convey teachings for a good part of their life spans. Then, when they die, they leave behind a series of signs—*tak*, signs—that through a process of seership or divination, the signs are readable and you can tell from the signs roughly where the person is going to recycle himself.

The signs are usually when the person dies and you take the physical form body and burn it; in the charred bones, usually in the charred skull, the configuration of ashes is readable in a certain way that is like a map. It tells you the regions that they're going to reincarnate in, which typically is the same region. If you want a pretty good documentary on that, look at a film called *Unmistaken Child*. It's about a very prominent teaching lama who dies, and his attendant, who is very devoted, searches to rediscover him. It shows you the whole process of how amongst the candidates, they read the signs and then determine … usually, the signs will tell you that a certain geographic area might be a cluster of villages. And then, based on the prophecies and the signs, they will look for certain things and they'll round it down to three or four candidates. And then, they'll show the three or four candidates' objects—usually mixed with objects that belonged to the former incarnation of that lama and other objects—with the idea that the correct child will pick out his own stuff, not the other stuff.

It's sort of like showing a lineup; you show the real assailant and a bunch of dummy pictures, and then they pick out the real one. It's more valid that way.

What Rahob has conveyed, as far as I can understand it, is the end of the lineage. Rahob emanated as a *tulku* in the fourteenth century. And then a monastery developed around his teachings, which is Rahob Monastery, which was destroyed in the Cultural Revolution. It was a very big monastery; it was for six thousand people. Now, it's got three hundred monks. It's a smaller, rebuilt monastery, but a viable working monastery. What he conveyed in this last trip is that he's not going to reincarnate as a *tulku* anymore in Kham, in Eastern Tibet, or his region. He told his people not to look for him; that's what he's conveyed. What he's been working on is their most important book in Indo-Tibetan Buddhism, their most popular book, *Shantideva's Bodhichayravatara* or "awakening to the path of enlightenment"—"entering the path of enlightenment."

What he's doing is he's been writing his own commentary on that, the *Bodhicharyavatara*, in Tibetan. He said he would like to make one more trip to visit his people and give that teaching as his last testament, but he's saying it's the end of the line. He won't be a *tulku* in Eastern Tibet or Tibet anymore. He's not saying he's going to stop teaching. He's basically, for years now since the early 1980s, been in America. The first time, which is four years ago, we went to Tibet with him. When we all finally arrived—and about fifty thousand people showed up to greet him, because he's the emanation of Padmasambhava, so he's a big deal there—they put him up on his throne and he did a traditional seven-line prayer.

When we went this last time, we arrived and he got up on the throne, and he didn't do the traditional seven-line prayer. He gave a talk about why he's teaching in the West. Basically, what he said was that the West had a great tradition of psychotherapy. And that his opinion is that Westerners, through psychotherapy, look deep into the mind. He thought that that was a good match for the teachings. That's why he was staying, to bring these teachings to the West. There was a kind of implication in that, but not directly stated, that Tibetan practice had deteriorated more to rituals and prayers, and not looking deep in the mind. Maybe, that's why the teachings were coming to the West, because Westerners, despite all the other stuff that we do—like the *dharma* flea market approach for one thing—there are at least a number of Westerners who are sincere enough about what they need to do in their own mind. Even though they're not devotional and they're not interested in all the rituals, in all that stuff, there's a way of getting to the depth of these practices, which is a good match.

So, all that he's conveyed is that he's not going to reincarnate in Tibet. That's the end of the communique of the line of transgenerational *tulkus*. He didn't say that he's not going to reappear, and he didn't say one way or another what he plans to do in the West after he meets his form body.

But, if you take the mythology of Padmasambhava, he never died. Since spreading the teachings in Tibetan in the eighth or ninth century, he has lived in the West and lives in the Copper Mountains. I thought it was interesting that in the years since Rahob was my roommate, maybe thirty years ago, we both traveled a lot and lost touch. In the years that we lost touch, he was living in Arizona in the Copper Mountains.

He has not said one way or the other whether he intends to reincarnate in the West. It's just not clear. I don't know what it means. With the Nyingma Dzogchen material that we're learning, I only teach up to him. So, the fact that he didn't go to Israel was a bit strange. It put me in a position of having to teach the full course without his transmission. I don't know what that means. They got the same material. I took the material that he usually reads and retranslated everything from the Tibetan, explained it in a way that I think is accurate to the text. But certainly his presence as a form body was missing, but not his presence.

So, I don't have any idea what that means, nor what I do with teaching Nyingma material after he leaves his form body. It's just not clear. All I'm doing is following what I've been asked to do and trying to do it the right way. We'll see what happens from here. Don't know.

Now, the Dalai Lama's position is quite different from that. He's also said that he's not going to reincarnate as the Dalai Lama, but I'm not sure it's for the same purpose. There are two things about that, both of which are political. He being a former head of state, that statement is much more politically motivated. Number one, as he's manifested many times over, he is a stronger believer in democracy. He doesn't think the Tibetans should have had a Dalai Lama or anybody as a ruler. They should, in this modern era, switch to election; and then the Tibetans, as a government in exile, have elected a prime minister, which was a former Tibetan Harvard Law student and now the prime minister, who is very smart and very good. The Dalai Lama was the first one to support this democratic process.

He stepped down from being the Dalai Lama head of state for that purpose. The Dalai Lamas were not always the head of state. The first four Dalai Lamas were not head of state, they were just head of the Gelugpa. And then, the fifth Dalai Lama was appointed. That's a complex part of history here. At that point, the Khan lineage of emperors, Genghis Khan and his descendants, had militarily conquered most of Asia. They had a massive empire. They understood that the best way of controlling a conquered empire was through religion.

The fifth Dalai Lama was actually appointed a puppet of the Khan emperor to control Tibet. He was not a nice man. There was a reign of oppression, where many practitioners were killed—mostly Nyingma, Bonpo, and Kagyu. Obviously, the Gelugpa flourished at that point. And the Sakya also flourished, because the head of the Sakyas was the personal lover of the Khan emperor. They reaped lots of wealth, so that the other three of the five great chariots were seriously oppressed. This current Dalai Lama does not like that history. He's tried to personally correct it by stepping down as head of state, by putting all five great chariots at equal footing, and respecting all of them equally.

Since the Bon were the most oppressed, he officially made the statement that the Bon were the indigenous and the oldest religion in Tibet. Therefore, all the other four great chariots of teaching had owed something to the Bon. In response to that really quite political statement, when Menri built his library, he didn't make it a Bonpo library. It has the Tengyur and Kangyur canon for all five great chariots equally represented in the library.

Then, to make sure that the other four sects went along with his wishes, he personally appointed Menri as his personal meditation teacher. That was a clear statement of good faith. It was a way of trying to heal a great rent in their own tradition.

Now ... the other part of the politics of the Dalai Lama as I understand it, and this is not something that's ever come out of the news, but traditionally, the Panchen Lama, who is sort of like the vice president, is the one who decides amongst the candidates when the Dalai Lama dies, and then several years later there are a number of young kids who are candidates. The Panchen Lama is the one who has to make the final call about who the real Dalai Lama really is.

The story with that that I know something about is that when, in the late '50s when the Chinese were at the border ready to invade Tibet, they knew that the invasion was inevitable. The young Dalai Lama—then in his, I think, early twenties, late teens, early twenties—along with the Panchen Lama who was somewhat older, they talked together and decided that the best thing to do would be to make a trip directly to Beijing and negotiate with Mao directly a peaceful settlement for the takeover.

The Panchen Lama and the Dalai Lama agreed that it was necessary to do to prevent a violent invasion of their country. They went on that trip. There was a lama that was an old, dear friend of mine, since deceased, called Gomang Lama. Gomang Lama led the expedition, and on the third day of the expedition, Gomang Lama had a prophetic dream about an ambush. He was very disturbed, and he told the Dalai Lama that if they continued on the trip, there would definitely be an ambush.

Everybody agreed that the Dalai Lama's life would be in danger if he was captured, and the country would clearly fall. It would be worse because it would be demoralized, and he had to lead, but the Panchen Lama felt that the negotiations were important enough that he would take the risk upon himself and go ahead with it. So, they put a dummy up in the place of the Dalai Lama in his carousel. Panchen Lama went on with the rest of the troops and then they disguised the Dalai Lama as a salt trader. Gomang took him back on a donkey personally, just the two of them. He basically saved the Dalai Lama's life.

Seven days later, there was the ambush that was predicted in the dream. The Panchen Lama was captured. He spent the rest of his life in house arrest in Beijing and died. The Panchen Lama then was reincarnated. Then, two years ago, the young Panchen Lama—now you've got to think about this, because this is really amazing—the young Panchen Lama who was determined by the Chinese and educated by the Chinese when he was eight years of age, personally escaped from China. Despite his education by the Chinese, he escaped as an eight-year-old boy himself. He ran away, dodged every way to get caught, and made his way to India. He showed up and presented himself to the Dalai Lama and said, "I'm back."

Only one person knows where the Panchen Lama is, and that's the Dalai Lama. Because, everybody knows that if the Panchen Lama's whereabouts were to be found, the Chinese secret police would certainly kill him. You see, what's going to happen now, is that the Chinese have to fake it. They're going to put in a double, a fake Panchen Lama, who is going to do what everybody has expected all along. The fake Panchen Lama, whose allegiance is to China, will choose the next Dalai Lama, which will be a Chinese Dalai Lama.

But what the Chinese have done is lost control over it. They won't mention anything about this, because they've lost control, and they want to save face. As long as the real Panchen Lama is alive and he's young, when this Dalai Lama dies, according to the tradition, the real Panchen Lama will decide the next Dalai Lama. Now, I don't know what that means, because the Dalai Lama decided that he was not going to be the Dalai Lama before this whole thing happened. He made that announcement a couple of years ago. I think that at the time, he was making it because he didn't want there to be a cat fight between the Tibetans and the Chinese about who the Dalai Lama was, because there are obviously two of them.

But, now the situation's changed. There's still only two of them. I think part of the reason why he's saying that he's not going to reincarnate as the Dalai Lama is that he doesn't want to have this cat fight between two nations, because they're going to have to get along together and heal. In that sense, I think it's entirely politically motivated. Whether a great being like that will return in the form of being an emanation of Avalokiteshwara or Chenrezig again, I think the answer to that is probably "yes." But it certainly will not be in the form of a head of state. It may not be in a form that we expect, but I have no doubt about his returning. So, you see they're quite different situations.

But the larger issue here is that this is the time when all will come to the West. That means all of the teachings. Therefore, we ought to expect two things. One, that through the fruition of his teachings, buddhas will develop in the West. We will have Western buddhas. As an egalitarian culture, I think that there's a certain promise here that we could have equal representation of girl and boy buddhas, which was the original tradition in Tibet, which got lost in the monasticism. But I think there's a very strong possibility that that can happen here.

And, that the full array of teachings will come to the West and that some of the undiscovered termas will likely show up in the West, secret treasure texts in the future. And that is already is happening. Some of these *tulkus* will continue their lineage of teaching. They'll just relocate themselves in the West and reincarnate in the West as Westerners. We've seen some of that already. Lama Yeshe and Thubten Zopa were a teaching team that was very popular amongst Western students in Nepal outside of Kathmandu in the '70s. Many Western students flocked there because they were the first to systematically offer real meditation teachings to Westerners about Mahāyāna Buddhism. It was very popular.

Lama Yeshe was a big roly-poly, wonderfully jovial warm cow. Thubten Zopa in those days was thin, and wiry, and fierce. They were like good cop, bad cop, teaching the *dharma*. And then, Lama Yeshe died of stomach cancer, and there's a movie made about him that's not exactly inaccurate, that he basically reincarnated as a boy in Spain. The parents knew nothing about this tradition, basically. When they learned more about what was at stake with all this, they gave up their kid and let this Spanish kid go get traditional training in a monastery to become the next Lama Yeshe, who he now is. The Western Lama Yeshe trained in the traditional way. I think you're going to see more of that kind of stuff.

The teachings are here now. Now, it's just a question of nurturing them, developing them more. So, good question.

We don't, as Westerners, put a lot of stock in reincarnation, but it's interesting because it's not a topic that Western science is willing to address. But, if you go back to the 1880s and 1890s, the great American psychologist from this area, William James, was terribly interested in the topic. His best friend F.W.H. Meyers from the UK wrote a rather extensive book of accounts called *Human Personality and Its Survival of Bodily Death*. That was a topic of interest to the scientists of that day.

[Some say] there could be a quantum of bioenergy left over that survives bodily death and recycles itself. It's what is called "indestructible essence." That little indestructible essence, according to Tibetan theory, is lodged in the center of the heart at conception—not at birth, at conception—and held there by four energy knots. And, at a certain point of the dying process, when every system systematically shuts down, at a certain point after physical death, those knots loosen and the indestructible essence leaves its lodging, and then floats in the central chamber for up to three days—not three days, up to three days. It could be a minute. Somewhere in that time span, it will leave the body through some orifice.

So, physical death is when the brain and the heart die, but spiritual death comes up to three days later—not three days later, it could be right away—when that indestructible essence, that computer chip, leaves the body.

That computer chip contains information that has a signature, it's like a fingerprint. That has the signature of all the memory, of all the common memory traces, of all of your lifetimes. So, everybody's indestructible essence is absolutely unique and not like anybody else's. It's like a carbon fingerprint. And that leaves the body, and depending on what root of exit, what orifice it leaves by, that has some influence—not entirely, but some influence over how it will reconfigure itself.

It's an interesting argument, because it has some scientific basis to it. So, the interesting question is about when a realized being does a practice like *phowa*. You can actually have voluntary control over the recycling process, not something that normal individuals can do, but at advanced stages of practice there are types of *phowa* practices that allow you to have voluntary control over how you want to recycle yourself. And, if you want to come back in certain planes of reality to help beings or to carry on a certain level of teachings, you have some control over how you come back.

And usually, great teachers will do that. Their intention is to continue teaching or serving beings in whatever way they're serving beings. They'll intentionally recycle themselves. They have to go through the whole process of being reborn and reeducated, and discover who they are again, but they still go through that process. Whatever that takes, they do it. It's an interesting theory from an evolutionary point of view, because it ensures that the teachings continue, and we bring out the best of human nature. Because those that get selected are the ones that are going to be the best candidates to carry on the teachings and to serve humanity the best.

Even if you don't believe anything about reincarnation, from an evolutionary point of view, it's adaptive. It's very adaptive, because it ensures the best people carry on the teachings and serve the greater social good.

What's lacking in that process, I think, is that it's limited to the spiritual. So, they recycle themselves for the purpose of conveying teachings and serving beings. There isn't reason to think that we could do that differently. But, if you take the myth of *Gesar* in human history, there have been three very long oral poems. The first and oldest is *Gilgamesh* from the Middle East. There's *Beowulf*. And there's *Gesar*. It's a very long oral poem that's passed down from mouth to mouth, heart to heart, from generation to generation.

What *Gesar* is about is enlightened leadership. It's about a king who through his practice becomes enlightened. He uses his spiritual realization to rule as an enlightened king to serve all beings. There isn't any reason why we couldn't develop a model of enlightened leadership. We certainly need it to survive. It might be useful if we develop a model of enlightened leadership to use the same kind of model of reincarnation. Enlightened leaders should keep on recycling themselves. So, we keep getting the best of leadership, if we're going to survive as a species.

Some people in the West are now reconsidering that, that there's the possibility, because there's a lot of courses in business schools and law schools teaching courses in leadership. Now that mindfulness has gotten enormously popular in the West, people are talking about mindful leaders. Why don't we go back to the tradition itself and take the *Gesar* model in talking about awake leaders, enlightened leaders, not just mindful leaders. Train enlightened leaders and use the same model for recycling them.

Student 2

This addresses this topic from a different direction. I've been moved this week hearing that Thich Nhat Hanh had a major stroke a month ago. My heart went out to him and his students.

Dan

I heard that he was recovering.

Student 3

I heard that he is recovering also. This week also I was shocked to lose a patient of mine whom I had a very close relationship with, who died suddenly at fifty years old of natural causes, completely unexpectedly. I'm moved by complicated—well, not complicated, but this is so pure—but unusual grieving in that it's somebody with such an intimacy in this relationship. In some ways, so I guess my question is what do we do if we find out something has happened to you? What do we do if we find out something's, you know, something happens to Rinpoche and we go to you and say, "Okay, what do we do?" In a sense, we pray, I know that. In a sense, my heart will tell me. I know that. But I really am very serious with this question. I feel like, you know, Gretchen will be tied up with her loss in a sense. Who will help us with that? Who are the leaders in this community who help us with that? It's a very simple, but heartfelt question.

Dan

Well, before I answer your question, since you talked about Thich Nhat Hanh, we should also acknowledge something else. That is two weeks ago, Denma Locho Rinpoche died. I taught with Denma Locho for twenty years.

He was the head of the Gelugpa. When the Dalai Lama stepped down as the head of the Gelugpa [in 2011], Denma became the head of the Gelugpa.

So, just so you know, all of what you learn of the Elephant Path comes from Denma Locho Rinpoche. Everything I learned comes from him: spinning the sword meditation, switching from mind perspective to event perspective, the Atisha emptiness of self meditation. So, except the Mahāmudrā piece, two thirds of that Level 1 course that we teach all came from Denma Locho Rinpoche. I wanted to acknowledge his contribution.

Student 3

Thank you.

Dan

Even though he's not in his form body anymore.

Well, there are two answers to your question. One answer to your question is that if your motivation is sincere, in your practice you will always get everything that you need along the way, but not usually in ways you expect. So, when I die, and not in my form body anymore, and Rinpoche is not in his form body anymore, if your practice is sincerely motivated, you will get what you need. It will just come and appear in a new form. You just have to recognize it. It doesn't stop. The *dharma* takes care of itself. It's always regenerating itself. It's infinitely regenerative.

As long as there are students who are worthy, the teachings and teachers will appear. Your task is to use your most metacognitive intelligence to recognize authentic teachers that represent the lineage. That's one answer to your question. There are actually three answers to your question.

The second answer to your question is what Rinpoche is saying, that not all teachings are done through oral transmission. A lot of the teachings are done through mind-to-mind transmission, especially for advanced students, which basically means if you go into your *samādhi*, whatever level of practice that you're doing, at a certain point, typically, if you've opened up *dharmadhātu* exhaustion and that's your path, you start to open "all-at-once-ness."

When you think about—okay, you take the view of Lion's Gaze, and it opens up awakened awareness as your basis, then you have to stabilize awakening. When you start to stabilize awakening as your basis of operation, then your mind turns from the ground aspect of awakening to the appearance aspect of awakening. Then, your view becomes liveliness until everything, every moment, is the liveliness of awakening; awareness, until you have a continuous flow of lively awakened awareness. Then, you have it all the time.

Then, you take the inseparable pair of the ground and appearance aspect of awakening, which is watching everything arise as spontaneously present from groundless ground, left completely alone. There you break karmic connections. If you don't form any new karmic impressions by not engaging anything, it forces the mind to release all the previous karmic impressions. You do that until you're on the path of *dharmadhātu* exhaustion.

At some point, as things get more pure, your next view is going to be opening to everything as basic space. When you do that, it opens up "all-at-once-ness." Now, your mind operates on many levels simultaneously. When you get to that level of practice, which many of you are now doing, it's *dharmadhātu* exhaustion. It's only one more view. When you're given the instructions for that view, which we're beginning to open up to, when you get the instructions from that view, that will open "all-at-once-ness." You have to stabilize that. Then, all of the teachings are downloaded, but they don't come from out there. They come from your own buddha nature.

That's what we call mind-to-mind transmission. If you're at that level of practice, Rinpoche is no longer in his form body as Padmasambhava, and you want to talk to Guru Rinpoche Padmasambhava, you want a certain teaching? He'll give you the whole thing. The whole thing will just come to you. I just finished in Switzerland teaching the 3B course, which is *Namjang*, *Buddhahood Without Meditation*. I've read it in Tibetan seven times, but I can't say that I understood it.

And then, in an instant, the whole thing came to me. I ran it by Rinpoche and I said, "Is this right?" He said, "Yes. You understand it." But I didn't sit down with him and have him explain each chapter. It didn't come from the reading; it just came as a complete structure without words. It was perfectly clear. That's mind-to-mind.

Now, the third answer is the most interesting one. I'll answer this personally, because when I started as a kid in my late teens and twenties living with Geshe Wangyal, that changed everything in my life. But, when he died, at first I had a lot of regret, because I was a young kid and I felt I wasted a lot of time there. I could have used it better. He was fierce and I was terrified of him, so I wouldn't press him for things. I got what he gave me. But I wouldn't pester him to get more teachings. Now, I would pester him, because it's precious, short, this life.

But I got what I got. And then, having gotten what I got before the practices, everyone had a chance to mature and then that was a time in my life that I was developing my professional career, trying to run some departments at the medical school, and trying to raise a family. Many times, I felt like there's a ... One of my favorite plays is *Camelot*. There's a scene where everything is going bad with the Round Table, everything is completely messed up. Richard goes out to the forest to look for Merlin. The poignant part of that scene is after searching everywhere, it's very clear that Merlin isn't in the forest anymore. There's no Merlin anymore. There are so many points in my life, particularly in my thirties and forties, that I kept looking for Merlin. Merlin wasn't there anymore. And then, at some point in my practice, it became clear to me that looking for Merlin was misguided. And then, what Geshe Wangyal had taught me is that the way that I would not miss his form body or his presence is because the real teaching is that you have to become that.

When you become that, there's nothing missing. And then, the whole thing seemed perfectly ridiculous to me, all that missing stuff. You understand exactly what I'm saying. You have to become that.

But, my personal experience, having gone through that, is when you have that loss all the doubt comes out. All that is just clouds. You have enough. You have enough in yourself with your own buddha nature, with your own intelligence, your own resourcefulness. You have enough of the teachings. We've given you a whole map that keeps spelling out details for you. But, what else do you need?

Just do it.

You understand now. You have to become that. That is "not missing." There's no missing. There's not a shred of missing left. I don't miss Geshe Wangyal anymore. I did for a long time. I don't miss Denma who just died, because they're never apart from me. I won't miss Rahob and I won't miss Menri, because they're never apart from me.

But it's not like it's an internalization of their being. It's more like they're never apart from me, because there's a certain level of understanding and realization of being that. So, what's the problem here?

APPENDIX 1

Interview of Dan Brown About His Unique Way of Teaching

by Susan Pottish in San Francisco, CA—2/16/2017

SP: I was hoping you'd give us a sense for how you developed your unique way of teaching.

DB: Well, there are a couple of things I think are useful in terms of background, personally I feel … that most people don't know. The first is that when I went to graduate school at the University of Chicago, I couldn't afford undergraduate school, I had to work my way through school; my parents didn't support me. So, I worked three jobs to get through undergraduate school at the state college because that's all I could afford. And I knew that the only way I could get a ticket to graduate school was to get a scholarship. So, I did a lot of research on different scholarships that were available, and in those days—they don't exist anymore—in those days the Danforth Foundation [whose founder developed Purina Dog Chow], Danforth gave ten a year for young promising teachers. And I researched that and I got it. And one of the things that was unusual is that they paid four years of tuition and living expenses in Chicago. So, I couldn't have gone without the Danforth. So, I want to give them some credit. They stopped giving those scholarships, but one of the things they did, a requirement of the scholarship, was that in the summer, for four years, we had to go to a conference for a month, and what they did is two things: they brought in the best teachers in the country in different fields to do live teaching, and then they would give lectures on how people taught and what was effective. And the second thing they did is they made us teach and they filmed it and they did live action coaching.

So, I actually was taught how to teach. It's not done anymore. But that was very important because you got to see some of the role models of the best effective teachers out there. So, I think this goes to your point because no one ever gets taught how to teach. But Danforth had a special mission for that and they selected people who they thought would be talented teachers and gave them the best training. So, I had that. It was really very fortunate to get that possibility in life.

SP: Was it teaching in a particular field?

DB: So, what they [taught] was how to teach across fields. Because when they role modeled, there were teachers that they took from every field—from physics to English. When we taught, we taught in our fields and then they broke it down.

The other thing that I think was helpful, more than my classes in four years of undergraduate study, is that I did four years of debate. And you've got to learn to think on your feet, and talk articulately. So, those were my undergraduate training experiences and graduate training experiences that I think were helpful.

The second thing that I think was helpful in terms of from a Western point of view, in terms of working with Tibetan stuff was that I've been working at Harvard Medical School for thirty-six years now. And I mostly taught, in the early days I taught mostly interns, post-docs and medical residents and interns. And what I learned was they're just too damned busy. So, whatever you want them to learn, spoon feed it to them. Don't make them look things up because they're not going to do it. They don't have time. So, as a senior teacher at the medical school, my task was to take a certain area and spell it out as clearly as I can so they didn't have to look anything up—because they're not going to do it!

And I think that that's not just applicable to medical school training, but in this culture where everyone is busy—I remember teaching with Denma Locho Rinpoche, who was the abbot of Namgyal Monastery in Dharamsala. And one time a student asked him, how do I deal with laziness in my everyday life, and he said, "No, laziness is for the monks in the monastery. For you guys in the

West, it's busy-ness. That's your laziness." And I think that's true. Most people who come to retreats are too busy. So, you have to start out with them, spoon feed it to them. So, that's the second thing I learned.

I think the third thing I learned was in working with Erika Fromm for thirty-five years—she was my main clinical mentor, who was in hypnotherapy—I learned how you word things matters —so, always changing the wording to get something that works effectively for this population of Western students. I'm not sure even nowadays that the wording—you know, this is relevant to you—the wording of what we do in classes in general may not be relevant to twenty-year-olds. This is a different culture. So, we have to do it completely for that generation, if we can. I'm not sure how to do that yet. But you know what I'm talking about. We're always working on how to word it.

And then the fourth thing I learned was that since 1990, that's what, twenty-seven years now, at Harvard my role is to teach continuing education. So, that's post-graduate. I don't teach the students anymore. These are fully licensed people. And my field is to review hundreds and hundreds of journals, outcome research journals to update and upgrade the standard of care in psychiatric diagnosis. So, I'm constantly updating what we know in terms of the scientifically important literature on what works.

So, those four influences I think are the most important things [about] what I do in a whole different field, which is teaching Tibetan Buddhism. But those are the things I learned most from the West.

What I've learned from the Tibetans is that it's a refugee culture. And being a refugee culture being invaded by Chinese over fifty years ago is that the culture is scattered all over the world, and dismantled, and as a result of that, when you get a refugee culture, they resist acculturation and they become very conservative. So, if you look at what happened, say, with the Nazi Germany culture, and the decimation of the Jewish culture in central Europe when they got scattered all over the world—what did they do? They resist intermarriage, they do the same old Pesach ritual, it's the same way every year. Nobody changes anything anymore. They resist acculturation and they try and speak still Yiddish. It won't work, but they become very conservative because that's what keeps the culture together. But what gets lost in a refugee culture is innovation.

So, I think the same thing is happening with the Tibetans. It's a refugee culture. So, the Tibetans go around the world and they teach the same old same old stuff the same way, and there's no innovation anymore. And they won't adapt to the culture. They refuse to adapt to Western culture. There are some important exceptions to that. Like, I think, Tenzin Wangyal has a pretty good sense of how to teach Westerners. Or Dzogchen Ponlop, who's in Seattle. But, most of the others don't, and they have no interest in how to adapt it to Western culture because they're trying to preserve it, and it's sort of sad. But, that's what the truth of it is.

So, I've learned that most Tibetans can't do this. So, the burden is on people like myself who live in both worlds, to bring innovation back but to preserve the tradition in a way that they would feel like I'm not disturbing it. And if I can do it in a way that they're happy with and still make it work for Westerners, then we've got something that works here.

SP: Have you had contact with the younger generation?

DB: Well, Asonam. He is forty-two, forty-three, something like that. And he's the next generation of very good teachers. And it's been a good learning process. His Holiness [Mentri Trizin] told Asonam and Chongtul, and Tenzin Wangyal, to teach with me, because they need to learn to teach Westerners. So, when we were teaching the Akhrid thing for the first time, he had that conservatism that's very much appropriate to the culture, although Menri is not that way. So, he said what should I teach? What are we going to teach them this week? I said, what we're going to teach them is all fourteen lessons. He said, what? Do all fourteen lessons? I said we'll do all fourteen lessons in a week. His eyes bugged out. I said, yes, we're going to do all fourteen lessons. We're going to do two a day for seven days. He said, that's not possible! I said, yes, it is. And these students are going to do well with that. So, we went through all fourteen lessons and most of the students understood experientially the first thirteen lessons. And he said, I see what you mean, it's possible to do. He completely changed his expectation of what could be done. And now I convinced him we're going to do the inner fire text. I said, look, we got as far as the first four of the eight verses in a week, and that wasn't far enough. I could redo this course with all eight of them. He said, okay, let's try it. So, he's open.

So, I think he and His Holiness trust that we're not going to distort it. And they understand very practically that if it doesn't get passed on in some form it's not going to last. So, it's kind of an unusual window of flexibility there. At least more with the Bon, I think.

SP: Is it your impression that Asonam can appreciate or see what you see in students' responses in the retreats?

DB: I think he's not as confident in terms of reaching students at different levels in students in the West because he still has a hard time somewhat with some words. So, he doesn't quite get some, a few of the words. But if you ask him a question about practice, he's got a lot of depth. To illustrate it, he'll show it. He knows much more than people would [figure]. Because I was translating the bypassing visions text, and some of it, the wording, was difficult. And I said, I don't understand this part. And he just went down and he explained the whole thing to me. Not from the text. Just from his own experience. And I was, whoa, this guy knows what he's doing.

SP: So, one of the first questions I have down is with respect to the Pointing Out Way, how and why did you start it and develop it, and what is it?

DB: Okay. Well, my first lama who was Gelugpa. In old Tibet the main Gelugpa teacher was Ling Rinpoche. And Ling was the senior tutor for the young Dalai Lama. And Ling had three main students: one was the Dalai Lama, the other was Geshe Wangyal—he was actually Mongolian—my teacher, and the third was Denma Locho Rinpoche, who was the head at Namgyal Monastery. My teacher was much older, so he died, I think seventy-nine or eighty, and then the Dalai Lama became my default teacher in the early seventies. Before he was a movie star I spent a lot of time with him. And that was great. And then I started teaching with the third of that group, Denma Locho, and then another of other Gelugpa lamas we taught the nine stages of the mind staying concentration in the Elephant Path. And we taught basic emptiness, but that's as far as we went.

And he struggled, and the other lamas I taught with struggled with how to teach it to Westerners. Like there was one point where I said we should use the breath because Westerners don't do well with visualizations. He said, no, we use the image of the Buddha. I said, no, they're not going to do as well with that. Use the breath. And I said, Tsongkapa says you can use the breath if you're too intellectualized. And Westerners are over-ideational, so use the breath. So, I pushed him on it, which is what I did. [Dan chuckles.] And to his credit, he said, okay, I teach visualization, you teach the breath, I come to your sessions, you come to my sessions, and we'll see which one works.

SP: Outcome study!

DB: And then he said, I see what you mean. The breath works better. So, we'll do that. I thought that was enormously flexible. It was unusual. So, after that we did the breath. So, we had little struggles with things like this, about how to make it available to Westerners because they don't change it. They do it the same old same old way of teaching it, and it doesn't work very well. So, after struggling for fifteen years, I was visiting His Holiness the Dalai Lama—I think it was 1986—and we had done the tachistoscopic research on the speed of the mind. A tachistoscope is a highspeed electronic board. Looking at the speed of the mind he gave us his best meditators. And we were measuring the speed of the mind in the meditators. And then after we finished the project, I went over the project with him. And apparently, he had talked with Denma Locho, but I didn't know that at the time. And he said, can you stay around a couple of extra days? There's someone else I'd like you to meet that's very unusual. He's from an old lineage, and he will explain things in great, great detail, in ways that you'll never hear in such rich detail. He said, most people won't talk about attainments. The etiquette is you don't talk about personal meditation experiences because it leads to spiritual pride. He said, but in this lineage, they explain it in great detail, and that's how it's taught.

So, he introduced me to a man who did six hours of live, continuous practice of inner fire, and gave me a live, technically, remarkably detailed commentary on what he was doing while he was doing it. It took six hours on the spot, live, an action commentary. And I'd never seen anything like it before. The Dalai Lama was right. There was nothing like it. And apparently, that's what he felt would be an approach of teaching to the West, where you explain things in detail and you walk them through it. And that was the style of the eighty-four mad wandering masters. It was popular from about the year 500 AD to about 1050, and then about 1050 is when you got the rise of the monastic tradition. And the wandering masters tradition didn't die out, but it became less popular.

So, that was the tradition that he had shown me. And I thought, although he wasn't explicit about it, I felt what he was trying to say was your great tradition in the West for growth is psychotherapy, which is highly relationally based. And this is a relationally based way of teaching. So, use this for Westerners. So, what am I going to do, say no? So, after he showed me this, I tried to teach what he showed me.

The guy who showed it to me, I never even knew his name. He died three weeks later of a tropical disease. Tibetans don't have much of an immune system for living in the jungles. So, that felt to me like it was as gift to the West. And I had some obligation to try and present it in the best way that I could. But, at that point, I had only done basic concentration and ordinary emptiness practices. I had never done anything advanced before. So, I thought, well let's just try this and just go for the whole thing. Teach ordinary concentration and ordinary emptiness, and then, well, what I knew was Mahāmudrā, so I'd teach Mahāmudrā up to awakening and see what happens. And with this "pointing out" style it surprised us because people started getting experiences of awakening, and not infrequently. So, it had a certain efficacy to it. So, I got more confident that this could be taught.

There's a funny story because I was teaching at Esalen at the time in, I think it was somewhere in the mid-90s, early '90s. We were teaching in the little Round House, which isn't very big, because that's how small the classes were—there were under twenty people. And this woman had this profound sense of awakening and remained stable for six months. And the next year, George Protos, he had taken that workshop and watched the woman get this profound realization. The next year he was sitting in the same place that she sat in in the Round House, and there was one point, about two thirds of the way through the course that he was getting a lot of spontaneous energy shifts in his body, but his posture was off, so I went over and shifted his posture, and boom, he had a taste of awakening at that point. So, after that, all the students—because it was the same students that we had earlier—they were all sitting there because that was the "awakened" site. Everyone would sit in that same spot.

So, then we began to think, well, maybe we should try and teach this up to awakening. So, I then worked in the late '90s and 2000s on trying to spell out this step-by-step sequence to awakening, from what are called the "extraordinary emptiness" practices—Ocean and Waves up to and really work out those stages, and you get a lot of experimenting here with changing the wording of things until we found what worked. And it was working.

And then it was around, I don't know, maybe 2008, that was the first year Gretchen taught with me, that was 2008, somewhere around there, we were at Kripalu when Rahob Tulku called us up. And he was my roommate some twenty years earlier, but we had both traveled a lot and we lost sight of each other from the traveling. And he said, I heard from a mutual student that you're teaching nearby, and I'm close by, come visit me. So, we did. And Gretchen came along and he treated us as a couple—and eventually he married us; we weren't thinking anything like that, but he obviously saw something there. But I said ... He asked me what I was doing with teaching, and I told him about this whole story, and I said to him, would you (he's Nyingma—but, he's also Rimed), I said would you forego the preliminaries and teach them at this level, give them the teachings that stabilize awakening? Nyingmas don't do that. They don't give out things easily. So, he said, well, normally I would say no, but I know you. So, I will come to your class and interview your students and take the class and see what I think about what you're doing. It was for his due diligence.

And he came, and he interviewed the students and he said, I see what you mean. You don't care about the preliminary prayers and the rituals. But, a lot of your students have awakening, and it's not stable. So, I'll do what you ask—under one condition: you have to follow them. You can't just do retreats.

SP: So, before that time you didn't follow?

DB: Well, duh, we were teaching in the relational style of teaching, but it never occurred to me that we should develop an ongoing relationship. [Laughter] It's just so easy, he reminded me, it seemed like ridiculously obvious what he was saying. It's just we hadn't thought about it before! But, it was one of those moments. [Laughter] So, we started teaching the relational style, including following them in the relationship. And we began to find with his additional teachings, which were precious, people were learning the tools to stabilize awakening. He first introduced Padmasambhava's self-liberation's pointing out instructions for awakening, and he introduced *The Lion's Gaze* book, which is mostly about stabilizing awakening, so you have it all the time. And, the instructions worked, but we had to find a way of putting them in wording that worked for Westerners. But, with a little experimentation it was mostly working.

Now we have lots of people who have awakening, a number, maybe 300 people who have stable awakening most of the time now, who are working on the third map. And this last year we convinced Fetzer foundation to give a grant to Judd Brewer's lab, who is an MD, PhD in neuroscience to do a study on the neurocircuitry of awakening. And we got our first results in!

SP: And?

DB: Well, we haven't done awakening yet, but we did the analysis of the scan of ordinary waking state versus Ocean and Waves, and we got very strong findings for Ocean and Waves.

SP: Across subjects?

DB: Across subjects. There were thirty subjects. And the strong finding is that relative to the [awakened] state there is a strong and stable activation of the ACC (the anterior cingulate cortex), and a strong and stable de-activation of the PCC. So, my interpretation of that is ACC is concentration, so what they're doing is they're holding a stable view, they're not falling out of the view. And secondly, with the PCC is the categorization and judgment experience so that they're in a state where they're letting everything come up and everything has, there's no reference point; there's no judgments. They're just letting everything just be there in the field of experience without any grab to it, and without any categorizing and where it all just comes and goes.

So, in just concentration meditation you get ACC activation, and in mindfulness you get mostly PCC deactivation, and some, because it's mixed with some concentration, you get a little bit of ACC activation. But, the strength of both of these is different from the combination of both. It's not something that's been seen before. So, this is working, from a neurocircuitry point of view.

SP: So, just out of curiosity, would there be, I don't know what the word would be, narrative interviews of people?

DB: We did that.

SP: Before and after?

DB: What we did is we had John and myself nominate students and we developed rating scales, 1-10, we rated the accuracy of their report of Ocean and Waves—let's see, four things—Ocean and Waves, Natural State, setting up the view of Lion's Gaze, and Awakening. And John and I had to come up with, we only accepted students that we both agreed upon. And we had about four students we didn't agree upon. But we ended up getting about, we tried to get forty students, but some people didn't follow through with it, but we ended up getting, who actually followed through and did the study, we ended up getting thirty subjects who we agreed upon. And they gave a narrative report in the laboratory of each of these states. And Poppy, who's Judd's research assistant has analyzed the narratives already. I had her come take the course in January so she learned what we were doing in the meditations. And she, the two research assistants both took the course now. So, they understand what we're doing and why, and they have a clear sense of what we're looking for.

So, I hope we'll get some, in the next couple of months, we'll get some sort of identification in the neuro-circuitry of awakening, but it's labor intensive because you have to come up with regions of interest, so you have to generate the hypothesis and then test it out.

SP: And differentiate between, if I remember correctly, correlations and causation? In other words, doing ...

DB: Well, you can't do that, but ... I suspect, because I did the study on myself at one point. And when I set up Lion's Gaze it was, there's an area of the infra-parietal system that has to do with shifting from local to global awareness. And I think that's what's probably involved in awakening. And when I did it on myself, I had, in setting up the Lion's Gaze I had strong activation in that area in the parietal system on the left side. And when I was in awakening it was the same activation on the right side, which makes perfect sense to me. I think it's a parietal issue, and that's why something like the gaze, the view, is so important. And the lower part of the parietal system is anticipating high speed movements into space, which is basically particularizing. But humans have a piece of the parietal system that is, one is perspective taking and empathy, and there's another one on global and localized awareness. So, I think it's an untapped area of the brain circuitry. And I think that's what, that's what I think we're going to find.

SP: So, that's kind of pioneering territory.

DB: I hope so. So, I don't know if that's my hypothesis, but I gave Poppy[1] and Judd the description of my own highlighting of this and said look for this here, so maybe we'll save some time here. We'll see what we find out. But who knows.

1 Poppy was part of the crew doing the EEG studies with Judd Brewer.

SP: So, this, without getting too much into the details, although it would be fun to do that, the presumption I've frankly made and I think some people make is that neuro-physiology is one thing, but the set of, or say, the network of connected aspects of the person, in terms of compassion, understanding, wisdom, are these actually related, in other words, is the neuro-physiology a state phenomenon, or is it also a wisdom phenomenon? Can you correlate …

DB: A what phenomenon? I didn't hear the word.

SP: Can you correlate the neurophysiological product in a test with something you could also call wisdom, or is it more, or is …

DB: Yeah, I think you can. There was a single subject study done on a Richard Davidson study with Mathieu Riccard, and what they found was when he was doing his compassion meditations, which is what Gelugpas do, there was very strong activation in the medial-orbital pre-frontal cortex. And the medial PFC is associated with emotional saliencies, positive emotions, and pro-social behavior. It makes perfect sense. So, he's trained himself with compassion to be more pro-social and to have more positive emotional states. That's what it looks like to me.

SP: So, you don't think that the ten or twenty years he spent sleeping next to Dilgo Khyentse had …

DB: No, I think it's the compassion meditation.

SP: Is that right?

DB: Yeah, I think so. And I think it's probably because if you use areas of the brain that changes volume and size, he's probably developed a structure of the brain that has to do with compassion now. He's a pretty happy guy.

SP: Yeah, we met him at the …

DB: Okay, so you know what I'm talking about.

SP: Yeah.

DB: So, I think that that's probably true for any of these things. There's probably, and the more I think what matters is that Westerners have a lot of skepticism. If suddenly we show that there's a neurocircuitry to awakening then people are going to start moving beyond mindfulness and start taking awakening seriously. Because mindfulness has become so popular that it's lost the heart of its meditation practice. What's the goal? I mean how many people who teach mindfulness ever talk about awakening? Nobody. Why are we doing this? It's about awakening.

SP: So, you think it's possible to approach awakening, could you use some kind of feedback mechanism, biofeedback type stuff?

DB: Well, Judd[2] and I have a respectful disagreement about that. He had me, when I played in the lab on this, he had me do the feedback and I told him it was a waste of time and it got in the way.

SP: Oh yeah, because you have to pay attention.

DB: Because it forces you to particularize. But, for people who are not capable of getting the awakening, maybe the feedback will work for them. But it doesn't work for people who have some propensity towards it. And, included in the protocol, even though I didn't agree with it, but he's found that with some of the people who we didn't put in the original study who wanted to be involved in the study but they were too intellectualized, the feedback worked for them. So, something for everybody.

SP: Interesting. Yeah.

DB: I told him that there were some studies on biofeedback in the seventies that showed that not everybody does well with it. High hypnotizables do poorly with biofeedback because they can make the mind-body connections internally. And the signals in the machine actually distract them, and they can do it better without it. So, you can't assume it's a good technology because there's technology there.

---

2 Judd Brewer, lead researcher with Dan in UMass EEG research.

SP: Right.

DB: It works for some people and not others.

SP: That brings this to the question of asking how this is different, other, you're kind of saying it already, but, like you pointed out, mindfulness is extremely popular, in fact I was going to ask you later how you would feel about our using, if we create a publication out of this, the answer you gave to Stephanie's question a couple, early January, where you gave a really, I thought, beautiful critique of mindfulness because of this deficiency, not having a sense of the goal being awakening.

DB: I don't know what I said, but I'm okay with that.

SP: Okay, this question is just to ask how the way that you teach is different, is it different, generally speaking, from the way that others teach.

DB: Yeah. First of all, it tells you explicitly what the goal is for the next stage of meditation just before you do it, so it's fresh in your mind. So, you get an orientation to what we're doing, so it gives you what the Tibetans call *gowa*—overall intellectual understanding of what we're doing next. And then, unlike most meditations, they're guided. It's not a silent meditation class where people sit there; what do we do next? Everything, we walk them along the path. And the art of that is to word it correctly, to judge where most of your group is, so they can follow what's happening. You're describing where they are, and they can say, "Oh, yeah, I can see that."

SP: And to make adjustments …

DB: So, if they know what to look for, so they don't waste a lot of time. There's so much idle time wasted in meditation and they don't get anywhere. And they're making a lot of bad habits in that time. When someone spells out for them what to look for, I mean, the traditional teaching of the Elephant Path, the sutra version of that, is that you get the instruction and then you go and practice it, and Alan Wallace teaches that way. It's the traditional way of teaching it. I mean there's a living Tibetan belief that it takes lifetimes for this stuff. So, his view is that when you teach the Elephant Path, it takes a year. We cover all nine stages in three days. And the difference is the "pointing out" style of teaching. Not that one's better or worse than the other. They're … it's just more explicit. So, people know what to look for. They say, "Oh," and once they get it, they don't have to waste all the time trying to wait for something to develop because they already got it.

SP: And as they're telling you their experience and you're mirroring or telling them …

DB: Exactly. It's more interactive. And you're also making explicit, most people cover the same map. There are not a lot of differences. So, if you say, "this is what's going to happen in this next meditation," they go out looking, "what he's saying is true, it's really happening." And then they get efficacy.

SP: Yes! And excited.

DB: Yeah, and they get excited and want to explore further because it's working. And they feel confident. Because the proof of the pudding was that we had this woman who came to us, who volunteered herself in a research study for Alan's program, an MD, PhD. And she got through the third stage of the Elephant Path in six months in that program, and with the same teaching, different style of teaching, she got the whole thing in three days. And the difference is the style of teaching. It's not my style of teaching. It's what His Holiness showed me. That was the way it used to be taught in the wandering masters' lineage. But, there's not very many people teaching it because the tradition became monastic. And I think what happened to meditation in Tibet is what's happened here in the West.

If you look at around the eleventh century, you get the rise of the monastic tradition in Tibet, and you've got big monasteries, three thousand, five, six thousand people in a pop. You can't teach that many people. So, nobody's followed carefully anymore. It becomes institutionalized. And then two hundred years later you get hundreds and hundreds of books written on the problems of meditation like the problem of the sinking mind. Hundreds of books. Why were they written at that given time? Because the institutionalization had developed so much that people were developing all these bad habits and it was poorly taught in the monastic tradition.

So, then people had to write all about the problems that were coming up. They were artifacts of the institutionalization of this. You didn't get that for five hundred years in the wandering masters who taught, because they taught either one on one or in small groups. And they corrected the bad habits as they saw them. It's part of the relationship. That's the difference.

So, what have we done? We recreated that same problem here in the West. We get mindfulness teachers, they teach one hundred, two hundred, three hundred people at a retreat. Every two or three days the people go for an interview, so-called interview, in a group of people—there's ten, twelve people in a group—they get one or two lines about their practice, they say, "Fine, keep on going." That's not teaching. There's no attempt to correct the bad habits that the students are making or even to inquire about what those bad habits might be.

The teaching is lazy. I'm sorry. I'm being honest about it. But that's what I think.

It's lazy teaching. They're not really taking their students seriously. They just want to create a big movement. That's what happens when you institutionalize something. I don't want a big movement. I want buddhas. We get a couple of buddhas in my lifetime then I figure I've done a good job. And I want girl buddhas in the West. That's where you have to come in. Girl buddhas.

SP: Girl buddhas, yeah.

DB: Just as many or more girl buddhas than boy buddhas. It's the West. This is what we need here. I'm not joking. I'm taking this very seriously.

SP: So, this brings up a really big question that, because when you talk about Westerners being skeptical, one of the things they have in mind, that I have had, too, is that the Western psyche, you know, meaning like epi-genetic influences, hormones, expectations and assumptions, these patterns, these programs running in the background that weren't there, in Tibet, or India for that matter, when these teachings as kind of or more guided instructions were happening. So, one wonders …

DB: Every culture has its own set of limiting beliefs. Tibet had its own limiting beliefs. They're just different.

SP: But they had an orientation to preliminaries, wasn't that part of it, to clean out …

DB: In the monastic tradition, but not in the lay tradition. The lay tradition didn't do preliminary practices. It's part of the monastic tradition.

SP: And not part of the wandering teachers.

DB: No, not part of the wandering teachers' tradition. The assumption was that everybody has buddha nature. Everybody is quite capable of doing this.

That's the assumption I operate out of, that everybody has buddha nature, and everybody has innate metacognitive intelligence. I expect them to bring out the best. I'm not going to assume … I'm not going to disempower them and think they can't do it. I think it's disrespectful to people. I try and very explicitly create the atmosphere that you can do this. And people get confident because they see they can do it. That's culture. Because in this culture people doubt themselves too much. So, they need a message that they have the ability.

SP: And to get the signs that they do.

DB: Do you think somebody's going to get somewhere if their teacher doesn't believe in them?

SP: Right.

DB: Do we ever get anywhere where we have a teacher who's got some sort of authority if they don't believe and have faith in the student? No. It's common sense.

SP: But, there's not a lot of it out there.

DB: What's the motivation for doing it? Self-importance? It's not about self-importance. If I've learned anything from the spiritual traditions in the last forty-five years it's that self-importance isn't terribly important. I don't care if I'm a teacher. I'm just trying to do the right thing because I was asked to do it. I'm honoring my teachers. That's all I can say. But it's important what we're saying.

SP: I know.

DB: Because students need to feel that if they have doubt, it's like, take an analogy here. A student in high school plays a certain sport. They need to have a coach who believes they can actually do their performance, because if the coach doesn't believe in them, they're not going to do it. But, if the coach says you can do this, and they say, "Huh? Me?" what's going to happen with that? They're going to discover they can do it. It's no different from that.

SP: And the opposite of that, where a person gets habituated to sitting with a teacher that has no personal contact with them, they feel that's it, and that's the enemy.

DB: Or the opposite of that is you get self-realized teachers in the West who talk about their own realizations. But they never give the technology to the students about how they can do it themselves.

When I was working with hypnosis, with Erika Fromm, she had a very unusual style of hypnosis because hypnosis, for most people, the stereotype is very authoritative. And she did a whole different style called "permissive hypnosis." And her fundamental assumption is that every patient has all the tools within them to get better. They have the wisdom to get better. And your task is to provide the relational conditions for the patient to discover that. So, if I'm working with a patient and I feel like the patient gets better and they feel like I didn't do very much, and they figured it out themselves, then I've done a good job. You know what I'm saying. It's like that. Same with the spiritual traditions.

SP: I have felt in, this is just personal, that this whole process of being with you has been getting permission, you know, more and more permission. That's …

DB: And the courage to act on what you know.

SP: Yeah.

DB: I don't treat people as stupid. I demand a lot from them. I demand the best from them. But not in a demanding way. You know what I'm saying. It works.

SP: So, that factors in sort of interestingly. The next question was, you know, like when you say why aren't we asking, why are we doing this, without exemplars in the West how does a person develop a clear understanding of the goal of practice is awakening and enlightenment? How do they, how do you introduce that to people as a legitimate question, what's the goal?

DB: The goal is to awaken and to stabilize that awakening. And the goal is the manifested awakening in terms of conduct.

So, William James, over a hundred years ago wrote his classic *Varieties of Religious Experience*, and somebody asked him, "How do you tell the authenticity of a mystical experience?" And his answer was, quote, "By their fruits ye shall know them." End quote. In other words, the true measure of the authenticity of any spiritual realization is always and necessarily conduct. If you want to see what I know about spiritual practice after forty-five years, it's not going to be in terms of what I have to say to the students. It's what I'm doing when I work in the courts for human rights and child abuse.

SP: So, the target of my question actually is somewhat different. It's that for people who don't have the understanding of a goal that way, they don't have exemplars, so when they hear that, you know, there's a retreat on the Pointing Out Way they may come or already have the expectation that they're going to get in the last mindfulness retreat, it was just …

DB: Yeah, and what they're going to get is more of the same kind of stuff.

SP: Right.

DB: So, that it doesn't lead anywhere. It's aimless. It doesn't lead to awakening. It's never talked about.

Self-important teachers are making a living from that. It's institutionalized. That's basically the name of it in the West. It's secularized and institutionalized. So, now, the emphasis of mindfulness is to make it accessible to more and more people. What purpose? For what purpose? Just to make it accessible? What are we making accessible?

SP: Stress management. That's what they say in the magazines.

DB: You understand that. You understand what I'm saying.

SP: I do.

DB: The problem is that we've lost the heart of it, the heart of it is to awaken.

SP: So, when students come to study in the Pointing Out Way, that's when they discover what the goal is? So, in other words ...

DB: I try to make that explicit the first night in terms of laying out the stages of the path, and say explicitly that it's not about technique in sitting there in meditation, it's about awakening. It's about stabilizing awakening, and living a life of good conduct. If it doesn't contribute to the greater social good, what good is it? Look at something like, you've seen the movie *Digital Dharma*, my friend Gene Smith—he'll never talk about his practice.

If you asked him about his practice he would grumble and change the subject. He would never ever talk about his practice. But, look at his life. He single-handedly reconstructed in a lifetime eighty thousand books that were lost in this spiritual tradition and preserved it forever in hyper-space. So, what does that say about his life? What does it say about his realization? See you can infer from there … Or as a Sufi called it, he says, great masters wander through the market place every day and no one recognizes them. Because they live the life; they live a good life. They don't try to make self-importance. They don't try to be teachers. They don't hang out shingles and say, "I'm a meditation teacher." None of that stuff matters. All that matters is they feel that they have a life helping people. It's not about self-importance. And that's where this thing is going wrong.

SP: So important. Important message. So, you've talked already about how after that first night already one gets the impression by being instructed what to do, getting help to look forward to what might happen, and then getting feedback and correction and so forth …

DB: What they're going to learn is, usually the feedback after the second day is nobody gives these kinds of detailed instructions because they don't. That's what we dig about this method. Or as one of the people who took it said, "This is GPS for the mind!" And that's a good way of describing it. We tell you how to stay on track. And we're fierce about busting people when they get in their own way. The art of doing that is to try and get them to listen without being too judgmental. Otherwise, they can't take anything in.

SP: And isn't part of the great, one of the great elements of this the role of metacognition and developing that right from the get-go.

DB: Right from the get-go. It's important. There was study done out of Richie Davidson's lab on concentration meditation. And they looked at beginning and advanced concentrators. And both groups activated the ACC, the anterior cingulate cortex, the concentration part of the brain. But only the advanced activated the right dorsolateral prefrontal cortex, which is metacognitive, and monitoring. And, beginning or advanced practice had nothing to do with duration. There were people in the advanced practice who had after several months of training because they had already activated the ACC and the dorsolateral prefrontal cortex. So, they already knew how to monitor and correct their mistakes. And other people practiced for twenty years and they were still in the beginning group because they couldn't do that. And the difference between the two groups was metacognitive monitoring. We use it in this tradition explicitly in every stage of the practice. It's called *shezhi*. Or metacognitive awareness.

SP: So, by becoming familiar with that, it becomes a kind of natural …

DB: Well, if you look at the mindfulness tradition, there's awareness, and then there's what they call total awareness, which is their translation of metacognitive, but it has nothing to do with, they misinterpreted it. They think it's when you're off the pillow you're trying to be aware off the pillow. They completely miss what it means. But the megacognitive awareness is important, in anything.

If people are aware of strategy in problem solving and they can correct their dysfunctional strategies they can solve their problems better and learning is quicker. There are a lot of studies in the West in education where you teach people to be metacognitively reflective in their strategies. And then they learn anything better, from driving a car to solving mathematical problems. And in doing meditation the same way.

SP: And in your book on attachment repair, is also …

DB: Correct. Well, the chapter on metacognition there, I was dissatisfied because there are four stages of metacognition in the West.

The first started at Stanford with John Favell's work. And he called metacognition "thinking about thinking." He did studies about how kids distinguish between reality and fantasy based on metacognitive capacity. And some of those early ideas were incorporated in Mary Main's work on the Adult Attachment Inventory, but she never really developed a scale fully. She promised that she would develop her revision of it, but she never got around to doing that.

And the second generation, the Tavistock people put together a general measure of metacognition called the Reflective Function Scale. Howard and Mary Steel, Peter Ferman, Valery Simonson, and what Howard told me when they did their research on in-patients at Tavistock, the scale was measured from minus 1 to plus 9. The average is about 5.5 in the general population. So, most people that are mild to moderately metacognitive, not terrific but not bad either. And then what they found was, Howard told me that they never found a patient who had a personality dissociative disorder that they diagnosed had above 3. And they were so un-psychologically mindful that that shocked them. So, they developed a whole treatment based on developing metacognition, mentalization-based treatment. And what they found is that when they developed metacognitive skills in those populations of patients that the patients were showing completely different reorganization of the mind, what we call coherence of mind. So, there was a profound effect.

The third generation was the Rome school. And they said, well, there's not just a general function of metacognition, there are different metacognitive skills and different diagnostic groups of psychiatric patients that are deficient in different skills. So, they developed what I would call, or they call it a marginal approach, I call it a condition-specific approach. In this patient you want to develop this metacognitive skill versus that one. And that was really the third generation of work. I was particularly interested in what they're doing, so I went over to Rome and studied with [the researcher who developed it] and brought him over to Harvard. And I liked what they were doing there. It was a good program.

But, all of that is based on looking at megacognition in young children. And the huge blind spot in the field is that none of the people in the clinical field have looked at adult, mature cognitive development and adult mature metacognitive development. And that's what we try to do in our book, saying that things like perspective taking, and taking the larger perspective on life have profound implications for mental health that go beyond the kind of more primitive metacognitive skills that they're teaching in, from the child-based state of mind. So, we've been trying to develop a more … Ken Wilber developed an integral model for seven stages of post-formal cognitive development. But he doesn't have the … he tried to spell out examples of that using Aurobindo, but it's not really a viable tradition. It was a synthetic tradition. And I've been telling Ken, look, this is in all texts spelled out in great detail in the Dzogchen tradition. We can give you subjects who can do all these seven stages, so you don't have to squish them all together and call them integral. We can unpack them. John Churchill is going to do that in his dissertation actually.

SP: So, I couldn't help but infer somehow reading about this in your book on attachment repair that there is, and I can testify in my own case, there is an effect by developing the metacognitive skills in the Pointing Out Way that affects all these other domains.

DB: Exactly. So, how many people have we had that have opened up something that's rather simple to open up with the right instructions—Ocean and Waves practice. So, you're operating, from a cognitive point of view, you're opening up a level of mature adult cognitive development that's post-formal, and it's beyond relativism. In the Reflective Function Scale, all knowledge bases are relevant. That gets high marks. And I'm saying you shouldn't give high marks for that. There's a perspective that supersedes all those relative perspectives that integrates everything, and that should be the higher marks; because everything ties together in a person's life, and that's when they have a central purpose and meaning in their life. That's what we should be teaching.

So, something like taking a perspective that supersedes our perspectives, or going from system to larger field, has profound implications for mental health. And most people who discover that say, "This is amazing. This changes everything in my life." It's simple teaching metacognitive skills that we should have mapped out a long time ago in the West.

SP: Yes, it's just interesting also to see how like in a lay, I'm sorry, I apologize for forgetting their names, but people who, there was as woman who commented on …

DB: Suzanne Cook-Greuter.

SP: It was a woman who noted that people who were actually successfully going through these stages of metacognitive development started to show transcendent states.

DB: Yeah.

SP: That really blew my socks off. Because she was talking about that as a kind of …

DB: I think that was Suzanne's work but she also said that in the West there were less than two percent of people who could manifest these states. Because we don't have the technology in the West, but we do in Dzogchen.

SP: So, in the Pointing Out Way you are doing this, maybe not towards psychiatric disorders, but towards the ordinary mind.

DB: Well, I think we've not raised the question, which I tried to raise in the attachment book is that post formal cognitive development, if we mapped out the metacognition for every one of those levels, those have profound implications for mental health that we should be tapping. And they are deeply positive.

Look at something simple in the West, in the positive psychology research. Bob Emmons' work on the psychology of ultimate concerns—that when people take a positive perspective and they operate out of that perspective there's a general purpose for their life, and they know what that is, and they're always there in the background of their awareness, they're operating out of that general purpose. And they're more resilient in the face of stress. They have greater wellbeing, and they do much better.

When I teach the course for the judges that's always the exercise that works best for them.

SP: Oh, wow.

DB: Because they need it. Then they can handle all the stresses that they're under on the bench, because they have a purpose behind why they're doing what they're doing. It's a simple perspective taken. It's shifting to a larger perspective that supersedes relativism. It's not hard to do. That's a piece of Western research that's consistent with what we're saying could be very effective.

SP: IMHO what's happening with the institutionalization and making business is creating an obstacle.

DB: It is an obstacle. Most people know that but they're not talking about the truth of it.

SP: Exactly. So, part of the impulse here was to try to stimulate a dialog kind of like what you described—I was thinking of the Gloria Project, but you just talked about somebody else interviewing, on the lectures on how to teach, across fields.

DB: Across fields.

SP: That there's an effective way.

DB: There's an effective way of teaching.

SP: And so, we have all these people sitting on cushions and spending thousands of dollars on their mats and their clothes and their retreats and everything, but where is the orientation to the greater purpose, the greater goal? And its potential effects for everybody?

So, it seems the role of metacognition is really important from the beginning and all the way through.

DB: Every step of the way. You have to use metacognition to determine whether you are… so you can detect thoughts during concentration. You have to use metacognition to determine whether you are developing bad habits of concentration. Or when you're doing emptiness, you have to use metacognition to determine whether you are doing it inaccurately, and you're not going off track with the emptiness practice. When you, later, when we get to the advanced practices, or what are called the "extraordinary emptiness" practices, you have to use metacognition to look into the underlying beliefs and be honest with yourself about, you know, and use metacognition to make sure you set up the view exactly right, because if it's a little bit off you won't awaken.

So, you have to use metacognition [in] the shift to awakening. We say that all creatures down to the smallest insects have buddha nature. They all have awakening. But only humans can recognize awakening because only humans have metacognition. So, metacognition is the necessary ingredient for recognizing awakened nature. Only humans can do that. That's why human birth is so precious.

So, then when you get more advanced you use metacognition to make sure you're staying on track with awakening. You use metacognition for self-arising, self-liberating, to make sure you're not subtly engaging things and forming new karmic impressions. You use metacognition to recognize awakened, or basis enlightenment with *dharmakāya*. And you use metacognition to recognize the pure buddha fields, which are always here, never been apart from here, but you can't see them because of the error of very worldly impurities instead. You have to be able to make that distinction. You have to use metacognition to recognize the residuals of the ordinary mind that interfere with seeing the pure realms, and awakened, and enlightenment. So, every step of the way you use metacognition.

SP: And part of what seems implied in what you're saying that's seems to be the worst injury you might say that people that are not trained in this, is that the practitioner doesn't know. If they don't have that they don't have the confidence.

DB: Well, it doesn't occur to them to use the metacognition.

SP: They're looking for someone else …

DB: Right, there's that Sufi tale: A log sits quietly on a wood pile for years and never realizes God. So, don't sit like a log. Sit intelligently. Many people they just sit and they think that that's good enough, but they never monitor the quality of the sitting, so they are making subtle and not so subtle mistakes. They don't even know it. And the practice bottoms out and it has for years. They waste a lot of time. And nobody else, no one ever tells them to put their metacognition online and to look at the quality of the meditation and use certain criteria to judge the quality of it so they keep it fresh and correct. Otherwise, they just, sometimes, they reach a plateau with bad habits. We've seen many people who've done that, who've been to the mindfulness, they're hard to teach because they've had twenty years of bad habits because no one corrected them. I'd rather have a meditation virgin who doesn't have any experience and they don't have a lot of bad habits to correct.

SP: So, this is a little bit off the point, but do you, it raises an interesting question about the people who come to you who've already had training in other methods. Do you have any observations about that?

DB: The mindfulness people in general have built up a lot of bad habits. They have very strong opinions about what they need to do, and they don't listen easily. The Tibetans generally, people with Tibetan training generally know the system better, but they usually have limiting beliefs that are particular to Tibetans that it takes lifetimes. So, they have to cut through all those limiting beliefs. But there are people who come from a Zen background who usually do well with the practice because Zen is minimalistic. They don't get the GPS map. And they respond to it pretty well, but there's a lot of experience. There's a lot of emphasis in Zen on real experience, and validating the authenticity of those experiences. They tend to do well with our system.

SP: They do?

DB: Yeah. And I have to say in all honesty that Zen has a better tradition for authenticating descriptions of awakening than we do in the Tibetan system. They're very good at it. They just don't have the step-by-step technology to get to it. The style … is minimalistic.

SP: That's really interesting. I never heard that.

DB: They're better at it.

SP: Is there a canon of Zen signs?

DB: It's a style of lineages that were passed down, testing the accuracy of people's realization. It's built into the system, which is very well evolved. I think we and the Tibetan tradition do better with step by step up to awakening. But they do a better job with how you authenticate the descriptions of awakening.

SP: Can you identify any bumps in the road in developing metacognition where people can be self-deceptive about what they're seeing? Do you run into that at all?

DB: Yes. The people that we have had most difficulty with, who've taken our courses, have been people who in Western terms would be strongly Narcissistic, which means chronic self-esteem failure. And they will, they have a need to call attention to themselves by talking about all their weird and wonderful realizations, which are not accurate, but they're embellished in order to handle their underlying, fundamental insecurity about themselves. And they don't listen to anything. They take a lot of group time up trying to get the group to validate their experiences, and see how important they are. And that's difficult. We've had to fire some of them because they take up too much group time.

SP: So, to that point, one of the questions I had here was …

DB: They're not using metacognition.

SP: So, how and why do clinical skills matter in a teaching?

DB: Well, there's going to be a percentage of people who come to retreats who are going to get into clinical issues. And I prefer to know what's going on so I can help them. There are lots of examples of that. Let's take something like panic attacks. Panic attack is the progressively learned fear of uncomfortable body sensations. They misread normal body discomfort as if their mind is going … it's going to get worse and worse and worse and they're going to spin out of control. So, when you focus on meditation, and they sensitize themselves to internal bodily experience, that means that panic people are going to be vulnerable to having attacks during the retreat, which is not infrequent. So, when I see that coming, I'll use Western techniques to help them with that on the side, apart from the meditation, in the breaks. It's not hard to do. It's simple exposure-based stuff.

We have, one of our better students, who took this last retreat, he took a course at Esalen years ago, and you know, we have a clear requirement that people come to the entire retreat, and they don't leave sessions. And somebody tipped me off and said that he was leaving in the middle of the retreat. And they said he was having a panic attack, and he was really uncomfortable. I said, well, where is he; so, I went to see him during the break and sought him out, and I said, look, I can help you with this. So, I gave simple exposure work for the panic attack and then I said, you sit up front next to me so I can watch you, so if something comes up with this, we can take care of it on the spot. And there were two times I whispered in his ear during the retreat about what to do. He didn't have any more panic attacks. And he actually mastered the panic attack.

SP: Wonderful.

DB: And now he has good awakening, and he's one of our better students, and I'm grateful, he's grateful he didn't leave. But I wouldn't have known that if one of the other students didn't protect him by telling me that he was about to leave. So, that's an example of when people who have things like irritable bowel stuff, I've had people who reactivate trauma, but we don't usually encourage that kind of stuff in the workshop. But some people get into enormous transference difficulties with teachers. And as someone who's been a clinician for forty-five years I'm used to dealing with that kind of stuff. And, I taught this now, well, this style of teaching since 1985. That's thirty years now, in the pointing out style. And I've had only one situation where I was worried about clinically. I had one guy come who was very over ideational, and he got more and more paranoid during the workshop, and dropped out halfway through, feeling that he was being hypnotized and we were taking away his mind, and I said this isn't a good sign, the guy's getting delusional. So, we met and said I think you should not do this. You're not tolerating it. He never came back. He didn't go psychotic. But we could see all the early signs of that. And what I did in that case is I called up the person who referred him to the course and said this is not an appropriate referral, and why.

SP: So, apart from people who have an actual diagnosis of some kind, from the standpoint of delivering, being able, if this is true—not having taught it I can't say—but, in terms of being sensitive to where the student is, at the edge of their connecting with the exercise is, is there a clinical, is there a role for a clinical skill in helping? Or is that in the teaching aspect that you talked about earlier?

DB: It comes out more in the teaching. But, you know, when you build into the compassion meditation the attachment stuff, because it's so, a necessary need for Westerners, and we do that in every retreat. And we usually use the third day, and most everybody settles down after we do that attachment stuff.

SP: Wow.

DB: There's a significant shift in the group after we do that.

SP: I'm excited to hear that because the impact of reading your book was enormous for me, and I couldn't help … So, I personally, this is sort of …

DB: You were talking about the attachment book.

SP: Yeah, it made such an enormous impact on me because I was in a spiritual community for, you know, three decades or whatever it was, where the focus, much of the focus was on dysfunctional love relationships and people's conviction of being unloved, and how they dramatized it and what to do about it, and how to act differently, and all this sort of thing, and it was completely missed, these core issues that I see when you're talking about "repair" in adults …

DB: You can repair it.

SP: I know! So, it doesn't have to be like …

DB: We were very pleased. We spent twenty years developing those protocols because we wanted to get them right. But, the pilot study we did, the treatment effect size was 6.2. Most, good outcomes, their treatment effect size is about .8. So, this is off the charts. It works.

SP: I get that. But you also point also, like you were saying rarely do you find metacognitive scores in psychiatric patients above three?

DB: Three, right.

SP: … sign really epidemic, you could say. In other words, we don't have to talk about psychiatric patients, just talk about …

DB: Well, the base rates of secure attachment in Europe and North America are about 62 percent across studies.

SP: Right.

DB: But, in other studies, there is one study in Russia, it's 9 percent secure attachment. That's pretty bad.

SP: So, of the people who come, who are spiritual seekers, I'm wondering how they fit in there.

DB: I don't think we have the vaguest statistics on that.

SP: Right. But I know that there are, there's some, you know …

DB: It definitely meets a need.

SP: Right. I think John Wellwood, for whatever else you might say, had the spiritual bypassing idea, that people with unresolved issues, childhood issues, are classically the spiritual seeker types that he was reporting on at the time back in the …

DB: Way back when …

SP: '80s or '70s or something? So, I don't know, I just thought that it's an insight which a lot of people may not have that could be very relevant and important …

DB: Well, Western psychotherapy is our version of preliminary practices.

SP: Okay, great, could you talk about that?

DB: It covers a lot of the same ground as preliminary practices. But, with some things missing. Traditional preliminary practices cover four areas: Motivational practices—what makes people reprioritize their life and makes spiritual practice that they put in their life with all the business, so it usually works out as *lözhi*, the Four Attitudes—precious human birth, analysis of the cause and effects of karma, visualizing the suffering of the six realms of *samsāric* existence, and impermanence, including visualizing your own aging and death, that will do it. That's comparable to what in the West we call states of change.

Some people are not ready for therapy. Most people go into therapy when they're thinking about the fact that they have a problem and can acknowledge it. And they're thinking about what would be best, effective to treat it. That's called the contemplative state of change. But there are a lot of people out there who are pre-contemplative. There are two types of pre-contemplatives: People who are not aware that they have a problem. Everybody else might be aware they have a problem, but they're not. Or, they're aware they have a problem but they're not ready to do anything about it. And that defines a lot of people. So, if those people go into therapy, it seems they go through the motions of it and it hardly ever works. So, there's a lot of research in the West in terms of how you get people to transition from pre-contemplative to contemplative, so they actually can tolerate and use therapy effectively. And that covers the same ground as the attitudinal practices, the *lözhi* practices in Tibetan Buddhism.

The second and third areas of preliminary practices are related—practices to reduce spontaneous negative states during the day and increase positive states. And those are seen as a set of practices. And in Tibetan Buddhism, the techniques to work with negative states and the techniques to work with positive states are not reducible to each other. They are separate sets of practices. So, if you just work with negative states, and you've got techniques that are effective for that, you get a relative reduction of, or, in the best, an absence of those negative states. The absence of the negative is not a positive. There are a whole other set of techniques that cultivate the positive. And that's the weak point in psychotherapy, except in the modern positive psychology movement.

SP: Very interesting.

DB: We have a lot of techniques to work with negative states, but nothing to work with positive states. And where we fail the most in Western psychotherapy is exactly in areas where, by definition, the problem is you have to develop something positive. So, look at self-esteem failure, narcissism. A good developmental definition of self-esteem is that self-esteem is the developmental linkage of positive emotions to the self-representation. That's a developmental achievement. And what that means for the older child or adult who has achieved that, when they evoke their sense of self they can evoke it against the backdrop of positive feelings. So, if I evoke Dan-ness, I can have good feelings associated with that. But, if I'm narcissistically vulnerable, and I evoke my sense of self I evoke it against a backdrop of no feeling, no sense of self that's articulated. I just don't have any feelings associated with it. So, I have the sense that something is fundamentally missing in my life.

So, if that were the case, I would compensate with self-agency. I would probably do a lot. But no matter how much I did I would never feel good about myself. A culture of narcissism, which is an epidemic in this country. So, going into, if you're narcissistically vulnerable, going into psychotherapy, which is based on, particularly a dynamic therapy based on meaning-making, and talking about mommies and daddies and all of that, things that happened in your life, that isn't going to make you feel good about yourself. It's going to make you feel worse.

Kohut, who was the grandfather of modern self-psychology, wrote a paper called "The Two Analyses of Mr. Z." And in that paper, he talks about a man who went into analysis and did a classic oedipal-based analysis, and he never got better. And then he came back to the same analyst some years later and said, "This is not what I need; this is what I need instead," and taught him about focusing on the positive self-development, self-esteem development. And that's how he claimed he discovered self-psychology. Now we know posthumously that there was never any Mr. Z as a patient. Kohut was Mr. Z. I know that because he was one of my supervisors.

SP: Wow.

DB: He was writing about his own personal experience and why the analytic tradition couldn't get it, because it was so focused on the negative it couldn't develop the positive, and why he tried to go in a whole different direction.

So, but if what if you're saying to somebody who has self-esteem problems, you know, "bring to mind a situation where you really like yourself, you really feel good about yourself, and generate a positive feeling," and you do that all the time, session after session, they get better. Or, look at the years of attachment research coming out of the psychoanalytic tradition. And what we focused on is interpreting the resistance to attachment. How is that going to get a person better? If they don't have a positive internal map for attachment, we're going to, interpretation is going to develop that positive map. You're going to develop it through positive visualizations.

So, a self-esteem failure and attachment failures are two areas of Western psychology where our bias toward negative states has meant that we have never developed effective treatments. But this is where the East comes in. If you cultivate positive states, it works for such conditions.

SP: So, you were talking about this as a …

DB: We call it "positive re-mapping" in the attachment field.

SP: Correlating with the preliminary …

DB: Yeah, so, with the preliminary practices what you're doing in traditional Tibetan practices, you use confession practices to acknowledge and purify negative states, you do that every day, many times a day. And you cultivate the mandala offering, which is the offering of everything positive in the world. So, but those practices are somewhat alien to Westerners. You know, we're offering all the good qualities in the world and the different continents and sub-continents. It makes no sense to us. Menri was quite flexible. Gretchen was talking with him and said, well, I don't understand this Mandala. And he said, "Nah, you're a Westerner," he says, "offer up New York City!"

SP: That's great.

DB: And he meant that!

SP: I know! I think he told a story, wasn't it he, or I don't know, when flying into New York and seeing the city at night, was it at Whippany, and he made some description …

DB: He did that, right.

SP: That was great. That's the second of the preliminaries?

DB: The second and the third are reducing negative states and developing positive states. We do a good job with the negative states, but we do a very poor job with the positive states of Western psychology.

And the fourth is planting the views. The views are keys that open up gateways to reality. So, you plant the keys, the gateways to the views through the guru yoga. You make the request for the view, for influencing you, you imagine these extraordinary beings are actually installing these views directly in your mindstream, like a download.

And when you have all the views, and if you put them into practice, then the view is the meditation and the meditation will develop because you're looking at it the right way. The teachings give you an orientation to how you view it. It's not about meditation. It's about viewing. The view is the meditation. So, it's very important that you get the right instructions on how you view the states of mind. Those are the four things we cover in the preliminaries. We do about half of that pretty well in psychotherapy. But, not all of it.

SP: What is the psychotherapy correlation with the fourth …

DB: There isn't any.

SP: Oh.

DB: So, we do motivation well. And we do handling negative states well. We do a poor job with positive states. And we do a poor job with, we do no job with the guru yoga and finding the views. Because most people have a utilitarian view of meditation: you just sit down and you do something in meditation. The idea that the meditation is really a way of looking at things is foreign to most Western institutionalized views of meditation. Explaining the view is the whole meditation. You get the view right, then you're going to get the realization correct. If you don't have the view right then meditation is not going to work.

SP: But you only get the view right …

DB: Transmissions. That's where lineage traditions come in.

SP: So, you prepare for the transmission by doing the preliminaries.

DB: Yeah, but now the Tibetans, at least some, are more flexible about that. They're not requiring a full set of preliminaries.

SP: So, just a curious thing, from your perspective, do you think it would make a difference if your students came and could do some kind of self-assessment on some sort of Western version of preliminary that they might do before?

DB: Well, Tenzin Namdak in the Bon tradition has done a huge creative job with that. He has now done away with the hundred thousand preliminaries. And what he does instead is he has people make a commitment to make a list of twenty personal things, personal relational things, and twenty job-related things that they want to change in their life.

Gretchen: I just want to say that we don't know the exact number, Dan.

DB: I think it's twenty, love. So, sixty things. And they have to say that in a public statement in front of everybody else who are doing the same thing; and they announce that, report back to the group how they are changing those things over time. It's very creative. And it fosters personal, relational, and job-related changes in significant ways in your daily life. It's part of the preliminary phase. Western preliminaries. It's creative. I like it. So, some people have tried to change that.

My approach is a little bit different. I was talking with His Holiness Menri Trizin about it. I said, look, we do it backwards. I said, Westerners aren't very devotional. And if you make them do the hundred thousand preliminaries, they're going to resist parts of them, or they're just going to go through them in a rote way, and it's going to be meaningless. So, don't even waste the time. But, if we're single-minded about awakening, and they get a taste of awakening, they grasp the preciousness of it, that's when they'll become more devotional. And then you can talk about these things. And he was quiet for a moment, and he said, "I like that." He was quite open to it.

SP: So, I think really this just points so perfectly to the question of efficacy, that that's what he was flexible about is actually delivering the awakening stance to people rather than clinging to …

DB: Well, he teases me about that. He affectionately gave me, but he's also busting me, he gave me like a Tibetan name, which is "Rigpa Kyandre," the one who is single-minded about awakening.

SP: What's the matter with that?

DB: Because he thinks it's narrow. He thinks I should be able to teach students of all capacity. He busts me about that. He doesn't have any problem with the fact that it works for awakening. And that people will get more devoted once they get awakened. But he thinks I need to be more flexible with a larger number of students who can't do that kind of stuff. And he's right. I'm not very patient with those who are disrespectful. I'm not very patient with people who don't try.

SP: Oh, I see.

DB: Yeah. You can't teach everybody, that's what I mean. He thinks you should be able to teach everybody. But, how do you reach them? I just finished a course a month ago, a Level 1 course, and a kid dropped out halfway through the week. No explanation. He said, it's not my path. But he didn't explain to the group that he was dropping out. So, the group felt sort of left, but there was another person in the group he was riding back with to where he was staying, and she said that he talked with her, and that what was really going on is he was heavy into doing psychedelics. And he thought this was too threatening to what he was doing with the psychedelics. And I mentioned attachment to states and he didn't want to hear that. So, he was attached to states and dropped out. So, how do you reach somebody like that?

SP: Right. So, I guess you answered this question, I was going to ask you why it is you begin with concentration but you combine it with a taste for the whole path, you know, the very first retreat.

DB: Because I'm trying to do something that's not being done in the West except maybe in the Zen tradition. So, they're my brothers and sisters because we think like-minded. Most of the commercialization of meditation doesn't mention the goal, which is the heart of this, which is awakening.

So, I tried to show people that they can get a taste of that in a week. And if they don't get a taste of it in a week—usually we kept good stats on this, and there's about a third of the people in any of the groups for the last ten years that get a taste of awakening.

SP: Wow.

DB: If they don't get it, they'll see other people getting it. But, one way or the other it goes to the issue of efficacy. They should leave the retreat knowing that this is quite possible and very real. That changes everything. And if we've been able to convey that as a real experience then I think I've done something useful to counter all the institutionalization of this stuff, and commercialization of it.

SP: Do you find that the numbers of people who are able to stay with the concentration practice is, what percentage would you say, if you have some idea of people—in the first retreat. Or is that also …

DB: Concentration typically deteriorates after retreat because of busy-ness.

SP: But, during the retreat, I mean.

DB: Yeah, they stay with the concentration.

SP: Most people?

DB: About 80 percent do. We have about ten percent of people who always struggle with concentration. But, one of the things we've found is that the people who struggle a lot with concentration are not necessarily the ones that drop out. In fact, they become some of our better students. Gretchen is particularly good with them. She'll hand hold them and walk them along through the concentration and give them a lot of support, and over time they become some of our better students. It was similar when I was working with hypnosis in the 1970s. There was a study done showing that when they started to use hypnosis at a local clinic at Harvard, not the one I was working with, a different clinic, and what they found in that study is that the people who, they were doing hypnotizability tests before, and the people who were low-hypnotizable wanted to be in the study more than the people who were high hypnotizable. Go figure. [Laughter] There was no explanation for why—and they did well.

So, perceived ability has nothing to do with motivation in that sense. And I think the same thing is true here. Some of the people who struggle the most with the concentration come back because they know they need it. A number of those people have ADHD.

SP: And they're getting a big dose of metacognitive training, aren't they?

DB: Yeah. And, I was talking with a new student this morning, first time. He told me he had ADHD and he really struggled with the concentration. So, I said, "It's going to be easier when you use the recordings." So, we worked out what recordings would be ideal because he needs to be reminded of what to focus on continuously. He's going to do better with it.

SP: Right. So, what common obstacles do students encounter?

DB: The main one in the West is limiting beliefs, thinking that they don't have the capacity or that certain problems will get in the way. And our task is to move them, all limiting beliefs, so they can … the sky is limitless.

SP: Are those beliefs, are they specifically related to awakening or to …

DB: The common limiting beliefs are, "I don't deserve it," "something will necessarily get in the way," "I really can't do this." It's all negative self-talk stuff. The Tibetans have their own version, [when] they say "it takes lifetimes, so don't even try." Limiting beliefs are just ideas. They don't define ultimate reality. And I would say that that's the thing that mostly gets in the way for most people, limiting beliefs.

SP: And you address that very explicitly.

DB: There's a practice that addresses it when they have enough metacognitive capacity to observe it. You have to build the metacognitive capacity because beliefs, by definition, operate in the background of awareness. So, they have to be able to see them. That takes a little work. But, you know, that's part of the course even though we're using emptiness practices. It's a good version of Western cognitive therapy. Covers the same ground. Although the beliefs here are not just general beliefs about themselves; they're beliefs that impinge upon the practice and limit it. But, that's the, I think that's probably the most common that we find. People don't take themselves seriously, that they have the capacity to do this.

SP: They show up for a retreat and yet they still have that …

DB: Yeah, they still have that; they don't have that motivation that thinks that they can actually do it. Most people don't show up for the retreat because they think they are going to get awakened.

SP: Why do they come?

DB: Because they've heard weird things about it. [Laughter]

SP: That's not why we came!!

DB: It's different from what they've heard from other places. So, that's why they come. But, they don't, I don't think we have a lot of students who actually show up because they expect they're going to get awakened. It's not something that Westerners think, and certainly in this culture with all the commercialization of it, of meditation. There's not a lot of talking about the goal is awakening. So, if you tell them that the first night, they get sort of shocked. That's what the course is about. And they don't really take it seriously until they start working at it, and then they start to see that there's something changing. And they start to take it seriously. And usually, you can see that in about two thirds of the week when we first introduce the crossing over instructions. Somebody will have a profound awakening. Most people don't take seriously that awakening is something possible. But, about two thirds of the way through the week, when somebody describes awakening, everybody quiets down and they start working a little harder because they actually think that this is possible. If the person who is just describing his experience is not somebody that they had ever dreamed would have this experience, then people start working at it.

SP: Do you think there's a field effect?

DB: Yeah. I think there's a field effect. They all influence each other because we're all part of the same field of awareness.

SP: I think maybe then it's possible that this is actually part of the efficacy configuration or whatever that field effect does contribute to a person's development. It helps ...

DB: It does. That's what we call chingyilap, the gift waves of influence. Non-ordinary beings can directly influence the mindstream of others—and if you ask them to … but only if you make the request. And only if you put what they influence … you have to follow it by practicing. It's like a matching grant. If you match it with your own effort then the influence will come to fruition.

SP: And, in what you were just describing, you could say extraordinary experience, the most ordinary people can be kind of transmission to ordinary people, that that confirmation that, this, too, this ordinary person, just like me …

DB: Well, that was the lineage of the eighty-four masters. The style of writing of all the masters is hagiography, and it's, they're the lives of people who are in one way or another substantially flawed. Some are illiterate, some are very poor, some are screwed up—look at Milarepa. He killed over fifty people. And the whole idea when you read a story like that is it inspires confidence. And when you finish reading the story your conclusion is that if that poor schlep can do it, I can probably do it, too. And they're written that way intentionally because they want you to identify with the story, and just see that it doesn't, people are not required to have special characteristics when they do this path. It's open to everybody regardless of race, ethnicity, caste, literacy, or gender. But nowadays we build a wall around all these people. [Laughter]

SP: I don't know if this is an appropriate question, but, what common obstacles do teachers encounter? Of the pointing out way, if any.

DB: That's a good question. I think the hardest thing as a Westerner trying to teach the dharma is that Westerners are not terribly respectful of teachers. So, they'll throw away precious realizations or they'll not take seriously the nature of the transmissions because you're a Westerner. So, I asked Rinpoche about that once. I said, look, you know, some of the students they just get so disrespectful. And he said, "In my country lamas like God. We get worshipped." He said, "What's the model for teachers in your country?" He said, "college professor," and he starts laughing and laughing, he can't stop laughing. And that's what it's like. It's a joke. Who takes a college professor seriously? He said, so, you won't get the respect anywhere close to what you're trying to teach. It just won't happen in the West, so get used to it.

SP: Wow.

DB: And when we were teaching at Mt. Madonna the first year, I had not met Hari Dass Baba, who I think is in a different tradition; he's a very realized being. So, I went to pay my respects to him and said "hi" to him. I'd not met him before. And just before I did that, we had this student who—this is an example of disrespect—she was doing dance and movement exercises in the back of the room while we were giving our lectures. It was very distracting. And Gretchen went up to her very nicely during the break and said, "Please don't do that, it's disrespectful when Dan's teaching. Sit down and at least appear like you're listening to the lecture." And, then we began the next class and she started doing it again, defiantly.

SP: Wow.

DB: So, in the middle of the class Gretchen says, "We asked you not to do this in class; it's disrespectful." And the woman with this fit of rage sort of stomped out, said, "Fuck you," left the retreat, after, this was the first day. She came at the last minute, and so she never paid, stuck us for the money, and just walked out on this precious teaching. So, I went up to Hari Dass Baba and I said, "I don't know," I said, "I'm here teaching a Tibetan meditation course, you don't know me. I've been teaching for a long time, but I have this struggle when Western students are disrespectful, and I get very fiercely protective of the teachings. And I don't know whether I'm being reactive or protective." And he writes—he doesn't speak; he took a vow of silence so he writes on this clipboard—"How are they disrespectful?" So, I gave him that example of the student that was doing the dance movements who stomped out, and another student who had, who was a Zen teacher, a Zen student for twenty years who was in Europe and came to a course we did in Europe and had a taste of awakening and stayed stable for about four or five months, and she wanted to take the 3A course, which was a little bit early, but since she had a stable awakening I said okay. But, the one we were doing in Europe she couldn't do because she had something conflicting with it, so she wanted to take the one we were doing with Rinpoche at Esalen. But it was full. And she wanted to visit Rinpoche, so I said, "Okay." I didn't mind fitting another person in the room, but there was no bed space at Esalen, so it was a lot of work with the staff to make an exception here to find her a place. And we finally found her a place and then I worked out for her to go have, fly over early and get an audience with Rinpoche. And then the day of the course she drops out. Stiffs us for the room space. Because the day before she came to here, she met somebody in the airport who was a Western Sufi teacher with no lineage and said, "This is the person from my previous life who is my teacher. I'm going to study with her." So, she gave up a chance to meet Rinpoche, who's the emanation of Padmasambhava; she gave up the precious teachings that stabilize awakening, gave up awakening, studied with some Western person who has no lineage. And things like that break my heart.

So, I told that to Hari Dass Baba and I said, "What can I do?" He said, "Those are good examples." And he wrote, he says, "Keep doing what you're doing. The good students will gravitate around you. And the bad students will go somewhere else. That's the best you can do." And it turned out to be rather sound advice. And without knowing that I had talked with him, Gretchen went up to him about an hour later to bring up the same incident. And she said, "What do I do with people like this?" And he said, "Honesty." And she said, "No, I'm too honest. That's my problem." And he wrote back, "No, that's your nature. You have to be." So, I was impressed with his answers. They were really right to the point. Crystal clear. So, since then I don't, I still get fiercely protective, but I don't see it as just being reactive anymore. I see it as being more protective. And I don't have the illusion that I'm going to teach everybody. And we have a lot of Diamond Heart students because we did a course for Diamond Heart teachers. But then I think the head of that got a little bit threatened by the meditations we were doing, so now they basically don't study with us. Study with them instead.

SP: Really.

DB: So, we don't have hardly any Diamond Heart students anymore. And I figure they did us a favor. If that's how fickle the students are I don't want them. I'd rather have a smaller group of people I can move along the path, and I'm not interested in the California approach where people are taking one workshop after another, and talking and gossiping about the teachers. It's totally uninteresting to me. It has nothing to do with the nature of these realizations. So, if that's what … Rinpoche calls it the "*dharma* flea market," I don't want any part of the *dharma* flea market. I'd rather have a smaller group of students who grasp the preciousness of this and can follow along to buddhahood. I mean that seriously.

I was, you know, I studied with Geshe Wangyal. In that generation, he was a couple of years before me, but his first students were Bob Thurman and Jeffrey Hopkins. And I was talking with Jeffrey once and he said that when he first started his dissertation on emptiness, the Dalai Lama made a comment to him. He said, "You're going to make a school in the West for Tibetan studies, modern Tibetan studies. And I want you to have twenty-five Tibetan scholars in this lifetime produced." And Jeffrey said, "I didn't think about it anymore," and he said, "Then when I retired," he said, "I counted the number of PhDs that were in Buddhist universities in the U.S., and he said, 'My god, it was exactly twenty-five!'" And then Jeffrey said, "You were always the yogi. You have to make twenty-five buddhas."

SP: [Laughs loudly]

DB: And by God, that's what we're going to do.

SP: By God!

DB: Twenty-five buddhas. Not in this lifetime. My role is to bring the teachings here to plant the seeds for that. And that will come to fruition after I leave this form body. But it will come to fruition. I have my role in this and have been given a clear assignment. My first Root Lama, when he was dying said, "Go out and teach. You won't understand why." This was in 1979. "You'll understand why you're teaching somewhere between 2008 and 2012." And that's when we started going from one retreat a year to about thirty retreats all over the world. He said, "You won't finish it." He said, "The fruition will come in the next lifetime; all the teachings will come to fruition as buddhas in the next lifetime. And you'll be the bridge figure for that." So, apparently, we're right on schedule here. So, I think it's been an interesting life. It's not boring.

SP: No.

DB: So, I take that seriously. And now it's not about awakening anymore. It's about developing the path to buddhahood. So, I'm trying to translate, and translate into meditations all the third map teachings that go from continuous awakening up to buddhahood, and make those available.

SP: Are those the ones you're working on now?

DB: Yeah. I'll finish the translations in the next two years and … The third map starts with automatic self-arising self-liberating of all karmic impressions. But, the whole point of the third map is purification of the residuals of the ordinary mind so that nothing gets in the way of the perception of the pure realm and enlightenment. So, there are three parallel tracks. You can automatically release karmic memory traces and emotions—that's the main track in the *trekchö*, or the thoroughly cutting-through version of Dzogchen. And that's the path of *dharmadhātu* exhaustion. And that will open up the threefold embodiment of enlightenment. But, it's not fully purified. It's enough to open it up, though. That's the quickest path.

Or you can purify perception—sights, sounds, tastes, smells, body, body sensations—using the bypassing visions. It's another map that's still, the common factor is purification of the residuals of ordinary perception. That's the *tögal* practices.

And then the third would be the purification of the residuals of the body using practices like Illusory Body and Inner Fire practice. Those are the three. You can do any one or all three of those maps. They all have the same common ground of purifying some aspect of the residuals of the ordinary mind and up to enlightenment; you can reach enlightenment.

So, all you need is the purification process along one of those maps. You do it long enough, and precious transmission instructions for enlightenment, and the threefold embodiment of enlightenment, and that's, it's really rather simple. Not hard to do. So, that's the stuff I'm working on now and would like to make available fully to the West. And you could see that that's consistent with what His Holiness Menri Trizin wanted when you went to Whippany. Because he basically gave you Lesson 14, which is the pith instructions for enlightenment. Not for awakening, for enlightenment. He thinks that this is the time that this is all going to happen in the West, and this is what we should be teaching. So, my task is to translate all these things and then translate them a second time into meditations. So, I hope in the next five years we'll have all this stuff translated and we'll have a complete set of meditations recorded. If I leave my form body, then I have left behind a complete set of teachings up to, through the whole path, up to buddhahood. So, that's my task. And people have to put it into practice. That's their task.

SP: Right.

DB: But I want to do my part here.

SP: I'm not sure this is something to talk about, but I'll ask the question, and that is, again this is, a lot of these questions were formulated in the context of thinking about developing more teachers. The question was how teachers approach assessing a student's practice. And the question that follows after this is how a student approaches assessing his or her practice, which I think you talked about with the metacognitive …

DB: Well, we all do that differently, so I can only speak for myself. So, Gretchen likes to have an hour just to get to know the students. I often don't know anything about their background, but just about their practice. So, we do that quite differently. But, part of that is because I follow seven hundred students, so it's a lot. But I know their practice well. And I keep notes on it, so I can remind myself when I talk with somebody. But I always begin the first time I meet with somebody by reviewing what they did in the Level 1 retreat and finding out at what point it stopped making sense, or they couldn't do it anymore, so I can locate where they are on the map. And then I'll work out an individualized meditation plan for the daily meditation based on where they are. And it doesn't take long anymore to figure out where students are. Sometimes I get in trouble with that because now I can just see it. So, if a student starts asking a question, sometimes they get irritated because I've already answered the question and don't let them finish what they're saying. I have to watch for that more. But, it's not hard to see anymore.

SP: One of the things that stood out to me more, particularly in the first retreat, is that it seemed that to a larger degree than I had seen before in any situation like that, students seemed to have, went home with a sense of what they could do and what they couldn't.

DB: There's our efficacy, right.

SP: Right. So, how much correspondence do you see when a student, where they assess they're at and when you assess they're at? Does it correspond often?

DB: I think it corresponds except with the people who are unduly narcissistic, who can't say anything correctly because they had a need to see themselves much more spiritually developed as possible. Those students don't work out well. But, they're difficult. With that exception I think there is a fair amount of congruence between how we see the student and where the students see themselves.

SP: I personally think that's remarkable. In looking at the general field ...

DB: Well, [with a mature student of mine], we did that when we were doing the neurocircuitry of awakening study, because we had never talked about it before. And we actually had to independently rate thirty students.

SP: Oh yeah.

DB: And I think we came up with four students that we differed on out of forty. That wasn't bad. And the differences weren't that big. So, we had a pretty good inter-rater reliability. So, I think we have learned something in this process. But I think that that said, I would fault myself and all the other teachers that sometimes we really miss it. We make mistakes. So that every time we do an advanced course, when we have thirty or forty people in an advanced course, there's always three or four people that shouldn't be there. And as soon as they, well, it's not a bad thing, we're not trying to correct it, because they're not fit for the course. They can't keep up with the meditations at the level we're doing it at. And then, but they learn something from it because they either misrepresented where they have a need to see themselves as further along, or they pushed to get into the course and then they realize that that was a little bit impatient because they didn't have the requisite requirements. So, that's not a bad thing to realize. So, we're not perfect with it, and sometimes we make mistakes. I think where we make mistakes are people who are tending to be over-conceptual. And they get all the words right. But, it's not clear about the nature of the authenticity of the realization because it's very difficult to base genuine or experience of awakening based on a verbal description. So, it's usually more authentic because it's accompanied by opening the heart. If it's accompanied by spontaneous compassion or gratitude or devotion they're probably on the right track. But, the only real test is conduct. If it changes the way they live their life, then we've done something useful. But we don't always get that right. We make mistakes.

Somewhere between 5 and 10 percent I think we're not correct on. I wish we could change that, but we're learning, we're still learning how to do this.

SP: I think by any measure of many disciplines that's not a bad rate. [Laughing]

DB: It's not a bad rate. I'd like to do better.

SP: Especially if, as you say, the student also has a good corresponding assessment.

DB: Yeah, I think mostly we're in congruence. But we have false positives and false negatives. The false negatives are ones that usually don't talk much. And then we find out that they really had this fantastic experience, but usually you have to catch them on the side because they don't talk about it in the group. So, we don't, we miss where they are. But they are really doing well. And the false positives are the ones that need to call attention to themselves or are over-conceptual or both. And they talk about it in a way that makes sense, so they get all the words right, but there's something missing about it. Sometimes I can get a feeling for that. Gretchen is better at detecting that than I am. She's got a better bullshit detector.

SP: Yes, she does. So, by comparison, without asking you to pass judgment on anybody else, every other type of community or members of communities that I have met in my checkered career, you don't see this. You don't see people having a sense of actually where they are. It's almost as though everybody is just starting …

DB: Well, I think the strength of the Tibetan system is it's a GPS map. It's a very detailed map. Even people like Hogen and Jan and some of the other Western Zen people, Zen masters, who have taken courses with us, they'll tell you, "Look, you guys got the map; we don't have the map." Judith who runs a Zen center near Minneapolis said, "Look, I want to take the map, and I want to line up all our koans to your map, because it tells us where to put the koans."

SP: Wow.

DB: Because it's a good map. The map is detailed. There's a deep structure to the mind.

SP: Right.

DB: And there's a natural unfolding of this, and I think I've done enough translation and enough sitting practice for forty-five years that I've internalized the deep structure. It's not hard to know where people are on the map.

SP: This is, I think, also a remarkable contribution because especially given your history with psychology, both in clinical practice and research and service in the trauma world of traumatized human beings, to be able to talk about this deep structure of the mind in a very different way than psychology does, and yet you also talk about parallels, I wonder if you have anything to say about that, how you've come to understand …

DB: Well, I think there's a map in psychology, too. In fact, since my field is for the last twenty-five years is Continuing Education, I have to read all the outcomes literature. And since a lot of the work I do in the Court is testifying in malpractice cases, the whole issue is standard of care and how we update and upgrade the standard of care. So, we're always giving the best knowledge of a certain treatment they're giving. So, I read all that stuff. So, with the exception of schizophrenia, for almost every, and maybe a little somatoform disorders, for almost every other DSM psychiatric diagnosis we actually have a pretty good idea what to do.

SP: How does that relate to a structure of mind?

DB: Because there's a map for each one of these conditions.

SP: Oh, okay.

DB: And that's what I used to do when I was doing my clinical teaching and supervision, I'd say, this is the path for depression. This is what you've got to do.

So, if you look at outcomes data, okay, there are four stages in the maturation of outcomes data. The first are efficacy studies. Does this work relative to wait-list controls, or some other control population? The second are clinical efficiency studies. Does it work in a way that the symptoms and the diagnosis no longer apply? And the third are, once you figure that out, then there are comparative efficacy studies—does this treatment work better than that treatment. If you leave out components of the treatment, you can find out what the active ingredients of the treatment are. So, that's very sophisticated. And outcome studies get very sophisticated and, say for this, say PTSD, these are the five things you have to put in the treatment. We don't care what you call them, but these things have to be addressed. And if you do all those five things, the probability can be very high in getting a successful outcome. If you drop any one of them out, and you're probably going to have to introduce them in a certain order ... So, we know that—if you read this stuff. Most clinicians don't do that because what most clinicians do is they do what they learned in graduate school, and they never learned anything else. But, as someone who reads all the journals, hundreds of journals, the deep structure is very clear to me. And I can say, this is the map and this is what you do. I've been having fun with my son because he's a resident in internal medicine now but most of his interfacing with patients is around psychiatric issues. So, he talks with me on the phone about patients he's seeing. And talking about the psychological and the psychiatric side of it, and he'll say, "Well how did you get that?"

SP: Yeah. [Laughing]

DB: I've done it for forty-five years, you know. So, he's really curious about it. I worked in primary care for ten years.

SP: That's great.

DB: My task on the wrap-up team was to handle all the psychological issues, which is 65 percent of primary care.

SP: Wow.

DB: So, it's not so different. There's a deep structure. Any one of these conditions in Western therapy, if you take the time to learn the map. But, you know, you're not going to do that in a ten-week teacher training, say. I've been translating for over forty years and I've been practicing that long, both West and East.

So, you develop a certain wisdom after a while about what the maps are. You just know. That makes all the difference in the world. And even with the teachers we are training—because I know that's relevant to you—it's taken on the average of twelve years to train each one of these teachers. We're not … there's no factory output here. And that's the difference between a lineage tradition. And when I was teaching in Israel, we added Ephraim. He's taught now for about ten years. He's done a really good job with it. So, we graduated him, but I didn't know what Asonam would think about him because he doesn't know him, and, he said, this is a good thing. We need more Western teachers. He was very favorable to him. And embraced him. So, this was good.

SP: Yeah. So, you talked about the maps, and you talked about how you're now working …

DB: I'm working on the third map. It's beginning to get pretty clear to me what needs to happen here. And the more clear the map gets, the better the teachings get because we know exactly what to do and what not to do.

SP: So, that would apply to the first and second that you've been teaching that now for …

DB: Yeah, the first map we got to the point that we could get people to a taste of awakening, but it wasn't very stable. That's easy now. Then we developed, with both Rahob Tulku and with His Holiness, we got introduced to all the teachings to stabilize awakening. That's easy now.

SP: Great.

DB: Now, I'm working on the teachings to enlightenment. And we're not finished with that yet. It's still a work in progress. But it's getting easier. And I hope we'll have that all in place in the next two or three years.

SP: So, do you feel that these, this understanding of these maps is something that could be, well, I'm getting ahead of the questions here. I'll back up … I'm not going to ask you that question yet. There's another question about that … What, if any, we don't have to spend a long time with this but I'm curious if you can comment on what cultural confusion arises around Eastern teachings for Western students.

DB: Well, we covered that in part around the issue of taking on a teacher. I look at this, see part of this, I work in psychiatry in the law field a lot, so … I do a lot of this court work stuff. So, I think the notion of *samaya* or "*damchik*" in Tibetan, which is very misunderstood in the West, I think it's very similar to the term "legal duties" or "duty zone" and legal ethics. It's very similar to that. So, I translate *samaya*, or *damchik*, as "spiritual duties."

A teacher-student relationship is a set of contractual duties. I have a duty to share freely everything I know about this path with a student, to put their welfare above my own personal interests, much like the code of ethics in psychology. I have to put my student's welfare above my own personal interests. And I have to use everything I know to move them along the path to enlightenment. That's my duty to them. They have a duty. They have to show up. They have to see the preciousness of these teachings so they don't disseminate them in a way that they lose their potency, because these are lineage teachings. And they have to put it into practice. And they have to show good conduct. They can't have conduct that's incongruent with the nature of the teachings and the preciousness. So, they've got to be good students, and they've got to work at it. And ultimately then they have to manifest it in their lives. That's a big contract.

I expect that of my students, and they can expect that I'll meet my duties. And there's a list in the Akhrid book that we just translated about what teachers to avoid and what teachers not to avoid. Find a teacher who can live it, who manifests the realizations, who respects the lineage, who can bring it alive in your own practice. But, watch out for teachers who are into power, money, misconduct of various sorts, like sexual misconduct. There's no place for that in these teachings. But, you know, it's not like that just happens in the West when lamas come over here. It happens in every spiritual tradition, you know. The history of Tibetan Buddhism is like the history of the Catholic Church. There's lots of intrigue, and lots of power and money and people killing each other off, and jealousy, and all this petty jealousy and all this crap. It's a joke that Tibetans are such a fiercely competitive people that they needed the dharma. They would have killed themselves off a long time ago without it. [Laughter.] I think there's some truth to that.

So, I think that, I tried in this lifetime to live a good life. And one of the things I've learned is that we are in a culture that is so morally bankrupt that there are very few moral exemplars out there. So that's really where my currency comes from. People will listen simply because I don't want anything from them. I'm not going to exploit them. And that's so unusual in this culture that that has a certain currency and weight by itself. That's what I've seen. And it's sad. But that's what this culture has come to. It's really a culture in decline. So, if you've been a moral light of any kind, people desperately want that. So, that's why I think this has some leverage.

SP: So, then there's the question for many people about what's the role of the teacher as distinct from guru?

DB: We don't make those distinctions.

SP: Okay.

DB: Guru means teacher. But you want a teacher who knows the path, who knows how to teach according to your capacity, and who can teach you in a very clear way, and will cut through, will help you to see all the ways you get off track. It's not enough just to sit there in front of a class and say, "Meditate now." They have to follow you and develop a relationship, and help you see with your metacognitive awareness when you're making habits that are not beneficial to the outcomes of the practice. It's no different from psychotherapy in that sense. A good therapist is active and keeps you moving along so you don't get stuck. But, a lot of therapists don't do that. They just sit and talk to you. They think that talking with the patient, listening is good enough. Really good therapists, who are seasoned, know where the patient needs to be, what the diagnosis is, where they need to get the patient and how to get them there, and then move them along. It's no different.

SP: And without that the student can end up …

DB: Getting nowhere or getting it to a place where they're making a lot of bad mistakes, or getting to a bad place. Ultimately, it's the teacher's responsibility. That's the duty owed.

SP: Right. Is there a Western view of levels of mind?

DB: Well, you certainly find it in Ken Wilber's stuff.

SP: Anything before Ken Wilber? I mean, is there any historical …

DB: No. You find some of it in the early Desert Fathers in the Christian tradition, but not very much survived. All that survived was student notes from a few of the teachers. But there was a viable tradition for a while. It didn't last that long. The difference is that the lineage tradition will last for thousands of years. So, you develop a rather precise technical language for this. There was—he was actually one of my teachers—when I was at the University of Chicago, I got a chance to study with many good people, but one of them was Stephen Toulmin, the great philosopher of science, master. And he made the distinction between, in science, being what he called "tight disciplines" and "would-be disciplines." And the distinction was how sophisticated the technical language becomes.

So, physics is a tight discipline because it has a formalized language. Everybody agrees on the language. But psychology is a would-be discipline because we can't agree on the language. We have thirteen different uses of the word "borderline." Nobody will agree on it. So, you see when you have a lineage tradition, the use of technical terms, we might disagree as translators in Western terms on how to translate them, but within the Tibetan tradition there is not a lot of disagreement on what the technical terms mean, because they evolved over twenty-five hundred years in Buddhism, and ten thousand years in Bon. So, the language is very sophisticated. But, if you look at something like Saint Theresa of Avila, it wasn't a lineage tradition. She discovered it and in the three times she'd write about it she uses completely different language. So it's confusing what she's referring to because she's using different terms each time because she doesn't really know; she's just discovering it for the first time. So, it never developed that kind of sophisticated language. So, that's why people like Walter Terence Stace, when studying his classical textbook on Western mysticism he says, "It's ineffable." Well, it's not ineffable! It's ineffable because they didn't have a lineage tradition. They didn't talk about it. But, in a lineage tradition where people talk about it a lot, then you have a sophisticated language. I translated a text on Rechungpa, a contemporary of Milarepa, that's forty pages on the moment of enlightenment, and what happens to body, subtle body and mind in great technical precision. It's not ineffable at all.

SP: That's a fantastic statement because I think the sense that ineffability still pervades and what you're saying …

DB: It's a cop out. It's lazy way.

SP: So, the precision …

DB: Precision is built into the lineage tradition because people evolve, as in science, where people talk about things and develop a technical language over time. It's no different. I learned that from Stephen Toulmin and just applied it to this field. It's not so different.

SP: So, then there's this remarkable and outstanding characteristic of the way that you're teaching is it has a very established language that the teachers and the students …

DB: Yeah, and what it means for the Westerner is they have to learn the language.

SP: Right.

DB: They have to learn the technical language, and then we have a common language—you're all talking about the same thing. Everybody knows what "partial staying" means. And there's not a lot of variance on that once you explain it to them. And many people find that useful because they have been doing it for years and they say, "Oh, nobody ever told me this before."

SP: Exactly. And they know it very quickly.

DB: Yes, very quickly.

SP: And discover the power …

DB: That's the metacognition. Because if you describe it to them in a way that they can understand, they should get it. It's an interaction between the clarity of the instructions and their own metacognitive intelligence. That's why I think if you describe things clearly enough then people are smart enough to get it. I don't dumb it down.

SP: And then having the language, they can actually also have a productive conversation about it.

DB: They have a productive conversation about it and they can also do it with other *sangha* members, and they all talk about the same thing. That's the value, I think, that we've learned about doing it in small groups. No matter where a person is in their practice during the week, there's always somebody else who's going to talk about where they're trying to get to in crystal clear terms, and a light will go on. So, they help each other.

SP: So, on the question of efficacy, do you see anything useful in the possibility of raising the question of efficacy with respect to practice for the explicit purpose of awakening via a colloquium of some kind, like with other teachers? Do you think there's any value now or in the future to open up the topic …

DB: The Garrison Institute did that about five or six years ago. They had a program for Western teachers. We got sort of invited at the last minute by Lama Surya Das, who actually heard of us. I didn't know him at the time, but he invited us. And it was a four day think tank where we all talked about, in small groups, about various topics about what it was like to be a Western teacher. We were clearly the minority, in the minority of the 250 teachers. Over two hundred of them were Western mindfulness teachers. And then there was as very small group of Vajrayana teachers and Zen teachers. And they put the Vajrayana teachers and the Zen teachers in the same group because there were so few of us. But it was clearly dominantly mindfulness.

GN: Rose and Ari were there.

DB: Yeah, and then the reason why it was good that it was set up that way is because we had close contact with a lot of very precious people that were like minded—not a lot, but that there was a small group of us. That's where I met

Hogen and Jan Bays, and others, Reggie Ray was there. So, it was a precious group. We just hung out as a small group together, and we had our own discussions about teaching, different from the mindfulness group. And I thought that it was nice to see that a lot of the Tibetan, or people teaching Tibetan stuff were struggling with the same stuff. We all were struggling with the same stuff. We all talked about disrespectful students, and the difficulty of teaching in the West. So, I found that symposium very valuable.

There was another one, I think two or three years ago, also at Garrison Institute, but it was at the time we were teaching somewhere out of the country so we couldn't do it. But I hope they do it again. I liked some of the format for it.

SP: I was thinking of an invitational event, something that you or the Foundation might want to think about to …

DB: Like how?

SP: Focus ... Well, you know, like Jan and Hogen and perhaps Surya Das or whoever that's congenial to raise the question of efficacy for their students. How do they feel about it?

DB: Like do a conference, maybe a couple of day conference?

SP: Yeah, something. I don't know.

DB: My only objection to that is that doing a conference means fundraising and I don't want to it to be something that's competing with our fundraising thing at the moment.

SP: No, of course.

DB: Because we're not doing very well with that.

SP: Yeah, I didn't mean this for some specific.

DB: But, it's a good idea. In spirit I like the idea a lot. I found that one time that we went it was very useful. I would like to have had more equal representation.

SP: Equal in …

DB: Rather than having it be a mindfulness conference where they had a couple of token minority people like myself.

SP: That's why I was suggesting an invitational.

DB: But, if you do it, if you did it with people teaching Mahāyāna Buddhism, I think you'd do a better job with it.

SP: Yeah, it could be like a test run. Just a first …

DB: Because the mindfulness people are just different … They don't care about these kinds of questions. Most of them don't.

SP: Right. So, assuming it's people who do care about these questions, if it were small …

DB: People like Reggie, and people like Jan and Hogen, who I met there, were very concerned about these questions. And a couple of Tibetan lamas that we met there that were very concerned about these questions. I liked the group a lot.

SP: And, so do you think that some kind of useful, productive conversation could come out of it about efficacy, that people could use and share and maybe meet again about it? Or is that a kind of Western way of thinking?

DB: I think that what we have realized, the value of that particular four-day meeting was, we discovered that we're all struggling with the same things, and we're all feeling pretty much alone with it. It's very hard to teach this on your own in the West. You get no support. You know, I may have the support of representing lineages so that gets the support from the lamas to some extent. And Jan and Hogen would say the same from their Zen Master in Kyoto. But, other than that there's not a lot of support.

SP: So, support group for essence teachers?

DB: Well, I don't know if I'd want that. I don't have time for that. But I'm saying there was a certain value talking about what we recognize, that we all struggle with the same issues and figure them out. I usually get together with Hogen and Jan. They come to the retreats just because they can talk about our experiences as teachers, and they struggle with a lot of the same things I struggle with. So, that's useful, I think.

SP: Okay, in other words, also in addition to that, I don't know if this is part of what you meant by that, is that on the question of, well, as an example, you were talking about Zen teachers, you mentioned a woman who is interested correlating the map with the koans. In the same way actually increasing efficacy in their own …

DB: Yeah, I think you're right to say that the underlying thing we do when we all got together as teachers at Garrison Institute, most of our discussions were around our, in our own ways, our sincere interest in proving what we do and offering better teachings to the students. Everybody wanted to do that. Everybody was, that was their main motivation. It's about efficacy.

SP: Right. And so do you think there might be a way of considering how to pose that, to structure …

DB: Yeah, I think it's a good idea.

SP: Okay. So, we'll just put it on the back burner until Mustang is …

DB: Yeah, I'm sort of burdened by this thing at the moment.

SP: Okay, good. That's great. So, in that group, did people talk specifically about outcomes with their student groups?

DB: Well, the Zen people do because they're concerned about awakening. They're the only people that I find who talk about outcomes.

SP: Wow.

DB: They take that very seriously.

SP: It seems shocking, actually. I mean I'm shocked to hear that, that they're the only ones that really …

DB: Tibetans don't talk about outcomes because they think it takes lifetimes. Mindfulness people don't talk about outcomes.

SP: So, without the pointing out, and without the reflection back from the one who knows what the outcome is supposed to be to the person who is learning, if they don't get that, what use is it? You know. You figured it out, but frankly I don't think …

DB: I didn't figure it out myself. I had help.

SP: Okay.

DB: I had a lot of teachers and I had a lot of *dākinīs*.

SP: So, in other words, the way it's taught is what's … there's the content that's taught but then there's the way that it's taught.

DB: The self can't teach. Dan doesn't teach. The teachings come from awakened dharmakāya space. All I have to do is put the intention into describing that experience from that state. Fresh. It's a kind of love.

SP: Yes, it is.

DB: That's where the teaching comes from.

SP: Yeah.

DB: That's what I'm conveying to the students.

SP: That makes all the difference.

DB: Yeah.

SP: Yeah.

DB: It's the only way you can teach it.

SP: That's a big statement because there's all kinds of people saying they're teaching it.

DB: Because it's coming from self. They don't understand that it can't come from self. Self can't teach. I don't teach. And I think that my duty, amongst others, is to do it in a way without spiritual pride. And the further you get along the path the more spiritual pride becomes a problem. And I think it's for people who have very legitimate realizations and self-realizations in the West, it's an epidemic problem here. At least in the lineage traditions there's some checks and balances. I remember going once to Menri and as soon as I show up, he says something to me, because he sees where I am. I don't have to say anything. And I walked in and he says to me, "You've been doing a lot of teaching, watch out for the pride." I said, "Busted, thank you." And I find that … because it works; keeps me honest. But if you understand the preciousness of this it's impossible to deviate too far from that. It's not possible. So that keeps it honest.

SP: And that's a perfect end to this interview.

DB: Okay. Did you get what you wanted?

SP: Yes. Thank you.

APPENDIX 2

Biography of Dan Brown

Daniel P. Brown, PhD
September 11, 1948 - April 4, 2022

The following biography was published as an obituary in the *American Journal of Clinical Hypnosis* [65(1):79-82] by D. Corydon Hammond, PhD (University of Utah)

The beloved educator, researcher, author, translator, hypnotherapist, psychotherapist, and meditation teacher, Daniel P. Brown, PhD, died on Monday, April 4, 2022, at his home in San Francisco, CA. He was 73.

Author of over 15 books, Dr. Brown made significant contributions in many fields of knowledge and clinical practice. He was also well-respected for his courageous work as an expert witness or consultant on high-profile cases involving complex trauma and abuse.

Born on September 11, 1948, in New Bedford, MA, Dr. Brown was the first person in his family to attend college, at the University of Massachusetts, Amherst, where he received his undergraduate degree in molecular biology. He went on to receive his Ph.D. in Religion & Psychological Studies at the University of Chicago, where he also received a Danforth Fellowship, given for promise in teaching excellence, and received specialized training in how to teach.

His first clinical placement was at Michael Reese Hospital in Chicago, and he also commuted part time to The Menninger Foundation in Topeka Kansas to work on the treatment of substance abuse. In the late 1970s he moved back to his home state of Massachusetts where he did a clinical internship at McLean Hospital and a Postdoctoral Fellowship in Clinical Research at Harvard Medical School at The Cambridge Hospital. His research focused on the long-term effects of mindfulness meditation.

In the late 1970s Dr. Brown became interested in the study of trauma and abuse largely through peer collaboration with Sarah Haley, one of the founding members of the International Society for the Study of Traumatic Stress.

In the 1980s Dr. Brown served as Director of Training and then as Chief Psychologist at The Cambridge Hospital. He helped develop a clinical psychology internship and postdoctoral training program to provide the best young talent in psychology the opportunity to work with a disenfranchised inner city chronic mental health population. He also developed and directed the Behavioral Medicine Program, a joint venture between psychiatry and primary care medicine.

In the early 1990s Dr. Brown became interested in the topic of memory for trauma and abuse. His textbook, *Memory, Trauma Treatment and the Law*, co-authored with D. Corydon Hammond, PhD and Alan W. Scheflin, is the recipient of awards from 7 professional societies, including the 1999 Manfred S. Guttmacher Award given jointly by the American Psychiatric Association and the American Academy of Psychiatry and the Law for the "outstanding contribution to forensic psychiatry."

Dr. Brown served as an expert witness or consultant on trauma and memory in over two hundred lawsuits, including testimony before the International War Crimes Tribunal for the prosecution of war criminals of the former Yugoslavia. He also worked on behalf of clergy abuse clients in Louisiana for 17 years with Roger Stetter, author of *In Our Own Words: Reflections on Professionalism in the Law*, which the Louisiana Bar Foundation distributed to every lawyer and judge in Louisiana.

Mr. Stetter said, "Dan was a brilliant guy and all of my clients thought the world of him. It became clear from my conversations with people in Newton, where he lived, that everyone there loved him as well. I think it was Dan's combination of brilliance and modesty that made him so special. He almost never talked about himself. His life was about helping others, showing respect and genuine concern for their welfare.

Dr. Brown also served on the Harvard Medical School faculty for nearly four decades, where he co-directed and taught courses on hypnosis, trauma, meditation, peak performance, and attachment. He worked to stay abreast of the latest scientific developments in assessment and treatment, and use these findings to offer clinicians practical, state-of-the-art methods to upgrade their standard of care.

Larry Lifson, director of the Continuing Education Program of the Department of Psychiatry at the Beth Israel Deaconess Medical Center, a major teaching hospital of Harvard Medical School, wrote that "Dan Brown was not only an enormously gifted clinician and highly esteemed teacher, he also was a beloved mentor to so many of his students."

Most of his clinical writing and teaching from the 1980s and 1990s focused on treatment for complex trauma disorders. He co-authored two books on developmental psychopathology—a book on affect development, *Human Feelings*, and a book on self-development from a cross-cultural perspective, *Transformations of Consciousness.*

In the 2000s Dr. Brown began to study adult attachment and received intensive training in the Adult Attachment Interview. His research focused on the relative contribution of early attachment pathology to the development of personality and dissociative disorders in adulthood. He is the senior author, with David Elliot, of a major textbook on the treatment of attachment disorders in adults, *Attachment Disturbances in Adults.*

Dr. Brown taught hypnotherapy for 38 years and wrote several important books on hypnosis, including Hypnotherapy and Hypnoanalysis with Erika Fromm, PhD, a noted hypnoanalyst who served as his primary clinical mentor—a relationship that spanned 35 years.

Dr. Brown's interest in meditation started while at grad school at University of Chicago. During that time, he also studied Tibetan, Sanskrit, and Pali in the Buddhist Studies Program at the University of Wisconsin in Madison. He spent ten years translating meditation texts for his doctoral dissertation on Tibetan Buddhist Mahāmudrā meditation.

Dr. Brown studied many forms of meditation practice over the course of his life, including Patanjali's Yoga Sutras with Mircea Eliade and Dr. Arwind Vasavada, and Burmese mindfulness meditation with Mahāsī Sayādaw and Achaan Cha.

Dr. Brown first learned Indo-Tibetan concentration and insight meditation with his root teacher, the Venerable Geshe Wangyal. He studied meditation practices from the Mahāmudrā, Nyingma Dzogchen, and Bonpo Dzogchen lineages with numerous Tibetan lamas, including H.H. The 14th Dalai Lama and H.H. The 33rd Menri Trizin, the spiritual head of the Tibetan Bon religion.

Dr. Brown also spent 45 plus years translating meditation texts from Tibetan and Sanskrit, and is the author of *Pointing Out the Great Way: The Stages of Meditation in the Mahāmudrā Tradition* (2006, Wisdom Publications) based on his doctoral dissertation of twenty-five years earlier He taught meditation retreats internationally for over 30 years, often in collaboration with Tibetan meditation masters including Denma Locho Rinpoche, Rahob Tulku Rinpoche, Tenzin Wangyal Rinpoche. Dan taught in the spirit of the ecumenical Rime movement, synthesizing the "greatest hits" of meditation instructions from various lineages to develop a comprehensive and precise path from ordinary dualistic consciousness to full enlightenment.

The latter part of his life was devoted to his goal of leaving behind a complete set of instructions to guide Western meditation practitioners along this path.

He was known for his unique integration of contemporary Western research on peak performance and positive psychology with the classical Buddhist meditation lineage traditions.

He spent 10 years conducting outcomes research on beginning and advanced meditators, and led the only scientific study identifying the neurocircuitry of the meditative experience of the awakened mind. He was especially interested in meditations designed to stabilize awakening in everyday life and to bring about the flourishing of positive qualities of mind.

Brown met his wife, Gretchen Nelson, in 2007 at a meditation retreat he was teaching in California. They began teaching meditation retreats together in 2007. They were married in 2010, by Rahob Rinpoche, and besides his wife, he is survived by two sons, Gabriel and Jeremy.

Dr. Brown was held in the highest esteem by his professional colleagues, yet he was perhaps even more deeply loved and appreciated by the many clients and students whose lives he profoundly touched. As prolific as he was, he had a way of making each individual he worked with feel deeply seen and respected for who they were and what they were capable of. His relentless commitment to helping others experience their true potential was unparalleled.

While any single one of Dan's many accomplishments would have made for a life well-lived, Dan never lost touch with his humble roots, and was known for enjoying good food, fishing and football with his friends and family.

Daniel P. Brown, PhD
CURRICULUM VITAE (abbreviated)

Part I. General Information

Date Prepared: July 16, 2024
Date of Birth: September 11, 1948
Place of Birth: New Bedford, MA
Date of Death: April 22, 2022

Education:

1971 B.S. University of Massachusetts, Microbiology
1973 M.A.University of Chicago, Religion & Psychological Studies
1981 Ph.D. University of Chicago, Religion & Psychological Studies

Training:

Internships:

1975-1976 Psycho-diagnostic Clerk and Clinical Extern, Psychosomatic and Psychiatric Institute, Michael Reese Medical Center, Chicago
1976-1977 Clinical Psychology Intern (APA-approved), McLean Hospital, Belmont, MA
1977-1981 Clinical Fellow in Psychology, McLean Hospital, Belmont, MA
Research Fellowships:
1978-1980 Research Fellow in Social-Behavioral Science, Harvard Medical School
Licensure and Board Certification:
1980 Licensed Psychologist, Massachusetts, #2399-PR
1990 Diplomate, American Board of Psychological Hypnosis, #209
Member, Executive Board, ABPH
Other Training & Certification:
2002 Certified Consultant, American Society of Clinical Hypnosis.2006
Successfully completed training in administration & scoring of the Adult Attachment Inventory; passed full 30-case reliability testing at high reliability level. AAI training with Deborah Jacobvitz, Ph.D. Reliability testing with Mary Main & Erik Hesse.

Academic Appointments:

1975-1976 Instructor, Religion and Psychological Studies, The University of Chicago
1980-1990 Adjunct Assistant Professor, The School of Social Work of Simmons College
1990-1991 Adjunct Associate Professor, The School of Social Work of Simmons College

1991-2006 Adjunct Professor, The School of Social Work of Simmons College

Hospital or Affiliated Institution Appointments:

1981-1986 Instructor in Psychology, Harvard Medical School at The Cambridge Hospital

1986-1990 Assistant Professor in Psychology, Harvard Medical School

1993-1997 Lecturer, Dept. of Psychology, Boston University

1990-2006 Assistant Clinical Professor in Psychology, Harvard Medical School

2006-2022 Associate Clinical Professor in Psychology, Harvard Medical School

Other Professional Positions and Visiting Appointments:

1974-1975 CIC Visiting Scholar, Dept. of Asian Studies, University of Wisconsin, Madison, WI

Hospital & Health Care Organization Service Responsibilities:

1977-1978 Staff Psychologist, Department of Mental Health, The Commonwealth of Massachusetts, Westboro State Hospital, Cambridge/Somerville Unit, Special Dual Diagnosis Treatment Team.

1978-1979 Psychology Associate, Highland Counseling Associates, Athol, MA

1980-1986 Supervisor, The Psychotherapy Center, The Cambridge Hospital, Cambridge, MA.

1980-1982 Director of In-Service Training, Department of Psychiatry, Central Hospital, Somerville, MA

1981-1985 Associate Director of Psychology, Department of Psychiatry, The Cambridge Hospital, Cambridge, MA.

1982-1983 Director of Hypnotherapy Service and Training, Department of Psychiatry, The Cambridge Hospital, Cambridge, MA.

1983-1992 Director of Behavioral Medicine Services, The Department of Psychiatry, The Cambridge Hospital, Cambridge, MA.

1985-1987 Director of Psychology Training and Clinical Services, The Department of Psychiatry, The Cambridge Hospital, Cambridge, MA.

1987-1990 Chief Psychologist, Department of Psychiatry, The Cambridge Hospital

1984-2000 Director, Daniel Brown, Ph.D. & Associates, The Center for Integrative Psychotherapy, 75 Cambridge Parkway, Cambridge, MA 02142

2000-2020 Director, Daniel Brown, Ph.D. & Associates, 796 Beacon St. Newton MA 02459

Major Administrative Responsibilities & Committee Assignments:

National/International:

2007 Chairman, Task Force, Division 56 American Psychological Association Liaison to DSM-V on Trauma-Related Disorders

2006 Executive Committee. Division 56 Psychological Trauma. American Psychological Association.

2006 Chairman, Task Force on Hypnosis and Memory, American Society of Clinical Hypnosis.

1998 Consultant, Expert Witness, United Nations, Office of the Prosecutor, International War Crimes Tribunal for the Former Yugoslavia, The Hague, Netherlands. Helped establish standard of evidence for what constitutes reliable memory in victims of severe war atrocities—standard upheld in two appeals

1998-2022 Member, Task Force on Hypnosis and Memory, APA-Division 30 (Psychological Hypnosis)

1998-2002 Executive Board, American Board of Psychological Hypnosis

1986-1990 Director, U.S. Center, Sino-U.S. Qi Gong Health Sciences Development Center, The Cambridge Hospital, Cambridge, MA and The Beijing College of Traditional Chinese Medicine, Beijing, P.R.C. Organized and led a delegation of scientists from HEW and the AIDs U.S. National Commission to China to educate the Chinese on stopping the spread of AIDs in China.

1989-1990 Vice President, World Academic Society of Medical Qi Gong

1987-1991 Association of Psychology Internship Centers (APIC), Post-Doctoral Membership Committee

1989-1991 Chairman, Post-Doctoral Training Site Membership Committee (APIC)

1988-1990 Education Committee, Division 30, APA

1980-1982 Occasional consultant on cross-cultural sensitivity for the Health Services Division, World Bank, Washington D.C.

Hospital:

1983-1990 Education Committee, The Cambridge Hospital, Cambridge, MA

1986-1990 Executive Committee, The Cambridge Hospital, Cambridge, MA

1986-1988 Executive Board, The Erikson Center, Cambridge, MA

Professional Societies:

American Psychological Association—-Divisions 30, 38, 41

American Society of Clinical Hypnosis (Fellow)

Society of Behavioral Medicine

International Society of Traumatic Stress Studies

International Society for Mental Training & Excellence

For a complete version of Dan's CV, please visit www.danielpbrownphd.com

APPENDIX 3

Daniel P. Brown, PhD Bibliography

Books/Monographs:

Wilbur, K., Engler, J. & Brown, D. 1985. T*he Transformation of Consciousness: Conventional and Contemplative Developmental Approaches.* Boston: New Science Library (Shambala/Random House).

Brown, D. & Fromm, E. 1986. *Hypnotherapy & Hypnoanalysis*, with a forward by Ernest R. Hilgard. Hillsdale, New Jersey: Lawrence Erlbaum Associates.

Brown, D. & Fromm, E. 1986. *Hypnosis and Behavioral Medicine*, with a forward by Gary Schwartz. Hillsdale, NJ: Lawrence Erlbaum Associates.

Fass, M. & Brown, D. 1990. *Creative Mastery in Hypnosis and Hypnotherapy*, with a forward by Martin Orne. Hillsdale, NJ: Lawrence Erlbaum Associates.

H.H. The Dalai Lama, Goleman, D., Brenman-Gibson, M., Brown, D., Bolen, J.S., Engler, J., Levine, S., & Macy, J. 1992. *Worlds in Harmony: Dialogues in Compassionate Action*. San Francisco: Parallax Press.

Ablon, S., Brown, D., Khantzian, E. & Mack, J. 1993. *Human Feelings: Explorations in Affect Development and Meaning*, Hillsdale, NJ: The Analytic Press.

Brown, D. & Scheflin, A.W. (Guest Editors). Summer, 1996. Special issue on the false memory controversy. The Journal of Psychiatry and Law, 24, 137-338.

Brown, D., Scheflin, A., & Hammond, C.D. 1997. *Memory, Trauma Treatment and the Law*. New York: Norton.

Goleman, D., (Ed.) with H.H. The Dalai Lama, Brown, D., Davidson, R., Kabat-Zinn, J., Salzberg, S., Valera, F. & Yearley, L. 1997. *Healing Emotions: Conversations with the Dalai Lama on Mindfulness, Emotions, and Health*. Boston: Shambhala.

Brown, D. & Scheflin, A.W. (Guest Editors) Fall-Winter, 1999. Special issue on interrelationship between factitious behavior, dissociative disorders, and the law, The Journal of Psychiatry and Law, 27, 363-706.

Brown, D. 2006. Forward by R. Thurman. *Pointing Out the Great Way; Meditation Stages in the Tibetan Mahāmudrā Tradition*. Boston, MA: Wisdom Publications.

Brown, D. 2009. *The Pointing Out Style of Indo-Tibetan Buddhism; A Guide to Awakening. Volumes 1-3*. Boston, MA. Private, publication manual, restricted access only to previous students and teachers of this style of meditation.

van der Linden, J., Brown, D. 2012. *Dissociation et memoire traumatique*. Dunod: Paris, France.

Brown, D., Elliott, D. et al. 2016 *Treating Attachment Disturbances in Adults; Treatment for Comprehensive Repair*. New York: Norton.

Bru rGyal ba g.Yung drung. 2017. Geshe Sonam Gurang and Brown, D. (Trans.). Translated under the guidance of His Holiness Menri Trizin. Pith Instructions for the A Khrid rDzogs Chen [Bon Great Completion Meditation]. Translated for the Pointing Out the Great Way Foundation.Occidental, CA: Bright Alliance.

Geshe Sonam Gurang and Brown, D. 2019. Translated under the guidance of His Holiness Menri Trizin. *The Three-fold Embodiment of Enlightenment; The Bon Yogi Texts of the Path of Liberation of Shar rDza bra' shis rGyal mtshan*. Occidental, CA: Bright Alliance.

Geshe Sonam Gurang and Brown, D. 2019. Translated under the guidance of His Holiness Menri Trizin. *The Twenty-One Nails, According to the Zhang Zhung Oral Transmission Lineage of Bon Great Completion*, Root text by Taphiritsa and Gyer spungs sNang Bzher Lod Po. Occidental, CA: Bright Alliance.

Geshe Sonam Gurang and Brown, D. 2019. Translated under the guidance of His Holiness Menri Trizin. *The Six Lamps, According to the Zhang Zhung Oral Transmission Lineage of Bon Great Completion*, Root text by Taphiritsa, auto-commentary attributed to Gyer spungs sNang Bzher Lod, Po, three additional commentaries, and Pointing Out the Six Energy Drops, transcribed by gTsang pa Bye Bral. Occidental, CA: Bright Alliance.

Geshe Sonam Gurang and Brown, D. 2019. Translated under the guidance of His Holiness Menri Trizin. *Heart Drops of Kuntu Zangpo*, by Shar rDza bra' shis rGyal mtshan. Occidental, CA: Bright Alliance.

Bissanti, M., Brown, D. & Pasari, J. (2020) *The Elephant Path: Attention Development and Training in Children and Adolescents*. Occidental, CA: Bright Alliance.

Geshe Sonam Gurang and Brown, D. (2021) translated under the guidance of His Holiness Menri Trizin. *The Precious Treasury of the Expanse and Awakened Awareness: The Ornaments of the Definitive Secret*, by Shar rDza bra' shis rGyal mtshan, Occidental, CA: Bright Alliance.

Bru rGyal ba g.Yung drung. (2022) Geshe Sonam Gurang and Brown, D. (Trans.). Translated under the guidance of His Holiness Menri Trizin. *Pith Instructions for the A Khrid rDzogs Chen [Bon Great Completion Meditation]*. Translated and revised for the Pointing Out the Great Way Foundation. Occidental, CA: Bright Alliance.

Chapters in Books and Other Monographs:

Brown, D. (1984) "A model for the levels of concentrative meditation," In D.H. Shapiro & R. Walsh (Eds.) *Meditation: Classic and Contemporary Perspectives,* 281-316, New York: Aldine.

Maliszewski, M., Twemlow, S.W., Brown, D.P. & Engler, J.E. (1981). "A Phenomenological Typology of Intensive Meditation: A Suggested Methodology Using the Questionnaire Approach", Revision, 4: 3-27.

Fromm, E., Boxer, A.M. & Brown, D.P. (1985) "Representations of Self-Hypnosis in Personal Narratives," In D. Waxman, P.C. Misra, M. Gibson & M.A. Basker (Eds.) *Modern Trends in Hypnosis,* pp. 215-222, New York: Plenum Press.

Brown, D. & Engler, J. (1984). "A Rorschach Study of the Stages of Mindfulness Meditation," in D. Shapiro & R. Walsh (Eds.) *Meditation: Classic and Contemporary Perspectives,* pp. 232-262, New York: Aldine.

Brown, D. (1988) "Hypnotic treatment of asthma," Advances, 5: 15-29.

Brown, D. (1990) "Erika Fromm: An intellectual history," In. M.L. Fass & D. Brown (Eds.), *Creative mastery in hypnosis and hypnoanalysis: A festschrift for Erika Fromm,* pp. 1-29, Hillsdale, N.J.: Lawrence Erlbaum and Associates.

Brown, D. (1990) "The variable long-term effects of incest: Hypnoanalytic and adjunctive hypnotherapeutic treatment," In. M.L. Fass & D. Brown (Eds.), *Creative Mastery in Hypnosis and Hypnoanalysis,* pp.199-229, Hillsdale, N.J.: Lawrence Erlbaum and Associates.

Fromm, E. & Brown, D. (1991) "The Hypnoanalytic Treatment of Unconscious Traumatic Memories and Developmental Deficit Caused by Early Incest," In. O. van der Hart (Ed.) *Trauma, dissociatie en hypnose,* pp. 221-248, Amsterdam: Swets & Zeitlinger, Publishers.

Brown, D. (1993). "Clinical hypnosis research in the past five years," In E. Fromm & M. Nash (Eds.). *Contemporary perspectives in hypnosis research.* New York: Guilford.

Brown, D. (1993). "Affective development, psychopathology and adaptation," In S. Ablon, D. Brown, E. Khantzian & J. Mack (Eds.). *Human feelings: Explorations in affect development and meaning.* Hillsdale, NJ: Analytic Press.

Brown, D. (1993). "Stress and emotion: Implications for illness development and wellness," In S. Ablon, D. Brown, E. Khantzian & J. Mack (Eds.). *Human feelings: Explorations in affect development and meaning.* Hillsdale, NJ: Analytic Press.

Brown, D. (1993). "The path of meditation: Affective development and psychological well-being," In S. Ablon, D. Brown, E. Khantzian & J. Mack (Eds.) *Human feelings: Explorations in affect development and meaning.* Hillsdale, NJ: Analytic Press.

Brown, D. (1995). "Types of suggestibility and their applicability to memory distortion in trauma treatment," In J. L. Albert (Ed.), *Delayed Memories of Abuse*, (pp.61-100) Northvale, NJ: Jason Aronson.

Brown, D., Scheflin, A.W., Frischholz, E.J. & Caploe, J. (2002). "Special methodologies in memory retrieval: Chemical, hypnotic, and imagery procedures," In R. I. Simon & D.W. Schuman (Eds.). *Retrospective assessment of mental states in litigation; Predicting the past.* (pp. 369-423) Washington, D.C.:American Psychiatric Association Press.

Brown, D. (2003) "The evolving standard of psychological testing in forensic evaluations," In. R.I. Simon & L.H. Gold (Eds.). *A textbook in forensic psychiatry: Guidelines for assessment.* (pp. 601-635) Washington, D.C.: American Psychiatric Press.

Brown, D. (2009). "Assessment of attachment and abuse history, and adult attachment style," In C. Courtois & J. Ford (Eds.). *Complex traumatic stress disorders: An evidence-based clinician's guide.* (Pp. 124-144) New York: Gulford.

Axelrad, D., Brown, D., Wain, H. (2009; 2016). Hypnosis, In. H.I. Kaplan, A.M. Freeman & B.J. Sadock, (pp. 2804-2832). C*omprehensive textbook of psychiatry.*

Brown, D. (2015). "Body meditation in the Tibetan Buddhist and Bon Traditions," In G. Marlock & H.C. Weise (Eds.) (pp.921-928) *Handbook of body psychotherapy and somatic psychology*. (2nd. ed.).

Brown, D. (2016) "Afterward". In A. Raz & M. Lifshitz (Eds.) (pp. 449-458) H*ypnosis and meditation.*

Steele, H., Brown, D. Sinason, V. (2017). "Bindung und complexes trauma" [Attachment and complex trauma: Essential conditions for treatment of survivors of child abuse]. In K.H. Brisch (Ed.). (pp., 92-112) *Bindungs-traumatisierungen: Wenn bindungspersonen zu tatern warden [Treating attachment disorders—Conference proceedings].* Munich, Germany: Klett-Cotta.

Journals:

Krippner, S. & Brown, D. Field Independence /Dependence and Electrosone 50 Induced Altered States of Consciousness, J. Clin. Psych., 1973, 29: 316-319.

Krippner, S. & Brown, D. Altered States of Consciousness and Mystical-Religious Experience: Methodological Perspectives, Research J. of Phil. & Soc. Sci., 1975, # (1): 39-76.

Brown, D. A Model for the Levels of Concentrative Meditation, Int.J. of Clin. & Exp. Hypnosis, 1977, 25:236-273.

Brown, D. & Fromm, E. Selected Bibliography of Readings in Altered States of Consciousness (ASC) in Normal Individuals, Int. J. of Clin. & Exp. Hypnosis, 1977, 25: 388-391.

Brown, D. & Engler, J. The Stages of Mindfulness Meditation: A Validation Study, J. of Transpersonal Psychology, 1980, 12: 143-192.

Fromm, E., Brown, D., Hurt, D., Oberlander, J., Boxer, A., & Pfeiffer, G. The Phenomena and Characteristics of Self-Hypnosis, Int. J. of Clinic. & Exp. Hypnosis, 1981, 29:189-246.

Shapiro, D., Shapiro, J., Walsh, R. & Brown, D. The Effects of Intensive Meditation on Sex-Role Identification: Implications for a Control Model of Psychological Health, Psychol. Reports, 1982, 51: 44-46.

Brown, D., Forte, M., Rich, P. & Epstein, G. Phenomenological Differences Among Self Hypnosis, Mindfulness Meditation & Imagining, Imagination, Cognition & Personality, 1983, 2: 291-309.

Brown, D.P. & Engler, J.E. An Outcome Study of Intensive Mindfulness Meditation, J. Psychoanalytic Study of Society, 1984, 10: 163-225.

Klagsbrun, J. & Brown, D. Getting the Picture: The Use of Imagery to Clarify Therapeutic Impasses, Psychotherapy: Theory, Research & Practice, 1984, 21: 254-259.

Brown, D.P., Forte, M. & Dysart, M. Visual Sensitivity and Mindfulness Meditation, Perceptual and Motor Skills, 1984, 58: 775-784.

Brown, D., Forte, M. & Dysart, M. Visual Sensitivity Differences Among Mindfulness Meditators and Non-Meditators, Perceptual and Motor Skills, 1984, 58: 727-733.

Brown, D. Hypnosis as an Adjunct to the Psychotherapy of the Severely Disturbed Patient: An Affective Development Approach, Int. J. of Clin. & Exp. Hypnosis, 1985, 33:281-301.

Forte, M., Brown, D.P. & Dysart, M. Through the Looking Glass: Phenomenological Reports of Advanced Meditators at Visual Threshold, Imagination, Cognition & Personality, 1984-1985, 4 (4): 323-338.

Forte, M., Brown, D. & Dysart, M. Differences in Experience Among Mindfulness Meditators, Imagination, Cognition & Personality, 1987-88, 7 (1), 47-60.

Brown, D. Pseudomemories, the Standard of Science and the Standard of Care in Trauma Treatment, American Journal of Clinical Hypnosis, 1995, 37, 1-24.

Scheflin, A.W. & Brown, D. (Summer, 1996). Repressed memory or dissociative amnesia: What the science says. The Journal of Psychiatry and Law, 24, 143-188.

Brown, D., Scheflin, A.W., & Whitfield, C.W. (Spring, 1999). Recovered memories—the current weight of the evidence in science and in the courts, The Journal of Psychiatry and Law, 27, 5-156.

Brown, D. & Scheflin, A.W. (Fall-Winter, 1999). Factitious disorders and trauma-related diagnoses, The Journal of Psychiatry and Law, 27, 373-422.

Brown, D., Frischholz, E.J., & Scheflin, A.W. (Fall-Winter, 1999). Iatrogenic dissociative identity disorder–An evaluation of the scientific evidence, The Journal of Psychiatry and Law, 27, 549-638.

Scheflin, A.W. & Brown, D. (Fall-Winter, 1999). The false litigant syndrome: "Nobody would say that unless it was the truth," The Journal of Psychiatry and Law, 27, 649-705.

Brown, D. (2001). (Mis)representations of the long-term effects of childhood sexual abuse in the courts, Journal of Child Sexual Abuse, 9, 79-107.

Van der Hart, O., Nijenhuis, E., Steele, K. & Brown, D. (2005), Trauma-related dissociation: Conceptual clarity lost and found, Australian & New Zealand Journal of Psychaitry.

Brown, D. (2007). Evidence-based hypnotherapy for asthma: A critical review, Special Edition on Evidence-Based Hypnotherapy. International Journal of Clinical and Experimental Hypnosis, 55(2), 1-30.

Brown, D. (2009). The energy body and its functions: Immuno-surveillance, longevity, and regeneration, New York Academy of Sciences, 1172, 312-337.

Brown, D. (2009). Mastery of the mind East and West; Excellence in being and doing and everyday happiness, New York Academy of Sciences, 1172, 231-251.

Baker, R.L. & Brown, D. (2015). On engagement: Learning to pay attention. Special edition on "Balance in Legal Education Symposium" University of Arkansas Law Review, 36, 337-385.

Schoenberg, P., Ruf, A., Churchill, J., Brown, D. & Brewer, J. (2018). Mapping complex mind states: EEG neural substrates of meditative unified compassionate awareness, Consciousness & Cognition, Jan, Vol 57, pages 41-53.